Web Site Design Made Easy

Learn HTML, XHTML, and CSS

3rd Edition

Dennis Gaskill

Morton Publishing Company
925 W. Kenyon Avenue, Unit 12
Englewood, CO 80110

http://www.morton-pub.com

Book Team

Publisher	Doug Morton
Project Manager	Dona Mendoza
Copy Editor	Kelly Kordes Anton
Cover & Design	Bob Schram, Bookends
Composition	Ash Street Typecrafters, Inc.

Printed in the United States of America

10   9   8   7   6   5   4   3   2   1

ISBN: 0-89582-735-2
ISBN 13: 978-089582-735-7

Preface

This book teaches the basics of web design. While it does assume that you've spent at least some time viewing web pages on the Internet and have basic computer skills, it assumes no other knowledge on your part. Not only will you learn to plan and create a working web site, but you will discover many of the "tricks" that take a web site from basic to cool and useful.

Web design is a broad area that can encompass many things: coding knowledge, graphic design, copywriting, page layout, and more—even server software programming. One book cannot teach it all. This book mainly focuses on teaching HTML coding and formatting using CSS. Other areas are touched upon, but these basic skills will carry you a long way toward your goal of web site design.

New to this Edition

This book is a complete rewrite from previous editions, except perhaps a paragraph here and there. It has been updated to the latest versions HTML (version 4.01) and CSS (version 2.1). The lessons teach web design that is XHTML compliant, and students even learn how to make a purely XHTML web page. While many web design books still teach deprecated (outdated) coding practices, they have been eliminated from this book, with only a few noted exceptions. It was necessary to make a few exceptions because nothing has replaced the deprecated practice yet that the major browsers support.

CSS, cascading style sheets, has been given an extremely thorough treatment with three chapters dedicated to the subject, along with it being referenced throughout the book. The chapter on "good design" discusses what makes for good and bad web site design.

Chapter 17 provides an overview of other web site technologies that students may want to learn, depending on which aspect of web design they want to focus on the most. A bonus chapter covers many good things to know—from spotting email hoaxes and netiquette to installing CGI scripts, working with Server Side Includes, and how to ask others for help in a way that gets results.

The book also includes some useful appendixes. Appendix A: HTML and XHTML is divided into five main parts: current elements, attributes and values; deprecated and obsolete elements and attributes; proprietary elements and attributes; an element browser compatibility and DTD chart; and a "valueless" attribute chart.

Appendix B: Cascading Style Sheets Chart is broken down into logical components and examples of usage are given for every CSS property. There are also new CSS charts showing units of measure and CSS terms and definitions. The appendices are designed using color in a way that makes it easier to reference. Other appendices include: Color Charts, an ASCII Character Chart, and Troubleshooting.

About the Author

Dennis Gaskill is an entrepreneur that earns his living either directly from the Internet or from writing about it. He started his first web site in 1997 as a hobby, and by 1999 he was earning his living full-time working from home via his www.BoogieJack.com web site.

He has since designed many successful web sites, both for himself and for clients, and has written three print books, several electronic books, and more than 500 newsletters for himself and others. His own newsletter, *Almost a Newsletter*, has received multiple industry awards including Newsletter of the Year. *Writers Digest Magazine* once cited it as one of the top three newsletters on the Internet.

Almost a Newsletter is about web design and life, because as Dennis puts it, you can't separate who you are from what you do—because you always make business decisions from within your character. *Almost a Newsletter* is an eclectic combination of information that has won him tens of thousands of loyal subscribers, many whom describe themselves as "fans" when they write to him.

Words from the Author

Greetings! I hope you enjoy this book and find that learning to build web sites is both fun and rewarding. The Internet has been very good to me—and not just monetarily. It can be for you, too. Some of the best rewards have been the online friends I've made over the years. I've also had well-known celebrities write to me, and have even been offered a small part in a movie. It's the "average, everyday people," however, that I appreciate the most. These are the unsung heroes in life—just good folks trying to help themselves as best they know how—whom I admire and am inspired by the most.

To get what you want in life, you have to help others get what they want. If you'll just remember that much you'll do well enough. Life isn't about what you accomplish though; life is about who you become along the way. Feed your mind. Feed your soul. Design your destiny.

Note to Instructors

An Instructor's Manual with additional questions and answers and chapter exercises for use in the classroom is available from Morton Publishing at:

www.morton-pub.com

You'll also be given access to an instructors-only online bulletin board/forum where you can interact with other teachers.

The author is also considering starting a FAQ page based on questions collected from instructors. He will consider each question submitted for a supplemental page to be added to his web site to help students and teachers alike. Be aware that he may not be able to answer all questions or respond personally because:

- He receives hundreds of emails per day, and often gets more questions than he has time to answer.

- The questions may be too specific toward one web host, one software program, or represents an unusual problem that wouldn't be an issue for many people.

- He doesn't have all the answers to every question—no one does.

He requests that teachers submit only frequently asked questions that are not already answered in this book. If you'd like to submit a question, please do so using the contact form at:

www.BoogieJack.com/contact.html

Please use the subject line of: **FAQ Suggestion** so the message is filtered properly in his email program. He also requests that you identify yourself as an instructor and identify the school and city where you teach to help prevent the general public trying to "cut to the front of the line," so to speak.

With instructor cooperation, a resource can be developed over time that will be a great benefit to teachers, students, and future editions of this book.

In Memory of Cinnamon

Contents

An Overview of Other Technologies. 367

Bonus Chapter 387

HTML and XHTML. 413

Introduction to the Internet and Web Design

1.1 In This Book

BUILDING A WEB SITE may seem difficult at first, but it can be easy and fun with just a basic understanding of how HTML coding works. HTML is the language most of the World Wide Web is written in, although a gradual migration to XHTML is occurring. (HTML and XHTML, as well as CSS, are explained in the next chapter.) These are the primary languages you'll need to learn to become an accomplished web author.

The lessons are broken down into simple, progressive steps that make it as easy as possible to learn web design. An overview of other coding languages that you may want to learn is provided, but this book is all you really need to build a quality web site. The other coding languages are beneficial if you want a career in web design or simply want to be more informed and versatile than the average user.

Several reference charts in the appendices—plus references to online resources and other good things to know—will help you learn the ways of web design.

1.2 The Internet

THE INTERNET BEGAN as an experiment in private computer networking with access limited to military personnel, researchers, and a few other technically literate individuals. It was little more than two computer networks connected by a phone line. This "early Internet" was known as ARPANET back then.

In 1990, Tim Berners-Lee, a British physicist and research scientist, invented a way to more easily interconnect information between computers. These interconnected documents were the forerunner of what we now know as the Internet.

When Marc Andreessen and Eric Bina invented the Mosaic browser in 1992, which was the forerunner to Andreessen's Netscape Navigator released in 1994, the Internet literally exploded in popularity and rapidly became a very important part of the worldwide culture and economy.

The Internet is quite simple in theory. There are computer servers that send files stored on them to client computers, which are the computers and devices you and I use to access the Internet. Our client computers and devices display the visual information or play the audio information the servers send if we have the right software installed.

Today the Internet is comprised of the World Wide Web, email, usenet, and many other lesser-known information and file-exchanging technologies. More than 200 million computer servers are connected to the Internet today, and that doesn't include client side computers, cellphones, televisions, and other devices. The Internet truly has enabled global communication on an unprecedented scale.

1.3 Web Sites

WEB SITES ARE NOTHING more than a collection of files on a web server. These files consist of the documents to be displayed, but also may include graphics, sounds, movies, and other files.

Web sites can be as small as one page or as large as thousands of pages. A web site may be publicly accessible or private. Web sites may be personal, informational, educational, editorial, commercial, or any combination thereof.

If you want to put a web site online, it has to be uploaded to a server for others to have access to it. Specialized software is used to transfer the files from your computer to your host's server. We'll discuss this in more detail later in the book.

1.4 Standardized Language

IN THE BEGINNING, web pages were written using a computer language called HyperText Mark-up Language, or HTML for short. As the Internet grew and other software became available to surf the Net with, it became apparent that the earliest version of HTML wasn't capable of rendering web pages in a consistent manner across different computer platforms and different browser software. A web site that looked great in one browser might look terrible in another, or may not display the content of the page at all.

Soon, experts realized that standards had to be set. The World Wide Web Consortium (W3C) was formed to address the issue of coding standards. Tim Berners-Lee, the inventor of the Internet, serves as the director of the W3C. The W3C defines the standards for HTML and other web page programming languages, and also has the mission of leading the web to its full potential. As web designers learned these new standards and browser software vendors began programming their browsers to adhere to the standards, the more serious problems with cross-platform display capabilities gradually disappeared.

With browser vendors finally adhering to standards, there was little to set their products apart from each other. To position themselves as the better browser, they added bells and whistles and even created their own unique browser extensions. Sometimes these extensions catch on well enough that other browser vendors add them to their own products; other extensions remain non-standard. Web designers need to take care when using non-standard browser extensions to ensure they don't design web sites that aren't usable in all browsers.

While I do mention a very few nonstandard code extensions, the overwhelming majority of the book uses official code standards. The few nonstandard features I include are those that do not cause problems in other browsers—they are simply ignored by them. The extensions are either very popular or highly useful, so I'd be remiss if I didn't include them. Notations are made when nonstandard extensions are used.

As you surf the web looking for design tips, be aware that there are many, many tutorials out there that teach nonstandard coding methods, deprecated code, and even obsolete code. Be careful of what you use or you could end up using code you will have to replace down the road. While building a web site is fun, it's not that fun to have to go back through your site to find and replace code that no longer works.

1.5 HTML Editors

An HTML EDITOR is a software program that helps you design web sites, although all you really need is any plain text editor such as Notepad on Windows or TextEdit on Mac OS.

> **Note**
>
> When designing web sites, keep in mind not only what the W3C recommended standards are, but what the current browsers actually support. Browser support for new standards often lags months to a year or more behind the W3C recommendations. Plus, consumers need to acquire the latest browsers once they're released.

An HTML editor provides a working environment where you can insert many code snippets by simply clicking a button, saving you from having to remember the correct syntax and typing the code in by hand. Most HTML editors also have a preview mode so you can see what you're creating as you create it, more or less. I say more or less because the preview mode is often not a true rendering of what the page will look like on the web.

While handy, there are some drawbacks to using HTML editors. Some are proprietary, which means they use nonstandard code that requires special server extensions in order to display the web site correctly. That's not necessarily a problem, but it can be.

What can be an even bigger problem with HTML editors is that sometimes the vendors make significant changes to their products without making them backward compatible. For example, if your host upgrades server extensions to newer proprietary extensions—which they usually will so they can offer the latest advancements and security—that simple upgrade can break your web site if your site uses outdated proprietary code that is no longer supported.

As I sit here writing this book, a friend who is a web designer has some unhappy clients. He created all their sites using a very popular, but proprietary, HTML editor. The software vendor recently made some changes to the HTML editor and server extensions, and now many of my friend's customers' web sites are in various degrees of disrepair. The real problem is that he hasn't a clue how to fix them. He never learned how to code by hand; he only learned how to use his HTML editor.

That's why I'm a strong advocate of first learning to code manually. If something breaks and you have studied how to create web pages manually, you'll have the kind of knowledge you need to troubleshoot and fix many problems.

This book teaches web design using manual coding. I still code all my sites manually because I can work faster than I can using an HTML editor. I fully expect, however, that many readers of this book will migrate to some type of HTML editor sooner or later. Nonetheless, you'll be far better off having a foundation of knowledge to fall back on than my friend who only learned how to use a software program.

You should be aware of other drawbacks to using HTML editors. For example, some HTML editors may change the code you add manually. This usually breaks the code for whatever you wanted to add that your HTML editor couldn't do—and sooner or later you'll find a few things your HTML editor can't do that you want to do. While some HTML editors are free, the most popular and comprehensive ones can be quite expensive. If you rely on one of these editors, you'll be tied to costly software upgrades every year or two.

Finally, some HTML editors do not produce valid code 100 percent of the time. Software developers do not have to pass a test as web designers before producing software for creating web design code. While the code they produce generally works, that doesn't mean it's valid. Browsers are very forgiving at this stage of development. As XHTML takes over as the language of the web, however, that forgiveness is supposed to become a thing of the past—at least according to envisioned XHTML standards.

1.6 Web Design with Word Processors

YOU CAN USE ANY TEXT EDITOR to create web pages, but I do not recommend using a word processor. While some word processors will convert word processing files into HTML files so you don't have to look at the code, these software programs insert so much extra code and formatting that the pages often don't work in all browsers. The unnecessary code, which can make the file size of a web page three times or more larger, can also slow down the speed at which your web site downloads to a visitor's browser, and they definitely make it much more difficult to edit if you have to work directly in the code at a later date.

1.7 Your Computer or Mine?

HTML STANDARDS greatly help web designers create sites that display properly across various platforms without having to resort to workarounds and code tricks. Many webmasters, however, are still surprised to find that web sites that look so nice on their computers can still look very bad on different computers.

The problem is no longer a lack of HTML standards but that each computer is different. One computer may be set up with an 800x600 display resolution, while another could be lower or much, much higher. Different computers also have different capabilities as to how many colors they can display. While HTML standards have helped with page rendering, the various browsers still have differences in the way they render pages.

All these things contribute to how web sites look on different systems using different hardware and software. By checking your web site using different browsers and, if possible, on different computers, we can fairly determine if it displays consistently on different computer systems. If you have more than one computer, you can check it on each one, or view it at the library or on friends' and relatives' computers. This will give you an idea of how well it displays on a few different systems. At some point, though, you just have to call it good.

1.8 What You Make It

IN THE END, WEB SITE DESIGN can be anything from a hobby to a very good living for you. What you make of it is mostly up to you. I started my first web site as a hobby in 1997. Two years later I was working for myself full-time from home. You'll find many resources on my web site that will help you along your road to enjoyment and success, no matter what your web design aspirations are.

You'll find my main web site at:

www.BoogieJack.com

You'll find this book's resource page at:

www.BoogieJack.com/book/resources.html

If you want to keep learning web design beyond what this book teaches, I recommend you subscribe to my ezine (an electronic newsletter) called *Almost a Newsletter*. You'll find the subscription form on my main web site.

1.9 Chapter 1 Exercise

I recommend this to instructors as an ungraded exercise. Because this chapter isn't conducive to having a web design exercise, I suggest students create a short essay on their reasons for wanting to learn web design. Also, because goals are important to success, they should outline what their goals are for one year from now and five years from now as it pertains to web design.

Further, I suggest that due to the personal nature of goal setting, that these goals are kept private from other students—unless a student volunteers to share them.

An Overview of HTML, XHTML, and CSS

2.1 What is HTML?

HTML FILES ARE LITTLE MORE than glorified text files. If you can type—or even hunt and peck—you can create a simple web page.

The HTML code tells the browser how to display the page content. It does this through the use of *markup tags* (referred to as simply a *tag* from this point forward). These tags are not visible to the viewer of the HTML page. Here's an example of an HTML tag:

That tag tells the browser to begin displaying the text that follows in bold type. This very basic tag consists of a left arrow bracket, the HTML element reference inside, and a right arrow bracket.

That is the beginning tag. For most HTML elements, there are also end tags:

That tells the browser to stop displaying text in bold type. The forward slash in front of an HTML element instructs the browser to cancel that element.

That's the basic idea of HTML; it is simply the little sets of instructions that tell the browser what to do with your content. To make one of my favorite sayings display in bold text on a web page, we'd code it like this:

If you do what you've always done, you'll get what you've always gotten.

On a web page, that would display like this:

If you do what you've always done, you'll get what you've always gotten.

As you can see, only the text shows up, and it shows up in bold type as the HTML tag instructed, but the code that made it bold does not show up. A large part of web design is simply learning how to write those little code snippets that tell the browser how to display your content.

Code instructions must use the proper *syntax*. Syntax is simply the rules that define the form the HTML tags must be written in to work.

That's how HTML works. Simple! There are other tags that cause the browser to create a paragraph space, display text in italic type, display a picture, play a sound, and do many other things. This book will teach you how to do all that and more.

2.2 Elements, Attributes, Values, and Syntax

THE FIRST PART of the text inside the arrow brackets is the HTML *element*. In the previous example that created bold text, the letter **b** is the element. Elements are simply the HTML identifiers that tell the browser which part of the page structure is to be affected. To change the page structure, you only need to code which element of the page you want to change, and, sometimes how it should be changed. And you need to code it correctly. The way these pieces of code are written is called the *syntax*.

Many *elements* can also have *attributes* and *values*. An attribute identifies the part of the element you want to modify, and the value identifies how to modify it. For example, to create a table with a width of 480 pixels, I'd code it as follows:

```
<table width="480">
```

In the above code, *table* is the HTML element, *width* is the attribute of the element to be modified, and *480* is the *value* of the attribute as measured in *pixels*. (A pixel is the default unit of measurement in HTML. We'll go into more details about units of measurement later.) Figure 2.1 shows how the syntax of this code breaks down into its individual components.

If I didn't add the width attribute and value, the table wouldn't have a set width. Instead, the width would adjust itself to the space available and/or the content of the table. The equal sign tells the browser the attribute is equal to whatever is given as the value, and the value of an attribute must always be contained in straight quotation marks.

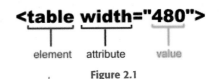

element   attribute   value

Figure 2.1

2.3 Multiple Attributes and Values

MANY HTML TAGS have more than one attribute that can be modified. Let's add two more attributes to the table tag we created previously.

<table width="480" **cellpadding="5" cellspacing="7"**>

As you can see, I've added *cellpadding* and *cellspacing* as attributes to the table. I've given a value of 5 pixels to the cellpadding attribute, and 7 pixels to the cellspacing attribute. For this one table element, we now have three attributes: the width, cellpadding, and cellspacing. Cellpadding and cellspacing are discussed in the chapter on tables.

2.4 Block Level and Inline Elements

IN WEB DESIGN, we use elements to define the structure of a web page—that is, how the web page content will be arranged. These elements are either *block level* or *inline*. A block level element is basically an element that creates a separation from other content. In other words, it creates a new "block" of content. An inline element does not create a separation of content; whatever the new element is supposed to do, it does so within the flow of the content into which it is inserted.

Let's look at two examples. To create a new paragraph of text, we use a paragraph tag. Here's a paragraph tag:

<p>

If we use a paragraph tag in the flow of text, the paragraph tag creates a new block of text, separated from the block of text before it, even if you type it on the same line in your code. Thus, it's a block level element because it causes a new block of content that starts on another line.

If we use a bold tag, the text within the opening and closing bold tags displays in bold, but the bold text flows in the same line of text without causing a new block of content. In other words, the bold element creates bold text **within the flow of the content** just like it appears in this sentence. A bold element, as you can see, is an inline element.

2.5 Elemental Hierarchy

ELEMENTS CAN ALSO be nested. That just means some elements can be placed inside other elements. Here's an example of two elements nested inside another element:

```
<div>
<b>Life is full of surprises.</b>
<p>We should not be surprised by that.</p>
</div>
```

Inside the <div> tag set (div = division), I placed a sentence inside a bold tag set, and then I created a paragraph line break and added another sentence. I then canceled the paragraph and canceled the division.

What I did is nested some bold text and a paragraph inside a division. On a web page, that displays like this:

Life is full of surprises.

We should not be surprised by that.

As you can see, the HTML code does not show up on the actual web page (unless a mistake is made). With nested tags, the outer tag set that surrounds the enclosed tags is called the *parent* element. The enclosed tags are the *child* elements. In the example shown, the <div> is the parent element, while the <b> and <p> tags are child elements.

Are you starting to sweat yet? Don't worry, it will get easier. You won't need to increase your deodorant budget.

Now then, for properly nested tags, you must close them in the reverse order they were opened. So, if you open:

```
<tag 1>
<tag 2>
<tag 3>
```

...they must be closed in the reverse order:

```
</tag 3>
</tag 2>
</tag 1>
```

The tags were opened in 1,2,3 order, so they must be closed in 3,2,1 order. See if you can spot what is wrong with the following code:

```
<b>This is bold type. <i>This is bold, italic type.</b></i>
```

Did you spot the error? I opened an HTML tag to begin bold text, and then added a tag to begin italic text, but when I closed them, I closed the bold tag before the italic tag. Since the italic tag was the last one opened and was a child element of the bold tag, I should have closed the italic tag *before* I closed the bold tag.

Here's how the code should be written:

```
<b>This is bold type. <i>This is bold, italic type.</i></b>
```

In the corrected code, I opened the tags in 1,2 fashion, and closed them in 2,1 fashion, just as they should be. I also changed the color of the second set of tags to give you a better visual reference. Here's how that code displays on a web page:

This is bold type. *This is bold, italic type.*

That is the basic idea behind HTML. It will become more obvious to you in the next chapter. Hang in there, kiddo, I promise not to break your brain!

2.6 What is XHTML?

As HTML WAS DEFINED and refined numerous times, it began to break down into a lot of inconsistent rules. Some HTML tags had to be closed, some didn't. Some attribute values were required to be enclosed in straight quotation marks, others weren't. Some mistakes were forgiven by some browsers, while other browsers were unforgiving of the same code errors.

Rather than having overriding structural concepts applied consistently throughout the language, HTML became fragmented into inconsistent smaller concepts that contributed to confusion and browser display inconsistencies. To correct this problem, XHTML was formed. XHTML is a meshing of HTML and XML, and both are derived from SGML. Here's what all those darned letters stand for:

HTML:	HyperText Markup Language
XHTML:	eXtensible HyperText Markup Language
XML:	eXtensible Mark-up Language
SGML:	Standard Generalized Markup Language

SGML is considered a metalanguage, intended as the parent language from which all other document markup languages should be created. You might call it the mother of all markup languages. SGML is very complex and the software needed to work with it is very expensive, so it's not a viable language for creating web pages. It was actually created specifically as the parent language for creating other markup languages from. SGML was not intended for actual web design nor was it intended to be used by the average person.

XML is also a metalanguage, derived from SGML, that isn't well suited to web design for the general public because of its complexity and specialization. XML is more of a way to define data so it can be shared across different platforms.

The W3C came up with XHTML as a way to bring uniformity and more strict standards adherence to HTML. If you're familiar with HTML already, you'll be pleased to learn that much of what you already know about HTML is valid in XHTML. You won't have to start from scratch, but you will have to learn a few new tricks.

Like HTML, XHTML is a document layout language that uses most of the same syntax as HTML. It defines how a document's content is to be structured. In a sense, XHTML picks up where HTML left off because the W3C has no plans to further develop HTML. You must learn XHTML to keep up with the changing times in web design. For those who know some HTML, you'll be pleased to know XHTML and HTML use the exact same elements, but some of the syntax has changed. These and the other differences are explained in the next section.

2.7 Differences Between HTML and XHTML

THE DIFFERENCES BETWEEN HTML and XHTML are not very difficult. In reality, you're still making HTML pages, but you're making them XML compliant. Here's a list of the differences, followed by an explanation of each.

- XHTML documents must be well-formed.
- XHTML must use the proper DOCTYPE.
- XHTML must include a NameSpace declaration.
- All elements must be properly nested.
- Empty elements must be closed.
- All attributes must be assigned values.
- All attribute values must be enclosed in straight quotation marks.
- Syntax must be in lowercase only.

Before explaining all these items, be assured that the majority of this book is devoted to making HTML pages that are XHTML *compliant*. We will make a simple XHTML page later, but most of you will simply want to make XHTML-compliant pages because that's the most practical solution for most situations and web authors. These brief explanations are only intended to provide a general overview; more details are given as it becomes necessary.

2.7.1 XHTML Documents Must Be Well-Formed

A well-formed (or sometimes called well-structured) document is one that follows all the rules of XHTML and doesn't have coding errors. In theory, if an XHTML document isn't well-formed, a compliant browser will not display the page. Whether browsers actually do this is another matter. In reality, HTML authors have always been encouraged to write well-formed HTML pages, but many browsers have overlooked whatever mistakes they could and displayed the pages as well as could be interpreted. Still, you should strive to create well-formed pages because if you don't, the pages may not work at some point.

Note

If you're already a web author and wondering if you should go back through your old pages to make them XHTML compliant, I wouldn't unless you are redesigning a web site anyway. I would start making new pages XHTML compliant, but there are billions of old-school pages out there and I doubt if browser makers will deprogram their browsers so those older pages won't display. If they did, someone else would come out with a new browser that displayed the old pages and grab a lion's share of the browser market with little trouble.

2.7.2 XHTML Must Use the Proper DOCTYPE

A DOCTYPE is a declaration at the top of your document that tells the browser which standard should be used to interpret the web document. In HTML, it didn't matter if you included a DOCTYPE declaration or not, unless you wanted to validate your pages through an HTML validator. In XHTML a DOCTYPE is required.

In the first edition of this book, I recommended not using the DOCTYPE because, ironically enough, even some of the W3C's own pages wouldn't validate. Since it wasn't necessary for the browser and seemed to only vex people, I shunned using it. Web design has come a long way since those days, and while I am neutral on its use now, I have no problem with those who recommend using it. For most of the exercises in this book, however, we will not be using a DOCTYPE to help keep things simple.

2.7.3 XHTML Must Include a NameSpace Declaration

In HTML, both the tag semantics and the tag sets are fixed. In XML, authors create their own sets of tags or use a schema that someone else already developed. A schema defines the language to create the structure for a database. A librarian may use a library schema to catalog book details; a mathematician may use a mathematics schema to be able to include data types not available in HTML.

The xmlns declaration, short for **XML NameSpace**, is simply a way to identify which schema to use in parsing the document. While the xmlns declaration can technically be left out of an XHTML-compliant document, it is required for XML documents. For the XHTML document you make in Chapter 14, you're given a line of code to use, and that's really all you need to learn about it unless you go on to write XML.

2.7.4 All Elements Must Be Properly Nested

We've already covered this in section 2.5 Elemental Hierarchy, and the same information applies for XHTML. The only difference is that in HTML, browsers generally forgive most nesting errors, while in XHTML browsers aren't supposed to forgive nesting errors.

To quickly recap, nesting is when you open one set of tags inside another set of tags. Nested tags must be closed in the reverse order they were opened. Here's an example of a pair of properly nested tags:

`<b>This is bold type. <i>This is bold, italic type.</i></b>`

The bold tag was opened, then the italic tag. The italic tag was the last opened, so it was closed first, followed by closing the bold tag. Nesting...it isn't just for the birds.

2.7.5 Empty Elements Must Be Closed

An empty element is a tag that doesn't have a corresponding closing tag in HTML. In a normal HTML tag, there are opening and closing tags:

`<tag>Content</tag>`

Between the opening and closing tags is a block of content. In an empty tag, there is no block of content; all the needed information is contained within the opening tag itself.

Here are three examples of empty tags:

`<br>` (break tag)

`<meta name="description" content="Describes the content.">` (meta tag)

`<img src="file.ext">` (image tag)

The break tag tells the browser to start the content that follows on the next line; no closing tag was needed. The meta description tag and image tag contain all the information the browser needs within the tag. In HTML, that's all you need because the tags have no corresponding closing tags. In XHTML, all tags must be closed. To get around the fact that there are no closing tags for these elements, a space and forward slash is added to the end of the tags just before the right arrow bracket. Here's how those tags are closed to be XHTML compliant:

`<br />`

`<meta name="description" content="Describes the content." />`

`<img src="file.ext" />`

Note

While adding a space and slash to the end of a meta tag is technically correct to be XHTML compliant, doing so may cause validation errors. In that case, we either have to accept the errors or use technically incorrect code.

This transforms the tags into self-closing tags. Take care to include an *empty space* before the closing forward slash or the tag will be invalid and may cause errors.

2.7.6 All Attributes Must Be Assigned Values

In HTML, some attributes have no value options. For example:

```
<input type="checkbox" selected>
```

In the above code, *selected* is an attribute for a form input checkbox that is not assigned a value in HTML because the value is the same as the attribute. To be XHMTL compliant, the *selected* attribute must include a value. Here's how that's done:

```
<input type="checkbox" selected="selected">
```

As you can see, it's just a matter of adding = "*selected*" to the attribute. This is how all valueless HTML attributes are treated in XHTML. You'll find a list of all the valueless attributes in Appendix A: HTML and XHTML Charts.

2.7.7 All Attribute Values Must Be Enclosed in Straight Quotation Marks

In HTML, some attribute values don't have to be enclosed in quotation marks. For example:

```
<table width=580>
```

In XHTML, all attribute values must be enclosed in straight quotation marks. The previous tag should be written as:

```
<table width="580">
```

2.7.8 Syntax Must Be in Lowercase Only

In HTML, it doesn't matter if you write code in **UPPERCASE** or **lowercase**. All five image tags below mean the exact same thing to a browser and display the image in the exact same way on a web page with them on it.

```
<img src="picture.jpg">
<IMG SRC="picture.jpg">
```

```
<img SRC="picture.jpg">
<IMG src="picture.jpg">
<iMg SrC="picture.jpg">
```

In XHTML, only the first tag would work because it's the only one in all lowercase. The *file name* and *file extension*, on the other hand, *do not* have to be in lowercase; they need to be coded as they were saved. The file name is not part of the tag syntax. The tag syntax is the part of the code that never changes.

2.8 What is CSS?

CASCADING STYLE SHEETS, or CSS for short, is a supplement to HTML. Whereas HTML defines the *structure* of a web page, CSS defines the *presentation* of the structural elements. In other words, HTML defines the layout of the page while CSS defines the way those elements appear (the color, for example).

That can be a difficult concept if you're new to all this, so let me break it down using a graphic for visual reference.

In Figure 2.2, you can see a heading without CSS styling. It's the default color of black and a predetermined size.

Below that is a heading I styled using CSS. I changed the font, color, and text size.

Under the heading is a paragraph displayed at the default setting. Below that is a paragraph I styled with a border, background color, and text color change.

The *structure* defines which elements are displayed and the *presentation* defines how those elements are displayed.

Clear as a foggy day in London? Great!

The syntax of CSS is similar, but different than HTML. See Figure 2.3 for a comparison.

The *element* in HTML is called the selector in CSS. The attribute in HTML is called the property in CSS. The value in HTML is also called the value in CSS.

You'll learn more about CSS in Chapter 4, CSS Kick-start. At the time of this writing CSS3 (CSS version 3) is still under

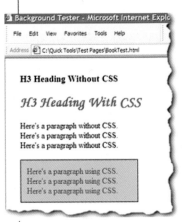

Figure 2.2

HTML Example	CSS Example
`<body bgcolor="black">`	body {background-color: black;}
body is the HTML element bgcolor is the attribute black is the value	body is the CSS selector background-color is the property black is the value

Figure 2.3

development. This book teaches CSS2.1, which isn't even fully supported by most browsers. Although CSS2 has been the standard since 2002, it still isn't fully implemented. When CSS3 is finalized, it could take years before it's implemented into browser software. This has been the history, and it isn't likely to change. To keep current on the progress of CSS3, visit the W3C web site at www.w3.org.

2.9 Deprecated and Obsolete Tags

IN A FEW PLACES IN THIS BOOK I refer to *deprecated* and *obsolete* tags. A deprecated tag is one that is destined to become obsolete. While the tag can still be used and should still render the element properly in most browsers, in most cases you should not use them. The reason for not using deprecated tags is simple—someday they will become obsolete.

Obsolete tags should never be used. While obsolete tags may be supported by some browsers (or all browsers) long after they become obsolete, at the software vendor's discretion sooner or later they are likely to become nonfunctioning. Once they no longer work, your pages will not render the same and may have to be redesigned. Save yourself the trouble by staying away from deprecated and obsolete tags to begin with.

2.10 Chapter 2 Exercise

All students will be building a web site about the same topic (unless the instructor allows other topics). The reason for using the same topic is so instructors can compare apples to apples. Otherwise, instructors have to compare how well each student has presented many diverse topics with which he or she may have no familiarity.

The topic I chose may even help make the world a better place. In fact, that is the topic—how we can make the world a better place. You can approach this from an individual, community, regional, state, national, or global level—or all of those perspectives if you're ambitious and bubbling with ideas.

Why this topic? Rather than using your mind in a passive learning mode, the mind is actively engaged in analytical and creative thinking. This better reflects the challenges of an individual's professional and personal life.

Also, we all live in the same world, so when we make the world better for another person or group, we make it better for ourselves. If everyone thinks about how to make the world better, there is a good chance some excellent ideas will come out of the class. I believe that at some point some of you will act on some of the ideas the class generates. Maybe someone will even come up with a brilliant idea that spreads out like ripples on the water, creating waves of positive influence that benefit an uncountable number of people. By encouraging you to do something to make the world better, if anyone acts on the ideas, I've also helped make the world better.

I recognize that this subject won't tickle everyone, so at the instructor's discretion, he or she may assign a different topic or throw it open to any topic. As an alternative, maybe you can create a web site showing how established groups such as Big Brothers/Big Sisters, Meals on Wheels, the United Way, the Salvation Army, the Red Cross, or other "help" organizations are already positively impacting individual lives and/or communities.

Because this chapter, like Chapter 1, isn't conducive to having a web design exercise, and to prepare you for the exercises in the coming chapters, your assignment is to think about how the world could be made better (or an alternative assignment if your instructor approves or assigns it). Decide if you want to approach the exercise from an individual perspective, if you want to think on a larger scale, or even if you want to offer one or more ideas at each level.

Jot down your ideas and some of your key points for making the world better. You can go into as much detail as you like. The more ideas for improving the world you have, the less detail you'll probably have time to develop, so decide if you want to present one or two comprehensive ideas or several less-detailed ideas.

Try to have fun with this. It's only an exercise; you can't really make any grievous mistakes.

Just because there is no assignment to turn in, do not take this chapter exercise lightly. After the next chapter, you'll be put to work on actual web design exercises. Those who skate now will pay the price for it later when you have to do this chapter's exercise before you can start the next one.

HTML Kick-Start

3.1 Getting Ready

THIS CHAPTER SHOWS YOU just how easy making a simple web page can be, and you'll be making your first web page just minutes from now! The first thing to do is to open the text editing program you want to use. I recommend Notepad on Windows or TextEdit on Mac OS.

To open Notepad:

1. Click the *Start* button.
2. Select *All Programs*.
3. Select *Accessories*.
4. Click *Notepad*.

See Figure 3.1 for a visual aid.

Figure 3.1

To open TextEdit:

1. From your Mac OS desktop, double-click the *hard drive icon*.
2. Double-click the *Applications* folder.
3. Double-click the *TextEdit* icon.

TIP

Once TextEdit is running, click on its icon in the dock and choose Keep In Dock. To launch TextEdit again, click the TextEdit icon in the dock once.

Figure 3.2

See Figure 3.2 for a visual aid.

Figure 3.3

In Notepad, if you don't have Word Wrap checked everything you type without a carriage return (pressing the Enter key) will be on one long line. This makes it more difficult to work with, so make sure Word Wrap has a check mark by it by:

1. Click *Format* on the menu bar.
2. Click *Word Wrap* if there is no check mark beside it.

See Figure 3.3 for a visual aid.

You are now ready to create your first web page! How do you feel? Are you almost dizzy with excitement? Calm down already, wow...you sure get excited easily.

3.2 The Basic HTML Skeleton

EVERY WEB PAGE has a basic structure. This structure comprises just a few HTML tags that are common to each page.

Here are the basic elements required for a web page:

<html>

<head>

<title>Page Title Here</title>

</head>

<body>

The visible page content goes here. This is the only part that will show up in a browser.

</body>

</html>

See Figure 3.4 to see how this looks in Notepad.

We'll cover each of these elements in a moment, but because I promised that you'd make your first web page in

Figure 3.4

just minutes, let's do it! Since you have your text editor open, go ahead and type those HTML elements into a new file—only where it says "The visible page content goes here..." type your name instead. You can add a little message or something else if you like, I'm flexible. Do it now, I'll wait.

3.3 Saving Your First Web Page

Done already? You are the speedy one!

Now we'll save that file as an HTML page and you can look at it in your browser. To save the file you just made as a web page:

To Save Files in Notepad

1. From the *File* menu, click the *Save As* option. See Figure 3.5 for a visual aid.

    Step 1 opens the *Save As* dialog box. You'll need to choose the location on your computer or removable media where you want to save your web page. For this exercise, we'll assume you're working on a school computer and need to save it to an external disk.

2. In the Save As dialog box, select the *external disk drive* (usually drive A). Be sure there is a disk in the drive before trying to save your file there. See Figure 3.6 for a visual aid.

3. Once you've selected where you're going to save your file, type: "index.html" ... in the *File name* field. Be sure to include the quotation marks around the file name and file extension. This prevents Notepad from appending a .txt (text) extension to the file.

    Instead of typing the quotation marks around the file name and extension, you also could click the down arrow in the *Save as type* field and select *All Files*. This also allows you to enter your own file extension, but without the need for quotation marks. See Figure 3.7 for a visual aid.

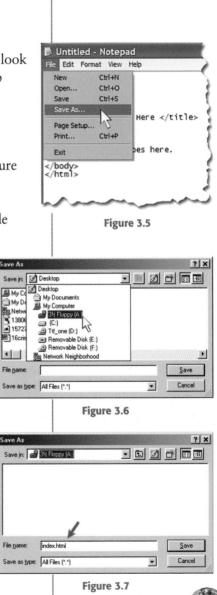

Figure 3.5

Figure 3.6

Figure 3.7

Note

When you reopen the index.html file in TextEdit, open it through *File > Open* (not by double-clicking it on the desktop) and be sure to check *Ignore Rich Text Commands.*

To Save Files in TextEdit

1. Choose *Format > Make Plain Text* or press Cmd+Shift+T. Click OK to bypass the alert.

2. Choose *File > Save As*.

3. Click the arrow next to the Save As field to expand the dialog box.

4. Choose Desktop from the scroll list at left or from the menu at the top.

5. Click the *New Folder* button to create a new folder on the desktop.

6. Type *My Web Site* in the Name of new folder field, and then click *Create*.

7. Type: index.html…in the *Save this document* as field.

8. Leave the *Plain Text Encoding* menu set at *Western (Mac OS Roman)*.

9. Uncheck *If no extension is provided, use ".txt"*.

10. Click *Save*.

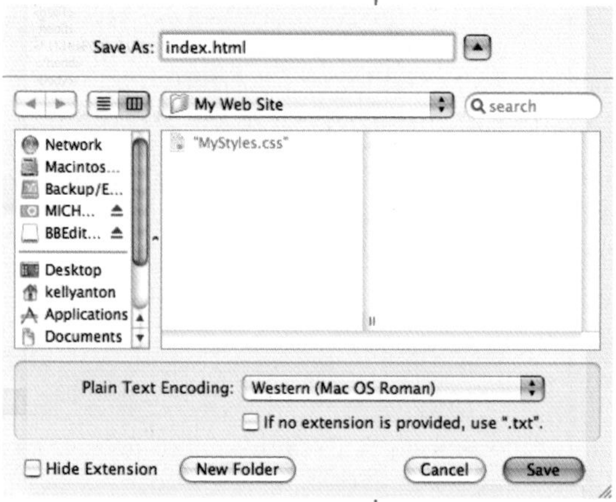

Figure 3.8

See Figure 3.8 for a visual aid.

The file you just saved is known as the *source code* of the web page document. Remember that term, *source code*, as I'll be referring to it again and again.

3.4 Viewing Your First Web Page

IF I TOLD YOU there were 400 billion stars in the Milky Way galaxy, you'd probably believe me. But if I told you that you've already made a fully functional web page, you'd probably want proof, and proof you shall have.

Open your browser and view the page you just made. If you don't know how to open the page you made, just follow these steps to open the page in Internet Explorer on Windows.

Opening Your New Web Page on Windows

1. With Internet Explorer open, select *File* from the main menu and click *Open*. An even easier method is to press

the *Control* key and the letter *O* on your keyboard. See Figure 3.9 for visual aid.

2. Step 1 opens the *Open* dialog box. In the Open dialog box, click the *Browse* button. See Figure 3.10 for a visual aid.

3. Navigate to the external disk or wherever you saved your *index.html* file. Click the index page in the main window so that its name appears in the *File name* field, then click *Open*. See Figure 3.11 for visual aid.

4. The step above returns you to the Open dialog box from step 2, only now the file you want to open should be listed in the *Open* field.

Click *OK*, and your web page opens in your browser window.

I told you that it was easy. Much easier than counting all those sparkling stars in the Milky Way!

Opening your web page in other browsers such as Netscape, Opera, and Firefox are very similar. You basically select the *Open* option from the *File* menu, and find the file you want to open.

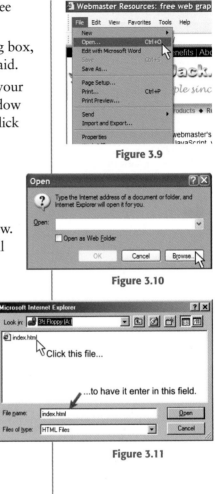

Figure 3.9

Figure 3.10

Figure 3.11

The instructions for Mac OS are a little different. To open a page in Safari on Mac OS:

Opening Your New Web Page on Mac OS

1. If necessary, click the Safari icon in the dock. Choose *File > Open File*.

   An even easier method is to press the *Command* key (aka the Apple key) and the letter *O* on your keyboard.

2. Choose *My Web Site* from the menu at the top of the *Open* dialog box.

3. Click on your *index.html* file to select it.

4. Click *Open*.

See Figure 3.12 for a visual aid.

TIP

If the new folder is not showing, click Desktop in the scroll list at left, and then click the My Web Site folder.

Note

Because technology can change at any time, these instructions may vary slightly from version to version of any browser or operating system. If they don't appear correct, don't be afraid to snoop around the menu options to find what you want.

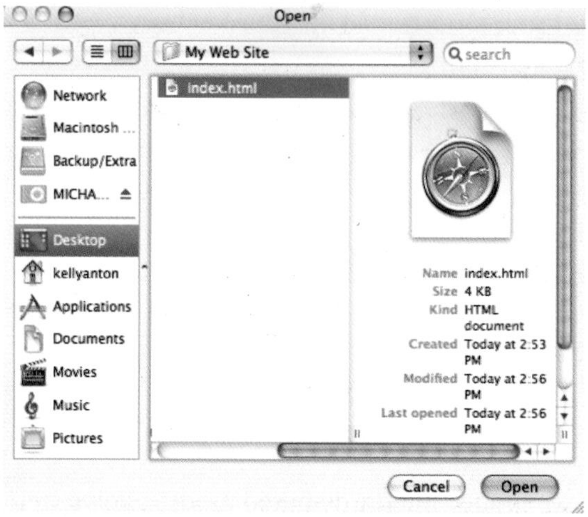

Figure 3.12

If you followed the instructions for making a simple web page, saving it, and opening it, you should have seen your web page in all its glory opened in your browser. Congratulations, you have successfully made your first web page.

In the following sections we'll break down each tag we used in the code for your web page so you understand what they do. Be sure to keep this practice web page you've just created —we will be working with it again in the next chapter.

3.5 The <html> Tag Explained

EACH WEB PAGE starts off with the **<html>** tag, which serves to identify the language the document is written with. The page ends by canceling the **</html>** tag. Everything else goes in between the opening and closing HTML tags. However, starting a web page off with only this simple language identifier means your web page will be displayed by browsers in what is known as "quirks" mode.

Once upon a time there were three little pigs. One little pig built his house out of…no wait, wrong story. Once upon a time each browser had its own way of interpreting and displaying HTML pages. Web designers had to use all kinds of tricks and workarounds to get their web pages to display approximately the same in each browser. Nowadays, though, most browsers closely follow the standards set by the W3C, so all those old browser tricks and workarounds are no longer necessary.

However, millions of old web pages still alive on the Internet rely on all those old tricks to display correctly, so most modern browsers have a "quirks mode" built into them so those old pages are still functional. At the time of this writing, however, Opera has no quirks mode.

With reliable standards in place, a browser needs a way to detect if it should operate in quirks mode, or according to one of several standards modes. This is where the DOCTYPE declaration (DTD) comes into play. If a browser finds a DOCTYPE declaration at the top of the page, it will use the standard mode specified in that DTD. If it does not find a DOCTYPE, it will default to the quirks mode.

Having a quirks mode and standards-based modes allows web designers to step into the future of standards-based design without compromising the functionality of older pages. If you want to ensure your web pages are standards compliant and will validate with an HTML validator, you will need to use a DOCTYPE declaration. For the exercises in this book, however, we will not be including a DOCTYPE in our pages simply because it's easier to work without it, and in most cases it just isn't necessary.

It should be noted that many web design authors (besides me) recommend only using a DOCTYPE if you are writing XHTML pages. They suggest leaving the DOCTYPE out of plain HTML pages. I'll leave that decision up to you, or to your instructor if you're using this book in a classroom setting. Personally, I have seldom used the DOCTYPE in the past, but I may start using it on future sites if for no other reason than to avoid having people ask me why I don't use it.

When you create a real web site on your own, you will need to decide if you want to use the DOCTYPE declaration. If you do, place it *before* the opening <html> tag, making it the first thing on the page. To give you an idea what it looks like, here's an example of a web page using a DOCTYPE declaration:

```
<!DOCTYPE html PUBLIC "-//W3C//DTD HTML 4.01
Transitional//EN" "http://www.w3.org/TR/html4/loose.dtd">

<html>

<head>

<title> Page Title Here </title>

</head>
```

```
<body>

The page content goes here.

</body>
</html>
```

The lines in red type *preceding* the <html> tag identify the DOCTYPE the browser should use is HTML 4.01 Transitional and English is the language of the page, and it identifies the web address where the standard is located. The rest of the code is the same basic HTML skeleton from Section 3.2 of this chapter.

3.6 The <head> Tag Explained

THE HEAD SECTION of a web page encloses other header elements. The opening <head> tag should be placed directly after the opening <html> tag. The TITLE tag set is placed between the opening and closing HEAD tags.

Other header information can be placed inside the HEAD area as well, which we'll discuss later. Header content is used to provide the browser and search engines with information about the document. It is also used to point the browser to other resources such as the style sheet the page uses and for coding JavaScript into the page.

3.7 The <title> Tag Explained

THE <title> TAG OFTEN GETS glossed over by amateur web designers, but it's actually very important. The text used between the opening and closing TITLE tag set is the text that appears in the Title Bar at the top of the browser window. See Figure 3.13 for a visual aid showing the browser's title bar.

Because search engines use the text from the title tag as the link for the web page, it's important to craft a good title that entices the searcher to read the description of your page. A good title can lure visitors to click the link without reading the page description. But at the very least it should encourage them to read the page description if they don't immediately click the link.

In addition to the TITLE text appearing in the Title Bar of the browser, it also shows up as the default text for the bookmark when users add your site to their favorites list.

A properly crafted title contains keywords that are relevant to the page it is on. Keywords are the words someone types into a search engine to search for something. By including 1–3 keywords in your title, the title becomes relevant for people searching on those keywords, and, to a lesser degree, for content closely related to the keywords.

Figure 3.13

A properly crafted title should also be free from hype. Search engines do not like hype, and most people don't either. Just make an honest representation of what your page is about and it will work for the search engines, web surfers, and your site. Keep the title to about 60 characters or less to avoid problems with the text being truncated.

You can find more information about search engine optimization on my web site at www.BoogieJack.com.

3.8 The <body> Tag Explained

THE BODY OF THE WEB PAGE is where you put all the content you want people to see—text, graphics, etc. The content is placed between the opening and closing body tags.

At one time, web designers included attributes and values into the body tag that controlled text color, background color and image, link colors, and other elements of the page. Nowadays, all that and more are all accomplished using CSS.

The body tag is still sometimes used to add certain JavaScript instructions to the page, but other than that, the body tag is pretty bare boned these days. It merely identifies the beginning of the visible content.

3.9 Meta Elements

META ELEMENTS ARE OPTIONAL elements that are not part of the basic HTML structure. It makes more sense, however, to talk about them here than in any other section of the book.

The meta element can be used to (a) identify properties of a document such as a page description, author, expiration date, list of key words, or copyright holder and (b) to assign values to those properties. The specification does not define a standard set of properties. With no defined properties, the author is free to create his or her own properties—but the value of creating meta elements that a browser or search engine doesn't understand is questionable at best. There are some meta elements that browsers and search engines do understand, and we will be using two of them in the practice site you'll make.

Each meta element specifies two attribute/value pairs. The *name* attribute identifies the type or purpose of the meta tag, and the *content* attribute is the description (value) attached to the name attribute. This is easier to understand when you look at an actual meta tag. Examples follow.

The two most common meta tags are the *keywords* meta tag and the *description* meta tag. Here's an example of how they are used:

```
<meta name="description" content="Define the
web page content here." />

<meta name="keywords" content="enter, your,
keywords, here" />
```

The first tag, the *description* meta tag, is used to describe the content or purpose of the web page where it's used. Some search engines use the content of the description meta tag as the description for your site in their search engine listings. For that reason, it's wise to take the time to write a good description that appeals to the kinds of users you are trying to attract to the page.

The second tag, the *keywords* meta tag, is used to list keywords and keyword phrases that are relevant to the page. Keywords and keyword phrases should be separated by commas.

Some say meta tags are no longer relevant because search engines ignore them, but that's not entirely true. While the keywords meta tag is no longer used by most search engines as part of their page ranking algorithm, at least one study indicates that it may help strengthen a site's theme. Having a theme, or primary focus, to your web site helps with search engine rankings. Also, I know of at least one search engine that will not include your site in their database if you do not include a description meta tag.

Meta elements are coded into the <head> section of the web page, and should be placed just after the <title> ... </title> tag set. There is no closing tag for meta elements, so they should be closed according to XHTML compliance, which is to place a space and forward slash before the right-arrow end character, as shown in the previous examples. As I mentioned in Chapter 2 though, closing a meta tag this way may cause validation errors, in which case you'll have to choose between error free validation or technically correct code.

3.10 Closing Remarks

IN CLOSING, STUDY the basic HTML skeleton in the following code example.

```
<html>
<head>
<title> Page Title Here </title>
</head>
<body>

The page content goes here.

</body>
</html>
```

Notice how each tag that was opened, was also closed. Notice too, how they were each closed in the proper sequence. All the tags that were opened after the <html> tag were closed before the </html> tag. The <title> tag was opened (nested) inside the <head> tag, so the </title> was coded before the </head> tag was coded. The <body> was opened, content was placed inside the body, then the </body> was coded before ending the document with the </html> tag.

This is the proper nesting of tags you'll have to use throughout your web pages. If you need a refresher on nesting tags, please review Section 2.5: Elemental Hierarchy, in Chapter 2: An Overview of HTML, XHTML, and CSS.

3.11 Chapter 3 Exercise

In Chapter 2, the exercise was for students to decide which level they want to approach improving the world from and to come up with some ideas. In this chapter, students have already created a web page using the basic HTML skeleton. Part of the exercise is to add a keywords meta tag and a description meta tag (as shown in Section 3.9) to that basic page.

● Description meta tag: Do your best to write a description that would entice a search engine user to want to visit your web site without using hype, all capital letters, or exclamation marks. Sell your site with your words, not with unsophisticated text gimmicks.

● Keywords meta tag: Be sure to use keywords and keyword phrases relevant to the topic of making the world a better place. Use at least five keywords or keyword phrases, but no more than 20 (8–12 is an optimal mark to shoot for). Do not repeat any one keyword more then three times. For example, if you were building a site about widgets, you could use "widgets" as a single keyword and then "metal widgets" and "wooden widgets" as keyword phrases, but you may not list the word "widget" again. Search engines consider excessive word repetition an attempt to spam their database.

● Next, change the TITLE text in the source code to words that are relevant to your class project. Be sure to use at least one keyword or keyword phrase in the title text. Save your page and then view it to make sure the title text shows up in the title bar of the browser.

● Finally, you are the head of a fictitious organization that is building this web site to promote ideas for improving the world. Decide on a name for your organization. Since you will not be using this fictitious organization's name outside of the classroom, don't be concerned if it's a name that is similar to or the same as one already in use. You'll put the name to use in the next chapter exercise.

CSS Kick-Start

4

4.1 Introduction

USING MY FINE COMMAND of techno-babble, CSS is a cross-platform, standards-based programming language supplement to HTML designed to facilitate page presentation capabilities. Got it? Would you like that explained in plain English now?

To refresh your memory from Chapter 2, Cascading Style Sheets (CSS for short) is a supplement to HTML. Whereas HTML defines the *structure* of a web page, CSS defines the *presentation* of the structural elements.

Let's make it even easier to understand.

HTML is used to set the placement of paragraphs, headings, and other elements in order to create the page structure or layout. Meanwhile CSS determines the way the elements that define the structure appear. CSS defines appearances such as font color and size, background color or images, word spacing, text alignment, page margins, and the borders around elements, for example.

If you think of a web page like a house, HTML is the foundation, framework, and other hidden structural elements while CSS is the floor coverings, wall coverings, and other visible elements. Unlike a house, however, web site owners don't have to pay property taxes on their web site property. Wahoo!

This chapter introduces you to the basic concepts of CSS and the three ways to apply the styles. In the chapters that follow you'll apply many styles to your practice web site. While the concepts may seem difficult to grasp at first, they will make sense when you see them a few times and actually start applying them in the chapter exercises.

4.2 Style Rules

THE STYLES ARE WHATEVER you decide—within the structure of the language, of course. For example, if you want all your H1 size headings to be in red text, and all your paragraphs to have the first line indented by 20 pixels, you can create style rules that define those styles. That's what style sheets are: the *rules you create* to control the appearance of the elements of your web page.

Creating a rule isn't as difficult as it sounds. A style rule is simply how you define an HTML element to appear. For example, to write the style rule so all H1 headings are rendered in red text, you create a rule in an external style sheet like this:

```
h1 {color: red;}
```

There now, that doesn't look too hard, does it? It really isn't hard. It's just a matter of learning bits and pieces of code as you need them, just as you did when learning the basic HTML skeleton. Once you understand the concept, you don't even have to remember most properties and values; you just have to know where to look them up as you need them. To refresh your memory from Chapter 2: An Overview of HTML, XHTML, and CSS, in the previous code *h1* is the *selector, color* is the *property*, and *red* is the *value*. That code creates the style rule for the h1 HTML element. Easy!

An HTML element is modified from its default value by either:

- Giving the HTML element an HTML attribute and value, or
- Giving the CSS selector a property and value.

Both modifiers work similarly, but they use different terms and formatting. The two biggest advantages of using CSS are:

- You only have to create one rule to affect the style of an HTML element each time you use it. With HTML, you have to code the change into each use of the element.
- With CSS you can change one file and have that change reflected on every page of your site. With HTML, to make a site-wide change, you have to find and make the change you want in every place and on every page where that element was used.

Obviously, CSS requires much less work to use and maintain, but CSS is much more than that. Following are just a few things you can do with CSS that can't be done with HTML alone—without resorting to quirky tricks or tedious coding that may or may not work the same in all browsers:

- You can set different page margins for all sides of a page.

- You can set the font size for any text element to the exact height you want—no more preset size limitations.

- You can highlight single words, entire paragraphs, headings, or even individual **LETTERS** with different background colors and text colors if you really want to go crazy.

- You can overlap words and make logo-type headers without making images. See Figure 4.1 for an example of this. The overlapping of the words "Online Edition" and "Almost a Newsletter," make the text look like an image, but it's not. This is all text made to look like an image through a creative use of CSS.

Figure 4.1

- You can color the scrollbars on your web site, which can't be done in HTML at all. Technically, changing the scrollbars appearance isn't a legal CSS provision and it doesn't work in all browsers. It is, however, a highly popular option many people elect to use and it doesn't cause problems in browsers that don't support it. Perhaps a future version of CSS will allow it if enough people use it.

- You can precisely position elements.

- Borders, border styles, backgrounds, margins, and padding can be set for almost any HTML element.

- You can set the font for whole tables—no need to recode the same font over and over into each table cell.

- You can make the first letter of each paragraph different, set letter spacing, change the space between lines of text, and much, much more!

The only disadvantage to using CSS is that not all browsers offer full support for it. Even that disadvantage, however, is minimal because every major browser does support most CSS quite well nowadays; for those that don't, your page will still render—just not in all its stylized glory.

4.3 Implementation of Styles

ONE OF THE BEST REASONS for webmasters to use CSS is that it can be implemented in three different ways—inline, embedded, and external—so it's also a very flexible language. Following are the definitions of each.

4.3.1 Inline Styles

An inline style rule is coded into an HTML tag within the flow of the source code. The purpose of inline styles is to allow you to override an embedded or external style rule. For example, you may have a rule that specifies H3 headings are the color blue. If you have a place on a page where you want an H3 heading to be red, an inline style rule allows you to override the embedded or external style rule that made it blue in the first place. To override an embedded or external style, an inline style must be coded into each HTML element each time you want to override the default display or embedded or external style rules.

4.3.2 Embedded Styles

Embedded styles are set in the HEAD section of a web page. Embedded styles allow you to override the rules defined in an external style sheet. The difference is that with an embedded rule, you don't have to create a rule with each use of an HTML element. An element given an embedded style rule will render that element according to the embedded rule each time it's used on the page (if no inline style is used to override it).

4.3.3 External Styles

External styles, also called *linked* styles or *remote* styles, are the least important in the cascading order but the most powerful! An external style sheet has a link placed in the HEAD section of a web page to a separate file containing your style rules. The advantage of external style sheets is that you can change one external file, and have the change reflected on every page of a web site that draws its style rules from it. Any or all methods of implementing CSS can be used on the same page.

4.4 Cascading Order

B Y NOW YOU KNOW that styles are simply the rules you create for how various HTML elements display. The term *cascading* refers to the order of rule importance the browser should follow when it encounters conflicting style rules.

For example, you may have a rule in a linked style sheet that specifies that the first letter of the first word in every paragraph is bold. You may have another rule in your embedded styles that specifies that the first letter is normal text but red. The browser uses the cascading order to determine which rule to follow.

Here's the cascading order, in order of importance:

1. **! important**
   This can be added to any style rule, and nothing will override it. For example:

   h3 {color: red ! important}

   If used, this rule should be written as shown, with a space before and after the exclamation mark. This feature isn't well supported and may cause more problems than it's worth.

2. **Origin of Rules**
   Both the web page author and the web surfer can specify style sheets. A reader may have poor vision, so he or she creates a style sheet that renders text larger than normal. When rules between author and reader conflict, the author's rule will override the surfer's rule of equal weight.

   The one exception to the author's rule taking precedent is if the reader makes a rule important, it will override the author's rule—even if the author also has the same rule set as important. It used to be that the author's rule would take precedence over the reader's rule if both were marked important, but that has changed.

3. **Inline Styles**
   Inline styles win out over embedded styles and external styles.

4. **Embedded Styles**
   Embedded styles win out over external styles.

5. **External Styles**

External styles are wimps, only coming out to play when no other styles challenge them. As low in the cascading order as they are, they are still the most powerful because of the ability to change one file and have that change reflected on all your pages. In case you missed it earlier, external style sheets are also sometimes called *linked style sheets* or *remote style sheets*.

6. **Specificity**

If the previous conflict resolution hierarchy hasn't yet solved the problem, conflicting styles can be resolved based on specificity. The more specific style wins out over the less specific one.

7. **Order of Specification**

As a last resort, when all the other conflict resolution specifications cannot determine which style should take precedence, the last style specified will be the style used.

Don't worry too much about all this. I provided the list in case you run into something quirky, but all most folks need to know is that inline styles take precedence over embedded and external styles, and that embedded styles take precedence over external styles.

Now let's look at how each method of implementation is actually used.

4.5 Inline Styles

INLINE STYLES ARE ADDED directly to HTML tags, so using them is very much like adding an HTML attribute and value to an element—except the word *style* becomes the HTML attribute. You can use inline style tags anywhere in the body of an HTML document. Here's an example:

```
<blockquote style="padding: 10px;">
```

In the above code example, I took the HTML blockquote element and created a padding of 10 pixels within the element. Don't worry about what a blockquote or padding is for now—you'll learn about them later. Just notice how the style, shown in bold text, was added to the HTML element.

As with any HTML element, to end the blockquote I need to cancel it. That's accomplished like this:

```
</blockquote>
```

Using inline CSS affects only the HTML element that it's coded into. If you want to repeat that style for another block-quote on a page, you need to code that style into the other block-quote tag.

 Before proceeding, let's give you some experience in using inline CSS with a quick exercise. Open the practice page you made in Chapter 3: HTML Kick-Start.

Mac OS Note: When you reopen the index.html file in TextEdit, open it through *File > Open* (not by double-clicking it on the desktop) and be sure to check *Ignore Rich Text Commands.*

Once you have your file opened, add the following to the body of the page just under the line where you typed your name:

```
<p style="color: blue; font-size: 28px;">
This text should be in blue.
</p>
```

Once you've added that code, save the page and then open it in your browser. It should look like Figure 4.2, except you probably have a different name on your page. I'm guessing your name is Nogustram Nigglesnorfer.

Figure 4.2

4.6 Embedded Styles

EMBEDDED STYLES ARE CODED into the <HEAD> section of the page, between a style declaration opening tag and a style declaration closing tag. Remember that for inline style rules, you have to code a style into each HTML element where you want it used. Embedded style rules, on the other hand, affect every usage of the HTML element you've created a style rule for on the page where the rule is embedded. Here's an example of an embedded style:

```
<head>
<style type="text/css">
```

```
div {font-family: Arial; font-size: 12px; margin-left:
30px;}
p {border-left: solid red 1px; padding-left: 5px;}

</style>
</head>
```

If the previous style rules were placed in the HEAD section of a page, here's how it would affect the page display:

- Each time you use a division tag (<div>) on a page with that style rule, the text within that division displays in Arial font at 12 pixels high, and the division has a margin of 30 pixels on the left side.

- Each time you use a paragraph tag (<p>), a 1-pixel thick solid red line displays on the left edge, and 5 pixels of padding are placed between the red line and the text.

You probably noticed that the formatting of style rules differs from HTML. Good job! Let's look a little closer at that.

As you learned in Chapter 2: An Overview of HTML, XHTML, and CSS, HTML elements are enclosed between the < and > signs. Confusion would abound for webmasters and browser programmers alike if CSS also used arrow brackets. Therefore, the opening tag **<style type="text/css">** and closing tag **</style>** identify the code in between as CSS code.

The CSS *selectors* (the HTML elements you wish to create rules for, such as the *division* element and *paragraph* element in the previous code example) are listed without any arrow brackets since they are already enclosed between the opening and closing style declaration, so the browser knows they are CSS selectors. Each selector is then followed by a space and curly braces { ... } that contain the property and value, which is the rule or rules for the chosen selector.

The property and value are separated by a colon and space. For example:

```
font-family: Arial;
```

A semicolon signals the end of a rule. Because each selector can have more than one rule, the semicolon also serves as a rules separator. For example:

```
font-family: Arial; font-size: 12px; margin-left: 30px;
```

In that example (taken from the style rules I created for the division tag), you can see there are three rules, each shown in a different color for easier comprehension. You should always include the semicolon after a rule, even if you're only creating one rule. The truth is, a single rule will work most of the time if you forget the semicolon, but results can be unpredictable. It's also a good habit to start. If you make a habit of always including the semicolon, there's less of a chance you'll accidentally leave one out where it's needed as a rules separator. Troubleshooting a large style sheet to find one little error is unneeded work.

Time Out! Before going any further, let's once again make sure you understand the concept. Open your practice page and add the following code to the HEAD section of your page, just under the *<title>* … *</title>* tag set:

```
<style type="text/css">
div {width: 150px; border: 1px solid green; padding: 10px;}
</style>
```

After that, add the following code to the BODY of the web page just beneath the place where you added the blue text from the previous exercise.

```
<div>
This text is boxed in!
</div>
```

Once you've done that, save it and open the page in your browser. If you still have the page open from the previous exercise, click the Refresh button to refresh the page content. If you don't know how to do that, simply close and reopen the browser.

You should see a page similar to the one in Figure 4.3, with a green box around the text in the division you just added to the page. If you see that, congratulations—you've now used CSS in two different ways. Are you ready to learn the third way?

Figure 4.3

4.7 External Styles

AN EXTERNAL STYLE SHEET contains the style rules you create. The style sheet is saved as a plain text file, but with a **.css** file extension instead of a **.txt** file extension. To save a file with a .css extension, in most text editors you can simply place quotation marks around the file name as you save it. For example:

"MyStyles.css"

The content of your external style sheet is the same as the style code you would place in an embedded style—minus the opening *<style type="text/css">* and closing *</style>* declaration. The opening and closing tags are unnecessary because the browser knows it's a style sheet from the link placed to the style sheet in the HEAD section of the page.

To link to an external style sheet, place the following code in the HEAD section of the page:

`<link rel="stylesheet" href="standard.css" type="text/css" />`

There is no closing tag for this link, but to follow the rules of XHTML, we closed the link by including a space and forward slash at the end of the tag.

Where I have **"standard.css"** in the code, you'd change that to reflect the name of your own style sheet (and if necessary, the server path to the style sheet). Don't worry if you don't know what a server path is yet—that's covered later. First things first, Elmo.

Following is an example of a real style sheet from one of my web sites, along with a couple explanatory notes I added.

Linked Style Sheet Example Contents

```
body {background-attachment: fixed;
     text-align: justify;
     font-family: Arial, Verdana;
     font-size: 12px;
     scrollbar-face-color: #423626;
     scrollbar-arrow-color: #A7C2B1;
     scrollbar-track-color: #000000;}

table {text-align: justify;
      font-family: Arial, Verdana;
      font-size: 14px;
      border-right: 2px solid black;
      border-left: 2px solid black;
      padding: 7px;}
```

```
/* You can line the styles up neatly like above,
or run it all together like below. */

/* This is how you make a comment in a style
sheet so that a browser isn't confused by it.
It's simply a forward slash, asterisk, and a
space followed by your comment; and it's ended
with a space, asterisk and forward slash. */

a:link {font-family: Arial; font-size: 12px;
font-weight: bold; text-decoration: none;}

a:visited {color: #7C7161; font-size: 12px;
font-weight: bold; text-decoration: none;}

a:hover {color: #36cc9a; background-color:
#000000; font-weight: bold; text-decoration:
none;}

a:active {color: #B70004 font-weight: bold;
text-decoration: overline;}

div.main {padding-left: 10px; padding-right:
10px;}

h1 {font-family: "Comic Sans MS", cursive;
font-size: 24px; font-size: 16px; font-weight:
bold;}
```

Don't worry about what each individual item means right now—you'll learn about them later. I just wanted you to see what the inside of a linked style sheet looks like. Writing the style rules follows the same format as an embedded style sheet, except the linked style sheet is kept in a separate file. It's just a text file containing the style rules, save as with a **.css** extension. In the previous example, my style sheet was saved as:

htmlville.css

I named the file *htmlville.css* because it's the style sheet for my www.HTMLville.com web site. You can name your linked CSS files anything you like as long as the name doesn't include spaces or special characters. Keep in mind, however, that using sensible naming conventions helps keep things organized, especially when you have a lot of web sites as I do.

To have that style sheet work on my www.HTMLville.com web site, I placed a link in the HEAD section of each page like this:

```
<link rel="stylesheet" href="htmlville.css" type="text/css" />
```

Notice at the end of that code I included a space and forward slash to make it compliant with XHTML. That's because this tag doesn't have a closing tag. Remember, any tag that doesn't have a closing tag should be self-closed in this way to be XHTML compliant.

Time Out! Before moving on to the next lesson, let's create and use an external style sheet with your practice page. Open Notepad or whatever text editor you're using, and type the following code into a new file (a blank page):

```
h5 {color: maroon; font-size: 22px;}
```

Once you've typed that, save the file as: **test.css**

Remember to save it according to the instructions in Chapter 3: HTML Kick-start, Section 3.3. Save it in the same location as your practice HTML page.

Once you've saved the external CSS file, open your practice page source code again. In the *HEAD* section of the page, just *under* the *<style type="text/css"> … </style>* code you added in the last exercise, add the following code:

```
<link rel="stylesheet" href="test.css" type="text/css" />
```

Next, in the *BODY* of the page, enter the following code after the boxed message you added in the last exercise:

```
<h5>This is fun!</h5>
```

Figure 4.4

Save your practice page and open it in your browser. It should now look like Figure 4.4. If so, you've just succeeded in implementing the third method of using CSS. If not, either you or I did something wrong. I'm not saying I never make mistakes, but I'm guessing it's you this time!

4.8 Style Classes

CSS ALLOWS YOU TO CREATE your own "class" of elements. That means you can create several styles for the same element, and code the *class name* into the element for the style you want it to have. For example, if I wanted to create some paragraphs of text in blue, some in red, and some in green, I could do so by creating a class for each desired style. Here's how those three classes would be created in an external style sheet:

```
p.red {color: red;}
p.blue {color: blue;}
p.green {color: green;}
```

By placing a period after the *p* selector (the HTML name for a paragraph element) and then adding a class name immediately after the period (using no space), I've created three different style classes for paragraphs.

The way to call these styles into action is by adding the class you want to use to a paragraph tag in your web page source code. Here's an example:

```
<p class="red">
```

By adding a *space* after the paragraph element and then adding *class="red"* to the tag, I instruct the browser to render the text according to the *p.red* class I created in my external style sheet. Since you used the name of the class as the *value* of the HTML *class attribute* with the element, the browser will use the rules you created for that class. If I wanted the next paragraph in blue text, I'd just cancel the first paragraph and start a new one—except this time I'd add the class of *blue* to the <p> tag.

Note that just because I named the class for red text as *red*, doesn't mean I had to name it that way. I could have named the red class *blue* if I wanted to, or *Silly Wiggles*, or *Mary*—whatever I want—but as mentioned earlier, it's easier to keep track of things if you use sensible naming conventions. If I want a paragraph to have red text, it's much easier to remember *class="red"* than it is to remember that *class="blue"* makes the text red. A class can have any name you want to give it *as long as it begins with a letter*. The first character of a class name cannot be a number. Also, class names are case sensitive, so a class named *red* is not the same as a class named *Red*.

To be compatible with older browsers, don't name a class with a name that matches JavaScript keywords. For example, you might want to use "default" as a class to define your normal page

Note

Because external style sheets are so convenient and powerful, most of the code from here on will be demonstrated using external style sheet examples.

text, but that will generate an error in Netscape 4. Here are the words you shouldn't use in CSS class names:

abstract	boolean	break	byte	case	catch
char	class	const	continue	debugger	default
delete	do	double	else	enum	export
extends	false	final	finally	float	for
function	goto	if	implements	import	in
instanceof	int	interface	long	native	new
null	package	private	protected	public	return
throws	short	static	switch	synchronized	this
throw	transient	true	try	typeof	var
void	while	with			

You probably won't need this list often, but it's the first thing to check if you name a class that generates an error message in Netscape 4 or other older browsers.

Time Out! By now you should realize that these little "Time Out" graphics mean you have an exercise to do. Later on, I may trick you. But for now, open the test.css file you created in the last exercise.

After the line that created the rule for h5 headings, add the following line:

span.hilite {background-color: yellow;}

Save your file once you've added that line, and then open the source code for the practice web page. Find this line in the body of the document:

This text should be in blue.

Add *<span class="hilite">* before the word "should" and add </span> after the word "should." The line should now look like this:

This text **<span class="hilite">**should**</span>** be in blue.

Save your web page document and open it in your browser. It should look like Figure 4.5 with the word "should" highlighted in

Figure 4.5

yellow. If that's the way it looks, great! If not, go stand in the corner and count to twenty and seven.

4.9 Generic Classes

YOU CAN ALSO CREATE generic rules. A generic rule is simply a style rule that is not associated with any selector. It can be applied to a selector by adding the class name to a qualifying selector. A qualifying selector is any HTML element for which it's legal to use the style rules you want to apply.

To create a generic rule, simply add a period and a class name to your embedded or external style sheet. For example:

.border {border: 2px solid black;}

By creating that rule, anytime we add *class*=*"border"* to an element, that element will have a solid black 2-pixel border around it. Let's try it!

 Open your test.css file. To the end of the file, add the previous line of code for creating a generic class. Save it and then open the source code for your practice page. Find the line that reads *<h5>This is fun!</h5>* and change it so that it reads like this:

<h5 **class="border"**>This is fun!</h5>

Save the change and then open the page in your browser. You should now see a solid black border around the words *"This is fun!"* that extends past the edge of my screen capture. The border will go the width of the page in most browsers unless a specific width is added.

Does your file look like Figure 4.6? If it does, you are a remarkable student who totally amazes me!

Figure 4.6

4.10 ID Classes

MOST HTML TAGS can have an ID attached to them. These identifiers are most often used as the target for some kind of action. The action could be a JavaScript function, an automated function involving data processing, or something else, including style rules.

The syntax to create an ID class is essentially the same as for creating a regular style class—except instead of preceding the class name with a period it's preceded by a hash mark (#). Here are two examples:

```
#border {border: solid black 2px;}
p#fontred {color: red;}
```

The first example creates a 2-pixel solid black border around an element by giving the element an ID. This is the same as the generic style from Section 4.9, but it's called into use with an ID instead of a class. Here's how you'd use it on a page:

```
<div id="border">
```

Using the previous code creates the border around the division. The example on the second line isn't generic; it has the paragraph element in front of the ID name, so the style can only be used with a paragraph. Here's an example:

```
<p id="fontred">
```

With that coded into a page, the text in the paragraph will display in red type.

 Guess what? I told you I'd trick you with one of these "Time Out" graphics, and I think I just did. There is no exercise for the ID class. Just admit it though; I can be a pretty tricky fellow sometimes.

The reason for no exercise is that using an ID class to implement a style rule is not recommended. There is a drawback to using the ID class for style rules: HTML and XHTML standards require that an ID can only be used once per document (you can use multiple IDs, but each must have a unique name). So, if you wanted to repeat the ID class rule elsewhere in a document, you couldn't do it and still remain compliant with the standards. It doesn't make much sense to create a style rule that you can't reuse when one of the main purposes and conveniences of CSS is to create reusable code.

4.11 Pseudo-Classes

IN ADDITION TO THE PREVIOUS classes, there's also something called *pseudo-classes*. These allow you to define a change in the display for certain states of specific elements. If you rest your cursor on some links, for example, the font color changes. This is an example of a pseudo-class rule.

Pseudo-class rules are coded like a regular class rule, with the following two exceptions:

1. They have predefined names; you can't make up your own name.

2. Instead of separating the element and class name with a period, they are separated with a colon.

The four following pseudo-classes are the only ones with browser support at the time of this writing:

a:link

a:visited

a:hover

a:active

In the preceding pseudo-classes, the letter "a" before the semi-colon stands for *anchor* because some sailor made it up. OK, I made that up, but I used to be a sailor so it's OK. The truth is that "a" is short for anchor because it represents the HTML anchor tag. An anchor tag is a link to another file or to a specific place within the current web page. You'll see how to create links later on, but for now we'll just go over how to code them and what they do.

After each anchor pseudo-class, you add the CSS property and value as you did with any of the previous CSS classes we've gone over. Here's an example:

a:link {color: blue;}

Simple! Just like with the other classes, we add a property and value to the selector, and that is all it needs. Here's a brief description of those four pseudo-classes:

a:link	This sets the properties and values of a link before the link has been visited.
a:visited	This sets the properties and values of a link that the browser has already visited.
a:hover	This sets the properties and values of a link when the cursor is resting on it. This is usually used to change the color of the link text while in the hover state.
a:active	This sets the properties and values of a link when it has been activated (clicked) until it is processed. With the advent of broadband Internet connections and faster servers and personal computers, many times this change of state isn't even noticeable.

While most of the time webmasters just use these four pseudo-classes to change the colors of the link text for each state, other properties and values can be added or changed as well, such as font weight, text decoration, font style, and more.

When creating a style sheet using these pseudo-classes, they must be in this order:

a:link

a:visited

a:hover

a:active

If they are not in this order, things can break down and changes of state won't work properly in some browsers.

There are three other pseudo-classes:

:lang

:first-child

:focus

No browsers support those three pseudo-classes at the time of this writing, so I will not go into details about them. They are not options most people would use anyway, but you can look them up on the Internet if you want to learn more. Frankly, at this point, you've already got your work cut out for you!

We will not be doing an exercise for these pseudo-classes because you haven't learned to create links yet. You will put them to use later on, however, when you go from a single practice web page to building a multi-page web site.

4.12 Multiple Selectors

SUPPOSE YOU WANT ALL the headings on a web page to display in the same color. Rather than list each heading size separately, you can list multiple selectors in one declaration. This style rule:

h1, h2, h3, h4, h5, h6 {color: brown;}

. . . means the same as this:

h1 {color: brown;}

h2 {color: brown;}

h3 {color: brown;}

```
h4 {color: brown;}
h5 {color: brown;}
h6 {color: brown;}
```

The first line of code is certainly much easier to write and edit than the other six lines. The two methods of writing the style rules, however, tell the browser the exact same thing. Any time you want multiple elements to have the same property values, just list them all, separated by commas, and at the end add the properties and values you wish to effect.

Time Out! Land ho! Avast ye matey, it's time for another exercise. Argh. I know you're amazed by my pirate imitation, but try to calm down enough to open your *test.css* file again and add the following line after the last entry:

```
p, h4 {margin-left: 40px;}
```

Save the change and open the source code for your practice page. In the BODY of the document, underneath the line that reads *<h5>This is fun!</h5>*, add the following line of code:

```
<h4>This should be indented.</h4>
```

Save that change and open the page in your browser. Two things should have happened. The heading, *"This should be indented."* is now added to the bottom of the page, and it should be indented as shown in Figure 4.7. The other thing that should have happened is the blue text should have been indented also. Because we added both the paragraph and h4 selectors to our rules, each time a paragraph tag or h4 tag is used they will be indented. Since the blue text is coded inside a paragraph tag from a previous exercise, it became indented without actually changing the web page source code for that element; it was changed because of the change to the linked CSS file. Abracadabra, CSS seems just like magic sometimes!

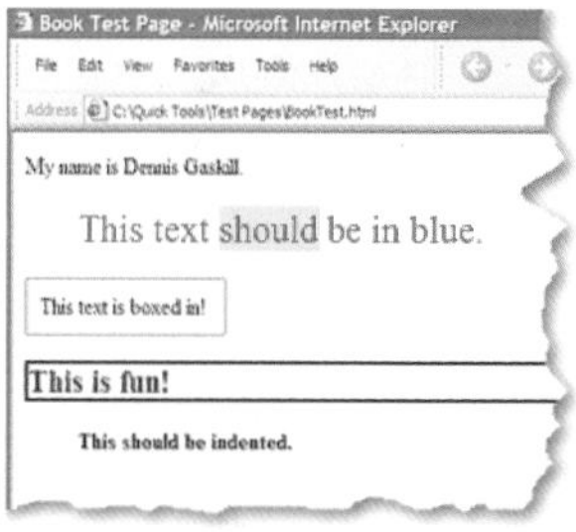

Figure 4.7

4.13 Contextual Selectors

A CONTEXTUAL SELECTOR IS WHEN a rule is applied to a tag only when it occurs within a specific context in the document. To create a contextual selector, list the tags in the nesting order they must appear in before the contextual selector kicks in.

For example, say I have places on a page where I want to use bold text, and places where I wanted to use italic text. And then perhaps I have a place where I want a background color behind the words when I use italic tags inside bold tags to create more emphasis than either bold or italic text will create.

To do that, I'd add the following rule to my *test.css* file sheet:

```
b i {background-color: burlywood;}
```

To make a contextual selector, do not separate the selectors with a comma as you do in creating style rules for multiple selectors. Instead, separate the selectors with a space.

In the previous code example, the contextual selector will kick in if I nest italic tags inside bold tags in my source code. If you look toward the bottom of Figure 4.8 you can see an example of how it looks in a web browser. I wrote a sentence with no CSS coding, then added a sentence in bold text, then added italic text without canceling the bold text. Because I hadn't canceled the bold text, the contextual selector kicked in and added the background color. If I had canceled the bold text before adding the italic text, the third sentence would have been in italic text only, with no bold and no background color. I showed how I wrote the CSS rule for that; now here's how I wrote the body content:

```
Here's a sentence with no CSS.  <br>

<b>Here's a sentence in bold type. <br>

<i>Here's italic type that should invoke a background
color.</i></b>
```

Notice how the <b> tag was opened, then the <i> tag was added before the bold tag was canceled. This order is what triggered the contextual selector to add the background color. Also notice how I canceled the italic tag before canceling the bold tag. This is proper nesting. Always cancel nested tags in the reverse order they were opened.

You also might have noticed the <br> tag in a lighter color. This is a break tag, which causes a line break in the text. You'll learn more about this in Chapter 5: Text Formatting, but I left it in to show the actual code I used. I used a lighter color to show that it isn't part of creating contextual selectors. If I hadn't used the break tags, the text would have continued on one line until it reached the edge of the screen before wrapping to a second line.

Figure 4.8

That would have made the screen capture graphic much too big for the book.

 Open your *test.css* file and add the following line to the end:

b i {background-color: burlywood;}

Save the change and open your practice page source code. In the BODY of the document, after the line that reads *<h4>This should be indented.</h4>* add the following lines:

Here's a sentence with no CSS.
Here's a sentence in bold type.
Here's italic type that should invoke a background color.

Save the changes and open the page in your browser. It should look like Figure 4.8, although the background color may not appear the same for various reasons.

As you progress through this book, you'll learn how to apply many more CSS styles to many more HTML elements than we covered in this chapter. The important thing to draw from this chapter is an understanding of how to implement the three methods of adding CSS to web page documents.

You may now holler "yippee wahoo" and dance a little jig.

4.14 Chapter 4 Exercise

For the Chapter 4 exercise:

- Open your source code for the ongoing chapter exercise and delete all the content in between the <body> and </body> tags. Also delete the embedded styles in the HEAD section of the page and save the changes. Open the external CSS file and delete all the code inside it and save the change.

- Now you get to start over—except this time you'll be adding code that pertains to the topic of your web site project. In your external style sheet, add the following code:

body {margin: 40px;}

Save the change and close the file.

You will learn more about margins later in the book, for now you just need to know that the purpose of that code is to add a margin (empty space where no content will be placed) of 40 pixels around all four sides of the page.

- Now that you've added an external style rule for the margin, add a link to your external style sheet on your web page (use the book for reference). This is also an exercise that will be of value to you later on. No one remembers every little piece of code—we only remember the most commonly used ones, so you need to learn how to find "how-to" information on your own.

- Next, add the following embedded style to the HEAD section of the source code for your ongoing web site project page.

<style type="text/css">
h3 {font-family: Arial, Verdana, Helvetica; font-size: 18px; font-weight: bold;}
</style>

You'll soon learn more about the font properties, too, but for now all you need to know is that the code sets the font face, font size, and font weight of an h3 size heading. The purpose of this exercise is to make sure you understand how to add embedded and external styles to your page, not that you understand what the actual styles mean at this point.

- Now add an <h3> ... </h3> (heading) to your page and place the name of your fictional organization on the page in lieu of a graphic logo or header. Replace the three dots in the heading code example with the name for the organization that you decided on in the last chapter's exercise. Following the heading, add a short paragraph of text that welcomes visitors to the site.

Once you've added all that, don't forget to save your changes and open the page in your browser to make sure it all works. You should see the h3 heading text at the top of the page and see a blank line followed by the paragraph you wrote after the heading. The heading text should be should be 40 pixels down from the top of the browser window and all the text should be indented 40 pixels at both sides of the browser window. Depending on your computer settings, 40 pixels will probably be somewhere between half an inch and three-quarters of an inch, give or take a smidgeon or three.

Text Formatting

5.1 Introduction

IF YOU HAVE FOLLOWED this book from the beginning, you've learned the basic HTML skeleton required to make a web page. You also learned how the syntax of HTML and CSS is written, and you made a simple web page. In this chapter, you'll learn how to format text.

By learning how to format text, you'll be able to add line breaks, paragraph breaks, bold type, headings, and more to the text on a web site. Before getting started, keep in mind that even though the majority of browsers follow the W3C standards for web programming languages, there still can be variations in how different computer systems display pages. These variations can be the result of software or hardware, so don't get too hung up on minor differences in how a page is rendered on different systems. Often, there is little you can do to iron out the differences.

5.2 Line Breaks and Paragraphs

UNLIKE TEXT EDITORS, browsers do not display the carriage returns (created by pressing the Enter or Return key) that you enter into the source code. Browsers also display a continuous series of blank spaces as just one space. If you typed the following two lines in a web page's source code:

It is wise to taste a great　　　diversity of thought, just be careful of what you swallow.

. . . a browser would display it like this:

It is wise to taste a great diversity of thought, just be careful of what you swallow.

As you can see, the extra spaces between the words *great* and *diversity* are reduced to one space, and both lines are displayed on one line (the indent, the format for examples in this book, won't show on the web page either). The browser will not start a new line of text until you either code a new line into the source code or the text reaches the end of the horizontal space available, at which point it wraps to the next line.

So, the first thing you need to know is how to tell the browser to start a new line. Amazing how I know just what you need to know, eh?

Two basic tags are used to create line breaks. One creates a single line break; the other creates a double line break. The tag for a single line break is called, appropriately enough, a *break* tag. It is coded like this:

The break tag used to be an empty tag, which simply meant it didn't have a corresponding closing tag. Wherever you coded a <br> tag into a page, the content that follows immediately dropped down to the next line and no closing tag was needed.

To be compliant with XHTML, you must now add the space and forward slash to the end of any empty tag to make it self-closing. Please review Section 2.7 in Chapter 2: An Overview of HTML, XHTML, and CSS if you need a refresher on self-closing tags.

The paragraph tag creates two line breaks. Text following a paragraph tag will drop down two lines, leaving an empty line in between the lines that precede and follow the paragraph tag. A paragraph tag is written as follows:

<p>

In HTML, a closing paragraph tag is optional, but to be XHTML compliant you must use the closing tag. Here's an example:

<p> ...paragraph of text goes here... </p>

Gee, this stuff sure is easy. As you learn more little bits and pieces of code like this, you can do more stuff—and the more you learn, the more you can do!

5.3 Divisions

A DIVISION ELEMENT IS A block-level element used to divide content into separate sections. The <div> element is a generic element that does nothing on its own aside from starting the content of the division on a new line like a <br> tag does.

While a <div> element may be used simply as a way to organize content, it is most often used with CSS *classes* or *IDs* to control several properties at once. A division tag is written as follows:

<div> ...content goes here... </div>

The division tag accepts several HTML attributes:

align | class | dir | id | lang | nowrap | style | title

Various JavaScript functions can also be added. This book provides only an overview of JavaScript, so we cover only the HTML attributes.

Align

The *align* attribute positions all the content within the division to the left, center, or right. This includes images as well as text.

In addition, by using the align attribute with a value of *justify*, text will be aligned evenly on both the right and left sides. However, justify only affects text; it has no affect on images.

Justified text looks very professional, in my opinion, if the horizontal space is wide enough. If the horizontal space is too narrow, lines can look silly with just a few words stretched out across a narrow column. If you look at the text toward the center of Figure 5.1, you can see how justified text in a narrow column doesn't look appealing.

Note that centering text is considered amateurish and is usually found only on personal web sites. By default, text is always aligned to the left. If you want left alignment, it isn't usually necessary to code an *align=left* attribute and value. Here's an example of a division tag with text justified:

<div **align="justify"**> ...content goes here... </div>

Don't overlook the value of small pleasures. Atoms too small to be seen compose the Universe, endless seconds fill eternity; so too, appreciation of small, daily joys render a happy life.

Figure 5.1

WARNING!

The align attribute is officially deprecated. Web authors are encouraged to use CSS to align the contents of a division element, but because of the widespread usage—and because nearly everyone still teaches aligning content this way—I mention it here for your enlightenment. You will know more than people who bought other books that still teach outdated coding practices. Cool beans, eh?

Class

The *class* attribute allows you to set the style for the division according to style rules you create for that class. See Section 4.8 in Chapter 4: CSS Kick-Start for a refresher on creating classes.

Dir

The *dir* attribute lets you tell the browser which *direction* the text should flow, either left to right or right to left. By default, text displays from left to right, but the right to left option is there for languages such as Chinese that are read from right to left.

When used with the division tag, text displays in the direction programmed only within that division. When used with the opening HTML tag, it controls the text direction for the whole document. Here's an example of how to use the direction tag:

```
<div dir="ltr"> …content goes here… </dir>
```

In the code above, *ltr* stands for **Left To Right**. Change the value of the *dir* attribute to *rtl* (**Right To Left**) to have text flow from right to left.

ID

The ID attribute allows you to set up a division as a target for certain actions or styles. See Section 4.10 in Chapter 4: CSS Kick-Start for a refresher on creating an ID.

Lang

The *lang* attribute lets you specify the language used within the division. There is very little browser support for languages other than English, so I won't waste space going into details. If you have a need to learn more about the language tag, you'll find links to official documentation on the resource page for this book. It's located online at:

www.BoogieJack.com/book/resources.html

Nowrap

The *nowrap* attribute stops word wrapping within the division. Line breaks occur only where you have coded them to occur with a <br> or <p> tag.

The nowrap attribute is used where you don't want lines to wrap to a second line, such as in song lyrics, poetry, or code examples. In HTML, the nowrap attribute is a *valueless attribute*. That means only the attribute is coded, but no value for the attribute is given. Here's an example:

```
<div nowrap> …content goes here… </div>
```

This kind of coding is not compliant with XHTML however, as each attribute must have a value. To give the nowrap attribute a value, code it like this:

```
<div nowrap="nowrap"> …content goes here… </div>
```

In XHTML, to give a valueless attribute a value, use the attribute name. While this makes it compliant with XHTML, it may mean older browsers will ignore the attribute altogether. It isn't a perfect world after all, but because web design is moving away from plain HTML and toward XHTML, I encourage you to create all new pages to be XHTML compliant.

Style

The *style* attribute allows you to add inline styles to a division. See Section 4.5 in Chapter 4: CSS Kick-Start for a refresher on creating inline styles.

Title

The *title* attribute allows you to add a descriptive comment to a division tag. Because there is no defined usage for the value of the title, many browsers simply ignore it. Internet Explorer displays the title text in a pop-up balloon for a few seconds when the cursor is placed anywhere within the division.

Few people use a title attribute with a division tag, but if used correctly the title either provides an overview for screen readers used by vision-impaired people or it provides some sort of help or directions to users. Here's an example of usage:

```
< div title="This passage describes the beauty of kindness.">

…content goes here…

</div>
```

A bonus to using title tags is that they can be used to enhance your web page's search engine rankings. To learn more about search engine optimization, please visit the resource page for this book at:

www.BoogieJack.com/book/resources.html

5.4 Spans

THE <span> ELEMENT, like the division element, is a generic element. It doesn't provide any formatting on its own, but unlike the block level division element, content within a span tag set does not start on a new line because it is an inline element.

The span element is often used to make changes to the display of text within the flow of content. The <font> tag used to cover this, but it has been deprecated and should no longer be used. In its place, you can make all the changes with a span tag that you could with a font tag by adding inline CSS or a CSS class or ID attributes. Here's an example:

Life isn't about what you get, it's about what you
<span **style="color: red;"**>become</span>.

On a web page, the previous sentence with a span tag and in-line CSS displays like this:

Life isn't about what you get, it's about what you become.

I used the span tag to change the text color to red for the word *become* to give it special emphasis. In addition to using the span element to change the font color, I could have also reduced or increased the font size, changed the font face, added a background color or image, or several other things.

5.5 Bold and Italic Text

AT FIRST GLANCE, HTML seems a little dippy when it comes to applying bold and italic styles because there are different elements that *seem* to do the same thing. The *bold* element and *strong* element both render text in bold type in most browsers. The *italic* element and *emphasis* element both render text in italics in most browsers.

Why? So guys like me can get paid the big bucks explaining it to good folks like you.

Seriously though, without getting bogged down in too many details, the bold element is intended to be visual while the strong element is intended to be aural. In other words, a bold element should be displayed in bold text, but won't necessarily be read aloud by screen readers any differently than normal text. A strong element, on the other hand, is supposed to be aurally stressed more than normal text by screen readers. The same applies to italic text (visual) and text with emphasis (aural).

Element	Example of Usage
Bold	We must **\<b\>never\</b\>** drive while blindfolded.
Strong	Joe was **\<strong\>that\</strong\>** close to winning the lottery.
Italic	I was \<i\>*not*\</i\> the one that fed the monkey caviar.
Emphasis	They never told me they were leaving town on a **\<em\>***mule***\</em\>**!

5.6 Headings

HEADINGS DRAW ATTENTION to important points, break up long passages of text into sections that seem less wearisome to read, label various sections of page content, and help with search engine optimization.

Headings come in six different sizes. From largest to smallest, they are written as:

```
<h1>heading text here</h1>
<h2>heading text here</h2>
<h3>heading text here</h3>
<h4>heading text here</h4>
<h5>heading text here</h5>
<h6>heading text here</h6>
```

Figure 5.2 shows how the heading sizes look in a browser. These aren't the actual sizes, but the graphic gives you a comparison of how they relate in size to each other.

As you can see, there is a good deal of space between each heading. A heading creates a blank line above and below itself,

Figure 5.2

so headings can't be used to create larger text for emphasis within the flow of a sentence.

The way headings are used online is similar to the way titles and subtitles are used in newspaper articles and magazine columns. Generally, the title uses a larger heading and subtitles use smaller headings.

Typically, the h1 through h3 size headings are displayed in a larger font than normal. An h4 heading is the same size as the default text, and h5 and h6 are smaller than normal text. All the headings are usually rendered in bold text, although some browsers may deviate from that and render them in italic, underline, or some other manner that brings emphasis to the heading text.

The h1 through h4 headings are typically used for titles and subtitles. The h5 and h6 headings are seldom used because they are so small, which makes them appropriate for use in disclaimers, copyright notices, and other boilerplate messages.

5.7 Image Use with Headings

YOU CAN USE IMAGES in place of headings to increase the visual appeal, but you lose some value in search engine optimization. Search engines place more value on the words inside heading tags than on normal text. Since headings often contain good keywords related to the content, using an image instead of text sacrifices any increased ranking the text heading would lend a page.

What most people don't know is that you can use an image with a heading tag. In Figure 5.3, you can see how I used an image of a tree in full fall colors inline with an h1 heading. If I coded the image outside the h1 heading, the image would not display on the same line as the heading text.

Here's the code for that little trick:

```
<h1>
<img src="tree.jpg" />
Fall Colors
</h1>
```

You'll learn all about adding images to web pages in the chapter on colors, images, and multimedia, so don't worry about

Figure 5.3

the second line of code at this time. For now, it's enough to know that by nesting an image tag inside an h1 heading you can add an image inline with the heading text. Because I placed the image before the text, it appears before the text on the web page. If I placed the image after the heading text, it would show up after the words *Fall Colors*.

I could have—and most webmasters probably would have—used that tree image and placed the words "Fall Colors" on the image to make it completely graphical, but that wouldn't help with search engine placement.

5.8 Acronyms

ACRONYMS ARE WORDS that are formed from the letters in other words. For example, *USA* is an acronym of United States of America; and *modem* is an acronym of MOdulator DEModulator.

The <acronym> tag provides a way to offer a visual clue that a word is an acronym. The tag itself, however, doesn't create a visual change in most browsers. This may change in future browser versions, but as of now we need to create the change using CSS. If I place the following code in my external or embedded style sheets:

```
acronym {color: blue; cursor: help;}
```

. . . then wherever I use the acronym tag set, the word enclosed between the acronym tag set displays in blue. In addition, if a user rests the cursor on the acronym, the cursor changes from the familiar arrow or text cursor to the help cursor. If I use a *title* attribute in my acronym tag, in most browsers a pop-up balloon appears when the cursor is placed on the acronym to explain what the acronym represents. Here's an example:

```
<acronym title="United States of America">USA
</acronym>
```

In Figure 5.4, you can see what the cursor looks like when someone rests it on the USA acronym. Notice how the cursor changed from the usual arrow or text cursor to the help cursor. The help cursor shows up immediately, but the pop-up balloon takes a second. Having the cursor change alerts the user that

Figure 5.4

something is different, which usually distracts them long enough for the pop-up balloon to show up. Figure 5.4 also shows a pop-up balloon in Internet Explorer.

5.9 Citations

CITED TEXT IS INTENDED for automated indexing programs to extract information from your web documents. Originally, it was to be used for the titles of cited works. In practice, however, it is incorrectly used for author names, quotations, and even in place of the italic or emphasis elements.

Cited text usually displays as italic text, but it can display however you choose with the addition of inline, embedded, or external CSS. Here's an example of how to code a citation:

> In **<cite>Almost a Newsletter</cite>**, Dennis Gaskill wrote that life doesn't promise us love, happiness, or even sufficiency. Life is simply opportunity, and it's up to us what we do with it.

By adding a *title* attribute to the <cite> element, a pop-up window appears in most browsers to display the text in the title's *value*. It isn't necessary to add a title, but it does give us the opportunity to offer additional information about the cited work without taking up page space. In the citation example, *Almost a Newsletter* is my newsletter about web design and life. I might use the title attribute to provide my web site address; information about the newsletter, author, and publisher; or some other notation.

Here's an example:

> <cite **title="Published by Dennis Gaskill"**>Almost a Newsletter</cite>

5.10 The Code Tag

THE <code> TAG WAS CREATED for software programmers to have a special style of text to present their code examples. Text within a set of code tags is rendered in a monospace font, such as Courier or Lucida Console. Monospace fonts align more readily, making them easier to work with in code samples.

Since the code tag was included for software programmers, it really doesn't have much use for the average webmaster. I don't recommend using it for anything else because, in the future, newer browsers may treat text in a <code> tag set differently than they do now. If you want to have a monospace font used on a web page, there are other options for that, as you'll soon learn. Figure 5.5 shows an example of a monospace font.

```
This is a monospaced font.
It looks like old-fashioned
typewriter text.
```

Figure 5.5

5.11 The Definition Tag

THE <dfn> TAG IS USED to denote unfamiliar or special words or phrases. While the popular browsers currently display text within a definition tag in italic type, in the future there may be options that help publishers create an index, create a glossary, or provide definitions for search engines. Here's an example of usage:

> The images of **<dfn>**nebulae**</dfn>** taken by the Hubble Space Telescope are so mysterious and beautiful that many people find them inspirational.

Of course, just having the text displayed as italic doesn't help the reader understand an unfamiliar term. We need to add a title attribute and value to actually provide the definition we want to convey to the reader. Let's add a title to our example:

> The images of <dfn **title="An immense cloud of gas and dust in interstellar space.**">nebulae</dfn> taken by the Hubble Space Telescope are so mysterious and beautiful that many people find them inspirational.

Just adding the title to the <dfn> tag doesn't tell the viewer that there's anything special about the word *nebulae* other than it's italic. However, if we add CSS formatting to it, we can make it visually unique so that a viewer is tempted to place the cursor on it to see if it does anything. Most experienced Internet users will know this, but less savvy users probably won't. You can always provide an explanation, or just let those who find it, find it; and those who don't, don't.

Whatever you decide, here's one example of how CSS can be used to change the appearance of the text inside a definition tag set:

> dfn {text-decoration: underline;}

If you add that line of code to an external style sheet or embedded style rules, each time you use the <dfn> tag, the text within the tag set is underlined.

5.12 The Keyboard Tag

THE <kbd> TAG IS SIMILAR to the <code> tag in that the content within the <kbd> tag set is displayed in a monospace font. The purpose of this tag is to indicate input the user should enter into a text field. An example of usage:

> Type **<kbd>**BoogieJack.com**</kbd>** into your browser's address bar and press the Enter key on your keyboard to go to one of my web sites.

Again, don't use this tag to specify a monospace font because in the future browsers may treat text in a <kbd> set differently than they do now.

5.13 The Sample Tag

THE <samp> TAG IS USED to indicate a string of text that should be taken literally, such as the output from programs or scripts. It, too, displays the text in a monospace font, but should not be used for the purpose of using a monospace font because in the future browsers may treat text in a <samp> tag set differently than they do now. Here's an example of correct usage:

> When the program first starts, you will see the **<samp>**¤**</samp>** prompt.

5.14 The Big and Small Tags

YOU CAN PROBABLY GUESS what the <big> tag does—it makes text a little bigger. If you just need a quick way to make a word or phrase larger than the default size, the <big> tag is perfect. If you want to change the font size for the entire page or need more control over the size, there are better ways to increase text size. You'll learn those methods in the next chapter. Example of usage:

> I'm not sure why, but I want **<big>**these words**</big>** in larger text.

Similarly, the <small> tag is used to make a word or phrase a little smaller. Here's an example of usage:

<small>Contact Dennis Gaskill for reprint rights to this article.</small>

5.15 Subscript and Superscript

THE <sub> TAG PLACES the text within it slightly lower on the line; the <sup> tag places text within it slightly higher on the line. Here's an example of each:

H₂O
E = mc²</sup>

Those display on a web page like this:

H_2O
$E = mc^2$

Of course, if you wanted to freak someone out, you could alternate subscript, normal text, and superscript to make a strange looking web page as in Figure 5.6.

You wouldn't really do that, would you?

Figure 5.6

5.16 The Teletype Tag

THE <tt> TAG RENDERS text in a monospace font. While many of the previous tags display text in a monospace font, this is the right tag to use if that's all you're trying to do. Here's an example:

<tt>This text would render in a monospace font.</tt>

The only change the <tt> tag makes is to the font. Unlike the <pre> tag in the next section, the browser still reduces multiple spaces to just one space and will not honor extra carriage returns.

5.17 Preformatted Text

THE <pre> TAG ALSO RENDERS text in a monospace font, but it honors multiple spaces and multiple carriage returns. This is the only tag browsers recognize that honors the way text is formatted in the source code.

In other words, if you wrote the following in your source code:

```
<pre>
    Name:          _____

    Address:       _____

    Phone:         _____
</pre>
```

It would display it like this:

```
    Name:          _____

    Address:       _____

    Phone:         _____
```

It isn't an exact science, though. You have to play around with the spaces and lines to get them to align evenly.

If you place that same text in the source code without using the <pre> tags, it displays something like this:

```
Name: _____ Address: _____ _____ Phone: _____
```

You can see the <pre> tag can be useful, but even so, it isn't used very often. It's probably used to create vertical white space (empty space) as often as it is for making things line up nicely. By placing an opening <pre> tag in the code, then pressing the *Enter* key a few times to create carriage returns, you can add that amount of vertical white space to a page.

5.18 The Blockquote Tag

THE <blockquote> TAG IS USED to set apart a text passage from the other body text. Usually, blockquote text is indented on the left and right sides. In some browsers, it may also display the text as italic. Using CSS, you can create rules to have the block-quote text display as you choose.

A blockquote, like it sounds, is often used to quote text from another person or another body of work. I also use it to highlight text from the work itself, much like a magazine or newspaper uses pull quotes.

A blockquote is written like this:

```
<blockquote>The man who succeeds has faced
failure more times than success, but he never gave
up. <br /> ~ Tom Dean</blockquote>
```

As you can see, you can use other HTML elements inside the blockquote. In this case, I used a <br /> tag before the man's name (who I actually heard utter that truism) to drop it a line below the quoted text.

By the way, Tom is a good friend, but I'm going to charge him for making him famous by quoting him in my book. Hey, I have to eat too, you know!

5.19 The Quote Tag

THE <q> TAG IS INTENDED for quoting short passages of text while the <blockquote> tag is intended for quoting longer passages of text. I use the blockquote for both.

The reason I prefer the blockquote tag is that different browsers display the text in a quote tag differently. Some designers insert quotation marks around the quoted text, and others do not. If you insert your own quotation marks so it looks like quoted text in one browser, it will have two sets of quotation marks in another. If you leave off the quotation marks so you'll have only one set of quotation marks in one browser, you won't have any in another. It's easier to just use the blockquote. Nevertheless, here's how it is coded:

```
<q>To have a bright future, don't waste the present.
~ Dennis Gaskill</q>
```

When the next generation of browsers comes out, I expect this quirky behavior will be settled one way or another. Only then would I start using the <q> tag.

5.20 The Address Tag

THE <address> TAG IS USED to define addresses, signatures, or authorships of documents. The address displays in italic text in most browsers. In addition, most browsers will add a line break before and after the address element, but you have to insert line breaks within the element yourself. Here's an example:

<address>Williewally Foofingoofer
123 Avenue Street
Somecity, WI 54321</address>

I wish I had a cool name like that.

5.21 Spaces or Not

ALLOWING TEXT TO WRAP in a browser usually doesn't pose a problem, but occasionally we need a way to better control where line breaks occur. Two HTML tags and one character entity help us solve those niggling problems.

The <nobr> (no break) tag prevents the text contained within the tag set from wrapping to a new line. We never know how much space visitors to our web sites allow for their browser windows, so we never know where the lines of text will wrap in their browser. If you have text strings, such as lines of poetry or code examples, that shouldn't break in any place other than where you intend, using the no break tag prevents the text string from breaking in unwanted places. Here's an example:

<nobr>This is a long and meaningless string of text written here to present a long and meaningless string of text as an example of a long and meaningless string of text.</nobr>

If you place that in your source code, the entire silly sentence displays on one line. If the line is too long for the browser window, a horizontal scroll bar appears at the bottom of the browser to allow viewers to scroll sideways to see the whole line.

The <wbr /> tag (word break) is used to indicate where it's OK for text to break within a <nobr> tag set. The text will not break at the <wbr> tag if it isn't needed. The tag only indicates where it's OK for the browser to break the line if necessary. In this example:

> **\<nobr>**This is a long and meaningless**\<wbr />** string of text written here to present a long and meaningless **\<wbr />** string of text as an example of a long and meaningless**\<wbr />** string of text.**\</nobr>**

...I inserted a <wbr /> tag after each use of the word *meaningless*. A browser would display the text string on one line, unless it would cause a horizontal scrollbar. If so, the text could wrap to the next line where the <wbr /> tag is inserted. The <wbr> tag has no closing tag, so it's made into a self-closing tag for XHTML compliance by adding the space and forward slash at the end.

Note that the <nobr> and <wbr /> tags were originally Netscape tags and not part of the official HTML standard. While they still don't seem to be a part of the HTML standard, instructions for using them are found on the W3C web site and most browsers seem to support them. Use them at your own discretion.

The character entity of ** ** (no-break space) is used to keep words or numbers from wrapping at illogical places. Often mistakenly called a "tag" rather than a character entity, it is perfectly legal to use in code. This character entity creates a space, but doesn't allow the browser to wrap a line at the space. Here's an example of usage:

> 2** **-** **5/8 inches

If you needed to write 2 - 5/8 inches on a page, you wouldn't want the line to wrap to the next line before or after the hyphen, which could be confusing to readers. By including the * * entity before and after the hyphen, the entire "2 - 5/8" string will stay together. If you want to keep the number with the word "inches," you could add another * * character entity to the string.

Note that the ampersand (&) starts the character entity and the semicolon (;) ends it.

One other common use for this character entity is to force browsers to display more than one space at a time. If you string together several of these character entities, a browser will display extra spaces. For example:

> **   ** If this were the start of a paragraph, this first line would be indented by the use of a string of three of the no-break space character entities.

That displays on a web page like this:

If this were the start of a paragraph, this first line would be indented by the use of a string of three of the no-break space character entities.

However, that's an old trick. Now, you can indent the first line of each paragraph using CSS. But old or not, it's a good trick to know—tuck it under your hat and save it for another day.

5.22 Other Text Formatting Tags

YOU MAY ENCOUNTER A FEW other text formatting tags. For the most part, they are not useful. I've listed them below along with a comment and the tag's status.

Tag	Comment	Status
<abbr>	For abbreviation. Unrecognized by most browsers.	Unsupported
<basefont>	Used to set the basefont properties. Use CSS instead.	Deprecated
<blink>	Blinking text. Deemed annoying and made obsolete.	Obsolete
<center>	Centers content on the page. Use CSS instead.	Deprecated
<font>	Used for setting font properties. Use CSS instead.	Deprecated
<listing>	Similar to <pre> tag except no other code is allowed in it.	Obsolete
<plaintext>	Once used to tell browsers no mark-up was allowed.	Obsolete
<s>	Strikethrough. Use CSS to create this text effect.	Deprecated
<strike>	Strikethrough. Use CSS to create this text effect.	Deprecated
<u>	Underlined text. Use CSS to create this text effect.	Deprecated
<xmp>	Similar to a fixed-width <pre> tag.	Obsolete

If you search for additional tutorials online, understand that while there are many good tutorials, a great many are sadly out of date or just plain incorrect. None of the tags listed are recommended for use, and obsolete tags should never be used.

5.23 Chapter 5 Exercise

In this chapter, you'll practice adding a few text formatting elements to your page. To do that, you'll need to add some new content. By the end of this book, the ongoing practice web site you've started creating will include more pages than the one you are working on now.

- For this exercise, in the <head> section of the page where you added the CSS rules for an <h3> heading, add a new line for an <h4> heading. Everything will be the same as for the <h3> heading except the font size should be set to 16 pixels instead of 18 pixels.

- Next, add at least two paragraphs of text explaining what the site is about. Separate the first paragraph from the opening paragraph welcoming visitors to the site using an <h4> heading. The text of the <h4> heading should be relevant to the site topic. Ideally it would contain a keyword or keyword phrase to help feed search engines (if you were building a real site, that's very important).

- Separate the first new paragraph from the second new paragraph using a paragraph element. Don't forget to use the cancel tags on all elements.

- At some place in the page copy, use the bold element and italic element on two different words or phrases to add emphasis to an important point.

- At the end of your two paragraphs, add a blockquote element. You may use this to quote another person that has written or said something that reinforces the need to help make the world a better place. Or, quote yourself by creating your own text for the blockquote. At the end of the quoted text, use a break tag and cite the source of the blockquote. If you don't have a favorite quotation and can't make one up, just do a search at Google for "famous quotations" and you'll find several sites where you can browse quotations by topic or author. Many of these sites have a search function as well.

Applying Styles to Text Elements

6.1 Introduction

IN CHAPTER 4: CSS Kick-Start, you learned how to add inline, embedded, and external CSS to HTML elements. In Chapter 5: Text Formatting, you learned many text formatting elements. In this chapter, you'll learn how to apply CSS styles to various text and font elements.

Because external style sheets are so powerful and useful, most of the examples that follow are written for coding into an external style sheet. You can use the same code for embedded style sheets by adding the opening and closing <style> declaration around the code. Any of the examples can be made into inline styles as well. Please review Chapter 4: CSS Kick-start if you need help creating inline, embedded, or external styles.

6.2 Changing Font Colors

WHEN IT COMES TO WEB DESIGN—the terms *text* and *font* are sometimes used interchangeably—this is incorrect. Text actually refers to the words you see on the web page and font refers to something about the code, such as the font weight or size.

How you change the color of the text from the default value of black depends on if you want to change the color for the entire page or for a portion of the page. To change the text color for the entire page, add this to the style sheet:

```
body {color: indigo;}
```

That code in the style sheet causes the body text to be rendered in the color indigo. Of course, you can change indigo to any color you choose. You can also create style rules that specify different text colors for other parts of the page. Here are a few examples:

```
body {color: indigo;}

table {color: darkblue;}

p.subtle {color: gray;}

.grassy {color: darkgreen;}
```

In the preceding style rules, I created four different text color styles. The body text is rendered in indigo. Any text inside a table is rendered in dark blue. No extra coding is needed to have the body or table colors display. Any text in a table automatically displays in dark blue, and any text not in a table automatically displays in indigo.

I also created a paragraph class called *subtle*. Any time I want to change the color of the text for a paragraph to gray, I only need to code the *subtle* class into that paragraph. Here's an example:

```
<p class="subtle"> content goes here </p>
```

Any text inside the paragraph tags with that class is rendered in gray text. I also created a generic class called *grassy*. Any time I want text rendered in dark green, I only have to add that class to any element that accepts textual content. Here are two examples:

```
<h1 class="grassy"> content goes here </h1>

<div class="grassy"> content goes here </div>
```

In those examples, the h1 heading and the text in the division tag are both rendered in dark green because I gave those HTML elements the *grassy* class that causes the text color to change to dark green.

Time Out! Up to this point I've used only color names. The color names in the examples are officially recognized names—you can't use just any color name you choose. You must use an officially recognized color name for a browser to support it. In Appendix C: Color Charts you'll find a chart of the official color names.

There are other ways to code color that make many more colors available. Color usage is covered in Chapter 8: Color, Backgrounds, and Images.

6.3 Changing Font Sizes

Font sizes can be set in four ways:

- By keyword
- By keyword relative to the containing element
- By percentage of size relative to the containing element
- By unit of measurement

Setting the size according to keyword is probably the easiest method for most people, but it also offers less control. Here's an example of how to code the font size by keyword:

```
body {font-size: medium;}
```

Here are the possible values for setting a font using the keyword method:

xx-small | x-small | small | medium | large | x-large | xx-large

If you're familiar with setting the font size using the deprecated <font> tag, this chart shows how the new coding compares to the old.

New Size	xx-small	x-small	small	medium	large	x-large	xx-large
Old Size	Size 1	Size 2	Size 3	Size 4	Size 5	Size 6	Size 7

Font size can also be changed by keyword as it relates to the containing element. The containing element is whatever controls the current font size at the place in the page you want to change. This could be the font size you already coded into a page via style sheets, or the default font size of the user agent.

By using either the keyword *smaller* or the keyword *larger*, you can change the size relative to the containing element. If you code the font size by keyword to be small, using the keyword *larger* changes the size to medium—or one size bigger than it was previously set for. Here's an example using an inline style with a paragraph element:

```
<p style="font-size: larger;"> your paragraph text
here </p>
```

Using a percentage to change the font size is similar to using a keyword relative to the containing element, only it gives you more

> **DEFINITION**
>
> A *user agent* is a browser, screen reader, mobile phone, or other applications used to access the web.

control. Rather than having specific bumps in sizes, you can use any percentage (other than a negative value) to change the font size. Here are two examples using an inline style with a division tag:

<div **style="font-size: 200%;"**> your content here </div>
<div **style="font-size: 50%;"**> your content here </div>

In the first example, the text changes to twice the size of the font size in the containing element. In the second example, the text changes to half the size of the font size in the containing element.

Now that those methods are out of the way, we come to my preferred method of setting the font size—by unit of measurement. There are several units of measurement you can use:

- px (pixels)
- pt (points)
- pc (picas)
- in (inches)
- cm (centimeters)
- mm (millimeters)

Pixels, points, and picas may not be as familiar to you as inches, centimeters, or millimeters, so let me give you an idea how they compare to inches.

The actual size of a pixel depends on the resolution of the display screen. If the display is set to its maximum resolution, a pixel will equal the size of the dot pitch. If the resolution is set to less than the maximum resolution, a pixel will be larger than the physical size of the screen's dot pitch—in other words, a pixel will use more than one dot. I know that's a little hard to wrap your head around, so for practical purposes, let's just say a single pixel is the smallest unit of measurement a computer can render.

Most computers display at either 72 dpi (dots per inch) or 96 dpi. That will get you close enough to reality to work. There are 72 points in an inch. There are 6 picas in an inch.

Having a background in graphics, where using pixels and dpi are standard operational units, I prefer using pixels to set my font sizes. You can use whichever unit of measurement you prefer.

Size values for pixels are set in whole numbers while size values for points, picas, inches, centimeters, and millimeters can be set as whole numbers or decimals. Here is an example of each:

```
body {font-size: 16px;}
div {font-size: 28pt;}
p {font-size: 4.5pc;}
h1 {font-size: 0.75in;}
h2 {font-size: 10mm;}
.smalltext {font-size: 0.5cm;}
```

Notice that in all the examples, there is no space between the number and the unit of measurement. Writing *16 px* instead of *16px* is incorrect syntax—there should be no space between the number and the unit of measurement. Got it? Great, you're really smart!

6.4 Fonts and Font Families

THE DEFAULT FONT most browsers use to display text in is Times New Roman on Windows and Times on Mac OS. That doesn't mean you're stuck with that. You can change the font to any font you choose, but there is a caveat. The computer viewing the page must have the font you choose installed in order to display the font in that typeface. That limits the fonts you can use and still expect the page to display in the font you want.

When specifying a font, you can choose specific fonts by name (such as Arial, Verdana, or Garamond), or you can choose a generic font family. You can even choose a specific font or fonts, and choose a generic font family for backup in case the viewing computer doesn't have the fonts you choose installed.

Here's an example of how to specify a font by name:

```
body {font-family: Arial;}
```

Using that in a style sheet causes the Arial font to be used on the page instead of Times New Roman. Note that if the name of the font is capitalized, you should capitalize it in your code. Most font names are capitalized. You can also specify more than one font:

```
body {font-family: Arial, Verdana, "Lucida Console";}
```

Separate each font name with a comma. If a font name has a space in it, then and only then, the name should be enclosed in straight quotation marks as I show for "Lucida Console" in the code example.

This may leave you wondering how to code a font such as Gill Sans using an inline style since an inline style already uses quotation marks. In that case, use the single quotation marks around the font name. For example:

```
<div style="font-family: Arial, 'Gill Sans', Verdana;">
```

In the inline code example, the viewing computer displays the page in the Arial font if it's installed. If Arial is not installed, it displays the page in the Gill Sans font. If Gill Sans is not installed, it displays the page in the Verdana font. If none of the fonts named are installed, the page reverts to the default font.

You can also choose generic font families. By choosing a generic font family, the computer chooses the font to use from within that font family. The generic font families are:

serif | sans-serif | monospace | cursive | fantasy

serif	Bodoni Georgia Times
sans-serif	Arial Gill Sans Verdana
monospace	Courier Lucida Con.
cursive	Brush Script Comic Pristina
fantasy	Broadway Chiller Juice

Figure 6.1

A picture is really worth a thousand words—see Figure 6.1 to get a better idea of what the font families look like rather than having me try to describe them to you.

To specify a generic font family in your code, code it the same as you would for specifying a specific font, except use the generic font family name instead. Here's an example:

```
body {font-family: sans-serif;}
```

You can also code specific fonts, and specify a generic font as a last alternative in case the viewing computer doesn't have any of the specified fonts installed. Example:

```
p {font-family: Chiller, Juice, Curlz, fantasy;}
```

In that example, if the fonts Chiller, Juice, or Curlz are not installed, the computer will select a fantasy font from the options available. The results can be unpredictable, so use this option with care.

6.5 Font Style

FONT STYLE REFERS TO normal, italic, or oblique (slanted) font faces within a typeface family. Normal style is sometimes referred to as *roman* or *upright* style. An oblique style is a forward slanted type. It's usually displayed as computer generated italic type due to a lack of true oblique fonts.

A value of *normal* means the browser or user agent selects a font that is classified as *normal* in the browser's font database, while *oblique* selects a font that is labeled *oblique*. A value of *italic* selects a font that is labeled *italic*, or, if that is not available, one labeled *oblique*.

Note that if an oblique or italic font isn't available, the browser usually generates one by electronically slanting a normal font. An electronically generated slant usually isn't as easy to read as a true italic or oblique font, so you are wise not to overuse the italic or oblique styles.

Here's how to set the font style:

```
.stressed {font-style: italic;}
```

In that example, I created a generic class named *stressed*. Anyplace I add that class to an element that accepts text, the text will display in italic type.

6.6 Font Weight

THE FONT WEIGHT PROPERTY and value sets the weight, or heaviness, of the font. While there are many options, the font weight is relative to the font used. Many fonts do not contain all the weights listed here, so you may not see any difference between some values. In fact, it's quite likely that you won't see a difference with most fonts. The font size used also plays a role in whether there is a display difference between different weights. As a general rule, the smaller the font, the fewer weights there are that can be displayed. Here are the font weight values:

normal | bold | bolder | lighter | 100 | 200 | 300 | 400 | 500 | 600 | 700 | 800 | 900

The first four values are keywords, whose meanings should be obvious. The values *100* to *900* form a sequence in which each number indicates a weight that is at least as dark as its predecessor.

The keyword *normal* is the same as a *400* numerical value, and *bold* is the same as a *700* numerical value. Here's how to set the font weight property:

```
div {font-weight: normal;}
h1 {font-weight: 700;}
```

6.7 Font Variant

THE FONT VARIANT PROPERTY is pretty much a one-trick pony allowing you to set text to normal or small caps. The small caps setting transforms lowercase letters into slightly smaller versions of their uppercase counterparts. It's not very useful for my purposes, but you may find a purpose for it (often, it's used to make things look official). Here's how to code the font variant:

```
h2 {font-variant: small-caps;}
```

Wherever you use an h2 heading with that style, it renders something like this:

HELLO WORLD

6.8 Text Indent

USING THE *TEXT-INDENT* PROPERTY lets you indent the first line of a block of text like the first lines of paragraphs are indented in a book. Here's how to code it:

```
p {text-indent: 20px;}
```

With that in a style sheet, each time you start a new paragraph the first line will be indented by 20 pixels.

You can use the *text-indent* property with any element that accepts text, but I suggest using it for paragraphs or creating a generic class that you can add to elements as needed. For example, using it with the body element may cause indents in some items you don't want indented. Using the *text-indent* property for paragraphs of text or as a generic class rule eliminates unwanted items from indenting.

Note

Because I prefer to use pixels for my unit of measurement I use them in my code examples. Wherever I use pixels, you can also use the other units of measurement.

6.9 Text Align

THE *TEXT-ALIGN* PROPERTY allows you to align text horizontally within an element. The possible values are:

left | right | center | justify

If you use the *text-align* property with a value of *right* with a division tag, all the text within that division lines up on the right side of the page rather than the left, which is the default value. Here's an example of that:

div {text-align: right;}

If that is in a style sheet, any time you use a division tag the text aligns to the right side of the page. Naturally, a value of *left* aligns text to the left, and a value of *center* aligns text in the center. The text-align value will also align images and other content unless they are overridden by other code. The value of *justify* aligns text evenly on the right and left side with no ragged edges, but it does not effect other content such as images.

6.10 Text Transform

THE *TEXT-TRANSFORM* PROPERTY controls the case of the text within an element. Values have the following meanings:

- *capitalize:* Sets the first character of each word in uppercase; other characters are unaffected.
- *uppercase:* Sets all the characters of each word in uppercase.
- *lowercase:* Sets all the characters of each word in lowercase.
- *none:* No text effects. Go figure.

Here's how to create a class using the *text-transform* property:

div.allcaps {text-transform: uppercase;}

To display a block of text in uppercase with that style rule, I only have to add the *allcaps* class to a division tag. Here's how:

<div **class="allcaps"**> content goes here </div>

> ### HINT
>
> Usability studies show that using all capital letters for a string of text makes it harder to read. In many online circles, using all capital letters is considered the equivalent of shouting in person, and is therefore considered rude.

6.11 Letter Spacing

I'LL BET YOU NEVER WOULD have guessed you had this much control—but using CSS even allows you to control the amount of space between the letters of words. In typography, this is called kerning. In CSS, it is called oatmeal...I mean, *letter-spacing*. Here's how to code the space between letters:

body {letter-spacing: 1px;}

In Figure 6.2, you can see what adding just one pixel of letter spacing does to the text. The font family and size used is the same in both paragraphs.

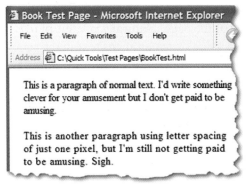

Figure 6.2

You can also use negative values to decrease the amount of space between letters, but I don't recommend it. It doesn't take much before the letters start overlapping each other, making your text impossible to read.

6.12 Word Spacing

OH YEAH, YOU WANT CONTROL, I'll give you control. The *word-spacing* property controls the amount of space in between words. In typography, this is called tracking. In CSS, it is called . . . *word spacing*. Thought I was going to write something silly, didn't you? I'm totally unpredictable! To use *word-spacing*:

body {word-spacing: 3px;}

With that code in style sheet rules, an *additional* three pixels of space is added to the normal distance between each word. You can also use a negative value to draw words closer together. For example:

p {word-spacing: -1px;}

If the negative value is too big, words can overlap, so be careful how you use this (if you use it at all).

6.13 Line Height

CONTROL, CONTROL, CONTROL—you are power mad! Yes, you can control the vertical space in between lines of text, too. Line height in typography is called *leading*. Unlike letter spacing in which the measurement is added to or subtracted from the default measurement, browsers take line height literally. If you code a line height of 3 pixels, it narrows the space between lines to 3 pixels, rather than adding 3 more pixels to the normal spacing. Here's how to add the *line-height* property to your style sheet rules:

    body {line-height: 24px;}

By the way, if you set the *line-height* to 0, the text disappears. Yes Mr. Zimpledorker, there is magic online. If you don't set the line height, browsers control the leading.

6.14 Vertical Align

IN FIGURE 6.3 YOU SEE two lines of text. The capital letter "B" in each line is an image. In the first line, the text that follows the image is vertically centered on the image of the letter B. In the second line, the text that follows the image is aligned at the bottom of the image. You do this by adjusting the *vertical-align* property coded into the image. In the first example, I set the vertical alignment to the value of *middle*; and in the second one I set it to *bottom*. Here's how I did the first one:

Figure 6.3

    <img src="B.gif" style="vertical-align: middle;" />e
    somebody nice.

The part of the code in bold text sets the vertical alignment. The vertical alignment is relative to the text in the same line. If a sentence wraps to a second line, the second line of text would drop down below the image in both examples. Here are the possible *values* of the *vertical-align* property:

baseline | bottom | middle | sub | super | text-bottom | text-top | top

Here's what each of the values mean:

Value	Description
baseline	Aligns the element (the image in my example) with the bottom of the letters in the same line of text.
bottom	Aligns the bottom of the element with the bottom of the surrounding text or other content, whichever is lowest.
middle	Aligns the middle of the element with the middle of the line of text.
sub	Subscripts the element; in this case the image is lowered, not the text.
super	Superscripts the element; in this case the image is raised, not the text.
text-bottom	Similar to the *bottom* value, only this aligns the element to bottom of the text. Other content is ignored for alignment purposes.
text-top	Aligns the element to the top of the text. Other elements are ignored.
top	Aligns the top of the element with the top of the text or other content, whichever is tallest.

6.15 Setting Multiple Properties and Values

RATHER THAN SETTING PROPERTIES and values one at a time, it's often preferable to set all the ones you want to use at once. Here's an example:

body {color: brown; font-size: 14px; font-family: Arial, Verdana;}

With that style rule, text is brown in color, 14 pixels tall, and rendered in Arial if available, Verdana if not, or the default font if neither specified font is available. Remember, each property and value is separated from the next one by a semicolon.

6.16 Text Decorations

TEXT DECORATIONS SOUND more fun than they really are. The possible values for the *text decoration* property are:

none | underline | overline | line-through | blink

While "none" may not seem like a useful value, it really is. It's commonly used to remove the default underline from text links. Many people, myself included, believe that links look nicer and are easier to read without the underline. Be careful about removing the underline from links *and* changing the default link color, however. Many people may not realize a link is actually a link without one of the normal visual clues.

An *underline* value underlines text, an *overline* value creates a line above the text, and the *line-through* value creates a horizontal line through the center of the text.

The *blink* value is supposed to make text blink on and off. *Blink,* however, doesn't seem to have support in the majority of browsers, although some do honor it. It's just as well that the majority of browsers ignore it because it's quite annoying. If you don't believe me, try reading this book while rapidly blinking your eyes.

Here's an example of how to use the *text-decoration* property and value to remove the underline from links:

```
a:link {text-decoration: none;}

a:visited {text-decoration: none;}

a:hover {text-decoration: none;}

a:active {text-decoration: none;}
```

If you remove the underline from links, you don't *have* to remove the underline from each link state (visited, active, etc.), but most professional web designers believe it's best to be consistent.

Text decorations can be used with any text element. You might use the *underline* value to emphasize a word or phrase or use the *line-through* value to cross out the regular price of an item before offering it at a lower sale price. Here's how to use an inline style to create a line through the old price of a sale item:

```
Our price: <span style="text-decoration: line-through;">$49.95</span> Sale! $39.95
```

On a web page, the text looks like this:

Our price: $49.95 Sale! $39.95

P.S. Did you try to read any text while rapidly blinking your eyes? If so…gotcha!

6.17 Chapter 6 Exercise

Now you get to make some choices and have a little bit of fun:

- First, remove all the CSS code from the HEAD section of your project's source code. For the most part, you're going to be working only with external style sheets from now on because that's simply the best practice.

- Add the h3 and h4 selectors to your external style sheet and set the font family, font size, and font weight properties. The values for these properties do not have to be the same as you used before, although they can be if you choose. Also add the color property to these selectors, and select any color but black for them. The reason for using any color but black is because black is the default color; by changing the color you can see if your code works. Refer to the color names chart in Appendix C to choose a color.

- Add the blockquote element to your external style sheet and change the font family to something other than the font used on the rest of the regular body text. Change the font size so that it's slightly smaller than the rest of the regular body text.

- Using inline CSS, set the font-variant property to small-caps and set the text-decoration property to "underline" for the h4 heading on your page. Need a hint? *Chapter 4: CSS Kick-Start, Section 4.5* shows how to add two properties to an element using inline styles.

- Finally, keep developing your ideas to better the world. You'll have to write about them later.

Applying Styles to Other Elements

7.1 Introduction

IN CHAPTER 6: Applying Styles to Text Elements, you learned how to apply CSS styles and fonts to various text. In this chapter, you'll learn how to apply many new styles to a variety of elements.

Once again, the examples that follow are written for an external style sheet, but they can be used as embedded or inline styles as well. Please review Chapter 4: CSS Kick-Start if you need a refresher about inline, embedded, or external styles.

7.2 The Box Model

TO UNDERSTAND MANY USES of CSS, you need to understand the CSS box model. Any HTML element can be considered a box. These boxes can be stacked on top of each other (block elements) or next to each other (inline elements).

The box model applies to all visual HTML (and XHTML) elements, so the properties and values of the box model can be used with all visual elements such as paragraphs, divisions, headings, images, etc.

Figure 7.1 shows a diagram of the box model. The green area represents the HTML element / content, such as a paragraph or an image.

The blue area surrounding the green area is a CSS property called *padding*. You can add padding to any visual HTML element. Padding places a cushion of space around the HTML element or content and the edge of the containing element. If the containing element is a paragraph, a padding of five pixels creates

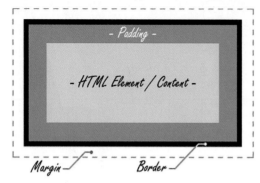

Figure 7.1

a cushion of five pixels of empty space between the text and the outside edge of the paragraph box. To relate this to the graphic, the text is the green area and the padding is the blue area; where the outer blue edge meets the inner black edge is the edge of the containing element.

The heavy black line at the outer edge of the padding is the *border*. Using CSS, a border can be placed around any visual HTML element. If the padding is set to 0 or isn't coded at all, the border goes around the HTML element or content. In other words, the blue wouldn't be there and the border would be at the outer edge of the green area.

The area between the black border and the gray dashed lines is the *margin*. The margin provides a cushion of space between the outside edge of the border and the edge of any surrounding content. The area outside the dashed lines may be the parent element or other content, such as text. (Note that the dashed lines are only there for visual reference; the dashed lines do not exist as a part of the box model.)

The margin is always invisible, so the background color or image of the parent element will show through the margin as if it isn't there. The border color and thickness are whatever color you choose. The padding is as thick as you set it to be also. The background color or image, if any, of the element using the padding shows as the background of the padding.

In other words, if the web page has a tan background color and we add the box model properties of padding, border, and margin to a paragraph element with a green background color, the results would be this:

- The text in the paragraph displays against a green background because the paragraph has a green background.

- There is a cushion of space between the paragraph text and the border; the amount of space is the width we set for the padding. This empty space is green, the same as the background color behind the text.

- The border is in the color and thickness we chose.

- There is a margin of space between the outside edge of the border of the paragraph and the surrounding content that is tan in color, the same as the web page background color.

That's the box model in a nutshell. It consists of four parts: *content*, *padding*, *border*, and *margin*. The content is needed to have the other three parts available, but you can use any combination of padding, border, and margin properties that you choose. None are required; any one or two can be used with or without the others.

This box model can be applied to divisions, paragraphs, headings, images, and many other elements—even individual words if they are contained in a <span> tag set. In the next three sections of this chapter, we'll apply the box model to an HTML division element.

7.3 Adding Padding

SORRY ABOUT THE RHYME, but hey, rhymes happen and life goes on, so tough it out. Here's how to add padding to an HTML division element in an external style sheet:

```
div {padding: 7px;}
```

Wow, that was easy. I can't believe I get paid to write this stuff. Anyway, with the above style rule, any time we create a <div> element on a page there will be 7 pixels of padding between the content of the division and the outer edge of the division.

In Figure 7.2 you can see the difference between a paragraph of text with no padding and a paragraph of text with 7 pixels of padding. I used a green background color to show the edges of the paragraph box. Notice in the top paragraph how the text butts up against the left and bottom edge of the paragraph box. The text on the right side would be at the edge as well, if the wording worked out right. There are always a few pixels of space at the top according to the default line height.

> Your life is an experiment from start to finish. Dare to explore what is possible for you.
>
> Your life is an experiment from start to finish. Dare to explore what is possible for you.

Figure 7.2

Now look at the bottom paragraph and see the padding between the text and edges of the paragraph box.

The sample code for adding padding to the division is the quick way to code it—provided you want the padding on each side of the content to be the same. Each side: *top*, *right*, *bottom*, and *left* can be set separately if different amounts of padding are desired.

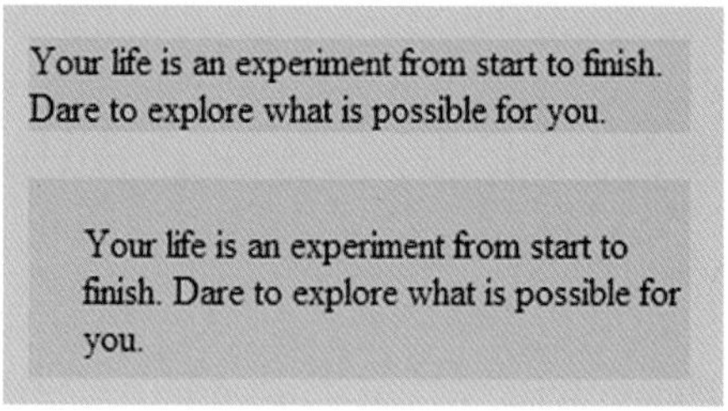

Your life is an experiment from start to finish. Dare to explore what is possible for you.

Your life is an experiment from start to finish. Dare to explore what is possible for you.

Figure 7.3

In Figure 7.3, I changed the padding in the second paragraph to 17 pixels on the top, 0 pixels on the right, 7 pixels on the bottom, and 23 pixels on the left.

When coding individual properties in the box model, you always work clockwise from the top. It's always *top*, *right*, *bottom*, and *left*.

Here's the code for setting the separate values used in Figure 7.3:

```
div {padding-top: 17px;
     padding-right: 0px;
     padding-bottom: 7px;
     padding-left: 23px;}
```

As a reminder, this code:

```
div {padding-top: 17px; padding-right: 0px; padding-bottom: 7px; padding-left: 23px;}
```

…is the same as the previous code. It's your choice whether you want to line up your style sheet code nice and neat or string it all together. Stringing it together is faster when you initially write code, but lining it up neatly makes it easier to edit later. Neatness may help as you are learning because the code doesn't look quite as crowded and confusing.

There's also a shortcut way to code the individual sides of the padding. Rather than writing *padding-side: numerical value* for each side, you can just write *padding* and code the numerical values for each side clockwise from the top. Have a look:

```
div {padding: 17px 0px 7px 23px;}
```

This tells the browser the same thing as the previous two code examples. When using the shortcut property, the individual values are still coded clockwise from the top, but do not use commas, semicolons, or any other separation characters—they should only be separated by a space. Are you loving this stuff, or what!

7.4 Adding a Border

NOW I'LL ADD A BORDER to that same test paragraph. Here's how that's done:

```
div {border: 2px solid black;}
```

In Figure 7.4 you can see what adding the border did to the second paragraph of text. Note that I reset the padding to 7 pixels on each side to make it a prettier picture. I'm always thinking of you!

As with the padding, each side of the border can be set separately. Again, work clockwise from the top. Figure 7.5 shows the border I added using a different color for each side.

As you can see, I made the top red, the right side green, the bottom blue, and the left side black. I could have changed each border width too, but it looks quite ugly, and again, I'm always thinking of you!

Here's the code for the multicolored border:

```
div {border-top: 5px solid red;
     border-right: 5px solid green;
     border-bottom: 5px solid blue;
     border-left: 5px solid black;}
```

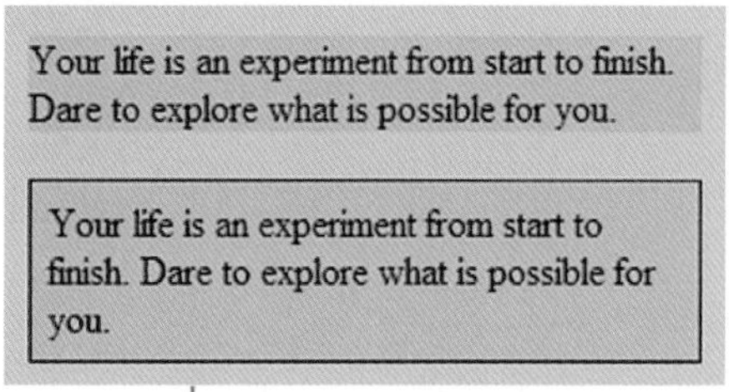

If you choose the border colors carefully, you can make it look like a beveled edge framing the content, but there are other ways to do that. The border itself has seven other styles in addition to solid. The styles are:

solid | dashed | dotted | double | outset | inset | groove | ridge

You can also use the values of *hidden* and *none*. *None* is the same as using no border. *Hidden* is the same as *none* except that it takes precedence over conflicting borders. Any border with the *hidden* value suppresses all borders at the location.

Figure 7.6 shows what each border style looks like at 5 pixels wide in sea green color against a lighter background color.

Some border styles will not look any different from others if the width is set too small. If you have a border that doesn't seem to be doing what it should, try setting the width to a higher numerical value. For example, the double border style has to be at least 3 pixels wide in order to have two lines.

Some of the styles may be hard to distinguish from the others here in print, so don't be afraid to experiment on your own.

Your life is an experiment from start to finish. Dare to explore what is possible for you.

Your life is an experiment from start to finish. Dare to explore what is possible for you.

Figure 7.4

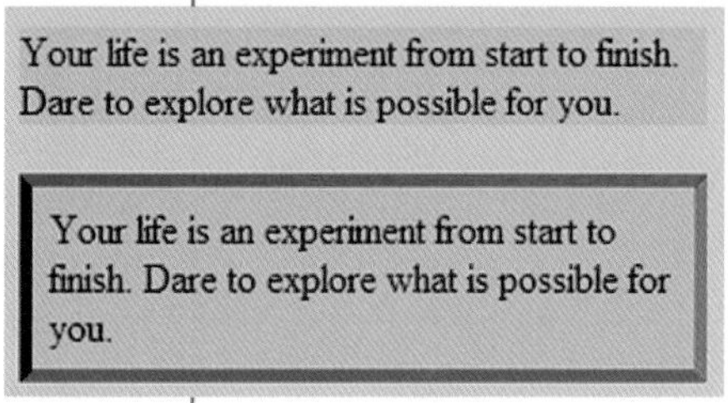

Your life is an experiment from start to finish. Dare to explore what is possible for you.

Your life is an experiment from start to finish. Dare to explore what is possible for you.

Figure 7.5

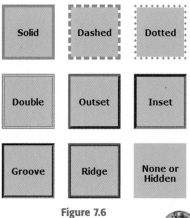

Solid | Dashed | Dotted

Double | Outset | Inset

Groove | Ridge | None or Hidden

Figure 7.6

To code the different border styles, substitute the style you want in place of the word "solid" in the previous examples. A couple more code examples follow, but this time I used inline styles instead of external style sheets:

<p **style="border: 3px groove blue;"**> content goes here </p>

<h1 **style="border: 5px double red;"**> heading goes here </h1>

While the shortcut way to code different widths, colors, and styles into just one rule is handy, you can use several individual settings when you need an extreme amount of control. In the following chart, you'll see all the individual border properties you can set.

Border Property	Description of Property
border-top-width: *value*	Sets the width of the top border.
border-right-width: *value*	Sets the width of the right border.
border-bottom-width: *value*	Sets the width of the bottom border.
border-left-width: *value*	Sets the width of the left border.
border-width: *top right bottom left*	Sets the width of all the borders at once.

Note 1: In the first four border width properties, substitute a numerical value and unit of measurement for the word *value*. **Example:** border-top-width: 3px

Note 2: In the last border width property, substitute a numerical value and unit of measurement for each: *top, right, bottom,* and *left*. Example: border-width: 2px 4px 2px 4px

border-top-color: *value*	Sets the color of the top border.
border-right-color: *value*	Sets the color of the right border.
border-bottom-color: *value*	Sets the color of the bottom border.
border-left-color: *value*	Sets the color of the left border.
border-color: *top right bottom left*	Sets the color of all the borders at once.

Note 1: In the first four border color properties, substitute a color value (color name, RGB color, or hexadecimal color) for the word *value*. **Example:** border-top-color: green

Note 2: In the last border color property, substitute a color for each: *top, right, bottom,* and *left*. Example: border-color: red blue red blue

border-top-style: *value*	Sets the style type for the top border.
border-right-style: *value*	Sets the style type for the right border.
border-bottom-style: *value*	Sets the style type for the bottom border.
border-left-style: *value*	Sets the style type for the left border.
border-style: *top right bottom left*	Sets the style type for all the borders at once.

Note 1: In the first four border style properties, substitute the border style (solid, ridge, groove, etc.) for the word *value*. **Example:** border-top-style: dotted

Note 2: In the last border style property, substitute the border style for the each: *top, right, bottom,* and *left.* **Example:** border-style: solid double solid double

7.5 Adding a Margin

YOU CAN PROBABLY ALMOST GUESS how to add the margin property and value by now. Just so I have something to write in this section, though, I'll go ahead and show you anyway. I know you're thrilled, but try to keep your composure. Here we go:

div {margin: 40px;}

If you place this code in an external or embedded style sheet, wherever a division tag is used, 40 pixels of transparent space are placed around the division area.

In Figure 7.7 you can see how a margin of 40 pixels created the space around the division element in the center of the text.

I added a background color to the division so you can see the margin is transparent space.

As with the padding and border properties of the box model, each margin can be set in one rule (if each side has the same value). Or, each side may be set individually and each may have different values.

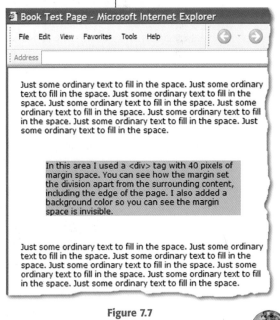

Figure 7.7

To set the margarine . . . er, I mean, to set the *margin* for each side individually, add this line to an external style sheet:

```
div {margin-top: 15px;
        margin-right: 30px;
        margin-bottom: 15px;
        margin-left: 30px;}
```

To set the individual margins using the shortcut method, just work clockwise from the top as in previous examples. The following shortcut code means the same thing as the long way of writing the individual margins in the previous example.

```
div {margin: 15px 30px 15px 30px;}
```

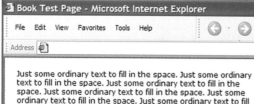

Just some ordinary text to fill in the space. Just some ordinary text to fill in the space. Just some ordinary text to fill in the space. Just some ordinary text to fill in the space. Just some ordinary text to fill in the space. Just some ordinary text to fill in the space. Just some ordinary text to fill in the space. Just some ordinary text to fill in the space.

In this area I used a <div> tag with 40 pixels of margin space. You can see how the margin set the division apart from the surrounding content, including the edge of the page. I also added a background color so you can see the margin space is invisible.

Just some ordinary text to fill in the space. Just some ordinary text to fill in the space. Just some ordinary text to fill in the space. Just some ordinary text to fill in the space. Just some ordinary text to fill in the space. Just some ordinary text to fill in the space.

Figure 7.8

Now let's put it all together using the padding, border, and margin in one declaration. Figure 7.8 shows how using the box model around a division of text really sets it apart from ordinary text. This is an effective way of drawing attention to something you want to emphasize—but be careful not to use it all over your page. When everything is emphasized, nothing is emphasized!

Here's the code I used:

```
div {margin: 15px 30px 15px 30px;
        border: 5px double brown;
        padding: 12px;
        background-color: burlywood;}
```

I used a margin of 15 pixels on the top and bottom, and 30 pixels on the right and left. The division has a 5-pixel width double border, brown in color with 12 pixels of padding on all sides. After adding the background color, the stage was set.

That sums up the box model. Remember, you can specify padding, borders, and margins for any visual HTML element. As you learn web design, this will be one of the most important things you learn. With a little imagination and creativity, you will be able to do things with your layout and design that amateurs only dream about.

7.6 Width and Height

ANY WEB DESIGN WOULD BE LOST without the ability to specify width and height in areas of need. Width can be added to some elements using HTML and a very few elements can also include height. However, width and height can be added to *any* block level element using CSS.

An example of using HTML to legally add the width and height to an element is with the image tag. A table tag can legally accept the width property only, although Internet Explorer will honor the height attribute as well, height is not a legal attribute for a table. You'll see how to do that in the chapters covering these elements.

Using CSS, we can legally add width and height to elements where it's illegal to add them the HTML way. Elements such as paragraphs, divisions, and form buttons all may be coded to size using CSS—but may not be coded to size using HTML. Using the width and height property and value is often done inline, rather than through embedded or external style sheets, because usually they are needed on a one-time basis rather than a repeating basis. Here's how to add the width and height to a division element:

> The words "legal" and "illegal" as used here refers to code being in compliance with the W3C standards for HTML and CSS, not to the laws of the land.

```
<div style="width: 350px; height: 200px;"> content goes here </div>
```

If you set the height too small for the content on a division tag, the division will expand in some browsers or the content will be cut off in other browsers. Most of the odd behavior

WARNING!

Kaboom! Sometimes our best laid plans blow up on our monitors. I have to warn you that setting the width and height of some elements sometimes causes unexpected things to happen. For example, if you set a width for a form button that is too narrow for the button text, the text will be truncated so people can't see the entire label.

can be controlled (you'll learn about that in the next section). Most of the time you won't have any problems. But, if you don't want unexpected results, be sure to watch for oddities such as these when setting the width and height of HTML elements that don't have their own width and height attributes and values available without CSS properties. When in doubt, refer to Appendix A: HTML and XHTML in the back of the book to determine which HTML elements have width and height attributes.

7.7 Overflow

IN THE LAST SECTION, I mentioned that if an element's height is too small for its content, you can get unpredictable results. For example, the containing element may stretch to fit the content in some browsers and scrollbars may automatically appear in other browsers. By setting the element's overflow property, you decide what happens when the content exceeds the space. The overflow values are:

visible | hidden | scroll | auto

Here's what those values mean:

- **visible:** The width and/or height of an element will be stretched to fit the content.

- **hidden:** The element is not resized. Content that is too large to fit in the element will be hidden from view and inaccessible.

- **scroll:** The element is not resized. A horizontal and vertical scrollbar is added to view the content—whether it's needed or not. If the scrollbar is unnecessary, it will be grayed out (inactive).

- **auto:** The element is not resized. Content that is too large to fit in the element will cause a vertical and/or horizontal scrollbar to appear. If the content is not too large for the element, no scrollbars appear.

Figure 7.9 shows four divisions with the width and height set to 120 pixels; there is too much content to fit within each division.

Each division has a different overflow value so you can see what each value does.

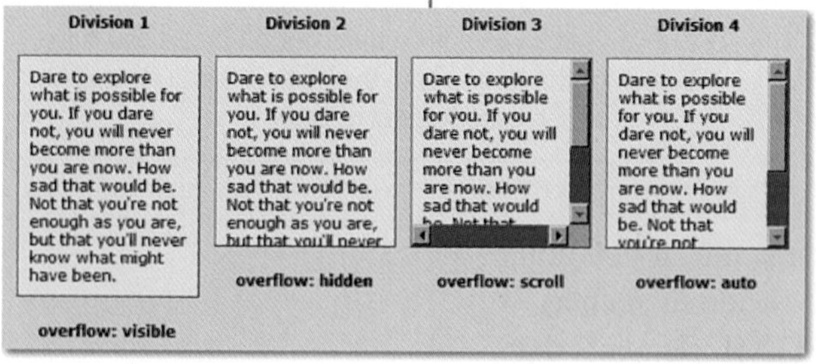

For comparison, Division 2 shows the division in the correct size: 120 x 120 pixels.

In Division 1, the overflow is set to *visible* so the division is expanded vertically to accommodate the content. In other browsers the content will bleed outside of the division box, causing the text to continue beyond the box's boundaries.

Figure 7.9

Division 2 shows the division container in the correct size, but with the overflow set to *hidden*. Some of the text is clipped off and cannot be accessed unless a reader viewed the source code of the document.

Division 3 shows the division container at the correct size as well, but with the overflow set to *scroll*. As a result, horizontal and vertical scroll bars are added to the container. The horizontal scrollbar is unnecessary, but the *scroll* value sets them both whether they are needed or not.

Division 4 also shows the division at the correct size, but with the overflow set to *auto*, only the vertical scrollbar is added. There is no content wider than the division container, so the horizontal scrollbar is not needed.

Adding the overflow property to an element is easy. An inline example:

```
<div style="width: 120px; height: 120px; overflow: auto;"> content </div>
```

In that example, I also set the width and height. If I didn't, by default a division expands vertically to accommodate the content, so the overflow property isn't needed or used. The code in red is what gives the element the overflow property. The following code shows an example of creating a class for a paragraph that sets the overflow property in an external style sheet:

```
p.testimonial {width: 200px; height: 100px; overflow: auto;}
```

In that example, I imagined using customer testimonials throughout a sales page to help sell a product. Since I don't want the testimonials to take up too much space, I limited the size of the testimonial class paragraph to 200 x 100 pixels and set the overflow to *auto*. Short testimonials will fit into the paragraph without causing scrollbars to appear. Longer testimonials will generate a scrollbar automatically if the content exceeds the space. Since there is only text in the testimonials, using the *auto* value for the overflow property means only the vertical scroll bar will be generated if needed (because the text will wrap to the next line, making a horizontal scrollbar unnecessary).

Note that the scrollbars appear inside the paragraph boxes rather than outside of it. This reduces the amount of horizontal space available for the text. Be sure to factor this into your decision-making process when working with narrow columns of text. If the space for text is too constricted, the text passage can read more like a list than sentences. The fix is to increase the width of the containing element and/or reduce the font size.

There are also *overflow-x* and *overflow-y* properties. Overflow-x tells the browser what to do when the content exceeds the element's width. Overflow-y tells the browser what to do when the content exceeds the element's height. Note that overflow-x doesn't seem to be supported in some browsers; the box expands horizontally instead of displaying horizontal scrollbars.

There is also a closely related property called *clipping*, which is addressed in Chapter 8: Color, Backgrounds, and Images. You have a few other lessons to learn first.

7.8 Display Style

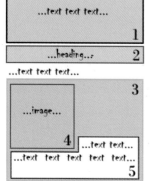

Figure 7.10

IF YOU THINK OF HTML ELEMENTS as blocks of content, it can help you understand the structure of a web page. As you read the description of the illustration in Figure 7.10, keep this block idea in mind.

The block labeled "1" represents a paragraph of text. The paragraph could have dozens of words, but I just used "…text text text…" to represent the content. That is the first building block on this example page.

The block labeled "2" represents a heading. The heading is a new block of content and it is stacked under the first block of content. Paragraphs and headings are both *block level elements*. Block level elements always start on a new line—unless their display property has been modified.

Under block 2, I added a line of text. Text is not an element—it is *content*. It begins on a new line because a heading always places an empty line above and below itself by default. After the line of text, I added a division, represented in green and labeled as block "3." A division is another block level element, so it begins under the bare line of text.

Inside the division I added an image, represented by block "4." An image is an *inline element*. An inline element remains in the flow of content; it does not start on a new line, so the text I add after the image starts on the same line as the bottom of the image. The next line of text wraps underneath the image. The white block labeled number "5" is not a really a block—I used the box shape to show the shape of the content flow.

With that prelude, I hope you can see how block level elements are stacked on top of each other, and inline elements are placed in the flow of the content. What if we need to change a block level element into an inline element—can that be done? Good question!

By changing the default *display* property, a block level element can be treated like an inline element. In the same fashion, an inline element can be treated like a block element.

In Figure 7.10, suppose the heading in block "2" was the title of an article and the text beneath it was the author's name. Normally, that would display as in Figure 7.11.

By changing the display property for the heading element, I was able to place the author's name next to the article title rather than underneath it as it would display by default. See Figure 7.12 to see how that looks.

I think having the author's name on the same line as the title looks nicer. It also sets it apart from the way most other web sites credit their writers. In a medium filled with billions of web pages written by millions of writers, finding ways to set yourself apart from the masses is of primary importance if you want to make a name for yourself.

I did two things to make my article title and the author's name look like Figure 7.12. First, I embedded the following style rules into the HEAD section of the page:

```
<style type="text/css">
body {font-family: Verdana;
        font-size: 14px;}
h2 {font-family: Broadway;
      font-size: 24px;}
</style>
```

With that code, I set the main page text to 14 pixels tall in Verdana font. That's what the author's name is displayed in. I also set an h2 size heading at 24 pixels tall in Broadway font.

Next, in the BODY of the page, I coded the actual title and author's name like this:

```
<h1 style="display: inline;"> Lip Service </h1> by
Betty Kisster
```

The sample code that is bold and red is what changes the heading tag from a block level element to an inline element, allowing the article title and author's name to display in the same line. Speaking of the article title and author, did you get it?

Lip Service by Betty Kister…Bet-he Kissed-her

Lip Service

by Betty Kister

Figure 7.11

Lip Service by Betty Kister

Figure 7.12

Come on, you have to pay attention, or my best stupidity will go for naught.

Silly humor aside, the values you can set with the *display* property are listed in the following chart. The chart is provided as a reference for future use— you're not expected to understand all the values at this time because we haven't covered all the elements the property covers.

Display Value	Definition
inline	Causes an element to be an inline element.
block	Causes an element to generate a block level box.
inline-block	Causes an element to generate a block level box, which itself is flowed in content as a single inline box. The inside of an inline-block is formatted as a block box, and the element itself is formatted as an inline replaced element.
inherit	The element inherits the display property of the parent element.
list-item	Causes the element to display as a list item (bulleted).
run-in	Creates either block or inline boxes, depending on context.
none	Causes an element to generate no boxes in the formatting structure (the element has no effect on layout). Descendant elements cannot generate any boxes either.
table group*	Causes an element to behave like a table element.

*The table group includes:

table | inline-table | table-row-group | table-header-group | table-footer-group

table-row | table-column-group | table-column | table-cell | table-caption

7.9 Positioning

ONE OF THE DRAWBACKS in the early days of web design was the difficulty in positioning elements precisely where you wanted them. This problem was finally overcome with CSS-Positioning or CSS-P for short.

When positioning elements, keep in mind that you are work-ing with the box model. There are three positioning schemes for the box model according to the W3C:

Normal flow	In CSS2, normal flow includes block formatting of block boxes, inline formatting of inline boxes, relative position-ing of block or inline boxes, and positioning of compact and run-in boxes.
Absolute	In the absolute positioning model, a box is removed from the normal flow entirely and assigned a position with respect to a containing block.
Floats	In the float model, a box is first laid out according to the normal flow, then taken out of the flow and shifted to the left or right as far as possible. Content may flow along the side of a float.

The first decision is to choose a positioning scheme. If you don't want the text and other content to flow alongside the posi-tioned element, choose either a *normal flow* position or *absolute* position. Choose the *float* scheme if you do want text and other content to flow next to the positioned element.

This section covers *normal flow* and *absolute* positioning. Floating elements are covered in the next section because they're coded in a different manner.

CSS-P consists of two parts. The first part specifies which type of positioning you want to use. The possible *values* are:

relative | absolute | fixed | static | inherit

To establish the type of positioning to use, the first part of the code is written like this:

position: relative;

Of course, if you want absolute positioning, type *absolute* in place of *relative* in the code. Here's what each value means:

relative	This value positions an element *relative* to its default posi-tion (where it would normally be positioned within the flow of content).
absolute	This value uses numerical coordinates to position an element.
fixed	This value also uses numerical coordinates to position an element, except the element doesn't scroll with the page—it stays "fixed" in place. Fixed is not yet fully supported by all browsers at the time of this writing.

Note

Keep in mind that even if you write perfect HTML and CSS code, browsers can still render pages differently from one to another. Remember, browsers are in a continu-ous state of development, as are web page standards. Always check your web pages in multiple browsers to ensure they display well.

static	This is the default setting and it's the same as not using positioning. It allows browsers to place elements in the flow of content as they appear in the source code.
inherit	With this value, an element inherits the position type from its parent element.

The other part of positioning an element using CSS-P is to name the coordinates where it will be positioned. This is where the guidelines get a little murky. I've pored over the W3C position papers and researched online and in book after book; everyone just kind of glosses over it. They all pretty much say the same thing—to position an element, use this code:

```
position: absolute; left: 50px; top: 40px;
```

Or, they'll use something like this for a model:

```
position: type; top: value; right: value; bottom: value:
left: value;
```

Excuse me, but should you use just the top and left properties, or is it sometimes necessary to use the top, right, bottom, and left properties? This is what gets glossed over every time, and no one gives concrete examples you can really wrap your mind around.

The easiest thing for me to do would be to gloss over it as well. However, I want to give you more than just few paragraphs that I know you'll ignore because you don't understand it. Instead, I've done some thinking and experimenting, and here's what I've determined:

Because the W3C standards are less than specific, so is browser support. In my experiments, code that validates perfectly was nonetheless rendered quite differently in different browsers.

I found only one method that allowed content to display as I intended across all CSS-aware browsers.

By using only the top and left coordinates, and using either an element's own width and height attributes or setting the width and height using CSS, the element will display as intended. Using the right and bottom positioning coordinates caused problems. In some browsers, the right coordinate was measured from the left side of the page, but in other browsers it was measured from the right side of the page. Using the bottom coordinate didn't work at all in some browsers. If the content was smaller than the coordinate, the box would shrink; if it was larger, the box would expand.

Obviously these inconsistencies made various page layouts look drastically different from browser to browser. I'm guessing this is why everyone seems to gloss over the position property.

Whew. I hope you appreciate all that thinking because it almost broke my head!

So, in view of what my experimentation showed, the only dependable way to set the coordinates for an element is to use the top and left coordinates—and be sure to set the width and height somewhere.

Figure 7.13 shows a division element positioned using *absolute* positioning. When using a division element, the size of the element must be set using CSS. While some browsers let you use HTML to code a size into the division element, the width and height attributes are not official HTML standards for the division tag.

Figure 7.13

One other thing—I recommend setting the overflow property when setting a specific division height. If you don't, any excess content is handled in different ways by different browsers. Some browsers expand the division box, others keep the box the right size but run the content out of the box, and yet others truncate the text. Setting the overflow property to allow scrollbars is the only way to be sure the division box stays the correct size.

I created a class for the division shown in Figure 7.13. Here's the code I used in the external style sheet:

```
div.fix {width: 150px;
        height: 110px;
        position: absolute;
        top: 75;
        left: 50;
        overflow: auto;}
```

I also set a border and background color for the division—so it would stand out on the test page—but I left those out of the code to keep the size and positioning code most prominent.

The *width* and *height* of the division are easy enough to understand without explanation. I used the *absolute* positioning scheme and set the distance from the top at 75 pixels and from the left at 50 pixels. The *top: value* and *left: value* properties and values should always follow immediately after the *position: value* property and value. In most cases, the top is measured down from the top edge of the browser window and the left is measured from the left edge of the window. In a few isolated cases, the top and left may be measured from the containing element, but it's rare. I only mention it in case things don't look right, so you'll know what to look for.

Lastly, I set the *overflow* property to *auto* to allow scrollbars as needed so the division will remain the correct size. If the content doesn't exceed the space the scrollbars will not appear. Since I created a class named *fix* for this division, the division is added to the page by naming that class in a division tag:

<div **class="fix"**> content goes here </div>

In Figure 7.14, I added a picture of our little puppy, Cricket. I used *relative* position, which means the picture is positioned *relative* to where it would normally be positioned in the flow of the content.

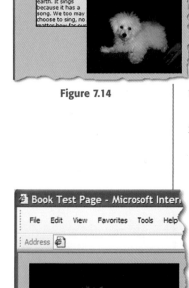

Figure 7.14

As you can see, the picture of our puppy overlaps the previous division I positioned on the page earlier. You need to be careful when using the *position* property because it's probably the fastest way to create pages that display differently in a variety of browsers and resolutions. Of course, a design may call for two or more elements to overlap, but be careful that the positioned elements do what you intend and aren't causing unintended problems in some browsers.

For the Cricket photo, I used inline CSS to position the little fluff ball on the page. Here's the code for that:

<img src="cricket.jpg" width="230" height="177" style="position: relative; top: 100px; left: 155px;" />

You'll learn about adding images to your page in Chapter 8: Color, Backgrounds, and Images. For now, the line in red text is what positions the picture on the page, and that's all you need to be concerned with for this lesson.

As mentioned earlier, *relative* positioning positions an element relative to its default position in the flow of content. Figure 7.15 shows where the picture would be in the normal flow of the content without the positioning.

In the source code, the division tag is coded before the photo, but because I positioned the division using the *absolute* positioning scheme, it is removed from the normal flow of content. That bumps up the photo of Cricket to the first content on the page, which in turn, placed it beneath the division tag.

Figure 7.15

Since I used *relative* positioning, the placement of the photo in Figure 7.14 was measured from where the photo would have been in Figure 7.15. The top of the positioned photo would be measured 100 pixels down from the top of the non-positioned photo to establish the positioned top; and the left edge of the positioned photo would be measured in from the left edge of the non-positioned photo. Sometimes it's easiest to just make a guess and then make adjustments.

As mentioned previously, there are times you may want content to overlap. Figure 7.16 shows the heading for my newsletter. It looks like an image, but it's really just CSS positioning that allows one element to overlap another. In this case, I used CSS to overlap three different headings. "Almost a Newsletter" is one heading and "Online Edition" is two headings, one in gold color over one in black color to create the shadow effect. In case you're interested, here's the code for the newsletter heading:

Figure 7.16

```
h1 {font-size: 32px; font-family: Impact, Arial, Helvetica;
    font-weight: bold; color: black; text-decoration:
        underline;}

h2 {font-size: 24px; font-family: Impact, Arial, Helvetica;
    font-weight: bold; color: black; position: relative;
    margin-top: -36px; margin-left: 189px;}

h3 {font-size: 24px; font-family: Impact, Arial, Helvetica;
    font-weight: bold; color: #B9B473; position: relative;
    margin-top: -49px; margin-left: 188px;}
```

This code is placed in my external style sheet. The h1 heading is coded in the normal flow of content, and the h2 heading is placed using the relative position scheme. This allows me to use negative values for the distance from the top of the window, which moves them into a position where they overlap the h1 heading. Here's how I coded the headings into my newsletter page:

```
<h1>Almost a Newsletter</h1>
<h2>Online Edition</h2>
<h3>Online Edition</h3>
```

Rather than using an image, I created the newsletter heading this way for two reasons. First, I wanted to show my newsletter subscribers how to do it, and second, text downloads faster than images.

7.10 Floats

THE OTHER WAY TO POSITION an element is to use the *float* property.

Sorry if you thought you were going to get a root beer float, but the publisher thought the soda would stain the pages. Instead, we'll use the float property to place a picture of a root beer float on a page.

In Figure 7.17, you can see how I floated the image on the right side of the page so the text would flow around it on the left side. Here's how I did it:

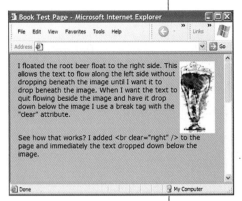

Figure 7.17

<img src="rootbeer.jpg" **style="float: right"** width="78" height="151">

I used an inline style to add the *float* property and value to an image tag. The part in red is what makes the image float to the right. The possible values for the float property are:

left | right | none

By default, images align to the left, but text will not flow alongside them without the *float* property. One line of text aligns with the bottom of the image element and the rest of the text drops down below it. Using *none* is the same as not coding a *float* property. By adding a value of *left* or *right* to the float property, the text is free to flow beside the image until it clears the image, at which point it drops below it.

To force text to stop running beside the image and drop down below, I added the *clear* property to a break tag. Here's how that works:

<br style="clear: right;" />

This code clears anything aligned to the right. The other values I could have used are *left*, to clear any left-aligned content;

clear *both* to clear both left- and right-aligned content; or *none* to clear, well, nothing. The *clear* property can be added to any block level element; it doesn't have to be a break tag.

7.11 Stacking Elements

A S I MENTIONED PREVIOUSLY, positioning can place elements on top of other elements, possibly causing one element to completely obscure another element. When elements overlap, the default placement is that those entered later in the code are stacked on top of those entered earlier in the code. Additionally, elements placed using CSS positioning are placed on top of content that is not positioned using CSS. This is called the *stacking order*.

Stacking order, however, doesn't have to be left up to the browser. You can specify the stacking order of elements using the *z-index* property:

z-index: *value;*

The value in this code is either a numeric integer (positive or negative) or the keyword *auto* to let the browser determine the stacking order. That would be kind of silly though, since the browser determines the stacking order without adding the z-index property.

Usually, you specify the z-index property with *inline* CSS. In Figure 7.18, you can see a web page I made with three over-lapping divisions. They are displayed in the default order, which is the same as setting the z-index to *auto*. By default, the last object in the code is the uppermost in the stacking order. The first object in the code is at the bottom of the stacking order. Of course, that leaves the middle object in the code at the middle of the stacking order.

Figure 7.19 shows the same divisions, except I changed the default stacking order. The box that was on the top is now on the bottom, the box that was in the middle is now on the top, and the box that was on the bottom is now in the middle.

Cools beans, eh McFloopingham? When setting the stacking order, the element with the highest z-index value is placed on top. The next highest z-index value is next, and so on.

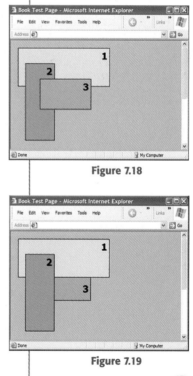

Figure 7.18

Figure 7.19

Here's the code for the three boxes with the z-index properties shown in red:

```
<div style="width: 250px; height: 100px;
             position: absolute; top: 20px; left: 20px;
             z-index: 2;">1</div>

<div style="width: 80px; height: 200px;
             position: absolute; top: 60px; left: 40px;
             z-index: 3;">2</div>

<div style="width: 140px; height: 80px;
             position: absolute; top: 100px; left: 80px;
             z-index: 1;">3</div>
```

Each division tag is on one line in my code, but is on three lines in this book to make it fit. In your style sheets, you can either let code wrap to the next line naturally or break it apart intentionally at convenient locations. Do, however, be sure to break it after a semicolon so no property and value becomes divided across two lines with a carriage return. While that shouldn't be necessary, I find that it prevents occasional unexpected quirks.

7.12 Hiding Elements

IT'S POSSIBLE TO HIDE ELEMENTS. Section 7.8: Display Style shows how to change an element's display property from *block* to *inline* and vice versa. One of the possible values for the display property is *none*. Using *none* as the value for the display property is one way to hide an element.

Another way to hide an element is to use the *visibility* property and set the value to *hidden*. At first, it sounds like *display: none* and *visibility: hidden* do the exact same thing, but there is a difference. With *display: none*, the page is displayed as if the element is not in the code at all. Other content shifts into the space the element would occupy if the display property was not changed. With *visibility: hidden*, the space the element would occupy under normal conditions is preserved, leaving a blank space in the page. See Figure 7.20 for a visual reference.

In this graphic, "Example A" shows how three blocks of content display with the visibility set to *hidden* for block 2. Block 2 is not visible to the user, but the position it occupies is preserved.

"Example B" shows how the same three blocks of content display with the display property set to *none* for block 2. As you can see, the content in block 3 shifts up and displays in the same place block 2 would normally occupy.

The following code shows how to hide a paragraph using the visibility property:

```
p {visibility: hidden;}
```

Here are the values you can use with the visibility property:

```
visible | hidden | collapse | inherit
```

Of course, when set to *visible*, the element shows as normal. *Collapse* hides a row or column in tables. *Inherit*, of course, inherits the property value from the parent element.

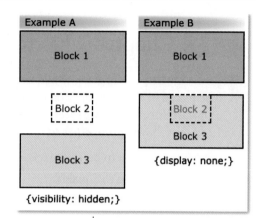

Figure 7.20

7.13 Chapter 7 Exercise

IN THIS EXERCISE, you're going to add testimonials to your project page. The testimonials are going to be placed in a narrow division on the right side of the page.

Open your external style sheet and create a division with a "class" (use any name you choose) and add the following properties to it:

- Set the division to be 180 pixels wide
- Set the padding to 7 pixels
- Choose a border color and set the border width, style, and color
- Choose a font family that's different from the main body text and set the font so it's visibly smaller than the main body text

Refer to previous chapters to see how to code anything you can't remember. Everything assigned has been covered in this chapter or previous chapters. Save your external style sheet with the changes.

Open the source code for your project page and perform the following:

- At the very top of your code, just after the <body> tag, add a division tag with the class name you used in the external style sheet.
- Use an inline style to float the division to the right.
- In the division, add the word "Testimonials" in bold text and insert a paragraph break.
- Make up three or four short testimonials that the beneficiary of your world betterment project might write to thank your organization for.
- Use a paragraph tag to separate the testimonials, and use a break tag to drop the name of the person giving the testimonial so that it's on the line immediately below their comment.
- Set the person's name in italic text.

Remember to close all tags.

Color, Backgrounds, and Images

8.1 Introduction

UNTIL NOW WE'VE WORKED mainly with text. Most web sites also use an assortment of colors, images, and sometimes multimedia to add visual appeal. This chapter teaches you about working with color and shows you how to add color, images, and multimedia to pages.

Included in this chapter is an introduction to color theory. This brief introduction is intended to give you a basic understanding of color theory and show you where to find more information about it.

8.2 Named Colors

IN EARLIER CHAPTERS, you probably picked up on the concept of using color names. Officially, the W3C recognizes only 16 color names. The recognized colors are:

aqua | black | blue | fuchsia | gray | green | lime | maroon

navy | olive | purple | red | silver | teal | white | yellow

However, most browsers, including all the major browsers, recognize a total of 140 named colors. Even the W3C lists these colors on their web site, so while unofficial, it's a pretty safe bet to use them. You'll find a list of all the color names along with color samples in Appendix C: Color Charts. The color samples may differ slightly on-screen from what you see printed in this book due to the differences among hardware and software, and because the printing process uses a different color model than computer monitors use.

While there are 140 named colors you can use, more than 16 million colors are available using other color coding methods, which we'll discuss in the next two sections of this chapter. Using color names is handy, but the range of color choices is severely restricted compared to using the hexadecimal color model.

8.3 Hexadecimal Colors

USING HEXADECIMAL COLOR VALUES, or *hex* colors for short, offers 16,777,216 unique colors. Hex colors are the most accurate colors to display from browser to browser. This is my preferred method of coding colors. The human eye actually can't distinguish that many different colors, but it sure gives us all the choices we need.

Hexadecimal color values are alphanumeric representations of red, green, and blue. A hex number is a six-digit code, with each digit having an alphabetical value from *A–F* or a numerical value from *0–9*. The format is #rrggbb (red-red-green-green-blue-blue).

In Figure 8.1 you can see how these alphanumeric values form a hex number.

The hex code is always preceded by a hash mark, also known as a pound sign. The first two digits represent the red value, the next two digits the green value, and the last two digits the blue value. You can use any combination of letters and numbers in any order in the code. The values represent a percentage. It works like this:

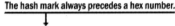

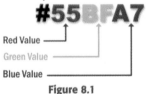

The hash mark always precedes a hex number.

Red Value
Green Value
Blue Value

Figure 8.1

- *FF* = 100 percent (full) intensity of the color

- *B0* = 75 percent intensity of the color

- *80* = 50 percent intensity of the color

- *40* = 25 percent intensity of the color

- *00* = 0 percent intensity of the color

A hex code of *#FFFFFF* is full intensity for all three color values. The result is the color white. A hex code of *#000000* is no intensity for all three color values. The result is the color black. Everything in between is confusing!

If you don't get it, don't sweat it. You don't really have to know all that. You can make up numbers and see what color it ends up looking like. Or better yet, you can use a software program that lets you pick a color and it will tell you the hex code. In addition, you can use one of two color generators available for free on my web site.

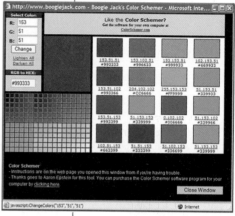

Figure 8.2 shows one of the color generators on my site, which not only provides the hex code for any color, but it also displays the hex code for 15 complementary colors to ensure your color scheme is sound.

In Appendix C: Color Charts, you'll also find a chart of several hex colors.

Let's say we want to change the text color for one paragraph using an inline style and a hex color. You code it like this:

```
<p style="color: #5E3A26;"> content goes
here </p>
```

Figure 8.2

Using that changes the color of the text in the paragraph from the default color to a color approximating chocolate brown.

8.4 RGB Colors

RGB COLORS MIGHT SOUND THE SAME as hex colors since they are also based on red, green, and blue colors, but there are differences. The RGB color model itself does not define what is meant by "red," "green," and "blue." Since the base colors are not defined, the base colors vary from platform to platform. Some companies have defined their own base colors to create a reproducible color model, but no industry standard has been defined. Each company's own color model differs from the rest, so the RGB palette is not consistent across various platforms. This is why I prefer using hex colors.

The RGB color model also offers 16,777,216 colors to work with, all the same colors as in the hexadecimal system, but they are enumerated differently and the code syntax is different. With the RGB color model, each color (red, green, and blue) can have a value ranging from 0 to 255.

Let's change the color of the text in an external style sheet for all paragraphs with the class name of "navy" using an RGB color this time.

```
p.navy {color: rgb(55,8,163);}
```

This code gives any paragraph with the "navy" class a nice navy blue text color. There are a couple things to note about using RGB color values. After *rgb*, the actual numerical color values are placed inside parentheses. There should be no space between the last letter of *rgb* and the left parenthesis. Each color within the parentheses has a value from 0 to 255 and each value is separated by a comma (with no spaces after the commas).

To remind you, here's how you code that class into a paragraph:

```
<p class="navy"> content goes here </p>
```

8.5 Color Theory

COLOR THEORY CONSISTS of three main aspects:

- The study of pigmentation and how to mix colors to achieve the desired result.
- The study of how individual colors affect human psychology.
- The study of how well different colors go together, or not.

This section is about the latter two aspects of color theory. What colors mean—color theory—has been debated for centuries, with the notion of which colors go well together changing with the times. Many color theories abound, many color models exist, and everyone seems to have an opinion. In the end, that's pretty much what it all is, a whole heaping helping of opinions about color.

Experts have written entire books on color theory. I'm not going to pretend I'm an expert, but I will give you a brief introduction. You can find all you want and more by searching for "color theory" online or for books at a good library or bookstore. Amazon and other online booksellers have plenty of books on color as well. Smart color use can help bring out feelings and some artists use colors for this purpose. Black is heavy and somber. Yellows are bright and cheery. Earth tones are warm and soothing. Reds can evoke anger or excitement. Greens might mean growth or continuance while blues are relaxing or professional, etc.

Other people use colors simply because they like the way they look. Many art and design instructors teach that it's wrong to choose colors just because you like them. I disagree. In my way of thinking, color always has meaning—even if the meaning is no more than the personal preference of the artist or designer. Why should that meaning have any less value than any hidden psychological meanings? After all, it's your work. Why should your personal preferences be dismissed just because you don't have a hidden meaning in your color choices?

Having said that, when choosing a color scheme, be sure it does not conflict with the purpose of the web site you're designing. No one in their right mind would build a web site for parents of preschoolers using black and red as the main colors. Using ominous and fiery colors just doesn't make sense on a web site for innocent children. Following the principles of basic color theory can help you decide which colors match as well as how colors make people feel.

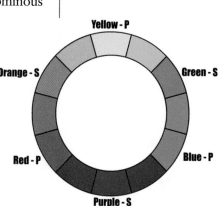

Figure 8.3

Figure 8.3 shows a basic color wheel. The yellow, blue, and red colors are primary colors. By mixing equal parts of red and yellow we get orange, which is a secondary color. Yellow and blue make green, another secondary color, and blue and red make purple, the third secondary color.

The colors in between the primary and secondary colors are called tertiary colors. To create tertiary colors, you mix one primary color and one secondary color in equal parts. They are red-violet, blue-violet, blue-green, yellow-green, yellow-orange, and red-orange.

Some definitions of tertiary colors include the mixture of two secondary colors, and others say tertiary colors are all the millions of colors not named as primary or secondary colors. Figure 8.4 might give you a small idea of how many in-between colors there are. Whatever you believe about tertiary colors, to me, that's where the fun is. Man cannot live on primary and secondary colors alone!

Figure 8.4

If musical harmony can be described as a mixture of tones that are pleasing to the ears, then color harmony might be described as a mixture of colors that are pleasing to the eyes. Some people have an instinct for which colors go together while others prefer to rely on various color models. I prefer to trust my eyes.

Following are the three most well-known and often-used color schemes.

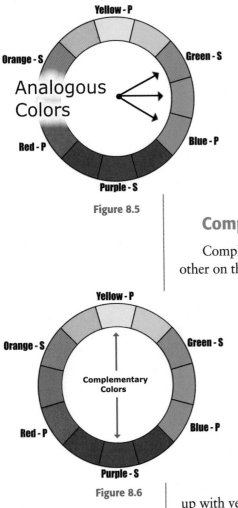

Figure 8.5

Figure 8.6

Analogous Color Scheme

Analogous colors are any three colors side-by-side on the color wheel, such as green, blue-green, and blue. Figure 8.5 shows a sample of analogous colors.

Analogous colors usually match quite well, but they often offer less contrast than other color schemes. They're good for creating serene designs where you want viewers to feel relaxed and comfortable.

Complementary Color Scheme

Complementary colors are those directly across from each other on the color wheel. Don't let the name fool you—complementary colors often don't "compliment" each other very well. They do offer high contrast and vibrancy, so they work best when you really want to make something stand out. Many businesses use complementary colors in their logos and sales offers. Figure 8.6 shows a sample of complementary colors.

There is also the split-complementary color scheme and double complementary scheme. With the split complementary scheme, you pick one color, and then across the color wheel you use the two colors next to the complementary color. For example, if you choose red, which is across from green, you end up with yellow-green and blue-green. The double complementary color scheme uses the colors on either side of both pairs of complementary colors.

Triadic Color Scheme

The triadic color scheme uses three colors spaced equally apart around the color wheel. This scheme offers strong visual contrast while retaining harmony and color richness. Figure 8.7 shows a sample of the triadic color scheme.

Personally, I'm one of those rebels who doesn't use any particular color scheme. I just choose colors that look good together to me. After all, my designs are a reflection of my creativity and taste, so why should I limit myself to someone else's color scheme?

Not everyone is a rebel, though. If you'd like to learn more about color and color theory, search for the following keyword phrases online: monochromatic color scheme, tetrad or tetradic color scheme, achromatic colors, color value, color brightness, saturation and desaturation, color theory, color analysis, color systems, additive colors, subtractive colors, color combinations, color contrasts, color intensity, color space, theories of color perception, color psychology, color harmony, color tint, color shade, color hue, color nuance, color meanings, and color studies.

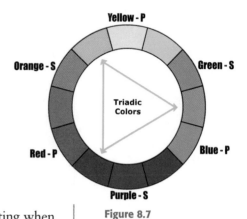

Figure 8.7

Searching online can be time consuming and frustrating when trying to piece together large concepts. If you'd like to skip all the searching and read a good book with a plethora of information in one place, try one of these:

- *The Art of Color* by Johannes Itten
- *Color and Meaning: Art, Science, and Symbolism* by John Gage
- *The Color Answer Book* by Leatrice Eiseman
- *Color: The Secret Influence* by Kenneth R. Fehrman, Cherie Fehrman
- *Interaction of Color* by Josef Albers
- *Theory of Colours* by Johann Wolfgang Goethe
- *Understanding Color: An Introduction for Designers* by Linda Holtzschue

Whether you use color theory or simply choose colors you like, the goal is the same. As web designers we want to create aesthetically pleasing web sites. When we achieve color harmony and balance, it engages the viewer and helps create an inner sense of order. When our designs are not harmonious, they are boring, disturbing, or chaotic and can create a sense of disorder or ennui.

Color has many emotional and psychological associations. Much of the feeling a viewer gets from the colors you choose in your web designs depends on these factors:

- Harmony or lack of harmony in the total color scheme
- The shades or hues of the color
- The message the graphics convey
- The tone of your written voice
- The actual message your words convey

In the following chart, you'll find the emotional responses the primary and secondary colors can elicit, as well as black and white.

RED	
Keywords:	Triumph, intensity, impulsiveness, action, warmth, hot, fiery, energetic, passionate, emotional, love, Valentines, stop, danger, war, alarm, warning, violence, blood, malice, competitive, stimulating, daring, aggressive, empowering, exciting, zest, erotic, arousing, awareness, saucy, spicy
Comment:	Emotionally intense, red stimulates and gets noticed.

YELLOW	
Keywords:	Joy, happiness, optimism, idealism, sunshine, cheerful, energy, revitalization, gold, summer, cowardice, jealousy, deceit, illness, hazard, elation, brightness
Comment:	Yellow can be a very difficult color for the eye and can be overpowering if overused.

BLUE	
Keywords:	Tranquil, serene, peaceful, relaxing, cool, cold, vulnerable, soft, passive, responsible, sophistication, richness, sky, ocean, harmony, trust, truth, confidence, water, spaciousness, comfort, sorrow, loyalty, calming, unity, stability, security
Comment:	Blue is the number one color for businesses because of the trust factor.

GREEN	
Keywords:	Growth, stability, balance, nature, generosity, kindness, approval, permission, health, good luck, renewal, youth, vigor, spring, fertility, jealousy, inexperience, envy, calm, conservative, masculine
Comment:	Green is easy on the eyes and is often used in hospitals because it relaxes patients.

ORANGE	
Keywords:	Warmth, heat, energy, summer, friendliness, youth, happy, motivated, cheerful, tart, tangy, tasty, health, appetite, strength, endurance, tropical, enthusiasm, creativity, determination, attraction, encouragement, stimulation, citrus, passion, pleasure
Comment:	Orange is the excitement and energy of red with the happiness of yellow.

PURPLE	
Keywords:	Royalty, noble intent, spirituality, ceremony, mystery, transformation, wisdom, enlightenment, cruelty, arrogance, exotic, moodiness, romance, luxury, wealth, sophistication, protection, comfort, security
Comment:	Because purple is rare in nature, take care that it doesn't appear artificial.

BLACK	
Keywords:	Power, weight, formality, elegance, mystery, fear, evil, anonymity, depression, depth, high style, remorse, anger, mourning, death, authority, timeless, submission, aloofness
Comment:	Black text on a white background provides the best contrast for reading.

WHITE	
Keywords:	Balance, reverence, purity, simplicity, cleanliness, peace, Godliness, innocence, youth, winter, snow, cold, goodness, humility, sterility, marriage, neutrality, illness, safety
Comment:	White is often associated with light, love, goodness, and purity. It is considered the color of perfection and holiness.

In the chart, many keywords for any given color may seem contradictory. The fact is, just as we all experience many different emotions, any individual color can evoke a variety of emotional responses. Speaking in very broad terms, the darker tones of a color tend toward the negative and lighter tones tend toward the positive. For example, a light red might initially evoke a feeling of spiciness, while dark red might evoke a feeling of anger. The actual feeling depends on the color harmony, the color shades, the message and tone of the message, and, of course, on the individual viewing it.

8.6 Foreground and Background Colors

IN WEB DESIGN, the foreground color usually refers to the text color, and the background color is the page color. Figure 8.8 shows a snapshot of a web page with the foreground color in a light yellow while the background color is a dark green.

I think your pet rock is shedding.

Figure 8.8

When coding the foreground color (text color), the term *color* is used to specify the CSS property. This differs from the background color, which uses the hyphenated term *background-color*.

The following code example demonstrates how to set the foreground and background colors for an entire web page:

```
body {color: #DAD9C2;

      background-color: #4D3722;}
```

With this code in the external style sheet, any web page linked to that style sheet displays text in a dark brown color on a cream-colored background.

Remember, if you prefer, you can code those two lines all on one line. In fact, all these code examples:

```
body {color: #DAD9C2;

      background-color: #4D3722;}
body {color: #DAD9C2; background-color: #4D3722;}
body

{

color: #DAD9C2;

background-color: #4D3722;

}
```

…mean the same thing, and all these ways of coding are used depending on each web designer's preferences. I prefer the first way of writing the code because it seems the easiest and fastest way for me to find what I'm looking for when I want to edit a file. With every line indented except the selector, it's easy to scan the left side for the selector you want to edit. It does take a little longer to tidy it up like that, so sometimes, when I'm in a hurry, I skip the neatness and put everything on one line for speed.

Now you know how to add text color and background color to web pages. According to the W3C standards, you can apply the *color* and *background-color* properties to any HTML element. However, applying color doesn't make a lot of sense for some elements and all browsers may not support odd color uses. Common color uses include paragraphs, divisions, spans, tables, table data cells, headings, and of course, the body element.

As with any CSS, you can also add the *color* and *background-color* to any element using inline and embedded styles, as well as an external style sheet. To make sure you understand the concept, we'll add foreground and background colors to a few more selectors to go with the body selector from the previous example.

```
body {color: #DAD9C2;
        background-color: #4D3722;}
h1 {color: #D77BA9;}
h2 {color: #E97443;}
div.special {color: #3708A3;
        background-color: #CFCDB4;}
```

With this code, we added text and background colors to the entire page linked to the external style sheet, changed the text color for the h1 and h2 elements, and created a division class with a foreground and background color we can call into use for any division element with the class name of *special*.

8.7 Image Formats

IMAGE USE IS AN IMPORTANT PART of web design. The right images can add visual interest, get your visitors' attention, provide direction and entertainment value, and delineate content sections. Only two image formats are universally displayed by graphical browsers: JPG format and GIF format.

If you download images from the web to use, they are usually in one of these two formats—although the format may not be the most optimal for the image. If you create your own images, you need to decide which format to use. The best format largely depends on the actual content of the image. Sometimes the JPG format is best and sometimes the GIF format is best.

Both image formats offer image compression, but the compression is performed in two different ways. Image compression is important because it reduces the image's file size. A reduced file size means the image will download faster, and download speed is important because people don't like to sit at their computers staring at nothing while the page loads. So, let's learn a little bit about each image format, JPG and GIF, along with taking a peek at the PNG format (PNG is not a new format).

JPG Images

The file extension, JPG, is an acronym for **J**oint **P**hotographic **E**xperts **G**roup (sometimes JPEG). As you might expect from the name, this image format is optimized for photographic images. JPG images use the full color range of 16.7 million colors, so the format also works well for images with a wide range of colors and textures.

JPG images use a "lossy" compression scheme, which means some image data is discarded in order to reduce the file size. The JPG compression scheme is designed to exploit known weaknesses in human vision. This weakness—that subtle color changes are not easily perceived—means that color subtleties can be discarded, resulting in smaller image files. The more the image is compressed, the more image information is discarded. Too much compression, however, results in a drastic loss of picture quality.

Optimized compression can reduce file size dramatically with only minute visual differences. JPG compression doesn't work as well on lettering, line drawings, large areas of continuous color, or images with color changes that have sharp edges.

One of the nice things about this format is that when you save an image as a JPG in a graphics program, most programs allow you to set the compression level. By controlling the compression level, you can optimize the image to the point at which the file is as small as possible without sacrificing picture quality.

Uncompressed   Heavily Compressed

Figure 8.9

Figure 8.9 shows an original, uncompressed photograph; next to it is the same photograph with heavy compression.

I'm not sure how well the defects in the heavily compressed photo will show to the naked eye in this book. You may have to use a magnifying glass to see the damage done by the compression. You should see pixilation, smudgy edges, and blotches of color rather than smooth color transitions. This is the result of over-compressing the image.

There are many degrees between the uncompressed image and the over-compressed image—you just have to experiment with different levels to find the right degree for each image. And actually, it can be better to not compress an image as far as it can be. This is because a browser has to decompress the image to display it, so an image that is too heavily compressed can actually take longer to display. My rule of thumb is to compress an image to the point where it starts losing too much quality—and then back off just a little bit. That has proven to strike a good balance between image quality, file size, and download speed in my testing.

GIF Images

The file extension, GIF, is an acronym for Graphics Interchange Format. A GIF image is limited to 256 colors and the compression is achieved by eliminating as many colors as possible. The more colors you eliminate, the smaller the file size.

GIF images are best for line art; images with solid blocks of color such as cartoons; images that typically have few colors such as icons, buttons, and company logos; and images with text such as page headers.

The GIF format offers two things that the JPG format doesn't. A GIF image can be animated and it can have one transparent color. There are actually two GIF formats: GIF87 and GIF89a. The GIF89a format is for images that use a transparent color, animation, and interlacing.

Interlacing is when a low-quality version of an image displays first, and then as more image data is received, the quality improves bit by bit. An interlaced image typically appears in full size but looks grainy and dirty at first, then clears up and becomes crisp and clean. A non-interlaced image is clean and sharp from the beginning, but gradually displays line by line from the top down. (The *progressive* JPG format offers an effect similar to GIF interlacing as well.) Interlacing increases file size as does animation.

PNG Images

The PNG (ping) image format was designed to replace the GIF format. PNG is an acronym for Portable Network Graphics. Like GIFs, images in PNG format can have animation, transparency, and interlacing, but they're far superior in quality. Unfortunately, browser support has been very slow. It's still not supported at all by some browsers, and only partially supported in others, so I don't recommend using PNG images yet.

Finding Images

It's beyond the scope of this book to teach graphic design, so you'll have to learn how to make your own images elsewhere.

Several graphics sites on the Internet let you download images to use. Some require payment, but many are free, requiring only a link to the site where you got the image as a way of saying thanks. You'll find many graphics on my site (http://www.BoogieJack.com) that you can use free of charge just for linking from your site to mine. Of course, you may use them in your school projects as well—no link is required for that, but it is appreciated.

8.8 Design Principles and Image Use

WHILE IMAGES CAN ADD HIGHER perceived value to a web site, misuse or overuse can devalue a web site. Images should complement your site and its content rather than overwhelm it.

Too often, especially with amateur web sites, there are just too many graphics on a page. Too many graphics, especially animated graphics, compete for attention and tend to distract and even confuse visitors rather than aid them in finding useful content.

Too many graphics also slow your web pages' download times considerably. I've seen web pages with a larger total file size than some software programs on my computer. Very few people will wait for a page like that to load unless there's a very compelling reason to wait. Remember that fact as you design—people hate waiting.

Generally speaking, a page's total file size is the size of the HTML file *plus* the file size of all the graphics on the page added together. If you use any remote files on the page, such as Java applets or sound files, count those as part of the total file size, too, because they need to download to make the page complete.

The general consensus is that a page shouldn't be more than 40K in size. You might consider making your index page even smaller. The faster it loads, the better chance you have of visitors staying around to sample your content. If users find something interesting, they will usually wait longer for a page to load, so you may have more latitude with interior page sizes. Until your index page loads though, they don't know for sure if anything interests them—unless they've been there before. What they do know is that they don't like waiting!

While much of the page-loading speed involves how well you manage the page's total file size, there are other factors. The speed of the visitor's Internet connection is one factor you can't control. But you can control the speed of your server to some degree. Pick a web host with fast servers and a good connection to the Internet backbone, and make sure they manage their systems well by not putting too many high-traffic sites on one server.

For every general rule, such as limiting total page size to 40K, there are always exceptions. Sites that offer an image archive (such as mine) are one of the exceptions. People expect a page full of graphics to take longer to load—and that's OK because they go there for the graphics. Of necessity, I make an exception for these types of pages. I compensate for the increased file size by keeping my site with a reliable host that has fast servers and high-speed connections to the Internet backbone. Because my site is on a fast server, I can also allow my index page to be a little larger than 40K. I have a large variety of content to present, but because my site is very fast, my page loads as fast or faster than most sites.

Using Java applets also runs up page sizes. Java applets are small programs that create special effects or do other tricks that aren't possible with HTML only. I always recommend against putting Java applets on the index page, perhaps with the exception of a small and well-behaved menu applet if that is the navigation system you prefer. Java runs off the user's computer system resources. Poorly written applets and applets that require a lot of memory can cause a visitor's computer to crash. You'll discover that doesn't please most folks. I recommend that you place any Java applets on secondary pages, and that you warn visitors there is Java on the page so they can assume the risk themselves rather than having the risk forced on them.

8.9 Server Paths to Images

A LOT OF PEOPLE THINK adding images to web pages is when it starts becoming more fun. But before you can add images, you first need to understand server paths. Typically, where you place your *index.html* page on your web host's server is the root directory for your web site. If you link to other files in the same root directory, the server path is simply the *file name* and *file extension*. For example, if you linked to another web page that you saved as *photos.html*, then the server path to that page is simply **photos.html**.

Because the photos.html file is in the same directory, the server path is simply the file name and extension. If you keep your web site's images in the same directory, then the image name and file extension is all that is needed as the server path. However, if you keep your images in a folder named *images*, then the server path to an image saved as *mom.jpg* is **images/mom.jpg**.

The server path just tells the browser where to find the file. The reference is always from the current location. Following are some other examples:

File Name/Server Path:	What it Means:
"page.html"	The file *page.html* is located in the **current directory**.
"tips/page.html"	The file *page.html* is located in a folder* named **tips** that is located in the **current directory**.
"tips/web/page.html"	The file *page.html* is located in a folder named **web** that is located in a folder named **tips** that is located in the **current directory**.
"../page.html"	The file *page.html* is located in a folder **one level up** from the current directory.
"../../page.html"	The file *page.html* is located in a folder two levels up from the current directory.

You probably didn't have any trouble following the first three examples in the table, but let me add a word or three about the last two examples. When you have a web page located in a sub-directory and you want to link to a page in a directory on a higher level, the path must point the browser in the right direction or it won't find the file. The two dots and forward slash (**../**) tell the browser that the file named in the link is one level up. For each additional level higher you need to go, add another set of two dots and a forward slash.

Remember, a server is just another computer. The path to files on the server works the same as the path to files on your computer. If your computer's hard drive is labeled the "C" drive, the C drive on your computer is the same as your web site's root directory on the server—only on the server you don't reference the drive label. On a server, it's assumed all files are in the root directory unless you reference a path to another location (folder) in the root directory. Or, if a file is in another directory, you have to work the server path backwards to the root directory.

*The terms folder and directory are used inter-changeably. A directory is a folder and a folder is a directory.

128

The server path, all files, and all file extensions are case sensitive. If you have an image saved as *Birds.jpg* and write it as *birds.jpg* in your code, it won't work because you didn't capitalize the letter "B" in the word *birds* the way it was saved. Likewise, if you save the image using capital letters in the file extension (JPG) but didn't capitalize the file extension in your code, it won't work. Same with the directory names in the server path, the uppercase and lowercase pattern in your code must exactly match the actual directory name, file name, and file extension.

One other thing about directory names and file names—never use a space in either. Some browsers will reach the space and determine that's the end of the code. If you link to an image named "my dog.jpg" some browsers will display a broken image icon because they stop reading the link at the space between the two the words. If you link to a web page with a space in the file name, some browsers will return a "file not found" error message because, again, they stop reading the link at the space.

If you must use two words in file names or directory names, use an underscore instead of a space. Browsers will not choke on the underscore, and "my_dog.jpg" still conveys the two-word meaning.

8.10 Downloading Images from the Web

BEFORE YOU CAN ADD IMAGES to a web site, you need to have some images to add. You could create your own images, buy a clip art package, or download images from the web. Since this book doesn't teach how to make graphics, and because downloading images from the web won't cost you anything, we'll work from that angle.

The first thing you need is a place to store the images on your computer. You can create a folder just for downloaded images on your hard drive, or if you are using this book in a classroom you may have to create a folder on removable media so you'll have it each time you get back on the computer.

Before downloading any images, create a folder called "images" on your computer or removable media. If you don't know how, I'll walk you through the process of creating a folder on a disk, but if you're on your own computer feel free to change the image folder location to your hard drive. Personally, I have all my web sites in folders labeled for each web site; all located in a folder on my C drive named Web Sites. Organization is the key to being well organized! Deep thought, huh?

To create an image folder on a floppy disk:

1. Insert a floppy disk into your computer's floppy drive (or other removable media).

2. Open Notepad and choose File > Open. This will open the Open dialog box.

3. In the Open dialog box, click the icon for your floppy drive (usually drive "A"). This will display the contents of the floppy disk. If there is no content it will display an empty window.

Figure 8.10

4. Click the New Folder icon. See Figure 8.10 for a visual reference. This action will create a new folder in the display window of the Open dialog box.

5. Next to the new folder icon will be a text box with the words "New Folder" highlighted in blue. Type "images" (without the quotes) to change the folder name from *New Folder* to *images*. If you accidentally lost the highlighting and locked in *New Folder* for the name, just right-click the name and choose the *Rename* option.

6. Once you've named the folder as *images* click the folder icon to lock in the name.

You can also create a new folder using Windows Explorer. Here's how:

1. Put a floppy disk in the floppy drive and then open Windows Explorer and click on the floppy disk drive, usually the "A" drive.

2. In the right pane of Windows Explorer, right-click a blank area and point to *New* on the pop-up menu.

3. On the secondary menu of the pop-up menu, click *Folder*.

4. That will create a new folder with the name "New Folder" highlighted in blue. While that is still highlighted, type "images" into the text label box for the folder.

5. Lastly, just click on the folder icon to make the name stick and you're done.

Now that you've created an images folder, you're ready to download some images from the Internet. Surf time—no swimming suit required! You can go to any search engine and search for images, or go to my site at www.BoogieJack.com and follow the Webmasters link to the web graphics archive. When downloading images, keep the following in mind:

> **Note**
>
> If you need to create a new folder in Mac OS X, Control-click the desktop and choose New Folder. You can also choose File > New Folder at the Finder. A new Untitled Folder is created on the desktop. Click on the name to type a new one; you can drag the new folder to any location you wish, including removable media or servers.

WARNING!

- Most web images are copyrighted; you can't just use any images you find. Wherever you get your images from, be sure you have permission to use them or you could be in violation of copyright laws. Look for a "terms of use" disclaimer or a link to one that outlines the copyright owner's terms of use, if any.
- If you can't find that, you'll need to ask for and obtain permission to use the images. You can also search for "public domain" images, but be aware that places offering them may have their own terms of use. Finally, be careful. Some rogue webmasters collect images from the Internet and offer them to the public in their own image archive, but they do not have permission to use the images they collect in the first place. If you use these images, you could still be violating someone's copyrights even if the site you found the images on gives permission.
- I created all the graphics in my graphics archive myself and I own the copyrights. So you're safe using images from my site as long as you follow my terms of use, which are listed on every page of the image archive.

You'll want to download at least one left border style background image and one full page style background to complete the exercise at the end of this chapter. You should also download some other kind of image to place on your page. This image should be relevant to what your practice site is about, if possible. Of course, if you can create your own graphics or have access to a clip art collection (many are available at office supply stores or software stores at a very low prices) feel free to use images from those sources.

Downloading images from the Internet is easy, but in case you haven't done it before, here are the instructions:

1. Find an image you want to download. D-oh!

Figure 8.11

2. Right-click on the image to bring up the pop-up menu (also called a context menu). See Figure 8.11 for a visual reference.

3. The pop-up menu will include many options. In Internet Explorer, choose *Save Picture As* (Windows). In other browsers, choose a similar command.

4. This opens the Save Picture dialog box.

5. Open the *Save In:* box to your floppy drive. See Figure 8.12 for a visual reference.

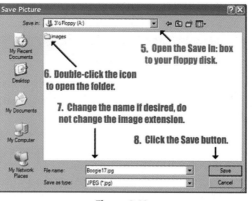

Figure 8.12

6. Double-click the *images* folder you created earlier to open it.

7. Change the *File name* of the image if desired, but do not change the image extension.

8. Click the *Save* button. Before leaving the web site containing the image, you may want to open Windows Explorer to your floppy drive and verify the image is there.

Congratulations, you just saved an image from the Internet.

Note

In Safari on Mac OS, Control+click the image and choose Save Image to the Desktop and you're done! You can drag the file to any location you wish.

8.11 Adding a Background Image

IN ADDITION TO ADDING a background color to an element, you can also add a background image to any element where background colors are legal. If you add a background image for the entire web page, you should also code a background color into the style sheet. The background image may take a little time to download. Adding a background color that is close to the overall image color makes for a smoother transition when the background image pops into view.

Sometimes glitches occur when pages load. If for some reason the background image doesn't load, you still want to have good contrast between the page color and the text. For example, if you are using a dark background image with white text and the background image doesn't load, the visitors will see white text on a white background in many browsers—unless you change the default background color. Obviously, white text on a white background is a little hard to read.

To add a background image to a web page using an external style sheet, code it like this:

```
body {background-image: url(images/marble.jpg);}
```

There should be no space between *url* and the left parenthesis. Earlier in this chapter you learned about server paths. The path (if any), image name, and file extension are enclosed in parentheses. In this case, the image named *marble.jpg* is kept in a directory named *images*, and the images directory is located in the root directory of the web site. Easy stuff!

Now, let's take a look at how a background color and image is coded in an external style sheet:

```
body {background-color: #DA46C2;}

    background-image: url(images/marble.jpg);}
```

That code gives the web page an apricot-colored background color until the apricot-colored marble background image loads. Peachy!

You can also add background images to other HTML elements. Just to have another pretty picture in my book, Figure 8.13 shows a screen capture from my web site.

Where it says "Almost a Newsletter," I added an inline style to add a background image to a paragraph tag and then added a border on the top and right side. The background fades from white to kind of a khaki color from left to right.

I use these headings to separate items in narrow columns of content. The whole thing looks like an image, but the only image is the fading background, which I reuse with other heading tags. Rather than having separate images download for each heading, only one image downloads. The image is reused so it helps the page load faster than it would if each heading was an individual image. Smart design!

Here's the code I used for the heading image:

```
<p class="bg" style="width: 210px; background:
url(images/fade.gif)">Almost a Newsletter</p>
```

Almost a Newsletter

Subscribe to my multiple award-winning ezine about web design and life for webmaster's tips and resources, a touch of humor, and my popular Life's Little Goodies column. It's packed with original content you won't find anywhere else. Live to learn and learn to live. [More Info]

Figure 8.13

The "bg" class sets the font properties and top and right border. I would have set the background image with the *bg class* as well, but when I created this design, one of the major browsers didn't support it through an external style sheet.

8.12 Background Image Options

WITH JUST HTML, the only option for a background image is to have it remain static and not scroll with the page. With CSS, there are several more options available.

The background image can remain static or scroll with the page, but it can also be repeated only across the top of the page, down either side, or it can be positioned anywhere on the page and coded so that it doesn't repeat. Technically, you can have it tile across the bottom, too, but it's not very practical to do so.

To understand why these options are useful, you need to understand how a background image works. A background image is usually much smaller than the browser window. It is a single image made so that the right side of the image matches up seamlessly with the left side of the image as it's repeated across the page, and the top of the image matches seamlessly with the bottom of the image as it is repeated row by row. By default, a browser starts the background image in the upper left hand corner and repeats it across the page. Then it starts a second row and repeats the process until the entire window is filled. Because the edges are seamless, that is, the left edge matches up with the right edge and the top edge matches up with the bottom edge without being able to see where the edge lines are, it looks like one big background image instead a small image repeated across and down the page until the document area is filled with the background image.

Now, let's say I'm building a web site called The Tree Garden. It's all about monkeys. I mean, it's all about trees. On this site, I want a big tree on the right side of the page that stays in place and doesn't scroll with the page. I want the text on the left side in a small column that doesn't interfere with the image of the big tree I love. There are ways to do this with HTML using some complicated coding, but it's much easier to do with CSS.

Figure 8.14 shows what my tree site might look like. The way it's coded, the tree always remains just as it is in this screen capture—it will not scroll with the page, only the text scrolls. That way, my beautiful tree is always right there as total eye candy as the text scrolls along the left side. The solid sky blue color you see on the left side is the background color. I faded that color into the left edge of the tree image so they'd blend seamlessly.

Let's first look at how I positioned the background image:

Figure 8.14

body {background-position: right top;}

With that code in the style sheet, the background image is started in the upper-right corner of the page. The format for coding a background position using keywords is:

background-position: *horizontal vertical*

When two values are given, the horizontal position comes first. The horizontal values you may use are: *left, center,* or *right.* The vertical values you may use are: *top, center*, or *bottom.* You may also set the position using a percentage or length; you're not locked into the three horizontal positions and three vertical positions.

With a value pair of *0% 0%,* the upper-left corner of the image is aligned with the upper left corner of the page (or the element the background image is being added to). A value pair of *100% 100%* places the lower-right corner of the image in the lower-right corner of the page. With a value pair of *25% 77%,* the image is started at a point that is 25% across the page and 77% down the page.

With a value pair of *20px 40px,* the upper-left corner of the image is started 20 pixels in from the left side and 40 pixels down from the top. If you're coding with percentages or length and only give one position, the browser uses the measurement for the horizontal position and centers the background vertically.

To lock the background in place so it doesn't scroll, use this code:

background-attachment: fixed;

The possible values are: *fixed* or *scroll. Scroll* is the default value, so there's usually no need to code that value.

I also want to make sure the tree background doesn't repeat on monitors with a very high resolution. That is accomplished like this:

background-repeat: no-repeat;

Using *no-repeat* as the value prevents the browser from tiling the background image, but you can also set values that make the background tile horizontally, vertically, or both. The four values you can use with the *background-repeat* property and what they mean are:

Value:	What it Means:
repeat	Default. Causes the background to repeat both horizontally and vertically.
no-repeat	Prevents the background from repeating both horizontally and vertically.
repeat-x	Causes the background to tile horizontally only.
repeat-y	Causes the background to tile vertically only.

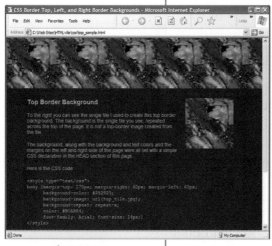

Figure 8.15

Now, since you're so darn good at supposing, let's suppose I want to use a small background tile, but I don't want it to fill the whole page. I only want it to tile across the top of the browser so I can have a top border style background.

Figure 8.15 shows the small background tile and how it looks tiled across the top of the page to create a top border background.

Here's how it's done:

background-repeat: repeat-x;

If I changed that to *repeat-y* it will tile down the left side of the page. I can also set the background to tile vertically down the right side of the page by positioning the background tile to the right to start off. Here's how that is done:

body {background-image: url(right_tile.jpg);

background-repeat: repeat-y;

background-position: 100% 0%;}

The last line of code is what moves the background image to the right side of the page. The *100%* value tells the browser to place the background 100% horizontally (all the way to the right). The *0%* value tells the browser to start the background at the top. The *background-repeat: repeat-y* tells the browser to tile the background vertically.

One additional note about background images before we move on—I've received many emails from folks trying to create a design where the default page margins interfere with their image placement. You see, by default a browser takes about 22 pixels of space around the edges of the viewing window for the page margins. While a background image will tile behind these margins, trying to place content to the edge of the screen is impossible unless you remove the page margins. The margins can be removed, or changed, in the *body* element. To remove the margins, add this to the external style sheet:

```
body {margin: 0px;}
```

You can also set the margin on each side separately. Refer to the box model explained in Chapter 7: Applying Styles to Other Elements, and specifically to Section 7.5 for the margin properties.

8.13 Placing Images on Web Pages

I CAN HEAR YOUR THOUGHTS—you're thinking it's about time you get to add an image to a web page. Eerie how I know that, isn't it?

Eerie or not, adding images to web pages is where the fun really begins for many folks. Up until graphics are involved, a web page looks very much like another boring text file in a basic word processing program.

A basic image tag is written like this:

```
<img src="graphics/mom.jpg" />
```

In that line of code, *img* is short for *image*, and *src* is short for *source*. What you're telling the browser is to open an image, and the source of the image is in a directory named *graphics,* which is in the root directory. The image is named *mom* and is in the *jpg* format. I'm guessing it's a picture of your mom.

An image tag has no closing tag in HTML, so to make it XHTML compliant the tag is closed with a space and forward slash as shown in the previous code example.

That will get the job done, but there are other attributes and values that every image except a background image should have. By adding the width and height attribute the browser knows how much space to reserve for the image before the image data downloads. This not only makes your page download slightly faster, but it prevents content from shifting around as image data comes in. Let's add the width and height to that portrait of good ol' mom now.

```
<img src="graphics/mom.jpg" width="480" height="360" />
```

Most portraits of a person are a little taller than wide. But because your mom has such a big nose, this one is wider than it is tall.

OK, all kidding aside, you should also add *alt* text, short for alternative text, to your images. Alt text provides an alternative for people using browsers that don't have native graphics capability or have images turned off in their browser preferences for faster surfing. Instead of showing an image, non-graphical browsers show the alt text. The alt text is also read aloud by screen readers so visually impaired people can understand what an image is about.

Alt text is added like this:

```
<img src="graphics/mom.jpg" width="480" height="360" alt="This is a picture of my dear, sweet mother and her big nose." />
```

Keep the description short. In most browsers, the text in the alt attribute pops up in a little balloon for a few seconds when the cursor is resting on it.

You can add alt text to any image except a background image. You should use alt text for any images that are part of your content, but you may want to make an exception for images that are part of your design.

For example, some sites use little images of rounded corners so everything isn't squared off. See Figure 8.16 for a visual reference. The rounded corners are part of the design framework, rather than part of the content. As such, you may not want to have alt text pop up when the cursor is over it just to offer the word "corner" or some other meaningless message.

If you decide not to include alt text on such images, you should still include the alt tag so the page will validate—just don't put text inside the quotation marks. For example:

```
<img src="corner.gif" alt="" />
```

Figure 8.16

Another attribute you may want to use at times is called the *low source* attribute. The low source attribute is a proprietary Netscape attribute; it won't work in all browsers, and in fact, may only work in Netscape browsers. It won't cause any problems in other browsers though, so I mention it here mainly because others teach it as official code. I want you to know it is not official and likely will cause a page to fail to validate.

Having said that, a *low source* image is a lower quality image than the original. You can make it lower in quality by compressing it more, using a smaller image, or combining the two methods. By coding a low source image into an image tag, the idea is that the lower quality image will load first—and faster—than the high quality image, giving the page the appearance of loading faster. When the higher-quality image data downloads, the browser replaces the *low source* image.

When I said the *low source* image gives the page the *appearance* of loading faster, it is only because of user perception. The low source image does show up faster than the high-quality image, but it actually takes longer for the page to fully load because the browser has to download all the same content *plus* the *low source* image.

You wouldn't want to use the *low source* option for every image—only on images with large file sizes that makes them slow to download. Even then it will only make a difference for a very small portion of visitors.

Coding a *low source* attribute and value into an image should look very familiar because it's almost like coding an image into a web page. The difference is it's written as an attribute and value to the image tag. Here's how to add the *low source* option to an image:

```
<img src="image.gif" lowsrc="image2.gif" />
```

The part in red is the *low source* attribute and value. I left out the other image properties so you don't have to wade through them, but they should be included as well.

8.14 Aligning an Image

THE HTML WAY OF ALIGNING an image with the align attribute and value (align="right") has been deprecated and should not be used on newly created pages. Using CSS to "float" an image is the correct way to align an image now, which works the same as floating other elements, which you learned in Chapter 7: Applying Styles to Other Elements.

Usually, you float an image using inline CSS so that you don't have to float all the images, or float them all in one direction. You can also float images by creating two classes for images, one that floats an image left and one that floats an image right. Since I used inline CSS to float an image in Chapter 7, in the following code I'll create two classes for floating images, one each for left and right floats for an external style sheet.

```
img.left {float: left;}
img.right {float: right;}
```

With that in an external style sheet, if I want to float an image left, I just need to add the *left* class to my image. Left class...how many of you wish you could have done that already?

```
<img src="tree.jpg" class="left" width="309" height="487" alt="Tree" />
```

As a free bonus, I included the image width, height, and alt text to remind you of the other attributes you should include. Mighty nice of me to do that for you for free!

To have the image float to the right, just change the word *left* to *right* in the code.

Sometimes we want the text to flow next to an image for a time, but then stop and drop below the image at some point. This was covered in Chapter 7, but let's run over it one more time to make sure there are enough tire marks on it.

Stopping the text from flowing next to a floated image is done with the *clear* property. You can add the *clear* property to any block level element such as break tag, a horizontal rule, a division element, span element, and others. Here's how to add the clear property:

```
<br style="clear: right;">
```

The values possible for the *clear* property are: *none, left, right,* or *both*.

Figure 8.17 shows three page layouts. The brown blocks represent text content and the orange block represents an image. The white space between the blocks represents where a paragraph tag was added.

Original Layout   Floated Image   Float Cleared

Figure 8.17

- The first page labeled "Original Layout" shows what happens to the flow of content when an image is not floated. One line of text flows next to the image then the remaining text drops below the image.

- The second layout labeled "Floated Image" shows how floating the image to the right allows the text to flow beside the image. The page is shorter because there is no blank space next to the image.

- The third layout labeled "Float Cleared" shows how the page looks when a <br style="clear: right;" /> tag is added. You can see how the text stops flowing next to the image and drops beneath it. You might want to use this when the text describes the image, and then drop the text under the image when the description ends and a new train of thought begins. Another use is to keep a disclaimer or page footer from shifting up beside an image.

8.15 Image Margins

WHEN YOU DON'T USE A MARGIN around an image, the text butts up right against the image, which doesn't look so nice. See Figure 8.18 for the difference between using a margin with an image and not using a margin.

As you can see, the first image has no margin. With the text so close to the image, it makes the whole thing look crowded and unprofessional.

The second image has a margin of 20 pixels on the left side and 10 pixels at the bottom. This creates a nice amount of white space around the image. White space, areas of the page where there is no content, offers the balance and visual rest stops necessary to good design.

Figure 8.18

If you remember how to add margins from the box model lessons in Chapter 7: Applying Styles to Other Elements, you already know how to apply margins to images.

You can add a margin using inline, embedded, or external style sheets, and the margin can be set for any or all sides of the image. For example, let's create two style classes for our images. One class will be for images on the left side of the page and the other for images on the right side. For this example, assume every image will come after a paragraph break, so we only need to add a margin on the right and bottom for images on the left side of the page, and on the left and bottom for images on the right side of the page. Here's how to code that in an external style sheet:

```
img.left {float: left; margin-right: 20px; margin-bottom: 10px;}

img.right {float: right; margin-left: 20px; margin-bottom: 10px;}
```

With that code in an external style sheet, you can set the margin for any image by adding which class you want to use. Notice I also added the *float: left* and *float: right* properties and values. That way, we don't even have to code that into each image. We know the images are either going to be on the left or the right when we use these particular classes so we can save ourselves from having to code it into each image. To use one of these classes, just add it to an image:

```
<img src="image.jpg" class="left" width="245" height="137" />
```

That code will float an image on the left. Change *left* to *right* in the code to have the image float on the right side of the page or containing element. If you are working with a design that uses the same size images, you can also code the width and height into the image classes to save yourself the trouble of adding it to each image. Pimple as sie…I mean, simple as pie. Too bad I don't know how to make pie because I really like it. Apple crunch, chocolate peanut butter, lemon meringue, cherry, pumpkin…mm-mmm good. Getting hungry yet?

8.16 Thumbnail Images

THUMBNAIL IMAGES ARE SMALL representations of bigger images. Rather than have a photo gallery of several large images on a page, smart webmasters make miniature pictures of the larger images. The thumbnail images serve as previews of the full-size images, and link to the full-size images on separate pages. A visitor can examine the thumbnails and decide which full-size pictures he or she wants to view. You have probably seen examples of this on shopping sites.

This makes the page load faster and doesn't waste your visitors' time by downloading full-size images they don't want to see. Plus, it saves you bandwidth, which, in turn, may save you money in bandwidth costs depending on your hosting plan and the number of visitors to your site.

There are three basic ways to make thumbnails:

Note

Bandwidth is the amount of data you can send through a connection, and/or the amount of bandwidth your site actually uses in sending data to visitors.

- The first method is to simply open the full size picture in an image editing program, resize it to a smaller size, and save it. This is also called resampling. Some webmasters cheat— instead of actually resizing and saving a second image to make a true thumbnail, they just use smaller dimensions for the width and height attributes of the image, giving it the appearance of a thumbnail. This isn't recommended because you don't gain any savings in download time or bandwidth. All the data from the full size images still has to download—even if you code them to smaller dimensions— because all the data in the full-size image is still present unless you actually resize the image.

- A second method for creating thumbnails is to crop a small thumbnail-size section from the image. When you crop an image, you use a crop tool to trim away unwanted or un-needed sections. Rather than the thumbnail showing a miniature version of the full-size image, it shows an interesting portion from the full-size image, with the rest of the image removed.

- I like to call the third method "logical thumbnails." It combines the first two methods. You crop out a larger section of the image than in the second method, and then reduce that to the desired thumbnail size. You get the best of both worlds this way. The thumbnail shows a greater section of the image than a full crop, and more detail than a simple resizing. Warning—if you get caught making logical thumbnails, you may be accused of being logical and smart. Goodness!

It's beyond the scope of this book to teach graphics, but I will give you a quick explanation of how to resize an image. In most graphics applications, you'll find a resize or resample option in the Image menu or the Edit menu. For example, in Adobe Photoshop, you'll find the Image Size command in the Edit menu. If you look around in your image program, you'll probably find the Resample/Resize command somewhere. When you find it, it's usually a matter of typing in the numbers for the new size or choosing a percentage. After resizing it to your satisfaction, choose:

File > Save As

...to save the thumbnail you just created. Be sure to use a different name for the file or save it in a different location from the original file or you'll end up replacing the full-size picture with the new thumbnail.

Cropping is a little more involved than resampling. Look for a tool like this ⊞ on your image editing program's toolbar. It might look different, but will probably have some kind of crossed lines showing a square center area. Click the tool icon to select that tool. Place the tool on one corner of the section you want to keep, and then drag it to the opposite corner of the section you want to keep.

You may need to play around a little to see how it works. In many programs, if you like the section you have selected, you just double-click inside the selected area. The rest of the image will be removed and the image size is reduced accordingly. Then, if you're creating a simple crop thumbnail, you can save the image as explained before. If you're making a crop and resize, you just resize it and save it. Even with a simple crop, you'll probably want to resize it a little to make all the thumbnails a uniform size. Your thumbnail gallery will look a little neater and better planned that way.

8.17 Clipping an Image

T HE *CLIP* PROPERTY IS SIMILAR to the *overflow* property in that it let's you have an element that is smaller than the content within the element. The difference is that clipped content cannot be viewed via scrolling; it is truncated at the dimensions you choose.

Hey, I've got an idea. Let's clip my wife!

Figure 8.19 shows a picture of my wife, Alison, standing in front of a huge rock. That's right guys—I get the big bucks *and* have a beautiful wife *and* I know where to find big rocks. Wow, life is good!

Figure 8.19

Figure 8.20 shows how I want to clip the photograph so I display just a head and shoulders shot of Alison.

To clip an object, start at the top and work clockwise around the image. Measure the horizontal clipping lines from the top edge of the element to be clipped, in this case the photo of Alison, and measure the vertical clipping lines from the left edge of the element.

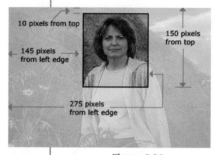

Figure 8.20

At the top, I want 10 pixels clipped off the image. From there, work clockwise. As shown in Figure 8.20, I want the right side clipped at 275 pixels from the left edge. The bottom is to be clipped at 150 pixels from the top. The left side is to be clipped at 145 pixels from the left side. These numbers are called clipping *coordinates*. These coordinates are used to tell browsers where to clip the element you want to clip, Chip.

There are two ways to determine the coordinates. The first is to just guess, enter the coordinates into the style code, open the page in a browser, and see what it looks like. From there you can adjust the coordinates until you get what you want.

The second way of determining the coordinates is to trick the Internet Explorer browser into thinking the image is an image map. When the browser thinks the photograph is an image map, the cursor becomes a hand pointer as you place it on the image, and then the key to the whole thing is that along with showing the pointer, the status bar of the browser will reveal the exact coordinates where the pointer is pointing.

By placing the pointer where you want the top clipping line, you'll easily have your first coordinate. Next move the cursor to where you want the right clipping line to be, note the coordinate, and finish the other two clipping line coordinates in the same way.

To trick the browser into treating the photograph as an image map, we need to do two things. The first is to add *ismap* to the image tag. Here's how to do that:

By adding the part in red:

```
<img src="Alison.jpg" ismap>
```

…to the image tag, the browser thinks the picture is an image map. To activate the browser into showing the coordinates, place a link around the image. We cover links in more detail in Chapter 9: Links and Multimedia, but for now all you need to know is a basic null link tag. Here's the image code with the link code added around it:

```
<a href="#null">
<img src="Alison.jpg" ismap>
</a>
```

With that little snip surrounding the image, you're ready to determine the coordinates.

In Figure 8.21, No. 1 points to the spot where I placed the cursor. The image coordinates of the cursor show up in the status bar at the bottom of the browser, labeled No. 2.

I've blown up the status bar so you can see it better as shown in No. 3. The first coordinate shows the how far the cursor is in from the left side of the image and the second coordinate shows how far down the cursor is from the top of the image. This gives the coordinates where I want to clip the left side and top. Now all I have to do is repeat the process to find the right and bottom coordinates. If you have trouble setting the cursor where you want for two coordinates at a time, you can just do one side at a time; it is easier for some people that way.

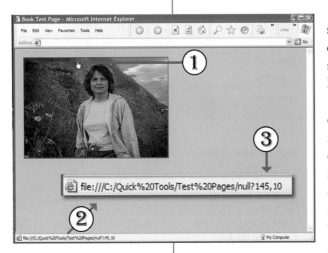

Figure 8.21

Clipping only works if the image is positioned using the absolute positioning scheme. Let's position the image and add the clipping code.

```
<img src="Alison.jpg" width="480" height="360" alt="Alison"
style="position: absolute; top: 20px; left: 20px;
clip: rect(10, 275, 150, 145);" />
```

The second line of code (in blue) shows the style attribute opened and the positioning of the image. Remember, only images positioned with the absolute positioning scheme can be clipped.

TIP

If you have Adobe Photoshop, you can see pixel coordinates on an image in the Info palette, which you can open from the Window menu. If necessary, change the ruler measurement system to pixels in the Preferences dialog box.

The third line of code (in red) shows the clipping property and values added.

The *clip: rect* part tells the browser the image clipping is rectangular. That's the only shape there is, but I anticipate a future version will include at least a circle shape.

There should be no space between *rect* and the left parenthesis. The coordinates are separated with a comma and space.

Figure 8.22 shows what the clipped image looks like. Be cautious using clipping—other content can disappear beneath the image, as with any absolutely positioned element.

Figure 8.22

8.18 Chapter 8 Exercise

For the Chapter 8 exercise:

- Open your external style sheet and change the body margin property from the Chapter 4: CSS Kick-start exercise to the following: 100 pixels on the left, 20 on the top and bottom, and 40 on the right. Refer to Chapter 7: Applying Styles to Other Elements if you don't remember how to add a margin to the individual sides of a box model element.

- Create a folder named "images" in the root directory of your web site (where your index page is saved).

- Next, surf the net and find a left-border style background image you like. You can visit any site you choose to find the background image, but you might save some searching by visiting one of my two sites: www.BoogieJack.com and surf to the Webmasters section, then the Web Graphics; or www.i-backgrounds.com and surf to the left border backgrounds. Note that most of the backgrounds on my sites are geared more toward personal pages rather than a business site (they're more fun to make!), so be selective. When you find an image you like, download it to your images folder.

- Choose an image bullet from my www.BoogieJack.com site or another site and download it to your images folder. The link to the image bullets is at the bottom of the Web Graphics index page. Choose one that will look good with your background choice.

- Next, code the background image into the body selector of your external style sheet and save the changes—but keep your style sheet open for now.

- Open your web page in a browser. It should now have a left border background image if you coded it correctly and have the right server path. If it works, in your external style sheet, adjust the left margin so that it is slightly wider than the border section of the background image (and the text is not on the border, nor too far beyond the edge). A half-inch past the border creates a nice margin.

- In your external style sheet, change the color of the h3 and h4 size headings so they more closely complement the background image you chose. Use a hexadecimal color value.

- Next, add the bullet image in front of the first line of each testimonial you added in the last chapter. Be sure to include the width, height, and alt text for each image, and don't forget to close it properly.

- Use an inline style to add a margin of 5 pixels to the right side of each bullet image.

- Save the changes and view your page to make sure everything works correctly.

In the next chapter exercise, you will detail your ideas for making the world a better place. Make sure you've got most of that worked out or you'll find yourself behind from the onset.

Links and Multimedia

9.1 Introduction

A LINK IS A SMALL PIECE of HTML code that connects one file to another. Clicking on a link to another web page takes your browser from the page you're viewing to that other web page. If the link is connected to audio, the link opens the default browser plug-in (if there is one) and starts playing the audio stream. A link can also connect to software, fonts, or many other types of files that can be downloaded to a computer.

This chapter shows you how to link to other web pages and files on your site, and to other sites on the Internet using hypertext links. It also shows how to incorporate multimedia into your site. This chapter, however, is not a tutorial on how to *create* multimedia files as that's beyond the scope of this book.

9.2 Understanding Web Addresses

THE TERM "WEB ADDRESS" is the same as:

1. URL, which is an acronym for:

   a. Uniform Resource Locator or
   b. Universal Resource Locator

2. URI, which is an acronym for:

   a. Uniform Resource Identifier or
   b. Universal Resource Identifier

All these things mean the same basic thing—they reference an address on the web to a file of some kind. The file might be a web page, a video, a font, a PDF document, a music file, a software program, a ZIP file, or many other things. I prefer to use the term URL, and I pronounce that acronym like my favorite uncle, good ol' baldheaded Earl, who wasn't really my uncle. I don't even know anyone named Earl. I do have an Aunt Lullabelle though. She isn't bald, but she does have six toes and a cat named Kootchie.

Anyway, a web address is a systematic way of keeping track of where everything is on the web. And there's a lot of stuff to keep track of—billions and billions of files at the very least. The web address to my first site is http://www.boogiejack.com. See Figure 9.1 to see what the different parts of that address mean.

http://www.boogiejack.com
1 2   3   4   5

Figure 9.1

1. The *http* stands for HyperText Transfer Protocol. It's a set of standards that enables computers to exchange information.

2. The *://* is a special separator. The two periods later in the address are also separators.

3. The *www* is short for World Wide Web. The web is the most popular part of the Internet, consisting of huge collections of documents and files stored on millions of computers around the world.

4. The *boogiejack* part is the domain name. Internet domain names are unique names that point to a specific Internet address. The domain name is really an alias. The real Internet address is a set of numbers such as 202.153.70.105. Since it's a lot easier to remember a name rather than a string of numbers, domain names are used.

5. The *.com* is the domain extension. In this case, it indicates that my site is a commercial site. Other domain extensions include:

   - *.org* for organization
   - *.net* for network
   - *.edu* for educational institution
   - *.gov* for government (U.S.)
   - *.mil* for military (U.S.)

There are other extensions, too, including two-letter country extensions, but the overwhelming majority of U. S.

sites fall into one of the previous categories. A link to a web address that ends in one of these extensions (with no other text after the extension) is linking to the main page, usually a page named *index* with an HTML or HTM extension.

Some links go deeper into a site than just the main page. See Figure 9.2 for a visual reference.

The gray text is the web address we already looked at. The colored text is a continuation of that address, and the point at which we'll pick up the explanation.

The "www.boogiejack.com" part is also known as the "server" part of the address.

http://www.boogiejack.com/**folder**/**page**.**html**
6   **7**   **8**

Figure 9.2

6. The forward slashes and period in the new code are again separators. Where it reads *folder* represents a folder (directory) located in the domain's root directory, and of course, *page* (7) is the file name and *html* (8) is the file format.

The folder that *page.html* is located in isn't usually named *folder*, but rather a name that has meaning to the site or at least to the webmaster of the site. Common folder names include *images*, *members*, *articles*, or any other name. There could be folders within folders as well. For example:

http://www.domain.com/photos/relatives/women/momsfamily/page.html

That web address means that *page.html* is located in a folder named *momsfamily*, which is located in a folder named *women*, which is located in a folder named *relatives*, which is located in a folder named *photos*, which is in the domain's *root directory*.

9.3 Relative and Absolute Paths

WE COVERED SOME OF WHAT a relative path is in the last chapter in Section 8.9: Server Paths to Images. Whether relative or absolute, the path refers to the trail on the server or Internet from one point to another. With web pages, a relative path points to the location of the page you're linking to within your own web site in relation to the page being viewed on your web site. A relative path is always between two files on one site.

If the page you're linking to is in the same directory as the page being viewed, then there is no real path—the "path" is simply the page name and extension. If it's in a folder one level deep, the path is the folder name/page name and extension. Look back at the chart in Section 8.9 if necessary.

Remember, when you have a web page located in a subdirectory and you want to link to a page in a directory on a higher level, the path must point the browser in the right direction or it won't find the file. The two dots and forward slash (../) tell the browser that the file named in the link is one level up. For each additional level higher you need to go, add another set of two dots and a slash.

An *absolute path* is the full Internet address. For example, if you had a link on your index page to a picture page, the absolute path might look like this:

http://www.yoursite.com/pictures.html

You may use a relative path or absolute path when linking to pages on your own domain from your own domain, but it's much better to use a relative path. By using a relative path, the browser knows to look within your domain space for the linked file. Since it's already at your domain space, it doesn't have to go anywhere to find your site. If you use an absolute path, the browser goes back out onto the Internet to find your site all over again, then finds the file within your domain, resulting in a longer retrieval time.

So, if you're linking to pages on your own site, using a relative path will make your site respond quicker. It's all about speed!

I know this relative path business is a little difficult to understand at first, so let me put it another way in case you don't quite get it. If the file you're linking to is in a different folder from the file you're linking from, then you must include the folder name in the path to the file—*if* the file is located in a folder on a lower level in the directory structure.

However, if the file you're linking to is in a folder located on a higher level in the directory structure than the page you're linking from, then use the ../ in the path to the file to indicate it's on a higher level. If the file is more than one level up, you must use the ../ for each level higher you need to go, just like climbing the rungs of a ladder.

9.4 Internal and External Links

AFTER TACKLING RELATIVE vs. absolute paths, this part will be easy. An *internal link* is to a file within your own domain space. An *external link* is to a file at another domain. You *must* use the **absolute path** when linking to web pages that are *not* on your own domain.

When linking to another web site, if you just use the domain name and extension in the link, the link will take you to the main page for the web site, usually the index page. If you want to link to a page other than the index page, place a forward slash after the domain name and extension, and then add the path to the file on the other domain's server.

How do you find out the path on someone else's server? If you right-click (or Control-click on Mac OS) a blank spot on the web page you want to link to and select Properties from the context menu, a dialog box displays the web address of the file among other things.

Another way to find the address is to look in the address bar of the browser, where it will tell you the location of the page your browser is displaying.

Figure 9.3 shows the address bar label circled in red in Internet Explorer. The red arrow points to a blow up of the address bar from a page on one of my sites. If you wanted to link to that specific page on my site, the address bar shows the *absolute address*.

Figure 9.3

However, if the site uses frames, the correct address probably won't show in the title bar. If this page was in a frameset, the address bar would reflect the address of the frameset rather than the main page. Fortunately, not too many sites use frames these days, so it isn't usually a problem. For sites that do use frames, you'll need to right-click/Control-click the page to find the web address of the page you're trying to link to.

9.5 Text Links

THE REAL POWER OF THE WEB lies in being able to connect documents anywhere in the world. Hyperlinks are the connecting

153

mechanism that ties it all together. A hyperlink, or just *link* for short, begins with this code:

```
<a href=
```

The "a" part of that represents the word "anchor" because it represents a specific address that connects one document to another—an anchor point so to speak.

The "href" part stands for Hypertext **REF**erence. After that part of the code, to use a relative address to a file on our own site, place the server path (if any) and file name and extension inside quotation marks (after the equal sign). If Joe Cool is linking to his contact page from a page in the same directory, he'd link to it like this:

```
<a href="contact.html">Link Text</a>
```

The "contact.html" is the file name and the extension of the page the link points to using a relative path. Because the file is in the same directory as the page the link is on, the path is simply the file name and extension. The part that reads "Link Text" is the text that becomes the hyperlink—the clickable words—that take us to the linked-to page. Following that is the link's closing tag.

If Joe kept his contact page with other fundamental pages in a directory named "basics," the link would be coded like this:

```
<a href="basics/contact.html">Link Text</a>
```

I added the part in red to reflect the path to the contact page, which is in the "basics" folder. Now, if Joe Cool is *really* cool, he'd want to link to my www.BoogieJack.com site. Since my site is at a different domain, he'd have to use the absolute path in his link. That is written like this:

```
<a href="http://www.boogiejack.com">Boogie
Jacks</a>
```

The link starts off the same as with a relative link, only the absolute path (full web address) is used. This includes the *http://www.* syntax before the domain name. With a browser using the default settings and a web page using the default settings, that link to my site appears on a web page like this:

Boogie Jacks

Many webmasters change the default settings. Often, the underline is removed and the link color is changed, to name two common changes. These changes can have a negative effect if the webmaster doesn't make it obvious in some way that the link text is a link. Without obvious clues, people may not understand which text is clickable, especially those new to the Internet.

9.6 Link Titles

A LINK TITLE, SIMILAR TO THE ALT attribute for images, lets you add a description to a link so screen readers can announce a description of the content at the other end of the link. Like alt text, most browsers will display the text inside the link title in a temporary pop-up balloon, so it can be useful to all visitors, not just the vision impaired.

Add a link title like this:

<a href="http://www.boogiejack.com" **title="Visit Boogie Jacks for web design tutorials, graphics, software and more.**">Boogie Jacks</a>

Figure 9.4 shows what that link and pop-up balloon looks like when the cursor is placed on the link.

The pop-up balloon lasts only four to five seconds, so you can't put too much text in there if you want visitors to be able to actually read the link title text.

Book Test Page - Microsoft Internet Explorer

File   Edit   View   Favorites   Tools   Help

Address

Boogie Jacks

Visit Boogie Jacks for web design tutorials, graphics, software and more.

Figure 9.4

9.7 Named Anchors

AN ANCHOR TAG CAN ALSO LINK to a specific place on the same page where the link is located. These are *named anchors*. You often see this used on FAQ pages (Frequently Asked Questions), where a question listed at the top of the page is linked to the answer somewhere further down the page.

Other common uses include linking from where an article is interrupted with an advertisement to where it continues further down the page, or from a lower part of the page back to the top of the page. I also use named anchors in my newsletter to link from a menu at the top to each regular column. This way my readers can go directly to the part of the newsletter they want to read first.

There are two parts to a named anchor. One code snippet links *to* a specific place on the page, and another snippet is placed at the location of the content the link points to. Let's use an example from my newsletter. At the top I have a list of all the columns in the newsletter. One of the regular features is my Life's Little Goodies column, which is toward the end of the newsletter. At the top of the page in my menu list is this link:

```
<a href="#goody">Life's Little Goodies</a>: The
Spark of Creation
```

In a link to another file, the part that reads "#goody" would be the relative path to another page on your site or the absolute path to a page on another site. When linking to a specific point in the same page, there is no path, per se, so the hash mark (#) tells the browser the link is on the same page. The word "goody" is the name of the anchor, which is the specific place on the page the browser displays when that link is clicked.

In this example, the text "Life's Little Goodies" is the link to the newsletter column as it's the text between the opening and closing <a> tag set. "The Spark of Creation" is the title of the article. If my readers want to read The Spark of Creation, they only have to click the "Life's Little Goodies" link and their browser instantly moves down the page to where that article is located.

That's the first part; the second part is to add the named anchor to the specific location on the page where the link is supposed to take the reader. To name an anchor, code it like this:

```
<a name="goody"></a>
```

Notice there is no text between the opening and closing <a> tag set. That keeps it hidden from the visitor. With that snippet hidden in the code, which is usually placed on the same line as the article's title or one line above it, the browser will jump to that named anchor point as soon as the link is clicked.

The name (*goody* in this example) can be anything you want. I usually try to keep it relevant to the content I want the link to target. Let's create another quick example of what is probably the most popular use of named anchors.

If you place:

```
<a name="top"></a>
```

...at the top of your page, just under the BODY tag, for example, and then place:

```
<a href="#top">Top</a>
```

...at various points down the page, each place where that link appears, clicking it will jump the page back up to the top. On long pages, this saves visitors from that pesky scrolling.

You can also link to specific places on other pages—if there is a named anchor at the location you want to link to. For example, if you want to link from your web site to the Spark of Creation article and you want the link to land at the article rather than at the top of the page, code the link like this:

```
<a href="http://www.boogiejack.com/news.html
#goody">The Spark of Creation</a>
```

The web address for the page (the part in green text) gets your visitors to the newsletter page. The "#goody" (the part in red) is what loads the page with that name target at the top of the page. Linking to a specific named anchor then is accomplished by simply adding the hash mark (#) and anchor name to the end of the web address of the page.

9.8 Opening Links in a Second Window

BY DEFAULT, CLINKING A LICK...I mean, clicking a link opens the linked page in the same browser window, replacing the current content. Sometimes you may want to have linked content open in a second browser window.

You shouldn't do it just to keep people trapped on your site, but there are instances when it's reasonable to open links in a new window. One example might be if you have an image gallery of some sort and use thumbnails on the main gallery page. The link to the full picture can open in a new window. When visitors are finished viewing it, they can close the window, but still have the thumbnail index open (without having to use the back button and wait for the thumbnail page to reload).

WARNING!

There will always be a small percentage of people who don't like it when you force a secondary window to open, so make sure you have a good reason for doing so.

I sometimes use a clever strategy for linking that works quite well—in fact, I've received many compliments on it. For links within my content that lead to external sites, such as my product reviews, I code two sets of links. One link opens in a new window and one link opens in the current window. Folks like the choice I provide them.

For the links that people are most likely to use when they are ready to leave my site, such as on a links page, I code only the one link that loads in the current window. When they are ready to go somewhere else, I let them go in peace.

Some webmasters act like it's a tragedy if someone wants to leave their site, so they do everything they can to prevent it. That's a big mistake. Everyone goes elsewhere sooner or later. If you let them leave in peace and give them good links to surf, there's a much greater chance they'll come back. After all, you've provided a value to them. If you make it hard to leave, there's a good chance they'll never come back. If it happens to be a site reviewer you trap, there's a chance he or she will discourage others from coming to your site by issuing a bad review.

To create a link that opens in a new window, add a target attribute:

```
<a href="http://www.ebookfarming.com"
target="_blank">eBook Farming</a>
```

The code in red causes the link to open in new window. Be sure to include the underscore preceding the word "blank" or the link will open a named window. A named window is when you give the target a name, such as:

```
target="chumbuddy"
```

If you include the above target of "chumbuddy" with the link, the browser opens that link in a new window named chumbuddy (provided there isn't already a window open with that name). If the user has a window named chumbuddy already open, all links with the name chumbuddy as the target open in the window named chumbuddy. If that named window is hidden behind the current window, the user may not realize the link opened in the hidden window and may assume the link doesn't work.

As you may have guessed, you can name the target to be almost anything you want. Keep in mind, though, that target names are case sensitive. The name *Chumbuddy* is not the same target as *chumbuddy*, *chumBuddy*, *ChuMbuDdY*, or *CHUM-BUDDY*. Case sensitivity simply means you must capitalize what is originally capitalized, and use lowercase where lowercase was originally used.

There is also a target called "**_self**" that ensures a link is opened in the current window. Here are the possible values for the target attribute:

Target Value	Description
"name"	Where "name" is any name you give it, opens a link in a window with that name.
"_blank"	Opens a link in a new unnamed window each time.
"_parent"	Loads the document (web page) into the immediate FRAMESET parent of the current frame. This value is equivalent to _self if the current frame has no parent.
"_self"	Opens a link in the current window.
"_top"	Loads the document into the full, original window, canceling all other frames.
"new"	Many people think this is what opens a new window, but it's only a "name" that opens links in a window named "new"—I've included it here so you won't be confused by other tutorials you see that incorrectly teach "new" is the magic word to open a new window.

9.9 Anchor Pseudo-Classes

P SEUDO-CLASSES ARE USED TO SET the link properties for different link states. The properties are the same as for any text element, such as font color, size, weight, text decorations, backgrounds, borders, and more. The link states are:

a:link

a:visited

a:hover

a:active

The "a" represents the anchor tag in CSS, followed by a colon and keyword. There should be no space before or after the colon. By using CSS to define the link states, we can program links to do anything from a simple color change when the cursor is on them to complex effects such as looking and acting like buttons, or even nothing at all.

Here's what each pseudo-class controls:

a:link	This sets the properties and values of a link before the link has been visited.
a:visited	This sets the properties and values of a link that has been previously opened.
a:hover	This sets the properties and values of a link when the cursor is resting on it. This is usually used to change the color of the link text while in the hover state.
a:active	This sets the properties and values of a link when the link has been activated (clicked) until it is processed. With the advent of broadband Internet connections, faster servers, and faster personal computers, many times this change of state isn't even noticeable.

When creating a style sheet using these pseudo-classes, they must be in this order:

a:link

a:visited

a:hover

a:active

If they are not in that order, changes of state won't work properly in some browsers.

After each anchor pseudo-class you add the CSS property and value as you do with any of the previous CSS classes we've covered. For example:

a:link {color: blue;}

With that, all the normal links are blue. Now let's create a set of style rules for each pseudo-class using an external style sheet:

a:link {color: blue; text-decoration: underline;}

a:visited {color: gray; text-decoration: none;}

a:hover {color: red; text-decoration: none;
background-color: black;}

a:active {color: purple; text-decoration: underline overline;}

Can you figure out what each link state would look like? You think about it while I go get some tea and when I come back I'll explain it.

I'm back. Did you figure out what the links would look like, or did you cheat and look at Figure 9.5 for a visual reference.

It should be pretty obvious, so it's OK if you peaked this time. The normal link state is blue, underlined text, just like a default link.

For the visited link state, I changed the text color to gray and removed the underline.

Figure 9.5

For the hover state, which is when the cursor is resting on the link, I changed the text color to red and gave it a black background color. Visitors will know for sure they have their cursor on that link.

And finally, for the active link state, I gave the link text the color purple and gave the link an underline and overline. Those codes are for demonstration purposes. It's not a good idea to have every link state do different things. Inconsistency can confuse your visitors; consistency makes them feel comfortable.

Pretty cool, huh? You haven't seen anything yet. In the next section I'll show you some link buttons that aren't even buttons— they're all fancy CSS pseudo-classes.

9.10 Fancy CSS Link Buttons

OK, TIME TO 'FESS UP. The following examples are not really buttons. I've just simulated the look and action of buttons using CSS pseudo-classes.

If you look at Figure 9.6, you'll see what looks like two button links. They are not buttons at all, however. They are coded to look like buttons using CSS. The second button with the cursor on it looks like a link button being clicked because I used a color change to simulate light change, but that too is CSS. As you

Figure 9.6

can see, using your imagination and CSS can create quite the illusion. Here's the CSS code for those fake link buttons:

```
WHOPPING BIG CODE EXAMPLE

a:link  {text-decoration: none; color: #ffffff; background-color:
#D72F40; border-top: 2px solid #E36F7A; border-right: 2px solid
#A01F2C; border-bottom: 2px solid #A01F2C; border-left: 2px solid
#E36F7A; padding: 3px; width: 120px; height="30"}

a:active {text-decoration: none; color: #ffffff; background-color:
#D72F40; border-top: 2px solid #E36F7A; border-right: 2px solid
#A01F2C; border-bottom: 2px solid #A01F2C; border-left: 2px solid
#E36F7A; padding: 3px; width: 120px; height="30"}

a:visited {text-decoration: none; color: #ffffff; background-color:
#D72F40; border-top: 2px solid #E36F7A; border-right: 2px solid
#A01F2C; border-bottom: 2px solid #A01F2C; border-left: 2px solid
#E36F7A; padding: 3px; width: 120px; height="30"}

a:hover  {text-decoration: none; color: #FFFF00; background-color:
#D72F40; border-top: 2px solid #8D1B26; border-right: 2px solid
#EC9BA4; border-bottom: 2px solid #EC9BA4; border-left: 2px
solid #8D1B26 padding: 3px;  width: 120px; height="30"}
```

This code creates the borders and background colors around the links, and it causes the border to change colors to simulate a button-down look when the cursor is over the link. The size of the fake button is also set, so they all have a uniform size. In addition, the link can be clicked without having a cursor on the text—it only has to be anywhere on the area with the button look, just like a real button. Most fake buttons don't have that as a feature. Shazam Gomer, that's cooler than tub full of crawdads on ice.

Fake buttons can be even fancier than this example, but you'll probably have trouble digesting that code so I won't throw something even more complicated at you. You don't really have to know how to make fake buttons like that anyway—I just wanted to demonstrate one possibility of what using your imagination with CSS can do.

9.11 Email Links

YOU CAN ADD AN EMAIL LINK to a web page that automatically opens the visitors default email program to a new message already addressed to you. An email link uses the same syntax as a standard link—the only difference is it uses a *mailto* email address instead of a web address. Here's an email link:

```
<a href="mailto:you@yourISP.com">email link text here</a>
```

Just substitute your real email address for the "you@yourISP .com" part and you're in business. Note that not all browsers will open the user's email client. If you use this kind of link, it's still a good idea to use your email address as the text of the email link. That way your email address appears on the page for those who need it. An address like that is coded as:

```
<a href="mailto:you@yourISP.com">you@your ISP.com</a>
```

The "you@yourISP.com" would be your email address *and* the text link in that example.

While on the topic of email links, do you know what a spambot is? Don't feel bad if you don't know—neither did my spell checker. A spambot is a small software program designed to surf the web and collect, or harvest, email addresses from web pages in order to build mailing lists for sending unsolicited commercial email, which is known as spam. Because of spambots, many webmasters don't put their email addresses on their web pages, but they still offer a contact method for visitors.

There are several ways to thwart a spambot. The email address can be encrypted, CGI software programs can be used to process email, JavaScript can be used, or an image can be used to display the address without linking it to an email address. It's beyond the scope of this book to teach encryption, CGI software, and JavaScript. I do, however, offer a low-cost program called Script Buddy that automatically encrypts your email address with JavaScript and generates the code for 26 other functions for you. You can learn more about it on my products page at www.BoogieJack.com.

Have you ever seen those email links that pop up with the subject line already filled in? Here's how it's done:

```
<a href="mailto:dork@dorky.com?subject=I am a Geek">Email Me</a>
```

It's a basic email link, but with a *question mark (?)* and then *subject=whatever* added to the end of the email address.

163

Well now, that's pretty easy isn't it? If you email someone from a link with that code, your email message opens with "I am a Geek" in the subject line—and the recipient just has to take your word for it.

You can change the word "subject" in the code to "body" and have a message automatically placed in the body of the email letter. You can also specify the subject and the body of the message at the same time.

```
<a href="mailto:ratboy@thedump.com?subject=
Rats&body=need love too">Rat Lover</a>
```

This code opens an email message with the subject line of "Rats" and "need love too" in the body. But wait, there's one more email trick! You can also send an email to multiple recipients:

```
<a href="mailto:me@here.net?cc=you@there.com&
bcc=joe@wherever.net">E-Mail</a>
```

In that example, one copy of the email goes to "me," one copy goes to "you," and a blind carbon copy goes to "Joe." I didn't want to leave Joe out—the poor guy doesn't have very many friends.

9.12 Creating Image Links

MANY WEB SITES USE graphical buttons as links, and this is very simple to do indeed. You already know how to add an image to a page and this chapter taught you how to create a link. To use an image as a link, you simply replace the link text with the image you want to use:

```
<a href="about.html">
<img src="images/about.jpg" /></a>
```

The code in red text shows the image button in place of the normal link text. By replacing the link text with an image tag, the image becomes the link. In this case, the link goes to a page named *about.html*, which in most cases is a page that tells a little about the company. The link button, named *about.jpg*, is located in the *images* folder. You should also use the image width and height attributes, but I left them out for the sake of simplicity.

The way the sample link is coded creates a blue box border around the link button graphic. The box is the same color as the text links. With graphic buttons, the default border isn't visually appealing, somewhat defeating the purpose of using a nice looking button. Most webmasters remove the link border. To remove the border using inline CSS:

```
<a href="about.html"><img src="images/about.jpg"
style="border: 0px;" /></a>
```

The code in red removes the border. Of course, if you're artistically indifferent or just a rebel, you can use the border attribute to create a larger border. To do that, simply code a number greater than zero—and there are lots of numbers greater than zero, so I've been told anyway.

Figure 9.7 shows an example of link buttons from one of my web sites. There are four buttons lined up on the left side of the page.

You can also remove the border from all images by setting the border property in your external or embedded style sheets. Just set the border to zero for the image selector:

Figure 9.7

```
img {border: 0px;}
```

Simple!

If you are really, really paying close attention, you might wonder what happens if you code a link title into the link tag along with an image alt tag for the link graphic. They both can't show up, can they? Nope. The image alt tag overrides the link title and is what shows when a visitor's cursor rests on a link graphic. Does that mean you should use only the image alt tag? Not necessarily. Screen readers may read both the link title and the alt text aloud.

9.13 Alternative Menu

I WEAR A LOT OF HATS in my business, including graphic artist. As a graphic artist, it is with great sorrow that I must tell you that some people just don't care a whit about your pretty little link buttons or other graphics. They turn them off in their browsers because they want pages to load as quickly as possible.

This is just one reason you should always include alt text with graphic links. Without it, users won't have much of a clue where the graphic links lead. If you use graphics for links, it's always a good idea to include a text menu as well.

On my site, I have a text menu at the bottom of every page. Each link leads to a major section of my site, making it easy to navigate even though there are hundreds of pages. By keeping the links consistent and in the same place on every page, you can quickly create familiarity for visitors. Before too long, they feel right at home. Of course, you can create familiarity with graphic links as well, but there are two other good reasons for using text links in addition to graphic links:

- Graphic links usually display on the first screen when a page opens. Pages are often longer than that, so as a visitor reaches the bottom of the page, the graphic links disappear. Rather than forcing visitors to scroll back to the top of the page to regain access to the links, text links at the bottom allow them to easily continue surfing your site.

- Text links show visitors the pages they have visited; graphic links don't do that unless you allow a border on link images. Text links make it easier for visitors to continue surfing to new content instead of accidentally revisiting pages they've already visited.

Thoughtful little touches like these go a long way toward creating a positive experience for visitors.

9.14 How to Make an Image Map

AN IMAGE MAP ALLOWS YOU to code two or more links into a single image using pixel coordinates. In other words, different parts of a single image can be linked to different pages.

An image map can be used for many things. For example, you might have a map of your county with each town linked to its own page or web site. On the personal side, it might be a group picture of your family with a link from each family member's head going to a page about or created by that family member.

Coordinates on image maps serve as reference points that specify the boundaries of "hot spots" that link to other pages or files. Hot spots are simply the areas of the image that are clickable. The entire image doesn't have to be clickable.

You can make three types of shapes on an image map: rectangular, circular, and polygonal. We'll take a look at the rectangular shape first. Refer to Section 8.17 in Chapter 8: Color, Backgrounds, and Images if you need a reminder on how to determine image coordinates.

Figure 9.8

Let's say that Joe Bumblebonker writes articles about gardening. In Figure 9.8 you can see the graphic he wants to make into an image map. He needs four hot spots, one each for the *Home*, *Bio*, *Contact*, and *Articles* links, and it's our job to create the code for the map.

The dashed lines around "Home" represent the area we want to make into the first hot spot. We only need to be concerned with the upper-left corner and the lower-right corner. The browser squares off the hot spot from there to create the rectangular shape. I've added arrows to the graphic to show the two coordinates we need for this hot spot.

Each coordinate point, the upper-left corner and the lower-right corner, for a rectangular shape has two measurements. The first measurement is the distance in pixels measured from the left edge of the image toward the opposite edge. The second measurement is the distance in pixels measured from the top edge of the image toward the bottom edge, thus forming a single coordinate.

For the "Home" hot spot, the upper-left corner coordinate is: 51 and 17. The lower-right corner coordinate is: 118 and 42. The Contact link will be a rectangular hot spot as well. The first coordinate for that hot spot is: 20 and 58; the second coordinate is: 96 and 88.

We'll use those coordinates to code the image map, but first we need to find the other two hot spots. The next hot spot will be a polygon shape for the Bio link, and the final hot spot will be a circular shape for the Articles link. A polygon is a closed plane figure bounded by straight lines on each side. It may have as few as three sides or as many as is practical. Also, the lines should not cross each other.

When creating a polygon shaped hot spot, I like to start with the upper-left coordinate and work my way around clockwise. With the polygon, we need the coordinates for each point where the line angle changes, not just the coordinates for the upper-left and lower-right corners.

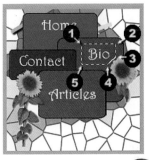

Figure 9.9

Figure 9.9 shows the shape of the polygon. I numbered each coordinate we need to create the polygon shape. It's really just another square with the lower-right corner cut off to miss the sunflower.

Here are the coordinates for each corner:

1. 117 and 48
2. 167 and 48
3. 167 and 77
4. 155 and 87
5. 117 and 87

Next, we'll find the coordinates for the circular hot spot. A circular area has three coordinates for an image map. The first two coordinates plot the center of the circle. The third coordinate is the radius of the circle.

Figure 9.10 shows the center point of the circle and the radius. The center is: 105 and 127. For the radius, I decided 38 pixels would create a circle that just encloses "Articles" without intruding into the coordinates for the Contact hot spot.

Now that we have our hot spot coordinates, all that is left is to code the image map. An image map starts off with the declaration:

<map name="navigation" id="navigation">

The *id* attribute is only needed if you want the page to be XHTML compliant. If so, just give it the same name as the *name* attribute; in this case, the name and id attributes are both named "navigation." While the name you give the map can be anything, I like to use logical naming conventions. Since this image map is for navigation, that's what I called it.

After the map declaration, we can start adding the area tags. An area tag consists of the shape, the pixel coordinates, and the link. The area tag tells the browser which areas of the map are hot spots, and which file each hot spot links to. Here are our image coordinates:

Rectangular Areas

    Home: 51, 17 / 118, 42

    Contact: 20, 58 / 96, 88

Polygon Area

    Bio: 117, 48 / 167, 48 / 167, 77 / 155, 87 / 117, 87

Circular Area

    Articles: 105, 127, 38

Figure 9.10

Note

Usually, I would use a rectangle for the Articles hot spot, but I do need to show you how to make a circular hot spot, so the circle wins the square.

Now that we've gathered all the information we need, let's code the image map for Mr. Bumblebonker:

```
<The image tag usually goes here; the how-to of
coding it for an image map is coming up.>

<map name="navigation" id="navigation">

<area shape="rect" coords="51, 17, 118, 42" href=
"home.html" />

<area shape="rect" coords="20, 58, 96, 88" href=
"contact.html" />

<area shape="poly" coords="117, 48, 167, 48, 167,
77, 155, 87, 117, 87" href="biography.html" />

<area shape="circle" coords="105, 127, 38" href=
"articles.html" />

</map>
```

The shape for an area is either *rect* for rectangle, *poly* for polygon, or *circle* for…you guessed it, a circle. The *coords* part is short for coordinates. As you may have noticed, the coordinate pairs aren't separated into pairs—all the coordinates are strung together and the browser sorts them out. However, you still need to input them in the correct order for it to come out right. The browser pairs the first two numbers to plot the first coordinate, the next two numbers to plot the next coordinate, and so forth. With the circle coordinates, you must put in the two coordinates for the center point of the circle first, followed by the radius. There is no closing tag for an <area> tag, so I added a space and forward slash to the end of each tag to make them self-closing for XHTML compliance.

Now that the image coordinates are coded into the page, all we need to do is add the image itself to the page. The image should be placed in the code where you want it to appear on the page, but it doesn't have to be near the map code. It does make sense to keep them together though—after all, if you need to edit one or the other or both, it makes sense to not have to hunt for two places in the code. I usually code the image just above or below the map code. Here's the image code:

```
<img src="images/navmap.jpg" usemap="#navigation"
    alt="Click the hot spots." width="210" height="214" />
```

> **Note**
>
> To be XHTML compliant each image map <area> tag should have an image alt attribute included. I didn't include them here to make the code easier to understand.

169

As you can see, it's just an ordinary image tag with alt text and the width and height coded into it. The code in red text is the part that activates the hot spots. Use the same name after the hash mark that you used for the *name* value in the map code.

In some browsers, the entire image map used to be surrounded by a blue border. I don't think it's a problem anymore, but it may still be in a minor browser or two. If you want to ensure that no one sees a border, use CSS to remove the border as shown in Section 9.12 of this chapter.

9.15 Access Keys

CLICKING A LINK ISN'T THE ONLY WAY to activate a link; you can also code access keys into links. An access key allows users to open links by pressing and holding down an accelerator key and then pressing the assigned key on their keyboard. The accelerator key is usually the Alt key on Windows or the Ctrl key on Mac OS. Adding the access key attribute is easy:

```
<a href="index.html" accesskey="h">Home</a>
```

The code in red text activates the access key. In this case, holding down the Alt key (or Ctrl key, Mac OS users) and pressing the letter "h" is the same as clicking the link in most browsers.

You can add a title tag to the link to identify the access key for visitors while keeping your page clean and free of explanations. Something like this works well:

```
<a href="index.html" accesskey="h" title="Access Key:
Alt + H">Home</a>
```

9.16 Changing the Base Location

THIS IS A COOL BIT OF CODE. Suppose you have a web page that you move to another folder. After moving the file, all your relative links will be broken because they no longer show the correct server path.

You have two choices: you can change all the relative links on the page so they point to the right place, or you can add one line of code to the HEAD section of the page that points to the old location of the file. All the links are then resolved from the old location, meaning all your links will still work correctly. Here's the code for that:

```
<base href="path" />
```

Where it says "path" in the code, change that to the path to the old page location from the new page location. With that in the HEAD section of the page, the browser will use the old location in referencing the relative links. Now that's *caws* for celebration, he *crowed*.

9.17 Linking to Other File Types

ONE QUESTION I'M ASKED over and over is how to link to file types other than HTML pages. Whether it's font files, PDF files, zip files, EXE files, text files, or most any other file you want to link to, the format is usually the same as for other links. All you need to do is change the file extension.

The behavior of the browser, however, will change depending on the file type. It may open or play the file, ask what you want to do with the file, warn you it could be an unsafe file, prompt you for the program to open the file with, or some other action, but the link usually remains the same:

```
<a href="path/file.extension">Link Text</a>
```

Where is says *path/file.extension* is where you substitute the server path, file name, and file extension. For example, say you are linking to a zip file of graduation pictures for your friends and family to download. The file name is "graduation.zip" and the file is in a folder named "compressed." That code looks like this:

```
<a href="compressed/graduation.zip">Link Text</a>
```

When a user clicks that link, they are asked what they want to do with the file—usually whether they want to save it or open it (if they have the software to open a zip file).

9.18 Adding an Audio File

AUDIO IS VERY POPULAR ONLINE, and many audio formats exist. It's beyond the scope of this book to teach how to create audio files, so I won't spend time going into the various formats.

You'll either learn about that when you learn to create audio files, or you'll use audio someone else created that is already formatted.

While there are many audio formats, some formats are classified into two types: streaming and non-streaming. Streaming audio starts playing after an initial buffer has been achieved, and then continues playing as the rest of the audio is downloaded. Non-streaming audio doesn't start playing until the entire audio file is downloaded.

A sound file can be included on a web page in two ways. One is to embed the file into the web page, which would then be played within the browser. The other way is to link to the file, which will then be opened in an external audio player. The external player that opens depends on what audio software the user has available and what the file format is. Most people will be able to hear the audio either way—but there will always be a few who can't due to the available software and system configuration.

The controls for the audio player can be hidden so an embedded sound file plays as background sound; or the player can be visible so the user has access to the controls.

Figure 9.11

Figure 9.11 shows the control panel for an embedded sound with the player controls visible, and an external player that opened for a linked sound.

Linking to a sound file is the same as linking to other file types as discussed in Section 9.17. For example:

```
<a href="guitar.mp3">Here my guitar riff.</a>
```

That code links to an MP3 file. Wav (wave) is another common format for music files.

Embedding a sound file has a couple problems. There are two different ways to embed a sound. One uses the *embed* element, and the other the *object* element. The problem is twofold. The embed element is supported by almost all browsers, but it's not part of the W3C specifications. The object element is recommended by the W3C, but is not very well-supported by browsers. This really only leaves one choice if you want to embed a sound—you need to use the embed element, knowing that your code won't quite be up to specifications. Here's how to embed a sound:

```
<embed src="guitar.mp3" width="300" height="28" autostart="false" />
```

That embeds the guitar riff and gives the user control over the player. You may have to play with the width and height values to get the control panel to turn out like you want. The "autostart" set to "false" means the music won't start playing automatically. I highly recommend that you never set this value to *true*. Many people surf the web at work and they don't want music they can't control. Others surf while listening to their own music and don't want your audio interfering with theirs. Others simply won't like your audio choice. The point is, most people don't appreciate audio being forced upon them—because most people like choices and having control.

9.19 Adding a Video File

AS WITH AUDIO, VIDEO COMES in several formats. It's beyond the scope of this book to teach how to create video files, so I won't spend time going into the various formats. You'll either learn about that when you learn to create video files, or you'll use video someone else created that is already formatted.

Also like audio, video formats are classified into two types, streaming and non-streaming, and they work in the same way. Streaming video starts playing after an initial buffer and non-streaming video must be completely downloaded first.

Like audio, video can be included on a web page in two ways. One is to embed the file into the web page to be played within the browser. The other is to link to the file, which is then opened in an external player. The external player that opens depends on what video software the user has available and the format of the video.

Figure 9.12 shows an embedded video player on a web page and the same video opened in an external video player.

Many digital cameras allow you to shoot video clips these days. That's how I took this video of my grandson playing in a mud puddle. Fortunately he was at home, so he had a change of clothes handy after he soaked himself from head to toe.☺

Linking to a video clip is done in the same way as linking to an audio clip:

Figure 9.12

```
<a href="bdayparty.avi">My Birthday Party</a>
```

That code opens the *bdayparty.avi* clip in an external program.

WARNING!

Video and audio files can have extremely large file sizes, thus taking a long time to download. A common courtesy is to place the file size beside the file link so users with slow connections can opt to not download clips they know will take too long.

Unfortunately, embedding a video into a web page poses the same dilemma as embedding an audio clip. The embed method works but isn't W3C legal, and the object method is legal, but isn't supported well by browsers. Again, if you want an embedded video, you have little choice but to use the embed element. The video is embedded the same way an audio file is:

```
<embed src="ethan.mov" width="320" height="254"
autostart="false" />
```

That'll do it!

9.20 Link Tips

THE FOLLOWING LINK TIPS fit here better than anywhere else— and more importantly, this way I get to use that pretty little checkmark I made.

 Surfing your web site shouldn't require a master's degree. Plan your navigation system in advance. Have a link on every page to your core pages, including: the home page, the contact page, and sub-indexes for different site sections. Try to keep it so a user doesn't have to click more than three links to get *to* any page on your site *from* any page of your site.

 While it's best to avoid extremely long pages, if you do have some, consider using a menu at the top that links to the content below. Also, include links from the content below back to the menu at the top of the page.

 Prioritize your content. Place links to the pages you most *want* people to visit in prominent locations. This might be your product sales pages, links to subscribe to your newsletter, or whatever else is important to you. The point is, if it's important to you, show it off with first screen, high-priority placement.

 Avoid using meaningless link text such as "click here" for links. The link text should be descriptive of the content at the other end of the link. This not only helps visitors, but it may help with search engine rankings as well.

Remember that the more graphics you have, the slower your site will load. Do you really need 15 different link buttons when you can use CSS and one reusable background image to make buttons that look like the real deal while keeping the page fast and lean?

 Consider using a program such as my Script Buddy to disguise your email address so spambots don't find it, causing a flood of unwanted commercial emails (spam) to fill your inbox.

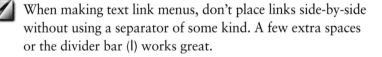 When making text link menus, don't place links side-by-side without using a separator of some kind. A few extra spaces or the divider bar (l) works great.

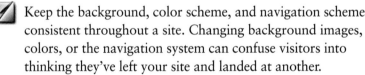 Never lead visitors down a dead end with no link out. Some users do not know about the back button. At minimum, always include a link to the home page on every page of a site.

 Keep the background, color scheme, and navigation scheme consistent throughout a site. Changing background images, colors, or the navigation system can confuse visitors into thinking they've left your site and landed at another.

Never use spaces in file names or directory names.

Make sure all your links actually work, as it's easy to commit a coding error. Broken links won't help you or your visitors.

Whenever possible, avoid putting too many links together in one large group. Too many options can create a feeling of clutter and confusion. Group content into logical collections and provide secondary indexes to the additional content. What constitutes too many links is subjective and many design variables come in to play, so you'll have to make your own value judgment about that.

If you use a graphical menu system, also provide alternative text links at the bottom of the page. This keeps visitors from having to scroll back to the top of long pages to access link buttons or an image map, and provides an alternative for users with non-graphical browsers. This is important for search engines as well, as they do not understand text embedded into graphic buttons.

 Never link to images, sound files, or video files on someone else's web site without authorization in order to display or play them on your own web site. That's called "hot linking" and it's illegal because it uses the other web site owner's bandwidth. A simple check of log files reveals this practice, so it's very easy to be caught. Of course, you can link to the web pages that contain these files because the visitor would be using the files while at the other webmaster's web site. That's fine.

Many web sites offer videos, sound files, and graphics you can use on your own site. Some are legitimate—that is, they create their own offerings and own the copyrights. Other sites simply collect graphics, sound files, and video files they like and put them online without permission from the copyright holders. If you use files from sites that do not have permission to offer them, you are still in violation of the copyright holder's rights. Ignorance of the law and ignorance of copyright status is no excuse. Penalties and damages can be as high as six figures—it's not worth the risk! The best practice is to create your own content. People will come to your web site to see what you have to offer that is uniquely you; they don't come to see what you could copy, borrow, or steal from someone else.

If you agree to exchange links with another webmaster—you link to his or her site and they link to yours—that's a reciprocal link. It's one of the key ways to begin drawing traffic to your site. The best way to obtain reciprocal links is to find sites you want to trade links with, and then post a link to their site before asking for a reciprocal link. Beware that many sites are overwhelmed with link requests. Some ignore them, some have specific guidelines for submitting your site for link exchanges, and some never exchange links. Do your homework before asking.

If you do ask for a reciprocal link and receive no response, your initial reaction might be to remove the link to that site. Not so fast—if it was a good enough link that you thought your visitors would like it in the first place, consider keeping the link to that web site anyway. *Good links are good content*, and good content shouldn't be dismissed easily. I have some sites bookmarked because they have good links, not because they have good content. Each time I go back to visit their link page, they have another chance to win me over with their content.

9.21 Chapter 9 Exercise

For the Chapter 9 exercise:

- Now you're thinking about adding new pages to your project site, and you've realized a background image isn't appropriate. Remove the background from your external style sheet and adjust the page margins to suit your visual sense of balance. Set the background color to white using the hexadecimal code for that color, and if necessary, adjust the color of any text.

- Since you've learned to make links, you need a page to link to. Create a new page that details your ideas for making the world a better place. Be sure to include the description and keywords meta tags, and format the text to include a heading for each idea. Be consistent in applying formatting.

- At the end of the content, place a link on this page back to the home page.

- Place a link to your new page above the testimonials on your index page. Separate the link from the testimonials with a paragraph element. Feel free to adjust the width of your floating division for your testimonials if necessary.

That's enough for this exercise; we don't want your brain to twist and contort in agony.

Creating Lists

10.1 Introduction

HTML HAS THREE TYPES OF LISTS: ordered lists, unordered lists, and definition lists.

- **Ordered list:** An ordered list is an indented list in which each list item begins with a number, a capital letter, a lowercase letter, an uppercase Roman numeral, or a lower-case Roman numeral. Other leading items for lists are available with CSS but they do not have full browser support at the time of this writing.

- **Unordered list:** An unordered list is an indented, bulleted list. The bullet types available are disc (a solid circle), circle (an outline), and square. This list is an unordered list using the disc. Image bullets are also available using CSS.

- **Definition list:** A definition list is an indented list without any numbers, letters, or bullets of any kind.

With all lists types, line breaks and indents occur automatically for each new list item. With an ordered list, the numbers or letters increase sequentially with each list item. A list can also be interrupted for commentary and restarted where the previous list left off.

10.2 Ordered Lists

AN ORDERED LIST BEGINS with the ordered list element **<ol>** (that's OL for Ordered List) and ends with the **</ol>** tag.

Each list item is prefaced with the **<li>** tag (that's LI for List Item) and ends with the **</li>** tag. If no list type is specified, a numbered list is displayed by default.

The following code:

```
<ol>
<li>First things first.</li>
<li>Second things not first.</li>
<li>Add a list item element for each list item.</li>
</ol>
```

...creates a list that reads like this:

1. First things first.
2. Second things not first.
3. Add a list item element for each list item.

A list can also be nested, which means you can put one list inside another list. For example, this code:

```
<ol>
<li>Item one.</li>
<li>Item two.</li>
   <ol>
   <li>Sub-item one.</li>
   <li>Sub-item two.</li>
   </ol>
<li>Item three.</li>
</ol>
```

...creates a list that reads like this:

1. Item one.
2. Item two.
    1. Sub-item one.
    2. Sub-item two.
3. Item three.

Note that the nested list items (sub-items) are not indented because they are indented in the code. The browser indents the list items automatically; I indent them in the code for visual clarity. Starting sub-items with the same marker isn't ideal. This is when you might use CSS to create the rules that specify different markers for the sub-items.

Using a different style marker for sub-items in a list is traditional and provides for an easier-to-read and easier-to-understand list. See the following example:

1. Item one.
2. Item two.
    a. Sub-item one.
    b. Sub-item two.
3. Item three.

There are two ways to create that style of list. The first is to use inline CSS as needed. Here's how to create the previous list using inline styles:

```
<ol style="list-style-type: decimal;">
<li>Item one.</li>
<li>Item two.</li>
        <ol style="list-style-type: lower-alpha;">
        <li>Sub-item one.</li>
        <li>Sub-item two.</li>
        </ol>
<li>Item three.</li>
</ol>
```

You can set up the same list style in embedded or external style sheets using contextual selectors. This code:

```
ol {list-style-type: decimal;}
ol ol {list-style-type: lower-alpha;}
```

…does the same thing as the inline code. The advantage of this method is that all the lists within lists will automatically switch from numbers (decimals) to lowercase alphabetic markers; there is no need to keep adding inline styles to multiple lists. You can continue using as many contextual selectors as you need.

A *contextual selector* creates a conditional statement that must be met before the style kicks in. In the previous example, two ordered lists must be opened (and none closed) before the conditions are met. The condition is created by two <ol> selectors in the same line with a space as the separator. Once that condition is met in the HTML code, then the list style is changed to lower-case alphabetical markers. Cool beans!

The marker options for an ordered list are:

list-style-type: *value*	Marker Created
Decimal	1, 2, 3, 4, 5…
Decimal-leading-zero	01, 02, 03, 04, 05… zeros dropped at 10
Lower-roman	i, ii, iii, iv, v…
Upper-roman	I, II, III, IV, V…
Lower-alpha	a, b, c, d, e…
Upper-alpha	A, B, C, D, E…
None	(no marker)

WARNING!

The *decimal-leading-zero* value was not supported in all browsers at the time of this writing. If you want to use this value, be sure to test it.

10.3 Unordered Lists

AN UNORDERED LIST BEGINS with the unordered list element **<ul>** and ends with the **</ul>** tag. Each list item is prefaced with an **<li>** tag and ends with a **</li>** tag. If no list type is specified, the disc marker displays by default.

The following code:

```
<ul>
<li>Carrots</li>
<li>Green Beans</li>
<li>Corn</li>
</ul>
```

…creates a list like this:

- Carrots
- Green Beans
- Corn

However, sub-items in an unordered list work differently from an ordered list. In the ordered list, by default the markers remain the same for sub-items. In an unordered list, Sub-items change from the disc marker to the circle marker; if you add a third unordered list, the marker changes to the square marker. Therefore, this code:

```
<ul>
<li>Carrots</li>
<li>Green Beans</li>
<li>Corn</li>
        <ul>
        <li>Cornbread</li>
        <li>Corn Syrup</li>
                <ul>
                <li>Sweeteners</li>
                </ul>
        <li>Cornmeal</li>
        </ul>
<li>Beets</li>
</ul>
```

...looks like this on a web page:

- Carrots
- Green Beans
- Corn
  - Cornbread
  - Corn Syrup
    - Sweeteners
  - Cornmeal
- Beets

As shown for ordered lists, you can apply contextual selectors to unordered lists using the following marker values:

list-style-type: *value*	Marker Created
Disc	●
Circle	○
Square	■
None	(no marker)

10.4 Image Bullets

USING CSS, YOU CAN USE images for markers (bullets) instead of the predefined markers. Suppose I'm making a list of my favorite musicians. I decided to use musical notes for the list bullets. After finding or creating the graphics, I'm set to the write the list.

Figure 10.1 shows what my list might look like with blue note symbols for the list markers.

Here's how I created that list:

Figure 10.1

```
<ul style="list-style-image: url(bluenote2.gif);">
<li>Paul Black and the Flip Kings</li>
<li>Pops Walker</li>
<li>Stevie Ray Vaughn</li>
</ul>
```

Of course, list markers (bullets) are not very big. You need to take care when choosing or creating images to use as markers. If they are too large, it looks confusing and amateurish. Markers should be the same size or smaller than the font height.

A list using an image for its markers displays with no markers in non-graphical browsers. The way around that is to code the image marker this way:

```
<ul style="list-style: disc url(bluenote2.gif);">
<li>Paul Black and the Flip Kings</li>
<li>Pops Walker</li>
<li>Stevie Ray Vaughn</li>
</ul>
```

Compared to the previous example showing how to create a list using images for markers, this list code has two differences. The first change is to change *list-style-image* to just *list-style* (remove "-image" from the property). The other change is to add "disc" or one of the other list marker types before "url," as shown in red text.

10.5 Marker Positioning

THE DEFAULT DISPLAY POSITION for list markers is outside the list text. This behavior can be changed with the *list-style-position* property. The values for this property are either *inside* or *outside*. Since outside is the default position, there is seldom a reason to include that value in code.

Figure 10.2 shows two short lists, one showing the inside position and one showing the outside position. As you can see, the outside position creates a neater looking list.

You can use the *list-style-position* with both ordered lists and unordered lists.

Here's how to code the list on the left:

```
<ol style="list-style-position: inside;">
<li>Smiles increase your face value.</li>
<li>Everybody is somebody, be somebody nice.</li>
</ol>
```

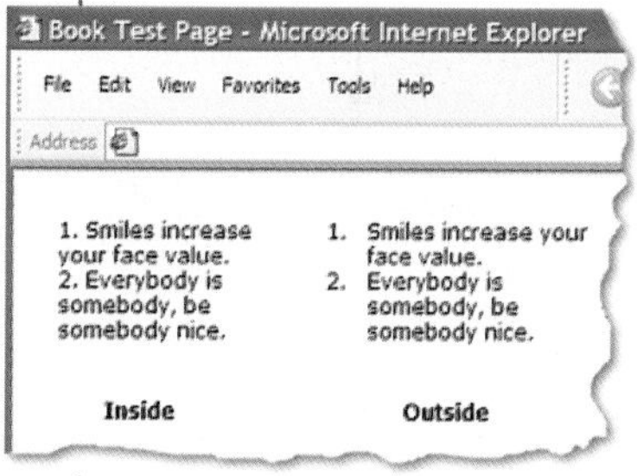

Change *inside* to *outside* in the code to create the list on the right.

Figure 10.2

10.6 Definition Lists

A DEFINITION LIST BEGINS with the definition list element **<dl>** and ends with the **</dl>** tag. Definition lists work differently from the other two list types—the syntax is different for list items and there are no markers used to precede the list items.

Rather than using <li> for each list item, a definition list uses <dt> for each list item. The "dt" is short for **d**efinition **t**erm, and a definition term needs a **d**efinition **d**escription. The <dd> tag provides the mechanism for that. Here's an example of a definition list:

```
<dl>
<dt>Bazantar</dt>
<dd>A Bazantar is a five-string acoustic bass, fitted with
    an additional twenty-nine sympathetic strings and
    four drone strings.</dd>
<dt>Udu Drums</dt>
<dd>Clay pot drums traditional in African folk music.
    </dd>
</dl>
```

That code displays similar to this on a web page:

Bazantar

A Bazantar is a five-string acoustic bass, fitted with an additional
twenty-nine sympathetic strings and four drone strings.

Udu Drums

Clay pot drums traditional in African folk music.

As you can see, the definition term is not indented, but the definition description is. Using CSS, you can format the terms or definitions for more contrast. For example, by making the definition term bold and the definition a slightly smaller font size, the same list looks like this:

Bazantar

A Bazantar is a five-string acoustic bass, fitted with an additional twenty-nine sympathetic strings and four drone strings.

Udu Drums

Clay pot drums traditional in African folk music.

To me, that's a much nicer looking and more readable list. To create that list, I added the following code to the style sheet:

```
dt {font-size: 14px; font-weight: bold; margin-top: 12px;}
dd {font-size: 12px;}
```

I coded the <dt> entries to display in bold and added a 12 pixel margin at the top to create separation between the <dt> and previous <dd> entry. I made the <dd> entry font size 2 pixels smaller to create further distinction between the definition terms and definition descriptions.

10.7 List Continuation

ONCE UPON A TIME, if you ended an ordered list to insert some content, and then wanted to start a new list with numbering continued from the previous list, it was pretty easy to do. Unfortunately, the W3C decided to make that much harder.

Suppose I have a list of books like this:

1. *Stupid People* by M.T. Head
2. *No Right or Wrong* by Seymour Gray
3. *Foreclosure!* by Anita Newhouse
4. *The Court System* by Sue and Bea Rich

To stop the list to offer an explanatory note or some other commentary, I need to end the list so the text is no longer indented. To restart the list with list item 5, I could use one of two easy methods. I could use this in the <ol> tag:

```
<ol start="5">
<li>...
```

Or I could use this in the <li> tag:

```
<ol>
<li value="5">...
```

Using either attribute started the new ordered list at the number specified. You can still do it that way, but the W3C has deprecated the *start* attribute for ordered lists and the *value* attribute for list items. It still works, but may not validate and may not work if the deprecated code is made obsolete.

Now the W3C wants you to restart lists using CSS, which would be just fine if they gave us an easy way to do it. Unfortunately, restarting a list using CSS is much more complex and isn't well supported by browsers at this time.

I understand some of their purpose in the change. The marker the browser inserts before list items is what is called "generated content." The W3C wanted to provide a way to allow other elements to be automatically numbered, such as headings, for example. With all the other changes, it really will be more a robust system *when* browsers start supporting it fully. The trouble is, I see no valid reason why starting a simple list at a specified value had to be made so complex.

I'll try to explain it. Here's the external style sheet code we are dealing with:

```
ol {counter-reset: books 4;}
li:before {
  content: counter(books) ". ";
  counter-increment: books;
  font-weight: bold;}
```

First, in order to have a counter (the list numbering system) start at the number you want, something has to be reset—the parent element, a surrounding <span> element, or something else as seems appropriate. For an ordered list, it makes sense to reset the *ol* selector.

So, in the first line of code, the *ol* selector has a *counter-reset* property, and then the word *books*. The word "books" is the counter name; since my list is about books that made sense to me, but the name can be almost anything. The number *4* that follows the counter name is the number the counter starts on. It seems, however, that the counter actually restarts at the number *after* the number you reset it to…and if you don't understand that, you're not alone. The point is, set this number to one number smaller than you want the list to start with.

The next line is the element we're going to apply the counter to, in this case a list item. That's followed by the *:before* pseudo-element. *Before* places the value the counter inserts before the list item content; *after* places the value the counter inserts after the list item.

In the next line, the content property identifies the counter as the content, and names the counter in parenthesis. After the parentheses, I included ". " What that does is insert a period and a space after the counter number. You could insert text, an image, or something else, but this is convoluted enough.

The *counter-increment* line lets you set the increments each list item increases by. If no value is given the default value is 1. If you wrote: *"counter-increment: books 3"* then the list items increase in increments of three. Since our list is restarting at 5, the list items would be numbered 7, 10, 13, etc. Remember, in increments of 1, setting the list to restart at 4 meant the list items actually start at 5; with increments of 3, the list item restarts at 7 instead of 5. Again, if this doesn't make sense to you, don't worry—you're not alone. I spent hours trying to find a good explanation for any of this and found none.

Simplicity is the ultimate sophistication. ~Leonardo da Vinci

Leonardo da Vinci was one of the smartest men in history, and the geeks would do well to remember his words. Anyway, in the last line of code in the previous example, sets the list markers in bold type. You couldn't do that with HTML lists without resorting to slight trickery, so that's cool.

So, if we started a list with that in our code, would the list work right? Not quite. Our previous list was an ordered list, so it numbers the list items on its own, it seems. If we don't take the automatic numbering away, our new list will be double numbered. It would look like this:

1. **5.** Visual Learning Skills by I.C. Howe
2. **6.** The Salvation Army by Belle Ringer

Now that is just goofy. To take away the original numbering that the new list causes, we need to start off the list with an inline style:

```
<ol style="list-style-type: none;">
<li>Visual Learning Skills by I.C. Howe</li>
<li>The Salvation Army by Belle Ringer</li>
</ol>
```

By setting the *list-style-type* to *none*, we finally have the list the way we want—except the numbers are in bold type when our previous list wasn't. So, we either have to remove the bold formatting or try something else.

If you need to restart a list several times instead of just once, the above code wouldn't quite work anyway. You could create a new class for each new list, but that's a lot of work. What to do, what to do?

Yeah, I've got you covered.

Let's start off our ordered list with the list-style-type set to none so we can specify the formatting from the beginning. After that, I'll show you how to reset the counter for each new list, and I'll toss in another trick or two for good measure.

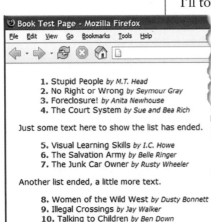

Figure 10.3

Look at the screen capture in Figure 10.3. The list is shown in the Firefox browser, which does offer good support for the CSS code that allows us to renumber lists. As you can see, I added bold type for the numbers, and also set the color to blue. The list items are still in black type. I also used the <cite> attribute to make the authors' names smaller than the book titles.

Speaking of authors and book titles, did you enjoy my silly combinations of titles and authors?

I used embedded CSS to create the list in Figure 10.3. Here's the CSS code from the HEAD section of the source code:

```
<style type="text/css">
body {font-family: Verdana; font-size: 14px;
        background-color: ivory; margin: 23px;}
ol {counter-reset: books 0;}
li:before {
   content: counter(books) ". ";
   counter-increment: books 1;
   font-weight: bold; color: blue;}
cite {font-size: 12px;}
</style>
```

This is the same code explained previously, except it shows the *body* property and the cite property, plus I added the blue color to the list items. The counter was set at zero because we are numbering all the lists with CSS only.

Now here's the code from the BODY of the document that created the lists:

```
<ol style="list-style-type: none;">
<li>Stupid People <cite>by M.T. Head</cite></li>
<li>No Right or Wrong <cite>by Seymour Gray</cite>
</li>
<li>Foreclosure! <cite>by Anita Newhouse</cite></li>
```

```
<li>The Court System <cite>by Sue and Bea Rich</cite>
</li>
</ol>
```

Just some text here to show the list has ended.

```
<ol style="list-style-type: none; counter-reset: books 4">
<li>Visual Learning Skills <cite>by I.C. Howe</cite></li>
<li>The Salvation Army <cite>by Belle Ringer</cite></li>
<li>The Junk Car Owner <cite>by Rusty Wheeler</cite>
</li>
</ol>
```

Another list ended, a little more text.

```
<ol style="list-style-type: none; counter-reset: books 7">
<li>Women of the Wild West <cite>by Dusty Bonnett
</cite></li>
<li>Illegal Crossings <cite>by Jay Walker</cite></li>
<li>Talking to Children <cite>by Ben Down</cite></li>
</ol>
```

The code in red text restarts the counting at the number I want. By setting the *list-style-type* to *none*, and adding the *counter-reset, counter name,* and numerical *value* to use, I finally came up with a workable series of lists.

However, using CSS to renumber lists is not supported well, so I recommend testing it before going live. If a technique isn't supported by Internet Explorer, Firefox, Opera, and Safari, I suggest using the deprecated *ol start* or *li value* HTML attributes.

Whew. That was a lot of work just to end up telling you that you probably shouldn't use this method until browser support catches up! Yeah, but you're well worth the effort.

10.8 Chapter 10 Exercise

F OR THE CHAPTER 10 EXERCISE:

- Now that you've learned about lists, open your index page source code. In the floating division where you added an image in front of the first line of each testimonial, change the structure so that each testimonial is a list item in an unordered list. Save the changes.

- Open the second page you made that details how to help make the world a better place. Create a division at the top of the page and float it to the right. Set the width to whatever seems appropriate, but it should probably be at least 200 pixels wide. Within this division, you will create a nested list.

- Create an ordered list with three list item entries. Each list item entry should be the (fictitious) name of a company that sponsors your ideas. Under each list item entry, nest an unordered list that indicates what kind of support or resources each sponsor has provided (financial, physical space, labor, donated services, etc.) to your company.

- Preface your list with a heading that identifies the list as "Sponsors."

- Add a title attribute to your list for screen readers.

- Move the link back to the index page to the top of floating division, so the navigation placement is consistent with the location of the navigation on the index page.

Tables

11.1 Introduction

IN HTML, TABLES PROVIDE a layout mechanism for arranging content in a grid of rows and columns to control the placement of content. Tables are often used to present rows and columns of data, but can also be used to control the entire page layout. You'll learn about both uses of tables in this chapter. You can also use tables to control white space, add background colors or images to portions of the page, and to add text to blank buttons.

11.2 Basic Table Facts

THINGS TO KNOW ABOUT TABLES:

- A table can be a single cell, but it is usually a grid of rows and columns forming multiple cells. See Figure 11.1 for a visual reference. The heavy black outline represents the table's outer boundaries. The thin black lines represent the table's grid of rows and columns. Each square within the grid is an individual entity called a *table data cell*.

- Tables can be as large or small as you need them to be.

Figure 11.1

- If you don't specify the size for a table, it will be as small as possible, but will expand to fit the content, which may produce unexpected layout results.

- If you do specify sizes for tables, the sizes must add up correctly. For example, if you code a table to be 500 pixels wide and have two columns that are 300 pixels wide each (for a total of 600 pixels), something will not display as intended because the width of the table does not match the combined width of the table columns.

- Tables can have background colors and background images independent from the background color or background image of the web page.

- Tables can be nested. That is, there can be tables within tables to further control the page layout.

- If you forget to close a table, some browsers will display the table and others will not. That's the first thing to check if your table isn't showing up on the page.

- The table border can be visible or invisible through the *border* property. Even if you want the final border to be invisible, it's often helpful to make it visible during the design process to help see where any problems are and make adjustments.

11.3 Basic Table Structure

THE SIMPLEST TABLE POSSIBLE consists of only one row and one column, resulting in just one table data cell. The code for this is:

```
<table>
<tr>
<td>
Content goes here…
```

The content of a table always goes inside a table data cell.

```
</td>
</tr>
</table>
```

Of course, a single-cell table like that doesn't give you the layout control we use tables to achieve. If you only want one cell, most of the time you're better off not using a table and just using a division or paragraph instead.

Tables always start with the opening table tag and always end with a cancel table tag. The <tr> tag is for *table row*, which starts a row of one or more table data cells. Every table must have at least one row. The <td> is for *table data*, which create columns when placed side-by-side. Every row must have at least one table data cell. All table content goes within the table data cells. Table data cells can hold anything—text, graphics, links, green fuzzy mugglewumpits…OK, *almost* anything. Mugglewumpits usually escape because they're so good at tunneling.

From a purely HTML standpoint, the </td> and </tr> tags are optional. However, leaving them out is not XHTML compliant and it will cause problems in some browsers. Since XHTML is supposedly the future of web design, I highly recommended you use the closing tags.

11.4 Sizing and Alignment

IF THE SIZE ISN'T SPECIFIED for a table, the table will be as small as possible but expand as much as needed to fit the content. If there are two or more columns in a table with no size specified, it's anybody's guess how wide each column will be. Each browser will determine the best column widths according to its own criteria, and the display isn't likely to be the same across browsers. Of course, that means you never know what your table is going to look like. That's why specifying the size is a good idea.

The width of the table can be set as a percentage or a numerical value using the HTML width attribute.

```
<table width="640">
```

That sets the width of the table at 640 pixels. Because *width* is an HTML attribute, the number value is always measured in pixels. Only CSS property values allow you to name the unit of measurement. You can also use CSS to set the width.

```
<table style="width: 640px;">
```

To be consistent, I recommend using CSS to set the width. Consistent with what you ask? Good question, Fleebermungle!

In tables with two or more table data cells, often you will set the width of the data cells in the first row so each column will be the width you want. While using the HTML attribute and value of *width*="*320*" for table data cells will work, it has been deprecated. I do not recommend using deprecated code unless it's unavoidable. Therefore, since you *should* use the CSS width property to set the data cell sizes, I recommend it for the table width as well.

It's best to be consistent whenever possible. Using inconsistent practices for specifying measurements can result in a quirky output in some browsers. Having said all that, here's how to use CSS to set the width of a table data cell:

```
<td style="width: 300px;">
```

You can also set the width using a percentage. The percentage is measured against the available horizontal space.

```
<table width="80%">
```

```
<table style="width: 80%;">
```

The first line of code shows the HTML method and the second line of code shows the CSS method, both for setting the width using a percentage. The display results are the same.

While a table's height is usually determined by its content—since the table expands to fit it—there are times when you may want to set the height. Some HTML authors say to add *height*="*x*" to the opening table tag as a way to set the height, but that attribute is not a legal attribute for a table. Some browsers will support it, but others won't.

The legal way to set a table's height is to use the CSS *height* property, but as with adding an HTML height attribute, some browsers don't support the CSS height tag either. In my opinion, the best practice is to not set the table height, but instead let the height adjust naturally to the content.

In a two-column table, such as in the magazine style layout demonstrated in the next section, if one column of content is longer than the other, the content in the shorter column aligns vertically in the center of the column. It's rare to want that result, so you can use the *valign* attribute with the TD element to set the vertical alignment:

```
valign="top"
```

That forces the content to begin at the top of the table data cell. The possible values for the valign attribute are:

top | middle | bottom | baseline

You can also set the horizontal alignment using the align attribute:

align="justify"

That justifies the text within the column, but has no affect on graphics. The possible values for the align attribute are:

left | center | right | justify

You're supposed to be able to align tables to the left, right, or center of the page. I say "supposed to be" because the only way that works reliably is using deprecated code. I'll show you the way you're supposed to do it first:

style="text-align: center;"

By adding that code to the opening table element, the table is supposed to center on the page or within the containing element. It works in some browsers, not in others. You could add it to a division tag and put the table inside the division but that, too, works only in some browser and not in others.

The float property is supposed to work with tables as well:

style="float: center;"

The *left* and *right* values work fine; *center* only works in some browsers. The possible values for the float property are:

left | right | center

The only way to center a table that works reliably is using the deprecated HTML align attribute with a table or division:

<table align="center">

<div align="center">

Pick your poison—or don't try centering tables until all the browsers catch up to the current CSS standards. By then, new standards will be out and we'll be waiting on the browser software developers again. I think it would be a good idea if the W3C wasn't allowed to deprecate code until the majority of browsers support the code's replacement!

Of course, there are always tricks you can come up with to work around browser inconsistencies and deprecated code, but trying to learn tricks while you're still trying to learn the basics adds another layer of complexity, so we'll skip the tricks.

11.5 Magazine-Style Table

A SIMPLE TWO-COLUMN TABLE is commonly used to create a magazine-style layout. It's also the style often used for laying out a page with a left-border style background. A magazine-style table is just one small step beyond the basic table structure.

Figure 11.2

Figure 11.2 shows a two-column table layout for a fictional magazine site.

I used the background positioning technique from Section 8.12: Background Image Options of Chapter 8: Color, Backgrounds, and Images to place the cattail as the background on the right side of the page.

Then I created a two-column table and set the width to a percentage of the page.

In the two-column table example that follows, I numbered (in red) each line of code so I can refer to each line separately. The numbers are not part of the code.

Here's the table code:

```
1 <table style= "width: 70%;">

2 <tr>

3 <td style="width: 50%;"  valign="top">

Column one content here...

4 </td>

5 <td  style="width: 50%;"  valign="top">

Column two content here...


6 </td>
```

```
7  </tr>
8  </table>
```

1. Line 1 opens the table. The width is set to 70 percent of the page to prevent the text from spilling onto the background image.
2. Opens the table row.
3. Opens the first table data cell, creating column one. The width is set to 50 percent so each column will be of equal width; the vertical alignment within the cell is also set.
4. Closes the first table data cell.
5. Opens the second table data cell, which creates the second column; the column width and vertical alignment are also set.
6. Closes the second table data cell.
7. Closes the table row.
8. Closes the table.

Well, that was certainly easy. To create more *columns* just keep adding more table data cells in the first row, but be sure not to make each column's size 50 percent if you have more than two columns or it won't add up 100 percent.

To create another *row* after you have as many columns as you plan to have, close the first row and open a second. Don't fret, Nanette, this will be demonstrated again in an upcoming section.

11.6 Table for Left Border Backgrounds

THE SAME TWO-COLUMN LAYOUT from the previous section is often used for a page with a left border style background.

Figure 11.3 shows a web site for a fictional rock band called Rock Quest. That's a great name—someone ought to use it (and I should get free CDs for life from them for coming up with it).

The left border background image has musical notes tiling down the side of the page. Obviously, if the text overlapped the left side of the background image, it would be very difficult to read. The magazine style two-column table is a popular way to keep the content off the left edge.

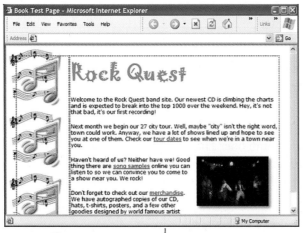

Figure 11.3

There are three differences between the previous two-column table and the left border style table:

1. The table width is usually either set to 100 percent or left out to allow the table to expand and contract to the various screen resolutions and browser sizes. This is called *liquid* design because it's a fluid structure.

2. The first column width is set much narrower and it should always be set to a numerical value rather than a percentage to keep the second column at the same distance from the left edge at all resolutions and browser sizes. Actually, that's a good idea when you use a background image on the right side, too, except the right column will have the hard-coded width while the left column is left liquid.

3. The width of the second column is *not* usually set; this is what makes the table liquid. It expands and contracts according to the horizontal space available.

You'll also notice a blue dotted line showing a narrow column and a wide column. That's the table border. By setting the border property so that it shows, you can see exactly where the boundaries are, making it easy to make adjustments to the width if you guessed at the size. When you have everything set right, you can go back and set the border to zero to make it disappear.

The code for the table in Figure 11.3 follows. Each list item below describes the corresponding line of code.

```
1 <table style= "width: 100%;" border="1">
2 <tr>
3 <td style="width: 160px;" valign="top">
    (Left border area)
4 </td>
5 <td valign="top">
Content area…
6 </td>
```

```
7 </tr>
8 </table>
```

1. This opens the table. The width is set to 100 percent so the design fills the screen. The border is set to "1" so it shows on the page temporarily.

2. Opens the table row.

3. Opens the table data cell and sets the width at 160 pixels to keep the content off the colored border part of the background image. A * * (no-break space) character entity is placed in this cell to keep the cell open; otherwise it would collapse with no content inside.

4. Closes the first table data cell.

5. Opens the second table data cell. No width is used for this cell so it can expand and contract according to the viewer's screen resolution and browser window size, thus making it a liquid design.

6. Closes the second table data cell.

7. Closes the table row.

8. Closes the table.

Note that this method is one of three common methods for using a left border background image. Other methods include using CSS to define the page margins or using the single pixel transparent GIF trick. Using CSS to define the page margins was discussed previously, and the single pixel transparent GIF trick is outdated trickery that's no longer necessary.

11.7 Multi-Column Multi-Row Data Table

WHILE THE PREVIOUS TWO table examples were for page layout, this example presents a table of data in a readable and logical format.

At the Lumpy Beds Hotel, Sue, Judi, and Darrel have to work the front desk for the weekend. The "Duty Roster Table" shows the shifts they were assigned.

The hotel manager, Ida Doorknocker, always puts the schedule on the company's

Employee	Saturday	Sunday
Sue H.	12AM - 8AM	2PM - 12AM
Judi J.	8AM - 2PM	12AM - 8AM
Darrel G.	2PM - 12AM	8AM - 2PM

Duty Roster Table

private web site so employees can access their schedule from home. Here's the code Ida used, along with my explanatory notes:

```
1  <table style="width: 300px;"><tr>
2  <td style="width: 100px;">Employee</td>
3  <td style="width: 100px;">Saturday</td>
4  <td style="width: 100px;">Sunday</td>
5  </tr><tr>
6  <td>Sue H.</td>
7  <td>12AM - 8AM</td>
8  <td>2PM - 12AM</td>
9  </tr><tr>
10 <td>Judi J.</td>
11 <td>8AM - 2PM</td>
12 <td>12AM - 8AM</td>
13 </tr><tr>
14 <td>Darrel G.</td>
15 <td>2PM - 12AM</td>
16 <td>8AM - 2PM</td>
17 </tr></table>
```

Line 1: This line opens the table and sets the width to 300 pixels. The first table row was also opened.

Lines 2–4: Each line opens and closes a table data cell in the first row, with the content included. The width for each cell/column is set here. The width need not be added to the cells in the subsequent rows because the width in the first row sets the column.*

Lines 5, 9, and 13: Each of these three lines cancels the previous row and starts a new row.

Lines 6–8: Opens and closes the three table data cells in the second row with the content included.

Lines 10–12: Opens and closes the three table data cells in the third row with content included.

*Setting the width of the table cells in row 1 sets the width for the rest of the column—unless you put in content, such as an image, that is too wide to fit in the cell. That will force the cell to open wider than specified in the code and will affect the entire column.

Lines 14–16: Opens and closes the three table data cells in the last row with the content included.

Line 17: Closes the last table row and the table.

For all my explanation, it's probably easier to understand if you just look at the lines of code and compare the cell content to the table to see where it displays in the table. Basically, I opened a table and started a row, then added three data cells. These are the three cells that display across the top of the table in the first row. Then, I closed that row, opened another, and added three more data cells (those are the cells in the second row). I repeated this for two more rows before closing the table and calling it done. Oops, I mean, Ida Doorknocker did all that.

That's a decent table Ida created, but it could be better. In a traditional table, the first row of column headers would be displayed in bold type.

Fortunately, HTML provides a very easy way to do this. By using the <th> tag, short for *table header*, the text in the header cells will display in bold text and be centered within the cell. What we need to do, then, is replace the table data cells in lines 2–4 in the code with table headers.

Previous Code	Changed Code
2 <td style="width: 100px;"> Employee</td>	2 <th style="width: 100px;"> Employee</td>
3 <td style="width: 100px;"> Saturday</td>	3 <th style="width: 100px;"> Saturday</td>
4 <td style="width: 100px;"> Sunday</td>	4 <th style="width: 100px;"> Sunday</td>

The changed code creates table headers from the first row. Table headers also center the content, so in addition to the text displaying in bold type it is centered. Here's how Ida's duty roster table looks now:

Employee	Saturday	Sunday
Sue H.	12AM - 8AM	2PM - 12AM
Judi J.	8AM - 2PM	12AM - 8AM
Darrel G.	2PM - 12AM	8AM - 2PM

Duty Roster Table

Now that's more like it. Ida is as happy as a clam with her finished table.

Hmm...I wonder how you can tell when clams are happy?

Before we move on to the next lesson, let's recap the table structure for multi-row, multi-column tables to make sure you understand what's been presented so far.

Code	Results
\<table\>	Opens a table.
\<tr\>	Opens a table row. Each table must have at least one row.
\<td\>	Opens a table data cell. Each row must have at least one data cell.
...Content...	The content goes inside the data cells.
\</td\>	Closes the table data cell. You may either close the row now or open another data cell. Each data cell will create a column if a second row is added. You may add as many data cells as you need, but you must have the same number of data cells in each row unless two or more data cells are combined (you'll learn how to do that later).
\</tr\>	Closes the table row. You may either close the table now or add another row. You may add as many rows as you need.
\</table\>	Closes the table. Game over.

11.8 Creating Row Groups

TABLE STRUCTURE CAN BE FURTHER DEFINED using row groups, which allow you to use different CSS formatting styles for different groups of rows. Any or all row groups can have CSS styles set independently through the use of *class* or *ID* attributes, or through the use of *inline* styles.

To use row groups, table rows are grouped into a table head, table foot, and one or more table body sections using the *thead*, *tfoot*, and *tbody* elements, in that order. It may seem odd to have a table foot coded before the table body, but this allows the table head and foot to be drawn before receiving all of the (potentially) numerous rows of data. The foot data will actually be displayed *after* the tbody elements in standards-compliant browsers, even though it's coded before the tbody elements.

A row group can also have the height set, and when combined with the overflow property, allows for scrollable sections within a table body that act independently of the table head and table foot. When long tables are printed, the table head and table foot information may be repeated on each page that contains table data. Not all browsers support the scrollable table or repeated head and foot information at the time of this writing, but the next generation browsers may. Test these two features in your target browsers before depending on them in table designs.

If used, each *thead*, *tfoot*, and *tbody* must have at least one row. The *thead*, *tfoot*, and *tbody* sections must contain the same number of columns unless data cells are combined. The table head should contain information about what is in the table's columns. The table body should contain the rows of table data. The *tfoot* element, which is optional, often contains copyright information, a disclaimer, or other pertinent information about the table content. If you do use the tfoot element, all the data cells in that row can be combined into a single cell, which contains the table foot content.

Figure 11.4 shows a table I created using the *thead*, *tfoot*, and *tbody* elements. I also used various CSS styles to show some of the possibilities of using CSS to create a table that's distinct and easy to read.

Here's is the code used for the table in Figure 11.4:

```
1 <table width="400"  style="border: 1px solid black;">
2 <thead style="color: #BEBFAA;
                 background-color: #000000;">
3    <tr style="text-align: left;">
4    <th width="70">Week</th>
5    <th width="100">Name</th>
6    <th width="130">Prize</th>
7    <th width="100">Value</th>
8  </tr>
9  </thead>
10 <tfoot style="text-align: center;
                 color: red;
                 background-color: #000000;
                 font-weight: bold;">
11 <tr> <td colspan="4"> - Weekly Winners - </td>
```

Book Test Page - Microsoft Internet Explorer

File   Edit   View   Favorites   Tools   Help

Address

Week	Name	Prize	Value
1	Courtney W.	Plasma TV	$5,995.00
2	Rich E.	Fishing Boat	$1,899.95
3	Autumn A.	Hot Tub	$4,779.00
4	Scott A.	Camper	$9,950.00
5	Alison G.	Room Makeover	$25,000.00
6	Judy P.	Piano	$4,389.95
- Weekly Winners -			

Figure 11.4

205

```
12 </tfoot>
13 <tbody style="background-color: #B4B69C;">
14 <tr>
15      <td>1</td>
16      <td>Courtney W.</td>
17      <td>Plasma TV</td>
18      <td>$5,995.00</td>
19 </tr>
20 <tr>
21      <td>2</td>
22      <td>Rich E.</td>
23      <td>Fishing Boat</td>
24      <td>$1,899.95</td>
25 </tr>
26 </tbody>
27 <tbody style="background-color: #9C9D7D;">
28 <tr>
29      <td>3</td>
30      <td>Autumn A.</td>
31      <td>Hot Tub</td>
32      <td>$4,779.00</td>
33 </tr>
34 <tr>
35      <td>4</td>
36      <td>Scott A.</td>
37      <td>Camper</td>
38      <td>$9,950.00</td>
39 </tr>
40 </tbody>
41 <tbody style="background-color: #B4B69C;">
42 <tr>
43      <td>5</td>
44      <td>Alison G.</td>
45      <td>Room Makeover</td>
46      <td>$25,000.00</td>
```

```
47 </tr>
48 <tr>
49        <td>6</td>
50        <td>Judy P.</td>
51        <td>Piano</td>
52        <td>$4,389.95</td>
53 </tr>
54 </tbody>
55 </table>
```

Now that you've seen how tables work, you may not need an explanation for the previous code, but I'll offer one anyway.

Line 1:   Opens the table and sets the border for the table outline.

Line 2:   Opens the thead section and sets the font color and background color. Note that I've included the line below as part of line 2 since it could be on the same line, but it is shown in two lines here in order to fit the code in the book.

Line 3:   Opens the table row and aligns the text to the left of the table data cells.

Lines 4-7:   Opens and closes 4 table header cells, sets the column width, and adds header text.

Line 8:   Cancels the first table row.

Line 9:   Cancels the thead.

Line 10:   Opens the tfoot and aligns the text to the center and sets the font color, background color, and font weight to bold.

Line 11:   Opens the table row and table data cell, and sets the colspan (column span) to 4 so that the words can be centered in the last row of the table without having separate cells.

Line 12:   Cancels the tfoot.

Line 13:   Opens the first tbody section and sets the background color.

Line 14:   Opens the first table row of the first tbody section.

Lines 15–18:   Opens and closes 4 table data cells listing the week, winner's name, prize, and value.

Line 19:   Closes the first table row of the first tbody section.

Line 20:   Opens the second table row of the first tbody section.

Lines 21–24: Opens and closes the next set of table data cells for the next week's prize information.

Line 25:   Closes the second table row of the first tbody section.

Line26:   Closes the first tbody section.

Line 27:   Opens the second tbody section and sets a new background color.

Line 28:   Opens the first row of the second tbody section.

Lines 29–32: Opens and closes the next set of table data cells for the next week's prize information.

Line 33:   Closes the first row of the second tbody section.

Line 34:   Opens the second row of the second tbody section.

Lines 35–38: Opens and closes the next set of table data cells for the next week's prize information.

Line 39:   Closes the second row of the second tbody section.

Line 40:   Closes the second tbody section.

Line 41:   Opens the third tbody section and sets the background color like the first tbody section.

Line 42:   Opens the first row of the third tbody section.

Lines 43–46: Opens and closes the next set of table data cells for the next week's prize information.

Line 47:   Closes the first row of the third tbody section.

Line 48:   Opens the second row of the third tbody section.

Lines 49–52: Opens and closes the next set of table data cells for the next week's prize information.

Line 53:   Closes the second row of the third tbody section.

Line 54:   Closes the third tbody section.

Line 55:   Closes the table. Life goes on.

11.9 Creating Column Groups

YOU CAN GROUP COLUMNS to set styles in an entire column or to set column widths, for example. Why would you want to set the column width using column groups instead of setting it in the first row of table data cells, you ask?

Hey, that's a pretty good question for a rookie—I'm proud of you! Suppose you had a table with 20 columns, each with a width of 50 pixels. Instead of entering the width 20 times, once into each data cell in the first row, you can enter it just once into a column group. Neat!

Figure 11.5 shows the same table as in Figure 11.4, except I used column groups to change some of the formatting. I centered the text in the first column, changed the font color to blue in the second and third columns, and changed the text to italics in the last column.

Column groups should be added just below the opening table tag, unless you use a table caption. If a table caption is used, the column group information goes under the caption information. Table captions are covered in the next section.

I made the following changes to the code from the table in Figure 11.4 to create the table in Figure 11.5:

Week	Name	Prize	Value
1	Courtney W.	Plasma TV	$5,995.00
2	Rich E.	Fishing Boat	$1,899.95
3	Autumn A.	Hot Tub	$4,779.00
4	Scott A.	Camper	$9,950.00
5	Alison G.	Room Makeover	$25,000.00
6	Judy P.	Piano	$4,389.95
- Weekly Winners -			

Figure 11.5

```
1 <table width="400" style="border: solid black 1px;">

2 <colgroup style="text-align: center;">

3 <colgroup style="color: #0B01C0;" span="2">

4 <colgroup style="font-style: italic;">

5 <thead style="color: #BEBFAA; background-color:
  #000000;">
```

Line 1: This is the same table opening shown in Figure 11.4 from the previous table.

Line 2: This column group was used to align the text to the center in the first column.

Line 3: This column group was used to set the text color to blue. Note the span attribute; the value of "2" sets the group to cover the middle two columns. The first column was set in the previous line.

Line 4: This column group sets the font to italic in the last column.

The rest of the table is the same as in Figure 11.4. If you use only one column group, it applies only to the first column. If you use a second column group, it applies only to the second column.

Each column can have its own column group, or you can group multiple columns together.

The *span* attribute is used to group multiple columns into a column group. For example, a *span*="5" indicates the column group includes five total columns. The five columns include the column where it's used plus four more columns, for a total of five. If *span*="5" is used in the first column group, it applies to the first five columns. A subsequent column group would start with column six. Column groups cannot overlap.

11.10 Spanning Columns and Rows

TABLE DATA CELLS CAN BE COMBINED across rows and columns so a cell can span two or more cells in the same row or span two or more cells in a column.

Figure 11.6 shows the layout of a table with three columns and three rows. This isn't, however, the final layout we want.

Figure 11.7 shows the final layout we want. This is the same table as in Figure 11.6, with two changes. The first change is that I combined cells 4 and 5 to create a larger cell in the second row. Combining them made what was previously cell 6 become cell 5, cell 7 became cell 6, cell 8 became cell 7, and cell 9 became cell 8, with cell 9 being eliminated through the process of cell combining. This is accomplished with the *colspan* attribute.

The second change is that I combined cell 5 in the second row with cell 8 (formerly cell 9 prior to combining cells 4 and 5) in the third row, thus eliminating cell 8. This is done with the *rowspan* attribute. A colspan attribute is used to combine two cells in the same row (because it's spanning two columns). The rowspan attribute is used to combine two cells in the same column (because it's spanning two rows). It sounds a little tricky, but it makes sense if you think about it. Here's the code for the table in Figure 11.7:

1	2	3
4	5	6
7	8	9

Figure 11.6

Figure 11.7

```
1 <table width="500">
2 <tr>
3 <td width="160">1</td>
4 <td width="200">2</td>
5 <td width="140">3</td>
6 </tr><tr>
```

```
7 <td colspan="2">4</td>

8 <td rowspan="2">5</td>

9 </tr><tr>

10 <td>6</td>

11 <td>7</td>

12 </tr>

13 </table>
```

You should have a pretty good understanding of the basic table properties by now, so I'll only explain the new code.

Line 7: The code in bold text is the code that combined cell 4 and cell 5 together. You'll notice that there are three table data cells in row one, but only two in row two. This is because the colspan set to 2 makes the first data cell count as two cells, so only a third cell was needed to complete the row. If the colspan was set to 3, it would be the only cell in this row.

Line 8: This is the second cell we needed for row two, which we combined with the cell below it using the rowspan attribute, so this cell spans two rows. Having used one cell from the bottom row, the last row now only has two cells.

When combining cells in a row or column, the cells edges must be in alignment with the cells in the other rows and columns. In Figure 11.8, you can see a table that attempts an improper cell alignment. This table won't display properly because the border between cell 7 and cell 8 do not align with the established cells in the top row. Each brand of browser would attempt to display this table in what it determines is the best choice—a choice that is most likely way off from what you intended.

Figure 11.9 shows how you might combine cells to make a custom table for a group of children's photographs.

Nice looking young'uns, eh? They smiled real nice for boompa.

Figure 11.8

Figure 11.9

211

11.11 Table Captions

A TABLE CAPTION IS USED to provide descriptive information about the table content. Table captions display centered above the table in bold type, but you can change the alignment using the *align* attribute. The table caption must appear directly after the opening table tag in your code. Here's how it's written:

<caption> caption text here </caption>

To use the align attribute:

<caption align="left"> caption text here </caption>

The values you may use with the align property are:

- **top:** The caption is centered at the top of the table. This is the default value.
- **bottom:** The caption is centered at the bottom of the table.
- **left:** The caption is at the top left side of the table.
- **right:** The caption is at the top right side of the table.

Note that the align attribute is not listed as being deprecated at the time of this writing (according to the list of HTML attributes at the W3C web site). However, on the page describing the align attribute, it *is* listed as a deprecated attribute. My guess is that it's deprecated but the webmaster forgot to add the deprecated designation to the attributes table. You may use CSS to align the caption to the left, right, or center, but there is no CSS option to have the caption placed at the bottom of the table.

11.12 Table Summaries

THE TABLE SUMMARY ALLOWS YOU to add a description about the table to the table tag. The summary doesn't show up in browsers, but is read by screen readers.

The code in red shows an example summary for the table in Figure 11.9:

<table **summary="This table contains pictures of my grandkids."**>

The summary can be as long or short as you need—but remember, it's usually best to write succinctly for the web.

11.13 Cellpadding and Cellspacing

YOU KNOW WHAT A TABLE DATA CELL IS. Cellpadding is the amount of empty space between the cell content and the edge of the cell. Cellspacing is the amount of empty space in between the cells.

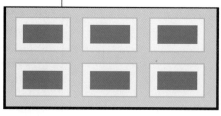

Figure 11.10 shows how cellpadding and cellspacing work in a table. The heavy black line represents the table border. The gray area represents cellspacing, while the green line represents the outer edge of each table data cell. The blue area represents the cell content, and the yellow area shows the cellpadding between the cell content and the outer edge of the cell. Cellpadding and cellspacing are attributes coded into the opening table tag:

Figure 11.10

```
<table cellpadding="10" cellspacing="12">
```

The numerals always represent pixels in HTML attributes.

11.14 Table Borders

YOU HAVE MANY OPTIONS for table borders. The first option is using the HTML border attribute. Figure 11.11 shows several samples of what an HTML border looks like at different sizes:

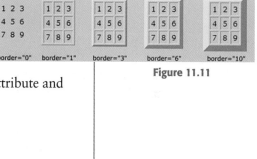

Figure 11.11

Setting the border in HTML is quite easy. The attribute and value are added to the opening table tag.

Here's the how:

```
<table border="7">
```

I told you it was easy. Just change the number to whatever you need for the border.

Internet Explorer allows for a light border color and a dark border color. Figure 11.12 shows how a table looks using the selected attributes and colors.

Other browsers will display such a table in various ways. Firefox, for example, displays the light color in white and the dark color in gray. I don't recommend using these proprietary attributes, but they are there if you choose to use them. To add light and dark border colors for Internet Explorer:

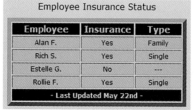

```
<table bordercolorlight="#A79C69"
bordercolordark="#524B30">
```

Figure 11.12

Using CSS border properties opens up further possibilities. With CSS, you can set any of the border properties for all four sides all at once or individually. The following table lists the many options for setting table border properties:

Property	Description
border	Shorthand property for specifying the border-width, border-style, and border-color for all sides of an element in one declaration.
border-bottom	Shorthand property for specifying the border-width, border-style, and border-color for the bottom border of an element.
border-bottom-color	Controls the color of the bottom border.
border-bottom-style	Controls the line style of the bottom border. Values are solid, dotted, dashed, double, groove, ridge, inset, outset, or none.
border-bottom-width	Controls the thickness (width) of the bottom border.
border-collapse	Table borders are divided into two styles in CSS2: *collapsed* or *separated*. In a collapsed border, adjacent cells share borders. In a separated border, each cell has its own distinct border.
border-color	Shorthand property for specifying border-top-color, border-right-color, border-bottom-color, and border-left-color properties in one declaration.
border-left	Shorthand property for specifying the border-width, border-style, and border-color for the left border of an element.
border-left-color	Controls the color of the left border of an element.
border-left-style	Controls the line style of the left border of an element.
border-left-width	Controls the thickness (width) of the left border of an element.
border-right	Shorthand property for specifying the border-width, border-style, and border-color for the right border of an element.
border-right-color	Controls the color of the right border of an element.

Property	Description
border-right-style	Controls the line style of the right border of an element.
border-right-width	Controls the thickness (width) of the right border of an element.
border-spacing	Specifies the distance between the borders of adjacent table cells in the separated table style. The space between table cells uses the background color or image assigned to the table element. Compare to cellspacing.
border-style	Shorthand property for specifying the border-top-style, border-right-style, border-bottom-style, and border-left-style properties in one declaration.
border-top	Shorthand property for specifying the border-width, border-style, and border-color for the top border of an element.
border-top-color	Controls the color of the top border of an element.
border-top-style	Controls the line style of the top border of an element.
border-top-width	Controls the thickness (width) of the top border of an element.
border-width	Shorthand property for specifying border-top-width, border-right-width, border-bottom-width, and border-left-width properties in one declaration.

As you can see from that lengthy list, it wouldn't be practical to demonstrate all the possible border combinations in this book, but I will show you a few combinations to get your imagination started. The first thing to look at is the difference between a collapsed border and a separated border (uncollapsed).

Figure 11.13 shows these two border styles, both using a solid line style. In some browsers, the collapsed style will render in only one color, that of the table border color (as opposed to the table data cell border color).

To create those two tables, I first used the following CSS in my external style sheet:

```
table {border: 2px solid #251DC9;}
td {border: 2px solid #1F821A;
```

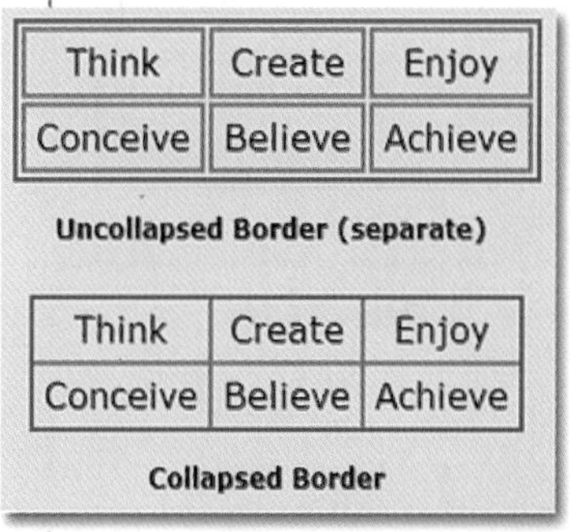

| Think | Create | Enjoy |
| Conceive | Believe | Achieve |

Uncollapsed Border (separate)

| Think | Create | Enjoy |
| Conceive | Believe | Achieve |

Collapsed Border

Figure 11.13

215

```
padding: 5px;

text-align: center;}
```

If you set only the table border property, the table will be displayed with an outline around the table. It's when you set the table data cell border property that a border is drawn around each table data cell. Here's the code (from the *body* of the page) that created the two tables:

Separated Border:

```
<table style="border-collapse: separate">

<tr><td>Think</td><td>Create</td>
<td>Enjoy</td></tr>

<tr><td>Conceive</td><td>Believe</td>
<td>Achieve</td>

</table>
```

Collapsed Border:

```
<table style="border-collapse: collapse">

<tr><td>Think</td><td>Create</td>
<td>Enjoy</td></tr>

<tr><td>Conceive</td><td>Believe</td>
<td>Achieve</td>

</table>
```

Figure 11.14 shows a slightly fancier table that uses separate border properties and a background color. Notice that the right and bottom border color is set to a darker shade than the top and left to simulate a light and shadow effect. The table code in the body is the same as the previous example; the only changes made were in the external style sheet. Here is the code for the style sheet:

```
table {border-top: 7px ridge #66DF60;

        border-right: 7px ridge #1C7517;

        border-bottom: 7px ridge #1C7517;

        border-left: 7px ridge #66DF60;}
```

| Think | Create | Enjoy |
| Conceive | Believe | Achieve |

Uncollapsed Border (separate)

| Think | Create | Enjoy |
| Conceive | Believe | Achieve |

Collapsed Border

Figure 11.14

216

```
td {background-color: #C8E4BE;
    border: 4px double #24931E;
    padding: 5px;
    text-align: center;}
```

Figure 11.15 shows a table with a double border on the top and bottom, and a solid border on both sides. The top and bottom borders are set slightly wider than the side borders. There is a double border around the table data cells, and the background color and text color are changed. Here's the code:

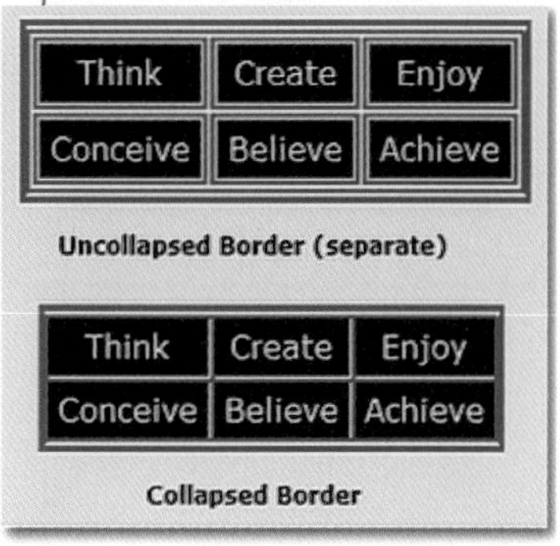

```
table {color: #CCE7FD;
       border-top: 7px double #0000A0;
       border-right: 5px solid #0000A0;
       border-bottom: 7px double #0000A0;
       border-left: 5px solid #0000A0;}
td {background-color: #000000;
    border: 4px double #0000A0;
    padding: 5px;
    text-align: center;}
```

Again, the table code is the same, but the CSS in the external style sheet has been changed. Here's one more example, using the same table:

As you can see in Figure 11.16, I used dotted lines for a really different look. Here's the code:

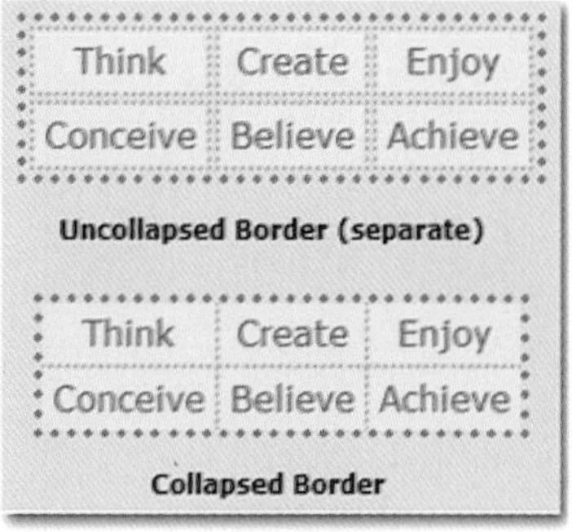

```
table {color: #285B77;
       border: 4px dotted #848348;}
td {background-color: #DDF0B9;
    border: 2px dotted #B3B175;
    padding: 5px;
    text-align: center;}
```

I could make up different looks all day; this doesn't even scratch the surface.

Figure 11.15

Figure 11.16

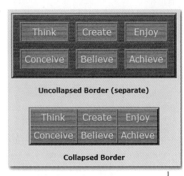

Figure 11.17

Figure 11.17 shows a table using two background images of a wood texture. Here's the code:

```
table {color: #D8DAC9;
        background: url(darkwood.jpg);
        border: 4px outset #CBB689;
        border-spacing: 12px;}
td {background: url(lightwood.jpg);
    border: 4px ridge #CBB689;
    padding: 5px;
    text-align: center;}
```

I threw these tables together rather hastily. But believe me, tables can almost be works of art if you take your time and use your imagination in creating them. I've made tables so beautiful and awe inspiring that grown men see them and weep. Mothers have named their newborns after me. People bow down before me in honor of my table skills.

No wait, they bent down to pick up food I'd spilled at the table. Oh well, at least mothers have named their babies after me. Only they spell the name differently…like "Roy" and "William" and all sorts of crazy things that don't look anything like Dennis. Silly people and the crazy ways they spell these days.

11.15 Adding Text to Blank Banners and Buttons

A TRICK NOT WIDELY KNOWN among webmasters is that you can add text to blank banners or buttons using tables. This is useful for those who don't have graphics software or graphics skills. You can find blank banners on my web site.

The trick is to use a blank banner as the background for the table cell. Here is the code from the sample on my site:

```
<table width="305" height="81" cellpadding="0"
cellspacing="0" border="0">

<tr>

<td style= "background: url(blank.jpg);" valign="middle"
align="center">
```

```
<span style="color: #6a570d; font-size: 36px;">Boogie
Jack</span>
</td>
</tr>
</table>
```

Figure 11.18 shows what text added to that blank banner looks like. Whether in this book or on my web page, you can't tell the difference between this trick and using a banner with text embedded using a graphics program.

Figure 11.18

As you can see from the code, it is just a simple, single cell table. The table's dimensions are set to the width and height of the blank banner. The cellpadding, cellspacing, and border are all set to zero to make sure none of the banner is cut off. The banner is then coded as the background image for the table cell. The valign and align attributes and values are set to center the text on the banner. The font size and color are set in a span tag using CSS. Then, just add the text and close everything out. It's pretty simple, but very effective. The only thing you have to be careful about is that the text you use on the banner actually fits within it.

The same trick can be applied on a smaller scale to blank buttons. If you have a page with 12 button links, and all the buttons are 4K in file size, that's 48K of data that needs to download before all the link buttons show. Using just one blank button, only that one button needs to download and all the buttons are there.

If you use the hover pseudo-property, the text on your link buttons will even change colors when a visitor places his or her cursor on the link text. The only difference between using this trick for link buttons instead of banners is the size of the tables and the fact that you'll be adding a link inside the table data cell instead of plain text.

11.16 Framing Pictures

HERE'S ANOTHER FUN WAY to use tables. You can add picture frames around images without knowing a lick about graphics programs. After all the hard stuff in this chapter, I had to give you something fun and easy.

Figure 11.19 shows a sketch of a weird little fellow I met a few years back while my wife and I were camping. His name was Ork Vrgldtz, that's what it sounded like anyway. I didn't have a

Figure 11.19

Ork Vrgldtz

Figure 11.20

map of the galaxy on me, so he jumped back in his funny round airplane and zoomed straight up. Man, that thing sure could go fast. He must have been from the big city.

Anyway, that picture would look a lot better if it were framed, but my graphics program must be with my map of the galaxy somewhere, so I'm going to have to use a table trick I know along with a regular background image.

Figure 11.20 shows the results of framing the picture of weird old Ork. Much nicer, don't you think?

Side note to class instructors: If anyone disagrees with me, fine them $10 and send it to me. We can't have that kind of dissension going on.

It looks like a lot of graphics work but it's just a single table with a healthy dose of CSS styling. There are two parts of the code to study: the external style sheet code and the code in the source code of the web page. Let's look at the external style sheet code first:

```
table {background: url(images/wood27.jpg);
        border: 9px outset #624D3E;
td {border: 5px inset #B0977B;
    padding: 22px;
    text-align: center;}
img.frame {border-top: 5px solid #413329;
            border-right: 5px solid #B0977B;
            border-bottom: 5px solid #B0977B;
            border-left: 5px solid #413329;}
```

In the *table* selector I set the background image. That's the wood look that fills in around the picture. I then added a 9 pixel border with an outset style. This is part of the border you see at the outer edge of the picture.

Next I added a border to the table data cell, which is the inner part of the border around the outside of the table. I also added 22 pixels of padding, which gives some space around the image for the nice wood background to display, and I set the text alignment to the center. While that isn't necessary to center the image—because the table data cell is only as wide as the image—it was necessary to center the "name plate" under the image. Because I don't want this picture frame on every image on my site, I created a class called "frame" for the image to create a border especially for this picture. I added a border to the image so it would look like it was sitting behind the image frame and matting. I colored it to create simulated light and shadow for depth. Pretty clever for a guy that once sat on a soaking wet lawn chair in the outdoor display area at a garden center and had to walk out looking like I...well, you know.

Now let's look at the source code for the picture frame:

```
1 <table border="7" width="180" height="210">

2 <tr><td>

3 <img class="frame" src="images\alien.jpg" width=
  "180" height="210">

4 <span style="background-color: #C0BE9C;

            align: center;

            width: 70px;

            height: 12px;

            font-size: 8px;"> &middot;   Ork
            Vrgldtz   &middot;</span>

5 </td></tr></table>
```

Here's what all that code means:

1. Line 1 opens the table.

2. Line 2 opens the table row and table data cell.

Employee	Monday	Tuesday	Wednesday	Thursday	Friday
Rory	9-5	9-5	9-5	Off	9-5
Eldon	9-5	9-5	9-5	9-5	Off
Judy	Off	9-5	9-5	9-5	9-5
Amber	9-5	Off	9-5	9-5	9-5
Brett	9-5	9-5	Off	9-5	9-5

Figure 11.21

3. Line 3 adds the image. I used the *frame* class to bring in the border I set in the external style sheet.

4. This is the "name plate" I added for realism. It's a span element with a background color sort of like dull brass. The text alignment is set to center and the width and height are set to control the size. The span content features Ork's name, but before and after his name is an *·* character entity, and you're probably wondering about that. That character entity is not available through the keyboard keys like other punctuation. It creates a dot in the middle of the line. I thought it would look like screws holding the nameplate on. I think it was reasonably effective. The * * entities were used to push each middot toward the ends of the span where the screws would be.

5. Table closed, put the silverware away.

As you can see, tables can be very simple or very complicated. Don't be discouraged if you don't master complicated tables right away—it takes a little practice for most folks.

11.17 Chapter 11 Exercise

GUESS WHAT YOU GET TO DO? That's right ladies and gentlemen—you get to build a table. You even get to build another web page. This has to be your lucky day!

- Open your text editor and start a new file for a new web page. In addition to the basic HTML skeleton, be sure to add the appropriate description and keywords meta tags.

- Create a table similar to the one in *Figure 11.21* showing the duty roster for your organization's call center for the coming week. Across the top row, include one column for the employees and then use column headers to list the days of the week, Monday through Friday.

Employee	Monday	Tuesday	Wednesday	Thursday	Friday
Rory	9-5	9-5	9-5	Off	9-5
Eldon	9-5	9-5	9-5	9-5	Off
Judy	Off	9-5	9-5	9-5	9-5
Amber	9-5	Off	9-5	9-5	9-5
Brett	9-5	9-5	Off	9-5	9-5

- Using a single colgroup, set the width of each of these table data cells so they are a uniform size and align the text to the center. Under that first row will be five more rows for five employees. Four are on duty each day, while one gets a rotating extra day off each week. List the employees using a table header for the first column of each row; show which employees are working and which are off. Use inline CSS to change the text color for each employee's extra day off.

I've shown many examples of different table styles, including background colors and border styles. I recommend you use CSS to dress up your table if you want to be above average.

- Pages with no color aren't much fun, so we need to add some color to the pages you've made so far. Open each page, and place a table across the top of the page using a background color of your choice.

- Use a heading tag to add your fictional organization's name inside the table. Set the color of the heading so that it looks nice with your background color and provides enough contrast to be easily read.

- For extra pizzazz, use CSS position as taught in Chapter 7, Section 7.9 to place a faux drop shadow behind the company name, as I did with the words "Online Edition" shown in Figure 7.18.

P.S.: Once you've set up your new header on one page, just copy and paste it into the other pages so you don't have to retype everything.

Frames

12

12.1 Introduction

FRAMES DIVIDE A BROWSER WINDOW into sections, and each section can display a separate web page. The sections can be visible or hidden, and each visible section can have its own scroll bar. As a result, a poorly designed site could have several scroll bars creating visual clutter and user confusion.

In the early days when the web was just becoming popular, many webmasters used frames simply because they learned how and wanted to show it off. Many web design "fads" like this have come and gone. This indiscriminate use of frames resulted in a resentment of framed sites by many (because they often weren't used properly and browser support was spotty), including a few "I hate frames" groups.

Those days are in the past, and today most webmasters only use frames when they have a legitimate reason. As webmasters learned the disadvantages of framed sites, many dropped them from their designs.

The primary disadvantage of using frames is that search engines often don't index framed sites well, and some not at all. If you do have a good reason for using frames, I recommend creating your index page without them for search engine purposes. Then, let your index page lead into the framed content. If you do use frames, some web designers advocate creating both a framed site and non-framed site to offer your visitors a choice. Of course, the larger your site, the more extra work that is.

Other disadvantages of using frames include:

● Because a framed site has to load two or more pages, depending on how many frames there are, it can be noticeably slower to load—depending on the content of the pages.

● Framed pages are harder for visitors to bookmark.

● Some browsers have problems printing framed content.

● Most people prefer non-framed content.

● Frames make navigating forward and backward less intuitive, and therefore more difficult for some users.

Given these disadvantages of using frames, it's wise to only use them if you have a very compelling reason.

12.2 An Example of Frames

Tom, Jerrod, and Dean were on a fishing trip when they had a close encounter of an alien kind. They decided they had to share their experience with the world, so they created the Alienz Zone web site to showcase their experience and research.

Figure 12.1 shows their web site, and not coincidentally, it happens to use frames.

As you can see, there is a scroll bar on the right side of the page where a scroll bar is normally found. If you look at the left side of the page, you'll see another scroll bar, just to the right of the navigation buttons. To the right of that scroll bar is a vertical divider bar, although it may be hard to see in the picture because of the reduced size.

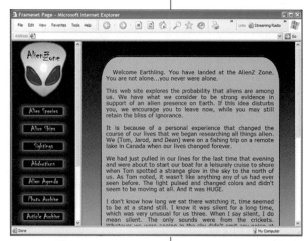

Figure 12.1

This web site is displaying two pages at once—one in the left frame that's used for navigation, and one in the right frame that contains the main content. When you click one of the links in the left frame, the page it links to opens in the right frame. This is probably the most common use of frames, and it makes updating the site's navigation easy because all the links are kept on one page. Other common uses include using frames to display a header or footer, and to display thumbnail images in one frame with the larger images opening in the main frame.

12.3 | Planning the Layout

BEFORE YOU CAN BUILD a framed site, you need to plan the layout structure. The primary considerations are:

- How many frames will the site have?
- What will be the size of the frames?
- Will any of the frames be static (no changes in content or display)?
- What content do you want your visitors to see in each frame when they first arrive at your web site?
- Will visitors be allowed to resize the frames?
- Will any of the frame borders be hidden?
- Which frame(s) will change in response to links being activated?
- Will your home page be framed or unframed for search engines?
- If the home page is unframed, will you offer visitors a choice between a framed and unframed site?

Before you start coding the web site, it's often more productive to plan it out on paper first. Draw a sketch of the layout, make notes as to the content in each frame, write down where the links will open, and try to foresee any problems that may occur. It's better to solve problems ahead of time than to discover them after you have several hours work into the project.

12.4 | The Basic Frameset

THE *FRAMESET* SPECIFIES THE LAYOUT, or views, of the frames. A standard HTML document has one HEAD section and one BODY section. A frameset document has a HEAD section, too, but it utilizes the FRAMESET in place of the BODY. Here's the basic frameset structure:

```
<html>
<head>
<title> Site Title Here </title>
</head>
```

```
<frameset>
    ...frames are described here.
</frameset>
</html>
```

Where it says "frames are described here," you code the structure, or layout, of the actual frames along with the frame sizes, frame sources, and a few other options.

This is the same structure of a standard HTML document, except the frameset replaces the body. This is because the frameset instructs the browser how to display the contents of other HTML documents; from a technical standpoint the frameset itself does not offer content.

Frames can be placed in vertical columns or horizontal rows, but not both. However, you can nest framesets, which allows you to have both horizontal and vertical frames.

12.5 The Alienz Zone Frameset

THE FRAMESET USED FOR THE Alienz Zone is very simple. It is composed of two frame columns. Here's the code for it:

```
1 <html>
2 <head>
3 <title>Web Site Title Here</title>
4 </head>
5 <frameset cols="212,*">
6 <frame src="nav.html" />
7 <frame src="main.html" />
8 </frameset>
9 </html>
```

Lines 1–4 you should already be familiar with, so we'll first examine the code in line 5. The Alienz site uses two columns. The "cols" part is short for columns, so we are setting the frameset to use columns and setting the width of the columns in this line. If we wanted two rows instead of columns we'd use *rows* in place of *cols* in this line of code.

The values for the cols attribute are (212,*). The 212 sets the first column width to 212 pixels wide, which is the space needed for the navigation buttons to display without creating a horizontal scroll bar. The asterisk (*) is a wild card that tells the browser to use the rest of the horizontal space available for this column after the 212 pixels are set aside for column one.

The columns are coded in order of appearance from left to right. For three columns, code another column into the *cols* value. For example, let's say we want one more frame of 180 pixels on the right side for advertisements. Our frameset would look like this:

```
<frameset cols="212,*,180">
```

That sets up three frames, with the frames on both ends a fixed width and the frame in the middle taking up the remaining space. The values are separated by commas. The W3C shows no space after the commas, but it doesn't seem to matter whether spaces are used. Still, I recommend following the W3C examples.

Frame widths can also be specified in percentages, or in any combination of set widths, percentages, and the wild card setting. I think it's best not to mix a hard-coded set width with a percentage width, but here's an example of the code anyway:

```
<frameset cols="212,*,20%">
```

In lines 6 and 7 after the frameset element, we add the source of the HTML pages to display in the frames. You must have an equal number of columns and frame sources or one frame will be blank. The syntax for adding the frame sources is:

```
<frame src="path/page">
```

Replace *path/page* with the path to the HTML page and the HTML page name and extension. The order you enter the frame sources in is the order in which they will display in the frames. Since "nav.html" is coded first in the Alienz frameset, it opens in the first frame on the left, the one set to be 212 pixels wide. That leaves "main.html" to open in the second frame. The first frame source displays in the first frame, the second frame source in the second frame, and so on. You can have as many frames as you need, though carrying it too far gets complicated for you and can be confusing to your visitors. Too many frames also creates clutter and can be constricting for content display.

Line 8 closes out the frameset and then the document is closed. That's the basics of creating a framed web site.

12.6 Targeting Links

ONCE THE BASIC FRAMESET is created and you can see your HTML documents load in the appropriate frames, you need to know how to target the links to open in the correct frame. If no link target is given, the links will open in the same frame where they appear.

To target a link, the frame where you want the link to open must have a name. In the case of the Alienz web site, the site navigation links are in the left frame and the content is in the right frame. In the frameset, the content frame was coded as:

```
<frame src="main.html" />
```

As it is, this frame doesn't have a name yet, so let's give it a name. Since this is the main frame, "main" is probably a pretty good name to use.

```
<frame src="main.html" name="main" />
```

As you can see, all we need to do is give it a *name* attribute and value. The name can be pretty much anything you like as long as it doesn't include any special characters. You could even name the frame "Dennis" after me—although I might be a character, I'm not special enough to cause a problem. ☺

Targeting a link to a frame works the same as targeting a link to a new window:

```
<a href="alien_ships.html" target="main">link text
or button here</a>
```

The code in red sets the link target, in this case the frame named "main." If you target a link with a name that isn't one of the real frame names, it will open the link in a new window.

There are four reserved target names for framed layouts:

Reserved Name	Frameset Action
_blank	Loads the linked document into a new browser window.
_parent	Loads the linked document into the immediate frameset parent of the current frame. This value is the same as "_self" if the current frame has no parent. The "_parent" is used where one frameset is nested inside another frameset. A link in one of the inner framesets with "_parent" as the target will load the new document in place of the inner frameset.

_self	Loads the linked document into the same frame the link is in.
_top	Loads the linked document into the full browser, replacing the frames.

It's not possible to open two different pages in two different frames from one link using only HTML (unless the link simply rebuilds the frameset, which usually isn't practical or desirable). While this book isn't intended to teach JavaScript, I am going to include a JavaScript that will load two different pages into two different frames from one link—because if I don't I'll receive emails asking how to do it. Here's part one of the JavaScript:

```
<script type="text/JavaScript">
function doubleLinks()
{
top.frameName1.location.href="upDate1.html";
top.frameName2.location.href="upDate2.html";
}
</script>
```

That part can be inserted in the HEAD section of the web page or the body of the page containing the link you want to use in order to change two different frames with one link. In each red line you'll need to change two things. Change *frameName1* and *frameName2* to the names of the frames you want to change. Change *upDate1.html* and *upDate2.html* to the names of the files you want to load into the two frames.

The second part is the link itself:

```
<a href="javascript: doubleLinks ()">link text here</a>
```

That's how it's done, but not all browsers will be able to activate the links. While very few browsers do not have JavaScript capability, some users may have JavaScript turned off in the browser preferences for security reasons. On my site, a fraction of 1 percent of readers do not have JavaScript capabilities, but it's something you may want to consider before using it.

As long as I'm at it, here's one more script. This one prevents your site from loading in someone else's frames. If someone tries to link to a page on your site and have it display as their own content inside their frames, this will rewrite the page, removing their frames and loading your page instead.

```
<body onLoad="if (self != top) top.location = self.location">
```

As you can see, the *onLoad* script (shown in red text) goes in the <body> tag of your web page.

12.7   Frame Borders

IN A FRAMESET, THE BORDER is a divider between frames. There are two ways to control this divider, one is W3C legal and the other isn't. The one that isn't legal seems to be supported by most browsers, and it gives you another coding option, so I'll show them both to you.

Figure 12.2 shows a close-up of the border between the two frames on the Alienz web site. That's the border I'm talking about. To remove the border the legal way, the attribute:

```
frameborder="0"
```

Figure 12.2

...is added to the frame element. The full code for the first frame of the Alienz web site would be:

```
<frame src="nav.html" frameborder="0" />
```

The possible values you may use are:

1 (tells the browser to draw a border)

0 (tells the browser not to draw a border)

The previous code removes half the border you see in Figure 12.2, but the same attribute and value needs to be added to the other frame source to remove the other half of the border—almost. What "almost" means is that it doesn't quite remove the whole border. In some browsers, approximately 3 pixels of the border is left behind—even more in other browsers. So much for doing things the right way; now let's look at what actually works.

Instead of coding a frameborder attribute into the frame source, you can code a simple border attribute into the frameset element:

```
<frameset cols="212,*" border="0">
```

That code completely removes the border in most, if not all, browsers. While it may not be XHTML compliant, it's what you have to do to remove the border completely. You can also set the border to be wider, although I don't know why anyone would want to do that. Well, hey, I don't know everything!

As long as I'm being sneaky and showing you unofficial code because it works better than official code, I may as well add one more unofficial log to the fire. You can set the border color using the *bordercolor* attribute.

```
<frameset cols="212,*" border="3" bordercolor=
"#329ad7">
```

The bordercolor value can be any hex color code or any named color. This should be tested in multiple browsers to make sure you like the look because it doesn't work the same in all browsers. In some browsers, adding a bordercolor to one frame affects the color of all the borders on all the frames. In other browsers, this code may only change the border color for the one frame. See what happens when you live outside of legal code... danger lurks at every turn. Danger Will Robinson, danger!

12.8 Margins

AS YOU MIGHT GUESS, the margins of a frame specify the distance between the page content within the frame and the edge of the frame. Sometimes the default value is too great or too small, so you can adjust the margin using the *marginheight* and *marginwidth* attributes with a frame source element.

The marginheight controls the space above and below the content, while marginwidth controls the space to the left and right sides of the content.

```
<frame src="nav.html" marginheight="0"
marginwidth="0" />
```

That code sets the marginheight and marginwidth to zero pixels. The marginheight and marginwidth values don't have to be the same, and you don't have to use them both. Using only one, however, causes some browsers to use whichever value you specify for both marginheight and marginwidth.

12.9 Scrollbars

THE DEFAULT SETTING FOR SCROLLBARS is that scrollbars appear only as needed. You can control this behavior, however, using the *scrolling* attribute with the frame source element.

```
<frame src="nav.html" scrolling="no" />
```

The values for the scrolling attribute are either *yes*, *no*, or *auto*. If you want the scroll bars to appear only when needed, you don't really need to set the scrolling value to auto—simply do not include the scrolling attribute.

12.10 Resizing

BY DEFAULT, IF USERS WANT TO resize frames, they can "grab" the border and move it—as long as the border isn't set to zero. If you use borders and don't want visitors resizing frames, you can prevent resizing using the *noresize* attribute with frame source.

```
<frame src="nav.html" noresize="noresize" />
```

There are no other values for the noresize attribute.

12.11 Nesting Frames

THE GUYS AT THE ALIENZ ZONE web site decided to add a graphic of outer space to the top of their frameset to create a little more color and visual interest. So they added a frameset with a narrow row across the top of their site and a large row below it that contained their old frameset consisting of the original two columns.

This is a fairly typical layout for sites that use both rows and columns. The header in the small frame row across the top is usually static (a frame that never changes). The second row under that usually contains a narrow navigation column on the left and a main content area on the right that utilizes the remaining horizontal space under the header. See Figure 12.3 for a visual reference.

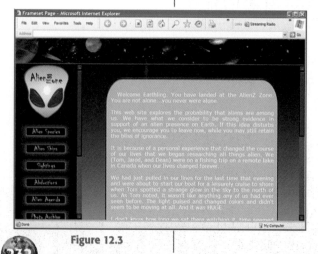

Figure 12.3

Here's the code for that:

```
1 <html>
2 <head>
3 <title>Frameset Page</title>
4 </head>
5 <frameset rows="80,*" border="0">
6 <frame src="head.html" />
7 <frameset cols="212,*" border="0">
8 <frame src="nav.html" />
9 <frame src="main.html" name="main" />
10 </frameset>
11 </frameset>
12 </html>
```

Lines 1–4:	These lines haven't changed.
Line 5:	This line opens the new frameset. Since this is coded for rows instead of columns, the first frame is measured 80 pixels from the top down rather than from left to right. The second row is coded with the wildcard so it will fill the remaining vertical space. This is the row under the skinny top frame.
Line 6:	This line provides the frame source for the first row at the top of the frameset.
Lines 7–9:	These lines are the original frameset with both frame sources.
Lines 10–11:	Up to this point, all the frames needed are opened. Because two framesets were opened, two framesets have to be closed, as shown.
Line 12:	This closes the frameset document.

A very common mistake people make when trying to build a frameset is that they code the opening frameset's first row and then try to add the vertical columns after that without realizing *the columns are contained in the second row*. So they fail to add the second row to the opening frameset.

That will not work at all. Some browsers repeat the first row over and over, others display a blank page, and I heard that one browser even jumps right out of your monitor and slaps you silly. Figure 12.4 may help you visualize how nested frames work. Frameset 1 is rows 1 and 2; frameset 2 is columns 1 and 2 and are placed in row 2.

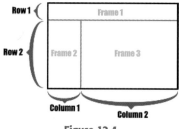

Figure 12.4

12.12 Noframes Element

THE *NOFRAMES* ELEMENT ALLOWS you to place content in a frameset for browsers that do not support frames. It is nested inside a frameset element.

```
<html>
<head>
<title>Web Site Title Here</title>
</head>
<frameset cols="212,*">
<frame src="nav.html" />
<frame src="main.html" />
<noframes>
<body>
...page content...
</body>
</noframes>
</frameset>
</html>
```

The code in red shows how to add the *noframes* option. Once the noframes declaration is made, the <body> tag is added because there is none for a frameset. In the body, place any content you'd normally place on a web page. This is the content that browsers that can't parse frames will display. Browsers that can handle frames will show the frameset. Once you've added your content, simply close the body and noframes tags and you're good to go.

Some search engines will look at the noframes content, allowing them to index at least part of your web site. Many search engines, however, do not do a good job of indexing noframes content and have a hard time following links in framesets. Again, be aware that using frames can have negative consequences with search engines.

12.13 Considerations

IN A NUTSHELL, consider the following when using frames:

- Don't play games with frames. In other words, make sure you have a good reason for using frames because the downside shouldn't be taken lightly.

- If you intend to use frames, consider an unframed version of your web site for those with browsers that can't parse frames and for visitors who don't like them.

- When linking to the home page from interior pages, do not link directly to the frameset page unless it's properly targeted or it will open a new frameset within the current frameset; instead, use the page source for the main frame and remember to target it to the main frame.

- Don't turn off the scrolling unless you're positive the content will fit in the frame with no need for scroll bars.

- Don't forget to name the frames intended for content that will be replaced by other content, and remember to add the target attribute to the links.

- Never display someone else's web page within your frameset. Either use "target=_top" so the link replaces your frames or open the page in a new window.

12.14 Inline Frames

AN INLINE FRAME OR IFRAME (sometimes called a floating frame) is sort of a "window" on a web page that you can look through to view content from another source. It allows you to have content changes on a portion of a page via links targeted to the iframe, without having to reload the entire page or making a frameset page.

Browsers treat inline frames as embedded objects, meaning they can be placed in the flow of text like images. Inline frames can have the following attributes:

Attribute	Description
frameborder	Set to 1 to display the border or to 0 to hide the border.
height	Sets the height of the iframe (in pixels).
width	Sets the width of the iframe (in pixels).
marginheight	Sets the distance between the content and the iframe's top and bottom edges.
marginwidth	Sets the distance between the content and the iframe's left and right edges.
name	Allows you to name the iframe in order to target links to load in it.
scrolling	Set to yes to have scrollbars, no to hide them, or auto to let them appear as needed.
Src	Sets the initial external file to load in the iframe when the page loads.
style	Use CSS to pretty up the iframe like a night on the town!

An iframe is coded into the *body* of an HTML document wherever you want it to appear on the page. The syntax is:

```
<iframe src="page_source.html"></iframe>
```

Not all browsers support iframes, so rather than opening and closing an iframe as shown in the previous example, it's wise to include alternate content as well. To do that, place a link to the alternate content between the opening and closing iframe tag set.

```
<iframe src="page_source.html">

Your browser does not support inline frames. Please

<a href="alternate.html">click here</a> to access
the content.

</iframe>
```

Hey, that was easy!

So that you're not left wondering forever what an iframe looks like, Figure 12.5 shows a web page with an iframe in the upper-right corner.

The styles I used in the iframe window were set in the page that loads into the iframe, page_source.html in this example.

To target links to open in the iframe, you need to give it a name. The name attribute is added just as you learned from other examples:

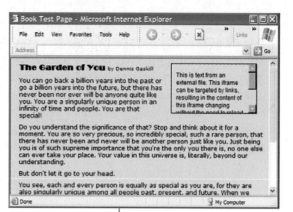

Figure 12.5

```
<iframe src="page_source.html" name="Fred">
alternate content </iframe>
```

As you can see, I named the iframe Fred. I name a lot of things Fred, and I don't really know why. I just do.

Now, to target a link to open in the iframe, add the target attribute to the link:

```
<a href="next.html" target="#Fred">Next Page</a>
```

Notice that the hash mark is included before the target name. This tells the browser that the target is on the same page as the link.

That's it…you've been framed.

12.15 Chapter 12 Exercise

I N THIS EXERCISE, you get to build a frameset and the corresponding web pages. The frame set will be a two-column layout with the left frame serving as a navigation frame and the right frame containing the main content area. You'll be making a total of five new web pages and modifying an existing page. Before you groan too loudly, don't fret, the new pages are all fairly simple and the modified page is only adding a link. Besides, you wanted to learn this, remember?

- Start by creating a two-column frameset. Use a set width for the navigation column and the wildcard character for the width of the main content area. In the left frame, set the scrollbars to none as there will be very little content. Set the frames so they cannot be resized by the user. Name the main content area so you can target links to it.

- For the navigation page, create a bare-bones web page with just three links. Make the first link a link back to the home page (your site's main index.html page). Be sure to target the link so that it opens in the entire window, and not into a frame.

- Make the second link to a page with a "forward vision statement." (A forward vision statement offers a brief overview of future plans). You will need to write this information.

- Make the final link to a page that contains a brief outline of your organization's history. Obviously you'll have to write this information as well.

Be sure to target the second and third link so they open in the main content frame. To summarize, the navigation page will have three links: Home, Vision, and History.

- For the content that loads in the main content frame (until users click a link in the navigation frame), create a page that thanks users for wanting to learn more about your organization and offers a synopsis of the current state of the organization.

- After you've made the frameset, the navigation page, and the main frame for content, you need to create the "vision" and "history" pages. To recap, this includes the frameset, the navigation page, the original main content page with the state of the organization, the future vision page, and the history page.

- Open the source code for your index page and add a link to an "About Us" page in the floating division on the right side of the page.

Make sure all your links work and that the frames work as intended.

Forms

13.1   Introduction

U P TO THIS POINT, this book has focused on how to present your information to others. Forms, on the other hand, provide an interactive way to obtain information *from* your web site visitors. Through the use of forms you can ask for suggestions, receive feedback, offer opinion polls, take product orders, add subscribers to a newsletter, and obtain other information about your customers and their opinions.

Forms can be processed by plain email or by server side scripts. CGI (**C**ommon **G**ateway **I**nterface) scripts are small software programs that can be (or often already are) installed on a web host's server when you open an hosting account. CGI server side scripts are the most common form processing scripts in use today. Because server side scripts are not part of HTML, and because of the variety of scripts and server configurations, this chapter covers only the email method of form processing.

If you choose to use a script to process your forms, you'll need to first find out which (if any) scripts your web host provides. Or, you can search for a script to install on your own. Once the script issue is settled, you need to learn to work with the specific script and web host you are using.

Forms consist of various form elements that allow for user input. These elements are called *control elements*. A control element in which users can enter information or make a selection is called a *field*. The information they enter into the field or input by selection is called the *field value*, or simply *value*, which is not the same thing as an attribute value.

The various form elements include:

- checkboxes
- form buttons
- input boxes
- radio buttons
- selection lists
- textareas

When planning which fields to include in forms, keep in mind that long forms tend to discourage people from filling them out. The more work it is to complete a form, the more people will simply not bother with it. Other reasons that contribute to a poor participation rate for completing forms include:

- Too many form field options that take time to read.
- Too many questions that require thinking (as opposed to questions that can be answered based on feelings or gut reactions).
- Too many text fields in which users have to type instead of clicking their mouse button to make a selection.
- Too much personal information requested.
- Poorly designed forms that are hard to figure out.
- Multipage forms that give no indication to users how many pages are included.

You can have more than one form on a page, and you can place regular content such as text and images within a form. Forms are often placed inside a table to tidy up the appearance—otherwise forms can quickly become quite ragged looking.

13.2 Planning a Form

IF A FORM WILL HAVE MORE than two or three fields, it helps to plan ahead before you start laying it out. If you plan ahead, you won't have to redesign the form when you realize it isn't working out well.

First, determine what form fields your form needs. Make a rough sketch of how it will be laid out on the page. Figure 13.1 shows the sketch I made for a subscription form for a newsletter.

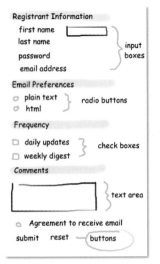

Figure 13.1

I divided this form into five sections:

- Registrant information
- Email preferences
- Frequency of mailings
- User comments
- An unmarked section that asks the user to agree to receive email along with the submit and reset buttons

Organizing a form in this manner will help encourage visitors to complete it. Rather than seeing a boatload of questions, they see a small number of specific sections, making the process of filling out the form seem simpler and less time consuming.

13.3 Beginning a Form

A FORM BEGINS WITH THE <FORM> element declaration. Amazing, isn't it? It may surprise you to learn that the </form> tag ends the form. Not a surprise? Good, that means you're catching on nicely.

A form can be placed anywhere in the body of a web page document. There are no special design rules or layout requirements for forms, so you need to use layout techniques such as tables and CSS styles to control the appearance and placement of forms and form elements.

There are two attributes to the <form> tag that *must* be included for a typical submission form to be processed. The *action* attribute directs the browser to the processing agent, be it a form processing script or an email link.

The *method* attribute specifies which HTTP method, *get* or *post*, to use to process the form data. The *get* method is used when the form processing is idempotent—that is, the submission doesn't cause any side effects such as modifying a database. A search engine query is a typical use of the get method. The *post* method is used when form processing does cause a side effect, such as adding a user name to a database or sending the submission via email. We will use the post method to build a form in this chapter since the form will be processed using email.

To begin a form and include the two necessary attributes:

```
<form method="post" action="mailto:you@your_
address.com">
```

Of course, on your own form you would need to change "you@your_address.com" to the email address you want the form data sent to. You can send form results to more than one email address by including a second address after the first, separated by a semicolon:

```
<form method="post" action="mailto:you@address1.com;me@address2.com">
```

While the above code will process a form submission and send an email to you with the submitted information, the results may be practically unreadable. In fact, the file may have so many extraneous characters that you'll decide it isn't worth your time to decipher it. This is because browsers encode form data before passing it on to the server. Without a form processing script, what you receive is the encoded data unless you set the encoding through the *enctype* attribute. To do this, add:

```
enctype="text/plain"
```

...to the opening form tag. You will then be able to read what arrives in your email inbox. If you use a server side script to process the form submission, you probably won't need the enctype attribute because the form processing script will take care of the encoding. If you use the email method for processing, however, you will want to use the enctype attribute. For this type of form processing, here's the final opening form element:

```
<form method="post" action="mailto:you@your_address.com" enctype="text/plain">
```

If you have more than one form on a page and need to know which one was used to submit data, you can include either a name attribute or id attribute with the opening form tag. Some processing agents may require forms to be named as well (rather than it being an option). This is as simple as adding one of the following attributes to the opening form element:

```
name="value"

id="value"
```

In either attribute, replace the word *value* with the name or ID you want to call the form. Which should you use? The *name* attribute is the older standard and offers the best compatibility with older browsers and older servers. The *id* attribute is the current standard for HTML and XHTML. It's best to use both for maximum compatibility.

Now that you've learned all about opening a form, let's start building the form.

13.4 Text Input Boxes

I AM NOT DEMONSTRATING HOW I BUILT the table that tidies up the form because of the extra code you will need to sift through. I did, however, include the entire table and CSS code at the end of this chapter so you can study it on your own. Since you have presumably read Chapter 11: Tables already, you shouldn't have too much trouble with the code if you study it carefully.

Most of the control elements that a user either fills in with text or chooses from multiple options are called *input elements*. The first part of our form calls for four single-line text input boxes. Figure 13.2 shows a screen capture of this section of the form. The syntax for a text input box is:

<input type="*value*" name="*value*" size="*value*" />

Where it says *value,* substitute the appropriate value for the given attribute. For the type attribute, the options are as follows.

Registrant Information

First Name:

Last Name:

Choose Password:

Email Address:

Figure 13.2

Input Type	Description	Appearance*
button	Displays a clickable button to perform an action.	Button Label
checkbox	Displays a selectable checkbox.	☑ (Descriptive text)
file	Displays a browse button for selecting a file to upload to the host site.	Browse
hidden	Creates a hidden form field.	(no display)
image	Displays an inline image that can perform an action when clicked. A common example is a custom submit button.	Order Now Click Here
password	Displays a text input box that hides the entered text behind anonymous characters.	••••••
radio	Displays a selectable radio button.	○ (Descriptive text)
reset	Creates a button that resets all form values.	Reset Form
submit	Displays a button that submits the form data.	Submit
text	Displays a single-line text input box.	

* These elements may look different from the examples shown here. The browser brand and version, computer operating system, and CSS styles in use all can affect the appearance of the input fields.

Since the first part of the form being built is a text input box, we enter *text* as the type value.

```
<input type="text" name="value" size="value" />
```

For the name value, the name can be anything. Since the purpose of using it is to identify the part of the form the user is responding to when the data is submitted, it makes sense to use a name that identifies the form field. As you can see in Figure 13.2, the first text input box is for the user's first name, so that is what we enter as the name value:

```
<input type="text" name="First Name" size="value" />
```

The last attribute in an input box is the size. The size for an input box differs from the other size values covered so far. A size value of "12" for example, creates a box length that is approximately the size of 12 text characters. That makes determining the size a bit of a guessing game at first. You first specify a size and then adjust the number up or down to lengthen or shorten the box until it is the size you want.

In the example from Figure 13.2, the text input box is set to size 40:

```
<input type="text" name="First Name" size="40" />
```

That is the complete code for the first text input box. The other four text input boxes are similar, with only the name attribute's value different, with one exception. First, here is the code for all four text input boxes:

```
<input type="text" name="First Name" size="40" />

<input type="text" name="Last Name" size="40" />

<input type="password" name="Password" size="40" />

<input type="text" name="Email" size="40" />
```

Notice the third line of code. Rather than using "text" as the type attribute value, the value is "password" for this input box. That hides the text the user enters behind anonymous characters so anyone watching the user filling out the form will not see the password the user enters.

When you receive a form submitted by email with these elements, it will look something like this:

```
First Name: Joe

Last Name: Somebody

Password: tr98z3mn

Email: joes@domain.com
```

Of course, each of those items returns the actual values of the submitted data. In other words, each first name, last name, password, and email address are unique to the user who submitted the data. I know this will be hard to believe, but not everyone that visits your web site will be named Joe Somebody. Really.

A text input box can already have text inside the box when the page loads. For example, if a text input box calls for the user's web site address, as a courtesy you might include the "http://" part in the box to begin the address. You do this by adding a value attribute to the input box code. For example:

```
<input type="text" name="URL" size="40" value=
"http://" />
```

The code in red shows how to add a value. On a web page, that appears as shown in Figure 13.3.

Web Site: [http://   ]

Figure 13.3

Whatever text you enter into the value attribute displays inside the text input box. You can also limit the number of characters a user can enter into a text input box.

```
<input type="text" name="Email" size="40"
maxlength="40" />
```

In the example above, the user is limited to entering 40 characters (spaces count as characters). You need to be careful in setting input limitations—for example, if you set a limit on a text input box for email addresses, some users with long addresses may not be able to enter their full email addresses. Limiting the number of characters a user can enter is typically used for data with a known quantity value such as a ZIP code or telephone prefix; this helps prevent users from making mistakes.

There is no closing tag for a text input box. To be XHTML compliant, you need to close it with a space and forward slash at the end.

13.5 Radio Buttons

Figure 13.4

THE NEXT ITEMS ON THE FORM are radio buttons. Figure 13.4 shows a screen shot of my form. In this example, the radio buttons offer the user a choice of receiving plain text email or HTML email. The buttons are coded like this:

```
<input type="radio" value="text" name="Email
Preference" />

<input type="radio" value="html" name="Email
Preference" />
```

Notice that both radio buttons have "Email Preference" as the *name* value. When two or more radio buttons have the same name value, it limits the user to selecting only one option. If the user tries to select a second item with the same name value, the first item is automatically deselected. In this case, it is assumed the user would prefer one or the other—plain text email or HTML based email—but not both.

The input *type* with the value of *radio* creates the radio input device because radio is the value entered for it. The *value* attribute identifies which choice the user made when the form is processed, in this case, either *plain text* or *HTML*. An email sent to you with HTML email as the selected option might look something like this:

```
Email Preference: html
```

Note

When I say it "might" look something like this, it's because the way it actually looks depends on how your email client is set up to display messages.

A radio button can be preselected. For example, if you know the greater percentage of your visitors prefer HTML-formatted email, you can have that radio button already selected. If a user prefers plain text, the preselected item is deselected when he or she clicks the plain text option. To preselect an item:

```
<input type="radio" value="html" name="Email
Preference" checked="checked" />
```

○ Plain Text

◉ HTML

Figure 13.5

With that code, the web page appears as shown in Figure 13.5. In this case, if the user doesn't change the selection, the *value* (HTML) of the *value attribute* is what is submitted via the email sent to you. It seems a little confusing to talk about the value of the value, but this is how the powers that be have decided it should be.

Note that some authors instruct you to simply add "checked" to the radio button without the "="*checked*"" part attached to it. In HTML that's OK, but it's not XHTML compliant. In HTML, that's known as a *valueless* attribute, or sometimes a *minimized* attribute. Valueless attributes are legal in HTML but illegal in XHTML. There is a list of valueless attributes in Appendix A: HTML and XHTML, along with the correct way to write them.

There is no closing tag for a radio button. To be XHTML compliant, you need to close it with a space and forward slash at the end.

13.6 Checkboxes

THE NEXT SECTION OF OUR FORM calls for two checkboxes as shown in Figure 13.6. Checkboxes are similar to radio buttons, but they allow the user to select multiple options. In this example, a user could select both the daily updates and the weekly digest if he or she wanted to receive both. Here's the code for the two checkboxes:

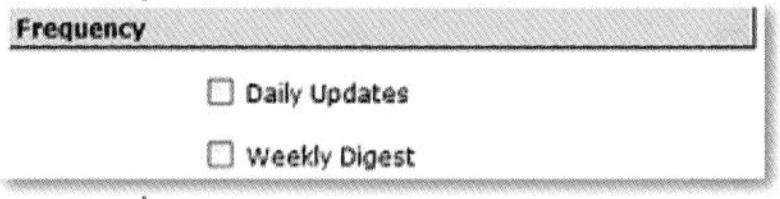

Figure 13.6

```
<input type="checkbox" value="daily" name=
"Frequency" />

<input type="checkbox" value="weekly" name=
"Frequency" />
```

In this example the *name* value is the same for both checkboxes, just as it was for the radio buttons, but with checkboxes the user isn't limited to just one choice. If a user opted to receive both the daily email and weekly digest it would show up in the email to you something like this:

```
Frequency: daily
Frequency: weekly
```

Checkboxes can also be preselected so they already have a checkmark in them when the page loads. The attribute and value to preselect a checkbox is the same as for a radio button, the difference is that if a user selects another checkbox, the preselected checkbox is not deselected. Here's the attribute and value to preselect a checkbox:

```
checked="checked"
```

There is no closing tag for checkboxes, so you must close them by including the space and forward slash at the end.

13.7 Textarea Box

THE NEXT ELEMENT ON THE FORM is a textarea box used for comments. A textarea box can be used for other purposes, but is mostly used for comments and feedback.

Figure 13.7 shows the Comments box on the form. Users are able to click inside the box and type the message they want to send. It's similar to a text input box, except a textarea box can be more than one row tall. The code for this textarea box is:

Comments

Figure 13.7

```
<textarea name="Comments" cols="46" rows="4">
</textarea>
```

The size of the textarea box is determined by the *cols* and *rows* attributes. The cols attribute works the same as for the text input box; with the "46" in this example being roughly equivalent to 46 characters wide. The rows attribute refers to how many rows of text can be typed into the box before the first line scrolls out of view.

You can also have a message appear inside a textarea box when the page loads. For example, if you want the message "Your feedback is valuable to us!" to appear inside the textarea box, to encourage visitors to send in comments, you add that text between the textarea opening and closing tags. See Figure 13.8 for a visual reference. Here's how to do that:

`Your feedback is valuable to us!`

Figure 13.8

```
<textarea name="Comments" cols="46" rows="4">
Your feedback is valuable to us!
</textarea>
```

Whatever text you include between the opening and closing tags appears inside the textarea box when the page loads. You cannot include images, links, or any other content—if you try to include other elements, visitors see raw code.

When a form is submitted, the words in a textarea box are normally submitted as entered, with line breaks only where the user pressed the Enter key. While the user is typing, text does wrap to the next line, but the text is not sent to you as he or she sees it. You can set word wrapping to change this behavior:

```
<textarea name="Feedback" cols="30" rows="5"
wrap="value">
```

There are three values for the wrap attribute:

Value	What It Does
Off	No word wrapping as the user types or as the information is sent except where the user presses the Enter key to start a new line.
physical	Text is wrapped within the textarea box and sent to you just as the user sees it. Many prefer this option because the user sees what you will see.
virtual	Text is wrapped within the textarea box for presentation to the user, but it is sent to you wrapped only where the user presses the Enter key.

Substitute one of the values from the chart for the word *value* in the code sample and you'll have the kind of word wrapping you prefer.

13.8 Submit and Reset Buttons

THE SAMPLE FORM, which is for subscribing to an email newsletter, ends with a radio button that is preselected to indicate the user agrees to receive email from the web site. This helps protect the newsletter owner from accusations of spamming by the user by getting the user's agreement in black and white. Since we already covered radio buttons, we'll go right to the submit and reset button code. Here's the code for those two buttons:

```
<input type="submit" value="Submit" style="width:
120px;" />
```

```
<input type="reset" value="Reset Form" style="width:
120px;" />
```

There are no closing tags for these buttons. To be XHTML compliant, you need to close them with a space and forward slash. By entering *submit* or *reset* as the value for the *type* attribute, the Submit and Reset buttons are automatically created by

☑ I agree to receive email from BoogieJack.com

| Submit | | Reset Form |

Figure 13.9

the browser. The text on the buttons is whatever text you place inside the *value* attribute. See Figure 13.9 for a visual reference.

I used inline CSS to add a uniform width to the two buttons. If I didn't, the button width is determined by the text in the value attribute. With an uneven length of characters in the two button values, the button widths are not uniform, and uniform buttons look better to me.

This code wraps up the form I sketched out. At the end of the chapter, I included a screen capture of the entire form and all the code for it. Before we come to that, however, there are more form elements to cover.

You can create a custom submit button using *image* for the input type. Any image button used becomes a "submit" button. There is no image option for a reset button, but as you'll soon see, you can use an image as a reset button as well. But first, here's how to code an image button that will act as a submit button:

```
<input type="image" src="YourButton.jpg" />
```

There is another kind of button you can use to create a reset button from an image to match a custom submit button. Here's how that's coded:

```
<button type="reset"><img src="images/order.jpg" />
</button>
```

It's simply a <button> element with a *type* value set to *reset*. Then, plug in your button image and cancel the button. I left the height and width out of the button to make it easier to read the code, but you should include them with an image button. If you do create a custom reset button using the <button> tag, do the submit button the same way if you want the buttons to match.

Figure 13.10 shows two buttons that use the same image. The top image is what the <button> tag does to the image. As you can see, it adds space and a border so it can work like a true form button, changing its appearance when clicked to look as if it's being pressed down.

| Reset |

| Reset |

Figure 13.10

The bottom button uses CSS to remove all the excess space, but it still allows the button to change appearance when it's clicked. The browser still adds a small border, but by setting the size right, it looks to be a part of the button graphic. If you use the input element with an image value, the button will look just

250

like the image, but it won't change its look when it's clicked. If you want to use image buttons and have them change their looks, using the <button> tag with CSS is the way to go for both. Here's the code I used for the bottom button:

```
<button type="reset" style="width: 108px; height: 24px;">

<img src="images/reset.jpg"></button>
```

It's just a matter of using CSS to set the width and height, then tweaking the numbers until it looks just right.

13.9 Selection Lists

SELECTION LISTS OFFER ANOTHER WAY to present a series of choices for users to pick from. They can be in the form of a drop-down list or scrollable window.

Figure 13.11 shows examples of both types. *Example 1* is an unopened drop-down list. *Example 1.2* shows the same drop-down list after the down arrow is clicked to expose the list. If the list is too long to fit on the page, a scrollbar is automatically added so all the options are visible and can be selected. Here's the code for the drop-down list:

Figure 13.11

```
<select name="TV">

<option>Comedy</option>

<option>Drama</option>

<option>Educational</option>

<option>Movies</option>

<option>Nature</option>

<option>Science</option>

<option>Sci-Fi</option>

<option>Soaps</option>

<option>Sports</option>

</select>
```

This drop-down lists offers options for the user's favorite kind of TV programming. I can't believe I left reality shows and game shows off the list.

Example 2 shows a scrolling list. The code for both a drop-down list and a scrolling list is the same with the exception of a size attribute added to the scrolling list. By adding the size attribute, a drop-down list is automatically converted to a scrolling list. *Example 2* shows the scrolling list with the size set to 3. The size determines how many list options can be viewed without scrolling. My selection list has nine options. *Example 3* shows the same list with the size set to 9—just enough to reveal all the list options with no need for scrolling (therefore, no scrollbar is present).

The code for a scrolling list is the same as for a drop-down list except for the size attribute added to the opening <select> tag:

```
<select size="3">
```

A selection list can also have a preselected option. Do this by adding the selected attribute and value to the option you want preselected.

```
<option selected="selected">Option Item</option>
```

Whichever option you preselect in the code is selected when the page loads.

By default, the user can pick only one option from a selection list. If you want visitors to be able to choose more than one option, you can allow it by adding the *multiple* attribute to the opening *select* tag.

```
<select multiple="multiple">
```

WARNING!

Note that adding the *multiple* attribute to a drop-down list automatically converts it to a scrolling list in most browsers. The size of the scrolling list is unpredictable. It will be a partial scrolling window in some browsers, and show the full list of options in other browsers. To maintain control over the display, only add the *multiple* attribute to a list with a size attribute.

With the part in red added to the *select* tag, visitors can choose multiple options—if they know how. To select multiple options, the user must hold down the Ctrl key (Windows) or Command key (Mac OS) when selecting additional options, or the Shift key to select several consecutive options. It's helpful to add a note to that effect for newbies. You might say something like: "To select multiple options, press Ctrl (Windows) or Command (Mac OS) while you click."

By default, a user-selected option sends the text between the <option> and </option> tags to you when the form is submitted (via email or to the server if you use a form processing script). Sometimes this is not ideal; you may want to have the user see an option worded one way while you receive it another way. This is accomplished using the *value* attribute with the option element.

Let's say you want the user to select from a list of states. Not all users know the postal abbreviation for each state, so you want to display the full names of the states in the list. Your office, however, uses the state abbreviations for your mailing labels, so you need postal abbreviations for your database. In the following abbreviated states selection list:

```
<select name="State">
<option value="AL">Alabama</option>
<option value="AK">Alaska</option>
<option value="AZ">Arizona</option>
...etc.
```

...the user sees the full state names to select from, but the state sent to you is the postal abbreviation shown in the value attribute. For example, if the user selects Arizona from the list, an email sent to you reads as:

```
State: AZ
```

13.10 Option Groups

THE OPTION GROUP, OR *OPTGROUP*, element allows you to logically group choices in a selection list. This is particularly helpful when users must choose from a long list of options; groups of related choices are easier to grasp and remember than a single long list of options. In HTML 4, all option group elements must be specified directly within a *select* element, so option groups may not be nested.

I don't know any browsers that fully support option groups at this time, but most do support one nice feature that makes them very useful. Browsers that don't support the optgroup just display an ordinary selection list, so there are no worries about using it.

Figure 13.12

Many web designers, myself included, believe future rendering of this element may include a collapsible/expandable nested list of options.

In Figure 13.12, you can see an optgroup list as it displays in Internet Explorer. In this list, Shannon owns a business with offices in seven different towns in two different states. She wants online users to select the office closest to them to get in touch with the right office. There are two option groups, one for Louisiana and one for Mississippi. The state names are added to the list with the use of an option group label, which is automatically displayed in bold type. The browser automatically indents the list of towns in each state.

The first list shows the option groups in a drop-down selection list. The second list shows a scrollable selection list, which is simply a drop-down list with a size attribute added. Shannon loved the list when she saw it, as did her two state managers, Dorothy and Samantha. Here's the code for the first list:

```
<select>
    <optgroup label="Louisiana">
        <option>Crowley</option>
        <option>Rayne</option>
        <option>Slidell</option>
    </optgroup>
    <optgroup label="Mississippi">
        <option>Abney</option>
        <option>Jupiter</option>
        <option>Pearl</option>
        <option>Shubuta</option>
    </optgroup>
</select>
```

The code is only indented to better show the groupings—it has no effect on the web page display. The *label="state name"* part creates the bold state names that head the option group lists. The label is not user selectable, but of course the individual towns are.

13.11 Fieldsets

WHILE YOU CAN USE TABLES or graphics to organize forms, another option is available as well. The *fieldset* element allows web authors to group thematically related form controls. Grouping controls make it easier for users to understand their purpose while at the same time making tab navigation easier for many users. Tab navigation is discussed in the next section.

The *legend* element allows authors to assign a caption to a fieldset. The caption is displayed with the fieldset and improves accessibility when the fieldset is rendered non-visually (by a screen reader, for example). Figure 13.13 shows a fieldset grouping—in this case, four radio buttons providing answers to the question in blue. The legend is the question in blue, although the text could just as easily be a field identifier rather than a question (*Sports*, for example). The line around the fieldset, which groups the buttons and butts up to left and right sides of the label, is drawn automatically by the browser.

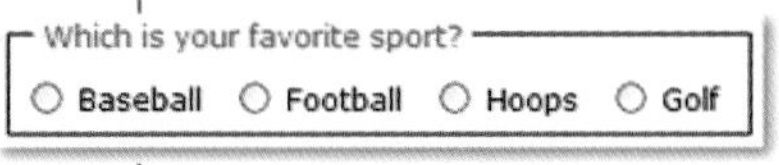

Here's the code for that fieldset:

```
<fieldset>

<legend>Which is your favorite sport?</legend>

<input type="radio" name="sport" /> Baseball

<input type="radio" name="sport" /> Football

<input type="radio" name="sport" /> Hoops

<input type="radio" name="sport" /> Golf

</fieldset>
```

Other form elements can be included as well; you are not limited to radio buttons. For example, you might ask users to name their favorite player in the sport they select, so you include a text input box. If you want users to explain why this person is their favorite player, you can include a textarea box. Figure 13.14 shows one way you could set this up, using CSS to dress it up a little.

With the fieldset element, the idea is to group other elements by theme. To pretty this up a little, I used CSS to change the font, font color, and font size of the legend, and I also changed the border style and border color of the fieldset.

Figure 13.13

Figure 13.14

font-weight: bold;}
font-size: 28px;
font-family: Pristina;
legend {color: red;
fieldset {border: 3px double #9D9C71;}

Figure 13.15

You're far enough along in learning about HTML that you should try to figure out how I coded the external style sheet for this effect. The text is Pristina font, bold, red, 28 pixels; the border is a 3-pixel double border with a border color of #9D9C71. Figure 13.15 shows the answer—upside down to make it hard to peak. Ha!

13.12 Tab Order

USERS CAN MOVE FROM FORM FIELD to form field by pressing their tab key. By default, browsers jump from element to element based on the order the elements are listed in the code, excluding any hidden elements.

You can change this order by assigning each element a *tabindex* attribute. With browsers that support tab indexing, pressing the tab key moves users through the form fields starting with number 1, followed by 2, 3, and so on. Any element with a tab index of zero is omitted from the tab order. Browsers that do not support tab indexing simply ignore it.

To add a tab index to an element:

```
<input type="text" name="First Name" tabindex="1" />
<input type="text" name="Last Name" tabindex="2" />
```

With the code in red added to the First Name and Last Name form fields, browsers jump to the First Name text box when the tab key is pressed. Pressing tab again jumps to the Last Name text box.

13.13 Access Key

ANOTHER WAY OF ACCESSING FORM elements is with an access key. An access key is a keyboard shortcut that involves pressing a single key while holding down the accelerator key. On Windows, the accelerator key is the Alt key; on Mac OS, it's the Control key; on Unix machine, it's the Meta key.

To add an access key:

```
<input type="checkbox" accesskey="C" />
```

Note that access keys are case sensitive. A capital "C" is not the same as its lowercase counterpart (c). Also, an access key not only jumps to an element—it also selects the element. When used with radio buttons or checkboxes, using the access key works the same as if a user clicked the button or checkbox to select it.

WARNING!

Be sure to test the access keys you select. Some browser menu items also have shortcut keys, so they may perform the menu action rather than the access key action when you code a menu shortcut for the access key.

13.14 Hidden Fields

HTML PROVIDES A FEW HIDDEN FIELDS you can use with forms, and they are quite useful. Unfortunately, they don't work with the *mailto* method. The mailto method of form submission simply uses your guests' default email program to send the form submission to the address specified in the form code. Most hidden fields require your web host to have a form processing script on the server—as most professional hosting services do. These scripts will have names such as formmail.cgi or sendmail.cgi and will be found in your CGI bin.

There are a variety of form processing scripts and different ways hosts can set them up, so it's beyond the scope of this book to go into much detail about them. The code used to point to a form processing script looks something like this:

```
<form method="post" action="http://www.yoursite.
com/cgi-bin/FormMail.cgi">
```

Consult with your web host to find out about the script processing they offer, and for the correct path to the script. Many web hosts offer this information in their FAQ. Most hosts offer FAQ pages (answers to Frequently Asked Questions) to help new hosting clients find the information they need.

If your web host does offer a script processing form, or you install one on your own, then the following hidden fields can be quite useful.

● This code fills in the subject line of the email you receive from a processed form:

```
<input type="hidden" name="subject" value=
"Feedback from Web Site" />
```

A form with that field sends an email to you with "Feedback from Web Site" in the subject line. You might use this information to sort your emails so you can easily find the ones most important to you.

● This code sends visitors to another page after they click the send button—often back to your home page or a thank-you page.

```
<input type="hidden" name="redirect" value=
"http://www.boogiejack.com/thanks.html" />
```

In this example, users are sent to a thank-you page after submitting the form.

● This code shows how to specify required fields, which must be completed before the form can be submitted:

```
<input type="hidden" name ="required" value =
"email, name">
```

WARNING!

Be careful when using required fields. Field names are case sensitive. For example, if you code "Email" as the name value of a text input box, but make "email" the required field, you'll create a form that cannot be completed. This is because there is no field named "email" as the actual field has a capital letter "E" to start the name value.

In that example code, if a user tried to submit the form without filling in the email field or name field, an error message lists the missing fields.

13.15 Tips for Forms

FOLLOWING ARE A FEW TIPS to help you create more useful and safe forms.

☑ First and foremost, if you use a script to process forms, make sure to use a high-quality script with spam protection. Many free scripts that you'll find are vulnerable to spam hack attacks. What that means is a spammer can exploit a poor script to send unsolicited email using your domain identity. If this happens, your site could be shut down by your host, or if you host your site with your ISP, you could lose your Internet access.

☑ Use field sets, option groups, horizontal rules, tables, images, and CSS to tidy up forms and make them easily understood. Grouping related items together makes a form more logical and inviting to fill out.

When planning a web form, design isn't the only issue. You need to decide the goal of the web form—and stick to that goal. The most common mistake made is probably an over-zealous webmaster trying to collect too much information—much of it often unnecessary, included more for curiosity than purpose.

 Use checkboxes, radio buttons, and selection lists as much as possible to make filling out a form easy for users. Requiring too many typewritten answers is a sure way to decrease the participation rate.

 Always view and test your form in multiple browsers to make sure the appearance is satisfactory and it works properly prior to taking it "live" for visitors to use.

 Use examples when appropriate to ensure that visitors understand the desired format. For example, for an order form requiring a credit card expiration date, you might show *mm/dd/yy* next to the input box.

To encourage visitors to complete a form, consider offering an incentive. Users need to believe it's worth their time, and a freebie of some kind often does the trick. Freebies of this nature should cost you nothing—maybe a list of 10 tips on a topic they are interested in, for example. Another incentive if you don't mind spending a little bit of money is to have the completed form qualify the user for a contest entry. Hundreds or thousands of people might fill out a form for a chance to win a prize that is of minimal cost to you. You also might convince a sponsor to donate prizes so it doesn't cost you anything.

 Every field, button, or box should be clearly labeled and associated with its proper purpose. Clearly identify all fields, buttons, and boxes.

 Use the "password" type for text input boxes where sensitive information is to be entered.

 Be sure to give those completing a form a thank-you message. It's discouraging to go to the trouble of filling out a form only to be shuffled off without a kind word of appreciation or acknowledgement of some kind. This can be done with a hidden redirect field to a thank-you page, an automated email reply, a personal reply, or by other means depending on your expertise.

13.16 Final Form Appearance and Code

AS PROMISED EARLIER, Figure 13.16 shows the screen capture of the entire sample form along with the external style sheet code and HTML code.

The external style sheet code:

```
table {font-family: Verdana;
        font-size: 12px;}
td.head1 {background-color: #DDDEB4;
        padding-top: 3px;
        border-right: 1px solid black;
        border-bottom: 1px solid black;
        font-weight: bold;}
td.head2 {background-color: #DFCAB3;
        margin-top: 8px;
        padding: 3px;
        border-right: 1px solid black;
        border-bottom: 1px solid black;
        font-weight: bold;}
td.head3 {background-color: #CFCEEC;
        margin-top: 8px;
        padding: 3px;
        border-right: 1px solid black;
        border-bottom: 1px solid black;
        font-weight: bold;}
td.head4 {background-color: #C5E6E9;
```

Figure 13.16

```
        margin-top: 8px;

        padding: 3px;

        border-right: 1px solid black;

        border-bottom: 1px solid black;

        font-weight: bold;}

td.input {width: 120;

        text-align: right;

        vertical-align: baseline;}

input,textarea {margin-top: 8px;}
```

We've covered everything in the CSS code and the following HTML code, so I'm not going to go over it all again. We have been covering code in smaller, bite-size pieces. The difference here is that a lot of small, bite-size pieces are strung together. When you start examining the large code sample bit by bit, it won't seem as complicated as it does at first glance.

The HTML code from the page body:

```
<form method="post" action="mailto:you@yourISP.
com;" enctype="text/plain">

<table width="400" border="0">

<tr><td class="head1" colspan="2"> Registrant
Information</td>

</tr><tr>

<td class="input">First Name:</td>

<td><input type="text" name="First Name"
size="40" /></td>

</tr><tr>

<td class="input">Last Name:</td>

<td><input type="text" name="Last Name" size="40">
</td>

</tr><tr>

<td class="input">Choose Password:</td>
```

```
<td><input type="password" name="Password"
size="40"></td>

</tr><tr>

<td class="input">Email Address:</td>

<td><input type="text" name="Email" size="40"></td>

</tr><tr>

<td colspan="2"> </td>

</tr><tr>

<td class="head2" colspan="2">Email Preferences</td>

</tr><tr>

<td class="input"><input type="radio" value="text"
name="Email Preference" /></td>

<td style="vertical-align: baseline;">Plain Text</td>

</tr><tr>

<td class="input"><input type="radio" value="html"
name="Email Preference" /></td>

<td style="vertical-align: baseline;">HTML</td>

</tr><tr>

<td colspan="2"> </td>

</tr><tr>

<td class="head3" colspan="2">Frequency</td>

</tr><tr>

<td class="input"><input type="checkbox"
value="daily" name="frequency" /></td>

<td style="vertical-align: baseline;">Daily Updates</td>

</tr><tr>

<td class="input"><input type="checkbox"
value="weekly" name="frequency" /></td>

<td style="vertical-align: baseline;">Weekly Digest</td>

<tr><tr>
```

```
<td colspan="2"> </td>
</tr><tr>
<td class="head4" colspan="2">Comments</td>
</tr><tr>
<td colspan="2"><textarea name="Comments"
cols="46" rows="4"></textarea></td>
</tr><tr>
<td colspan="2"><input type="checkbox"
name="Agreement" checked="checked" />
 I agree to receive email from BoogieJack.com</td>
</tr><tr>
<td><input type="submit" value="Submit"
style="width: 120px;"></td>
<td style="text-align: right;"><input type="reset"
value="Reset Form" style="width: 120px;">
</td></tr></table>
</form>
```

There you go!

13.17 Chapter 13 Exercise

YOU GET TO MAKE ANOTHER NEW PAGE! This time, you'll be creating a contact page with a working contact form. Use the "mailto" method for processing the form. The form elements you need to include are:

- User name text input box
- User email address text input box
- Two radio button options for "reply requested" or "no reply necessary"
- Selection list for choosing email priority level (low, medium, or high)
- Text area for comments

If you code the form so that it sends the mail to your actual email account, you can test the form to make sure it works and see what the form submission looks like. Remember to add the "enctype" to the form element so the message doesn't come in looking like gibberish. It's your choice whether to design the form using tables or fieldsets.

- Include your organization's other contact information (1-800-number, mailing address, fax number).
- Add a link from your index page to the contact page.

Creating an XHTML Document

14

14.1 Introduction

WHILE I'VE MENTIONED and demonstrated creating HTML documents with XHTML compliance throughout this book, this chapter pulls it all together in one place and shows you how to create an actual XHTML document. What we have been doing so far is creating HTML pages that are XHTML compatible. This is about to change.

Development of HTML stopped at version 4.01 in favor of XHTML. Eventually XHTML may replace HTML, but that shouldn't worry you because it's almost identical to HTML. While it is stricter and unforgiving of coding errors, there are two reasons for that:

- Creating a stricter standard reduces compatibility issues between user agents.

- The strict standard can be used on a variety of different devices without the need to write special pages for each type of device.

User agents, more commonly known as browsers, consist of far more than Internet Explorer, Netscape, Firefox, Opera, Safari, and other browsers of this type. User agents also include mobile phones, smart phones, web TV, voice response systems, PDAs— even some microwave ovens can access the web these days. Most of these devices do not have the ability to interpret sloppy markup language. The end goal of following strict standards is to create web pages that are not device dependent. Instead, you'll create pages that are device independent, allowing access from a whole range of diverse devices.

XML was designed to *describe* data while HTML was designed to *display* data. XHTML combines the strengths and functions of both. XML is a markup language in which everything has to be marked correctly. Correct markup results in "well-formed" documents that can be read by any XML-enabled device. This means XHTML is a markup language that is useful now and into the foreseeable future.

XHTML gives you the platform to write well-formed documents now—which work in all browsers and are backward compatible—while waiting for the rest of the world to step into the future.

Just as a reminder, this is what XML, HTML, and XHTML stand for:

XML = eXtensible Markup Language

HTML = HyperText Markup Language

XHTML = eXtensible HyperText Markup Language

14.2 HTML/XHTML Differences

THERE ARE SEVERAL DIFFERENCES between XHTML and HTML, but none are difficult to understand. With XHTML:

- All documents must have a DOCTYPE.
- All elements and attributes must be in lowercase.
- All tags must be closed.
- All attributes must be added properly.
- All tags must be properly nested.
- The *name* attribute has changed.
- All documents must be well-formed.

If any of these items are not complied with, the document will not be well-formed and will not display as an XHTML document. We'll examine each one of these items in detail so you know exactly how these things work.

14.2.1 DOCTYPE

In HTML, the DOCTYPE, also referred to as DTD or Document Type Definition, is recommended but not required.

In XHTML it is required. The DOCTYPE declaration should be the first line in an XHTML document. There is an optional line that can precede the DOCTYPE, which we'll discuss in Section 14.3 of this chapter.

XHTML has three DOCTYPEs you can use:

- transitional
- strict
- frameset

Let's look at each one:

XHTML 1.0 Transitional

Webmasters writing web documents for general public access might want to use the Transitional version. It allows you to take advantage of XHTML features, including style sheets, but still allows you to make small adjustments to your markup for the benefit of those viewing your pages with older browsers that do not parse style sheets. This includes using deprecated elements and attributes.

To use the Transitional DOCTYPE, use the following code at the top of the document:

```
<!DOCTYPE html PUBLIC "-//W3C//DTD XHTML 1.0
Transitional//EN"

"http://www.w3.org/TR/xhtml1/DTD/xhtml1-
transitional.dtd">
```

XHTML 1.0 Strict

Use the Strict DOCTYPE when you want clean structural markup, free of any markup associated with layout and free of deprecated HTML elements and values.

To use the Strict DOCTYPE, use the following code at the top of the document:

```
<!DOCTYPE html PUBLIC "-//W3C//DTD XHTML 1.0
Strict//EN"

"http://www.w3.org/TR/xhtml1/DTD/xhtml1-
strict.dtd">
```

XHTML 1.0 Frameset

Use the Frameset DOCTYPE when you want to use Frames to partition the browser window into two or more frames.

To use the Frameset DOCTYPE, use the following code at the top of the document:

```
<!DOCTYPE html PUBLIC "-//W3C//DTD XHTML 1.0
Frameset//EN"

"http://www.w3.org/TR/xhtml1/DTD/xhtml1-
frameset.dtd">
```

Note

The DOCTYPES should be written as shown, preserving the uppercase and lowercase.

14.2.2 Lowercase

In HTML, it doesn't matter if you type element tags and their attributes in uppercase or lowercase. Whether you type <html> or <HTML> or even <HtmL>, it doesn't matter—it all means the same thing.

In XHTML, all element and attribute names must be in lowercase. The values assigned to attributes can be in uppercase, lowercase, or mixed case. For example, PICTURE.JPG or picture.jpg are fine for the value of an image tag because that may be the way the file name and extension are saved. In other words, the *attribute name* must be in lowercase, but not the files and extensions (values) the attribute includes.

See if you can spot what's wrong with the code on the left before looking for the answers in the corrected code on the right. The correction is highlighted in bold red text.

Wrong Code	Right Code
<img SRC="Images/PICTURE.jpg" />	<img src="Images/PICTURE.jpg" />
<div Width="420">	<div width="420">

14.2.3 All Tags Closed

In XHTML, all tags must be closed. HTML tags that actually have closing tags must include the closing tag, while HTML tags that have no closing tags need to be self-closed by adding a space and forward slash at the end (/). Tags with no closing tags are sometimes called empty tags, one-sided tags, open elements, or empty elements because there is no content between an opening and closing tag.

See if you can spot what's wrong with the code on the left before looking for the answers in the corrected code on the right. The correction is highlighted in bold red text.

Wrong Code	Right Code
<img src="images/picture.jpg">	<img src="images/picture.jpg" />
<hr>	<hr />
<li>Item 1	<li>Item 1</li>
<li>Item 2	<li>Item 2</li>
<p> ...	<p> ... </p>
<p> ...	<p> ... </p>

14.2.4 Proper Attributes

In addition to the requirement for attribute names to be in lowercase as mentioned in Section 14.2.2, all attribute values must be enclosed in straight quotation marks.

See if you can spot what's wrong with the code on the left before looking for the answers in the correct code on the right. The correction is highlighted in bold red text.

Wrong Code	Right Code
<table cellspacing=3>	<table cellspacing="3">
<img src="pic.jpg" width=90 height=110 />	<img src="pic.jpg" width="90" height="110" />
<div width=420>	<div width="420">

In addition, attribute minimization (or valueless attributes) are forbidden in XHTML. That's when an HTML attribute has no *value* associated with the attribute.

See if you can spot what's wrong with the code on the left before looking for the answers in the corrected code on the right. The correction is highlighted in bold red text.

Wrong Code	Right Code
<option selected>Item</option>	<option selected="**selected**"> Item</option>
<input type="text" readonly />	<input type="text" readonly= "**readonly**" />
<frame src="2.html" noresize />	<frame src="2.html" noresize= "**noresize**" />

While attribute minimization is legal in HTML, you need to comply with the XHTML way of doing things to be compliant in the future. As you may have noticed, you can make a minimized attribute legal by simply adding the attribute name as a value to the attribute. Here's a handy dandy list for reference:

HTML	XHTML
checked	checked="checked"
compact	compact="compact"
declare	declare="declare"
defer	defer="defer"
disabled	disabled="disabled"
ismap	ismap="ismap"
multiple	multiple="multiple"
nohref	nohref="nohref"
noresize	noresize="noresize"
noshade	noshade="noshade"
nowrap	nowrap="nowrap"
readonly	readonly="readonly"
selected	selected="selected"

14.2.5 Name Attribute

In HTML 4.01, a name attribute can be used with all elements except the base, head, html, meta, script, style, and title elements.

In XHTML, the name attribute is deprecated and webmasters should use the *id* element instead.

Wrong Code	Right Code
<table name="vacation schedule">	<table id="vacation schedule">
<form name="Feedback">	<form id="Feedback">

This leaves one problem—the id attribute isn't backward compatible with older browsers. Anything in your code that relies on the name attribute will fail if the id attribute is in its place. So for now the best thing to do is include both the name attribute for older browsers and id attribute for XHTML compliance. Example:

<table **id="duty roster" name="duty roster"**>

Older browsers will ignore the id attribute, but it's there for XHTML compliancy.

14.2.6 Proper Nesting

Tags should be properly nested in HTML and XHTML, but many nesting errors that are forgiven in HTML will not be forgiven in XHTML. Therefore it's imperative that you avoid sloppy nesting practices.

Nesting is simply the process of placing one tag set inside another tag set. The problem that often happens is that you open element 1, then open element 2, but close element 1 before closing element 2—the reverse of the proper order. The result is that the end tags overlap rather than nest. Remember, nested tags should be closed in the reverse order in which they were opened.

See if you can spot what's wrong with the code on the left before looking for the answers in the corrected code on the right. The correction is highlighted in bold red text.

Wrong Code	Right Code
<b><i>message</b></i>	<b><i>message</i></b>
<tr><td> ... </tr></td>	<tr><td> ... </td></tr>
</html></body>	</body></html>*

*I realize I didn't show the opening tags in the third example, but the HTML tag is never canceled before the body tag is canceled. If you figured this one out, you done good!

271

If you just remember to close the tags in the reverse order in which you opened them, you'll have properly nested tags. Life is easy when you have it all figured out. ☺

14.2.7 What is Well-Formed?

What is "well-formed"? Well, it's all of the above. You've been learning what it takes to create a well-formed document from the beginning of this book. But there is just a little more.

- All elements must be contained in a single root element. For XHTML, that root element is the <html> and </html> element.

- While the Transitional DTD allows for the use of deprecated elements and certain proprietary elements, they are not allowed using the Strict DTD. The following elements are prohibited in the Strict DTD:

XHTML Prohibited Elements	Definition
applet	Java applet
basefont	base font size
center	centers content
dir	directory list
font	local change to font
iframe	inline sub-window
isindex	single line prompt
menu	menu list
s	strike-through text style
strike	strike-through text style
u	underlined text style

- The Strict DTD also prohibits some elements from being used as child elements with other elements. The following list shows which elements are prohibited from having which child elements:

Element	HTML Prohibited Child Elements
any inline element	any block level element

body	a, abbr, acronym, b, bdo, big, br, button, cite, code, dfn, em, i, img, input, kbd, label, map, object, q, samp, select, small, span, strong, sub, sup, textarea, tt, var
button	button, form, fieldset, iframe, input, isindex, label, select, textarea
blockquote	a, abbr, acronym, b, bdo, big, br, button, cite, code, dfn, em, i, img, input, kbd, label, map, object, q, samp, select, small, span, strong, sub, sup, textarea, tt, var
form	a, abbr, acronym, b, bdo, big, br, cite, code, dfn, em, form, i, img, kbd, map, object, q, samp, small, span, strong, sub, sup, tt, var
label	Label
pre	big, img, object, small, sub, sup
all page elements	big, small

- All XHTML documents must have:
  - <html> ... </html>
  - <head> ... </head>
  - <title> ... </title>
  - <body> ... </body>
- The Strict DTD prohibits deprecated attributes as well. The following list shows which attributes are prohibited in the strict DTD:

Element	XHTML Prohibited Attributes
a	target
area	target
base	target
body	alink, bgcolor, link, text, vlink
br	clear
caption	align
div	align
dl	compact
form	name, target
hr	align, noshade, size, width

Element	XHTML Prohibited Attributes
img	align, border, hspace, name, vspace
input	align
li	type, value
link	target
map	name
object	align, border, hspace, vspace
ol	compact, start
p	align
pre	width
script	language
table	align, bgcolor
td	bgcolor, height, nowrap, width
th	bgcolor, height, nowrap, width
tr	bgcolor, height, nowrap, width
ul	compact, type

● Lastly, XHTML has some required attributes. The following chart shows which elements have required attributes and what they are:

Element	XHTML Required Attributes
applet*	height, width
area	alt
base	href
basefont*	size
bdo	dir
form	action
img	alt, src
map	id
meta	content
optgroup	label
param*	name
script	type
style	type
textarea	cols, rows

*These elements are prohibited in the Strict DTD, but allowed in the Transitional and Frameset DTDs. When used with an allowed DTD, the attributes listed are required.

14.3 Your First XHTML Page

NOW THAT WE'VE GONE OVER all the rules, it's time to actually make an XHTML page. Open your text editor and type in the following line of code:

```
<?xml version="1.0" encoding="UTF-8" standalone="no" ?>
```

Earlier I mentioned that there was one line that could be placed before the DOCTYPE declaration. That is the line. Although it is optional, because all XHTML documents are also XML documents, it's a good idea to include it. It makes the document easier and faster for the XML parser to decode and removes any guesswork on the part of the browser. Let's look at what all that slobber-gobber means:

- Obviously the first part declares that it's an XML document and establishes which version of XML the parser should use. There are only two W3C approved XML standards, version 1.0 and 1.1. You should always use version 1.0 for XHTML.

- The encoding tells the browser which character set to use in reading the document. Without going into details you have no reason to be concerned with, the two most common characters sets are UTF-8 and UTF-16. For Western language XML documents, UTF-8 files will be smaller and faster than UTF-16.

- The standalone attribute is always set to *no* for documents that rely on the W3C for validation. If you don't know whether to set it to *yes*, the answer is set it to *no*!

Note

As an alternative to the opening XML declaration, you can also include the character set and encoding in a meta element in the HEAD section of the page. The syntax for this is:

```
<meta http-equiv="Content-Type" content="text/html; charset=utf-8" />
```

Note that the *content* attribute has two values separated by a semicolon. Don't assume this is a typing mistake and insert extra quotation marks. Other possible values for the charset are: *us-ascii* or *iso-8859-1*.

The next element to add after the opening XML declaration is the DOCTYPE. Because the Strict DOCTYPE can be difficult for even seasoned professionals to validate, I recommend using the Transitional DOCTYPE to get started. After adding the

DOCTYPE, the start of your first XHTML page code should look like this:

```
<?xml version="1.0" encoding="UTF-8"
standalone="no" ?>
<!DOCTYPE html PUBLIC "-//W3C//DTD XHTML 1.0
Transitional//EN"
  "http://www.w3.org/TR/xhtml1/DTD/xhtml1-
  transitional.dtd">
```

Next, we can finally add the opening <html> tag to begin our XHTML document—only the <html> tag is a little different as well. Included in the <html> tag is a *namespace* attribute and value. A *namespace* allows elements from other XML languages to be used in an XHTML document. For example, a scientist might need to use mathematical symbols to demonstrate equations so he or she would include the MathML namespace to have access to mathematical elements not found in standard character sets. This book doesn't teach XML, so I will just give you the standard namespace to use with XHTML documents:

```
xmlns="http://www.w3.org/1999/xhtml"
```

When you add that to the HTML declaration as the third item of an XHTML page, the code now looks like this:

```
<?xml version="1.0" encoding="UTF-8"
standalone="no" ?>
<!DOCTYPE html PUBLIC "-//W3C//DTD XHTML 1.0
Transitional//EN"
  "http://www.w3.org/TR/xhtml1/DTD/xhtml1-
  transitional.dtd">
<html xmlns="http://www.w3.org/1999/xhtml">
```

After this, the document uses standard HTML elements and attributes. If you include any special namespaces, you can use the properties they bring to the document. You can add as many namespaces as you need to a document, but that's a subject for another book if XML interests you.

Let's finish off our XHTML document:

XHTML Page Code

```
<?xml version="1.0" encoding="UTF-8" standalone="no" ?>
<!DOCTYPE html PUBLIC "-//W3C//DTD XHTML 1.0 Transitional//EN"
```

```
"http://www.w3.org/TR/xhtml1/DTD/xhtml1-transitional.dtd">
<html xmlns="http://www.w3.org/1999/xhtml">
<head>
<title>XHTML Page</title>
</head>
<body>
<h3>Hello world.</h3>
This is my first XHTML document.
</body>
</html>
```

That's it. If you finish off the code in your file and save it as "*name*.html" you'll be able to view it in a browser and validate it with the W3Cs XHTML validator. Substitute whatever file name you choose for "*name*" and save it with the .html extension. You read that right—XHTML pages are saved with the HTML extension. To validate your page go to:

http://validator.w3.org

You can upload the file using the Browse button—you don't even need to have the file stored online, you only need Internet access. You can also validate the code by pasting it directly into a textarea box.

14.4 Style Sheet Problems with XHTML

BROWSERS PARSE TWO TYPES of text: parsed character data (PCDATA) and unparsed character data (CDATA). Most code is PCDATA, which is why symbols such as the arrow brackets that surround HTML element tags don't show up on pages. CDATA, on the other hand, is not processed in the same way. While there is little concern about this issue in an HTML document, it can present a unique problem in an XHTML document.

Fortunately, it isn't a problem that comes up often or affects too many webmasters. The problem occurs when certain characters are used in an embedded style sheet. An embedded style sheet is treated as PCDATA, so a character such as the right arrow bracket in an embedded style can confuse the parser. For example, take a look at this code showing the parent-child relationship between a paragraph element and ordered list:

```
<style type="text/css">
p > ol {font-size: 75%;}
</style>
```

The code reduces the font size to 75% in an ordered list that follows a paragraph tag, however the right arrow bracket would most likely confuse the browser and invalidate the page.

You can use a special delineation called a *CDATA section,* which allows you to mark a block of text as CDATA. This means that parsers won't treat it as PCDATA. For example:

```
<style type="text/css">
<! [CDATA[
p > ol {font-size: 75%;}
]]
</style>
```

Adding the code in red text around the potentially troublesome code should cause the parser to ignore it. I say *should* because unfortunately, many, if not most, browsers aren't programmed to understand the CDATA section.

In the end, it's best not to use embedded styles in XHTML documents if they have any characters that could be processed by the parser. Using external style sheets is the only solution that works reliably at this time.

14.5 A Cautionary Tale

A FEW WEB DESIGNERS BELIEVE that XHTML will never fulfill its promise and end up dying on the vine. Some have even pronounced it dead now—far too prematurely, I'm sure.

They do make a good point. If XHTML is supposed to clean up sloppy coding practices, how will making it backward compatible with old browsers and sloppy coding practices change anything? After all, the very fact that it must be backward compatible allows, and even encourages, those with bad practices to continue coding as though XHTML doesn't exist. Many webmasters figure there is no need to learn something new when the old methods serve their purposes just fine.

I'm not pronouncing XHTML as a needless exercise in learning—because it does help webmasters create better code. I'm just saying it may not become all it's cracked up to be, at least not for a long, long time. After all, it's been around since the year 2000 and relatively few even understand it, let alone design their sites using XHTML documents.

As for me, I'm still writing HTML pages, but I do make any new HTML pages XHTML compatible.

14.6 Chapter 14 Exercise

TIME TO CREATE A NEW PAGE, this time an XHTML page. If you have Internet access in your classroom, or wherever you're learning this, test your page against the W3C's validator at:

http://validator.w3.org

- First, create a basic XHTML page using the code demonstrated in Section 14.3. Validate it to make sure you have everything correct and it passes validation.

- Once the page passes validation, change the "hello world" content so the page contains a public acknowledgement to three lists of donors: a list of individuals who gave more than $100, a list who gave more than $500, and a list who gave more than $1,000. Use the monetary levels as headings, and use embedded styles to change the heading colors to ones that get attention, such as red, green or blue. Include at least three names of donors in each list (either an unordered list or ordered list, your choice).

- Once this is complete, validate the page again. If it fails, fix it. If it passes, your assignment is nearly complete. All that remains is to add a link to the new page from the home page of your project web site.

Good Design

15.1 Introduction

NOW THAT YOU'VE LEARNED the nuts and bolts of web site design, it's time to go into the details of what "good design" is all about. While other authors and I can list what we think constitutes good design, there are thousands of web designers whose only voice in the matter are the sites they design. Even experienced web designers surf the Internet for new ideas and inspiration. So look around—not just to see what sites offer as part of their content, but examine them from a design standpoint. See what you like and what you don't like, and think about what you might do differently to make them better if they were your sites.

When you see things on a web page that arouse your curiosity, feel free to look at the page's source code to learn from it. Everyone does it—there's nothing wrong with that. Of course, it would be wrong and illegal to steal others' pages, content, or graphics, but it's all well and good to learn from them by studying their source code.

15.2 Rule Number One!

RULE NUMBER ONE IN WEB DESIGN is simple: content rules. Not that your design style and presentation are unimportant, because they most certainly are, but quality content is the most important thing.

I know, I know—content is not design—but you could be the worst designer in the world and still have an audience if your content is above average. Conversely, if your content is poor, the best design in the world isn't likely to save it because most people surf the web for content, not to see pretty web site designs. A good design is like a little salt on your food, it adds a little flavor (but no one wants to eat a bowlful of salt). Your design is the salt; your content is the food. Remember that.

Part of creating quality content lies in knowing something about your intended audience's expectations. For example, academicians aren't going to visit your site for long or often if you write only broad overviews of topics. They already have a general idea about the topic they're researching; they want and expect detailed and new information they don't already have. A consumer visiting a product review site may glance at product specifications, but they can get that from the product manufacturer and merchandisers. What they really want from a review is honest expert opinions, comparisons with other products, and analysis of user expectations vs. actual results—things they can't get from the biased manufacturer or a commissioned salesperson.

When you create content, always remember that unless you are interested in a rare and little-known niche topic, you are competing for eyeballs with hundreds of thousands (if not millions) of other web pages.

When I say you're competing with millions of web pages, I'm not exaggerating for emphasis.

Figure 15.1 shows a search I performed at Google for "left border backgrounds" (the first thing I ever optimized my web site

As a side note, the first and third listings in that list of more than 25 million in Figure 15.1 are my sites. If you want a high-ranking web site, you might want to visit www.boogiejack.com and check out my Search Engine Optimization Strategies eBook (SEOS).

Figure 15.1

for) as I was writing this chapter. I circled the search results in red. In this screen capture, Google is showing the first 10 results of about 25,200,000 for my search term. That's a lot of web pages to compete with, and the numbers for many topics are more daunting.

To give you a broader idea of the competition, here are the Google numbers for a few other search terms at the time of this writing:

- Web design: 470 million
- Hotels: 896 million
- Electronics: more than 1 billion
- Pet care: 9.4 million
- Gardening: 87.5 million
- Music: more than 2.7 billion
- Books: more than 2.3 billion
- Poetry: 204 million
- Computers: more than 1.2 billion
- Healthy recipes: 34.9 million

Even esoteric or downright silly search terms such as *cosmic dust clouds, life on other planets, moon men, flat earth society, weird animals, dirty socks, friends of monkeys, big toes, monsters in my head, smelly old you, soft concrete*, and *really bad recipes* all produced millions of search results. Can you imagine that, more than one million search results for *dirty socks!*

Now that you know the competition is fierce for most any and every topic you can think of—and most of those you wouldn't think to think of—don't let the competition bother you one little bit...the next section explains why it shouldn't.

15.3 Writing YaYa

M Y PUBLISHER AND EDITOR both would probably question the use of "Writing YaYa" as a heading for this section if I wasn't making any possible objections moot by making a point in using it. Since there is no such thing as "writing yaya" except in my mind—and now yours—it's only natural they would try to dissuade me from using it.

So what is writing yaya?

It's just an attention-getter. By definition, publishers and editors are more concerned with proper form and phraseology than function, so they naturally and logically are against inventing terminology. I used "yaya" for the title of an article I wrote for my newsletter a few years back. I wanted to draw attention to the article, which was about what I saw as the differences between writing for the web and writing for print. I've included that article later in this section because it's still relevant today, but first I'll follow up on explaining why you shouldn't let the competition online bother you.

In the first place, the numbers are somewhat misleading. Many search results won't be relevant to the purpose of the searcher. Most people have bad search habits, and bad search habits often produce poor search results.

Secondly, and I don't mean to insult anyone, but most of the competition just isn't that good. Most people settle for mediocrity because they see mediocrity everywhere online, and so, mediocrity becomes the de facto standard. People emulate what they see—without even knowing if what they see is successful. When I wrote the first edition of this book, about 90 percent of online-only businesses were *not* profitable. I'd guess the failure rate isn't as great today, but I'd bet money it's still 50 percent or better. Why copy that?

People aren't going to frequent your web site because you copy what others are doing. Or because you copy their content, or copy their style, or copy their anything. Would you go to sites after site knowing they all say the same thing in pretty much the same way? Or, would you rather go to sites with unique content written in the author's own voice? You, and most everyone else, looks for unique content that you can't find on a thousand-and-one other web sites.

The expression "use your own voice" is well known, but not well understood. Most people think jotting their thoughts and their ideas down is writing in their own voice. It could be, but more often than not it's only raw thought expressed in an un-developed voice. Few people online write with a distinctness and personality that sets them apart from other writers, which is what I consider writing with your own voice. If you take the time to develop your own voice, you'll be well ahead in the game.

Developing your own voice does take some thought and effort...and practice. It's also a singular process—meaning that no one but you can discover, invent, and define your own unique style. It's a lot like figuring out what you want to do with your life. No one can tell you what will make you happy; only you can figure that out. No one can tell you what your own writing voice is either; you must figure that out for yourself as well.

Once developed though, your unique style will come through in your writing no matter what you write about. For me, it's a relaxed style and conversational in tone as if I'm talking face to face with the reader. And because I'm a bit of a joker, I like to toss in little bits of humor and even absurdity here and there just to shake things up a little.

In addition to publishing my own newsletter, I "ghost write" another newsletter for a large publishing company. I've had people ask me if I wrote a particular article in that newsletter because they recognized my writing style...they know my writing voice that well. I've also been blamed for things I didn't write, but that's another story!

Having said that, here's my "yaya" article:

> There are a few differences in writing for the web and writing for print publication, and the differences can make or break your success. While good writing is good writing if the right people read it, if you don't get it in front of the right eyeballs and present it in the right way, it won't matter how well written it is.
>
> When writing for the web, try to keep the following important points in mind.
>
> 1. **Understand your reader's style, Kyle.**
>   Online reading habits usually differ from reading print material. Out of necessity, readers online tend to scan articles looking for catchwords, while readers of print material are more likely to read word for word. There is so much more poorly written, poorly researched, and poorly conceived material online that users need to discriminate quickly to find what they want. Only when a reader finds those catchwords of interest is he or she more likely to slow down and read word for word.
>
> 2. **Presentation is key, Lee.**
>   Because online readers scan content for catchwords, it's important to use short, punchy paragraphs that are easy to scan. Using headings and pull quotes that make it easy to pick out key words and key ideas is smart presentation.
>
> 3. **Keep your writing focused and snappy, Slappy.**
>   Content not crucial to the storyline is better off used in sidebars or listed as additional reading rather than used within

the article. Allow no digression to the progression of your expression! A conversational style works well online as long as the "conversation" isn't too insipid nor strays too far afield.

4. **Save the punch line for the end, my friend.**
You wouldn't tell a joke by telling the punch line first. Jokes are told by setting up the punch line with a buildup. Write so that each paragraph builds anticipation, and then deliver the bang at the end. Finish with the "wow" factor rather than delivering the wow too early and having the article fizzle out. Too many online writers don't build the anticipation. Though they make good points, they deliver the wow too early and the rest of the article disappoints. If you do that, it's the fizzle, not the sizzle, that's often remembered. The two impressions that matter most are the first and the last.

5. **Set yourself apart, Bart.**
Many people feel information overload. There are tens of thousands of people saying the same things in nearly the same way. Those who are able to think differently, add new insight, provide better explanations, or write in a more exciting or entertaining way have a better chance of being noticed and remembered.

A good example of thinking differently is in this very article. Starting off each list item with a point, then rhyming a name with the last word of the point being made is an example of thinking differently. That doesn't mean you should copy that gimmick. There are many ways to create a unique presentation, and you should find your own voice to set yourself apart.

6. **Explain yourself, Ralph.**
When people watch the evening news on TV, they want to know what happened. Online, more often than not people want in-depth information, but you should never assume your reader knows the basic facts. Some will be just "tuning in" for the first time. They'll want to know who, how, why, what, when, where, and more.

If it's a common-knowledge subject or heavily covered news item you're writing about, you can keep the basics brief, link to them on another page, or present them in a sidebar so you don't wear out the majority of your audience repeating well-known information.

7. **Give them a clue, Lou.**
If your article is a continuation of previous work, reference the first articles (use links to the material whenever possible) so they can see what brought the story to the point where the new article picks up. Or, at least provide a recap of the previous article(s). Links need clues, too. People want to

know what to expect if they click a link, so use link titles. If they have doubt, they may tune out.

8. **Show them the distant light, Dwight.**

If you can link to related articles on other sites that back up what you are saying and provide additional insights, it gives you more credibility. Credibility is a crucial asset. This is important for everyone, but especially if you're still trying to make a name for yourself. Someone with an established name can be his or her own authority more readily than an unknown writer. Quality links related to your content at credible sources are an additional important component to your writing. You can always have the link open in a new window if you fear losing your visitor, so there's little reason not to provide the most comprehensive material you can.

Before linking to backup information, be sure you have written an original story with your own ideas. If all you do is parrot others, rather than gain credibility, you'll probably lose credibility with readers who suspect plagiarism or mere bandwagon jumping. Most professional writers make intentional efforts to offer unique points of view because they understand this truism.

9. **Take a chance, Lance.**

Remember, online writing is a fairly new and still evolving discipline. Don't be afraid to be the first with an idea, you may be onto something big. Don't be afraid to make up your own rules, you may be a trendsetter. Don't be afraid to be yourself, be afraid to be like everyone else. Our egos want us to fit in with others in person, but we need to stand apart online.

10. **Finally, do the boring work, Dirk.**

Check and verify facts. Use a spell checker and proofread. Use proper punctuation, proper capitalization, and good grammar. Give credit where credit is due. Ask for permission to include someone else's work or words if you need to use it, and don't use it if they don't give you permission (the fines and penalties for copyright infringement can be in the six-figure range). The boring work is the glue that affixes a measure of authority to your writing.

Even if you only keep half these items in mind when you write, you'll be ahead of most others. If you also have a little bit of talent, you'll be well on your way to becoming a voice others want to hear more from. Retaining readers, web site visitors, and customers is a huge factor in online success.

Your web site design is important, but if you design your words and content with at least as much care as you design the look of your web site, you will be well on your way to realizing a measure of online success.

15.4 Site Planning

NOW WE'LL GET TO THE THINGS you probably expected when you turned to this chapter—the actual qualities of good web site design.

The first thing to do when designing a web site is stop thinking about the site design! Hey, how did that comment feel—odd maybe? It's a true statement, though. The place to start with is *site planning*, not site design.

A car manufacturer doesn't make a bunch of auto parts without first planning how the parts all fit together. Likewise, you shouldn't start designing your web site until you plan out how everything fits together either—unless you prefer becoming frustrated and confused, and you think it's more fun to redo your work rather than get it right the first time!

Since there are millions of web sites and trillions of web pages, why would anyone want to visit your site? What do you have to offer that will make it unique? What can you do to make those who arrive at your digital doorstep become regular visitors?

Because clicking away from your site to another site is so easy, anyone building a new web site needs to ascertain three things before starting the design process.

1. Determine your primary goal for the web site.

2. Determine who your target audience is based on that goal.

3. Determine what their needs are and how you can fill them.

The number one principle of usable web design is to meet the immediate needs and expectations of your visitors. You may not have realized it until now, but their immediate need is information. Even if you're selling a product or service they want or need, they first need information to decide whether or not to purchase your product or service.

Too many webmasters design their web sites around their own goals and desires rather than the visitors' experiences and needs. That goes a long way toward explaining the high failure rate of commercial sites and the high abandonment rate of personal and hobby sites. A lack of initial success diminishes hopes, diminished hopes dampen enthusiasm, dwindling enthusiasm lessens interest, and lack of interest kills the site. Avoid that typical death cycle for a new site by starting off on the right foot and doing the research and planning before the designing.

Since you're studying web design, let's pretend you want to start your own web design company so you can make a decent income working mostly from home. You've studied the craft and made some practice sites, and you're ready to build the web site for your design company. Think about this question for a minute before reading the next paragraph—what is the first thing your potential customers want?

Don't cheat and peak, just think.

They want the answers to questions like:

- Can I trust this company?
- Can they build the kind of site I need?
- Will they get the work done to my satisfaction?
- Will they get the work done on time?
- Are they good people to work with?
- Will they be responsive to my needs?

As you can see, these questions center around one key—you, the business owner or business entity. Before your web site can sell your services, *it has to put your potential customers' fears to rest.* This is best accomplished by demonstration. You can talk about your qualifications all day long, but that won't paint as good a picture as showing web sites you've designed and offering testimonials from real clients.

I know what you're thinking—your business is new so you don't have a portfolio to show yet. Building a few web sites for free for local charities, churches, community organizations, or even your community is one way to get started. You could go to a few small businesses and offer to build web sites for them for only your out-of-pocket expenses (domain registration and hosting mainly), donating your labor to build a clientele. If they agree, you may get your first paying gig by updating their site later on.

After you design a handful of sites like this, if you do quality work, you'll have a nice portfolio to show. At the very least, you may have some great recommendations and testimonials from the beneficiaries of your work. Client testimonials are an excellent way of demonstrating that you're good to work with, are trustworthy, and provide satisfactory results.

Site planning begins with sizing up your goals and your target audience, determining how you can fulfill your target audience's needs, and planning how you can overcome any fears or objections your potential audience may have.

The second part of site planning is to make a list of all the content areas of the web site and then draw a mock-up of the site on paper. Planning it out on paper will help you visualize potential problems before they become real problems—problems that turn into lost work because parts have to be redone.

Part of this planning is to design the site navigation. I don't mean designing the look of your navigation system— I mean planning how each page and content section connects with the rest. Navigation planning is about creating an easy-to-use information flow based on your goals and your customers' needs.

Going back to the web design company example, you might divide your web site into three content groups off your home page:

1. Portfolio, customer testimonials, design philosophy: Answers a potential customer's questions about trusting you, whether you do good work, etc. We'll call this section "Calming Fears" in our mock-up.

2. Harder sell section: Why every business and organization needs a web site in today's business environment, what you do that many of your competitors don't, etc. We'll call this section "Hard Sell" in our mock-up.

3. Company contact information, staff introductions and experience, and other "about the business" information. We'll call this section "About Us" in our mock-up.

With that in mind, the sketch of your company web site mock-up might look like the one in Figure 15.2.

At the top of the mock-up is the home page. The next level of pages are labeled A, B, and C. These represent the content sections mentioned earlier:

A: Calming Fears

B: Hard Sell

C: About Us

Pages A, B, and C represent sub-indexes. Each contains links to the pages in that section. There can be many more than two pages in the sub-indexes, but I limited it to two here for illustration purposes. Pages a1 and a2 represent the content progression in that section, likewise for the other two sections. The LP represents the Last Page in each section.

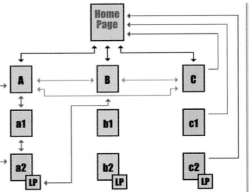

Figure 15.2

From the home page, you can see how the black arrows point from the home page to each sub-index and each sub-index points back to the home page. This represents the link relationship between the pages. The home page has a link to pages A, B, and C, and pages A, B, and C link back to the home page.

The green arrows show how the three sub-sections link to each other. Each sub-section has a link to the other two, plus links back to the home page.

The red arrows show how the pages in that content section link to the other pages within the section. The page A sub-index links to pages a1 and a2 and both link back to the sub-index page. In addition, page a1 links to page a2 and a2 links to page a1. This represents the "next" and "back" page relationship.

If the site had a page a3, I would not link page a1 to page a3 and vice versa. While we do want to make navigation as easy and logical as possible for visitors, we also don't want to create a nightmare for ourselves when it comes to updating. Suppose you have 30 pages in this content section. If you link every page in this section to every other page within the section, each page ends up with so much link clutter that it's confusing to visitors. Unless you're using "server side includes" to insert the navigation into each page, you end up having to add a new link to 30 separate pages when you add one new page of content. That's too much work.

Because there is a link to the sub-section index on each subsequent page of each section, the visitor only has to go back to that sub-section index to have access to all the pages in that content section (if he or she chooses not to follow the progression).

If a section has only two or three pages, you may be able to skip having page A be a sub-index. Instead, you can simply start your content progression or have links to the two or three pages from the home page. This navigation example assumes more than two or three pages in each section, yet produces a clean looking navigation system. With a well-planned navigation system, you can have a 1,000-page site with any page reachable from any other page with no more than two to four clicks, and still have a minimum set of links on each page.

I didn't show all the arrows on each content section because too many lines and arrows would make the graphic too hard to follow, but each content section (A, B, and C) would be structured in the same way I outlined for section A.

The blue arrow from the last page in section A has a one-way link to the next content section's sub-index page. If you do that from the last page of each section to the sub-index of the next section, a visitor could not only follow a progression from page to page within any content section, but he or she could also follow a progression from content section to content section.

Lastly, the purple arrows show one-way links back to the home page. The same applies to the other content sections. At a bare minimum, each page on the site should link back to the home page; I also add a link from each page to my contact page.

More often than not, users will *not* follow the progression through your site as you imagine. However, making your site as easy as possible to navigate will please everyone. It allows your visitors to find answers to the questions they need answered in order to do business with you.

15.5 Usability Testing

USABILITY TESTING? You're probably thinking I'm either joking or have gone dingy. News flash, I've been dingy for a long time, but I'm not joking. Usability testing doesn't have to be expensive and it isn't just for big companies.

According to Jakob Nielsen, a usability expert, it only takes five test users to find 85 percent of a web site's initial problems. While you can't actually perform a usability test without building the web site, you can discover problems before you build it by first conducting your own "preview-ability" study.

Once you have a mock-up of your web site, ask five people with a variety of web-surfing experience to preview your plan and mentally surf your site. At this stage, you'll probably want just family and friends to do this so it doesn't cost anything. You're really just looking for glaring mistakes in strategy and navigation planning at this point. Be sure they know you're not looking for compliments—that you're looking for potential problems to correct before you actually start building the site.

You might offer them an inexpensive reward for each problem they find to ensure the proper mindset. Give them a couple days to work at their leisure, and ask them to jot down their findings. Your mock-up will probably need more detail than my example illustration shows. Each page will need a summary of the content of the page. The summaries can be written on a separate paper so your mock-up drawing isn't too cluttered. When you get back with the testers, ask each person if he or she understands the primary purpose of your web site. You can discuss any problems they found after that.

Once you've actually built your web site, you can conduct a real usability test. For this, try to find five people that roughly fit into your intended target audience and ask them to surf your site. Try to find people you don't know by recruiting them online or through a local newspaper ad. If you have a college in your town and the students fit your profile, try students—they often work for cheap.

Have two or three of the five people surf your site and observe the process. Tell them not to ask you questions, but instead to jot down any questions they have. Observe how they navigate the site, what content sections they go to first, if they end up accidentally going back to a page they've previously visited, if they seem confused at times, etc.

Have two or three other people surf the site while not in your presence. The idea is to conduct some unmonitored surfing and some monitored surfing since your presence may affect how testers behave on your web site. In addition, monitoring may show you something the testers wouldn't have told you on their own.

After each test, be prepared to ask questions. Make up a list ahead of time so you're prepared.

- Did they understand your site's primary purpose?
- Was the navigation intuitive? Did they have any problems getting around?
- What content interested them the most? The least?
- What questions did they have that they couldn't find answers to?

- How does it compare to other web sites covering the same subject matter?
- Were they confused by anything, even for just a moment? If so, what?
- Did everything work, including links and images?
- Did they find the information credible?
- Did the design suit the content and purpose?

That should get you started. You can probably think of more questions that are specific to the type of site you build. Be ready to ask additional questions based on your observations and the test users' feedback.

By conducting a preview-ability study and a real usability study, you should have the majority of potential problems solved before you open the digital doors to the public.

15.6 The Template

DO YOU KNOW WHAT A TEMPLATE IS? A template is a pattern used to make duplicates of something so each new item matches the original. In web design, a template serves several purposes:

- It provides a pattern you can use over and over to create new pages.
- It prevents mistakes that can happen when creating new documents from scratch each time.
- It saves time by providing a basic page; you only need to add content without duplicating your efforts from other pages.
- By validating the finished template at the W3C validator site, you can be sure you are starting each new page with valid code and no coding errors of any kind.
- Working smart makes you feel smarter. Feeling smarter makes you more confident. More confidence makes you more attractive. And we all know feeling more attractive makes your feet smell like chicken!

Uh...sorry, I lost my train of thought for a moment. Anyway, if you follow the advice here, you're now at the stage at which you actually start designing the look for your site.

To make a template, include only the items that are common to each page. This includes the basic structure tags: the DOC-TYPE if you decide to use one; html, head, title, meta, and body tags sets; as well as the link to the external style sheets if used. This also includes the graphics common to each page such as the page header or logo graphic, any page divisions it will have (such as a two-column table), the navigation system, and any other items you want repeated on each page.

You can also use placeholders. If you know each page will have a heading at the top of the main content area, include a placeholder heading there.

<h3>heading placeholder</h3>

With the placeholder set, all you have to do is remember to change the text. I like to use the <pre> tag set to space multiple placeholders apart as this gives me the approximate final look (minus the actual content). As I add the content to the new page using the template, I remove the <pre> elements.

Figure 15.3 shows a template I created a few years back for my www.boogiejack.com site.

It's a little bit on the wild side for a commercial web site. I spent hours on this design and then decided not to use it. That's why I picked it to show as a template example here; I finally get some payback for my work on it. ☺

Once you've saved your template, I recommend flagging it as a read-only file. This will prevent you from adding content to the template and accidentally saving it that way. As a read-only file, once you make changes, you'll only be able to save it with a new name.

To save a file as read-only on Windows, locate the saved file in your web site folder, right-click it, and then choose Properties. When the Properties dialog box opens, check Read-only and click the Apply button. Close the Properties dialog box and you've got a damage-proof template. In TextEdit on Mac OS, open the file and choose Format > Prevent Editing. When you open a template, save it as a new file and then choose Format > Allow Editing.

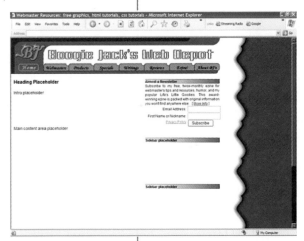

Figure 15.3

15.7 Site Consistency

NAVIGATION IS A KEY ELEMENT in how well your web site will be received. The navigation system should be consistent throughout your site. The idea is to help visitors become familiar with the navigation structure as soon as possible so they feel comfortable finding their way around. The easier your site is to surf, the more content your visitors are likely explore—as long as the content is of sufficient quality to hold their interest.

Consistency in the navigation structure helps people learn a site quickly, but it isn't the only area that requires consistency. Keeping a consistent look from page to page on a site is highly important as well.

You'll rarely find a professionally designed site that changes backgrounds, fonts, colors, or other design elements from page to page. If you make changes like that, users may begin to feel lost and not even know if they're still on the same site. You want visitors to feel at home as soon as possible, and consistency is the key to that.

Adherence to industry norms is part of the consistency users expect. When pages generally look and behave the same as users have experienced on other sites, they will have a basic comfort level from the beginning. Remember, every user's experience comes from an accumulation of time spent visiting hundreds or even thousands of other web sites, but not too much from yours.

When user expectations are in harmony with your delivery, they will feel more in control and more comfortable with your site. The more your web site breaks their expectations, the less comfortable they will feel. While innovation can be a wonderful thing, be careful about deviating from standard practices and expectations.

If you're trying to earn money online, consistency is particularly vital. If you change design elements from page to page, as hobbyists who create personal home pages often do, you will be thought of in the same group as amateurs. Don't take that wrong—there's nothing wrong with personal home pages; in fact, I enjoy them. However, I'm probably not going to send money to someone who appears to have no business experience and whose site may be gone tomorrow. To make money, you need to earn trust, and you accomplish that through professional design as much as anything.

15.8 White Space

AN IMPORTANT PART OF GOOD DESIGN is white space. Of course, white space isn't necessarily the color white—it simply refers to empty space on a page. If you run text from edge to edge and fill up all the space with something, the page will look cluttered to the point of being tiresome. While your intent may be to pack as much information as possible into the space, it actually makes everything harder to find. With no visual "rest stops" for the eyes, everything becomes a jumble of confusion for visitors.

Smart design includes ample white space on each side of the page. Keep in mind that reading text on a monitor is different from reading text on paper. While a standard sheet of paper is 8.5 inches wide, monitors are often 17 or more inches wide. Because of the extra width, when you read on a monitor and come to the end of a line, it can be much harder to find the beginning of the next line if the line length is too long. With margins on both sides, you not only create a cleaner and more professional look, you make it easier for visitors to read your text.

Vertical white space is equally important. Running on and on without paragraph breaks or headings creates an endless wall of text that looks overwhelming to most users. Few will read it all. By creating short paragraphs and adding appropriate headings in the right places, visitors can grab bite-size chunks and are more likely to read what you have to say, you gabby little thing, you.

Figure 15.4 shows a web page from an ebook compilation of some of my Life's Little Goodies stories I'm working on. Notice the white space on each side (filled with a nifty stone background texture) for horizontal breathing room. While you probably can't read the text in the graphic, you can see the short, easy-to-follow paragraphs in the main body area, and you can see the vertical white space between the main body text and the sidebar text. Everything is broken up into easy-to-digest pieces with plenty of resting places for the eyes,

Figure 15.4

yet it maintains a consistent flow of thought and design. It's this kind of design that makes reading a pleasant experience instead of a mental workout—it allows the visitor to concentrate on the message rather than the task of reading.

As I've already mentioned, surfers tend to skim pages to look for chunks of meat rather than starting at the top and nibbling away. Short bursts of words are more conducive to the way surfers view web pages, so this design technique helps prevent visitors from skipping over your important points.

Long paragraphs are tiring to the eyes and more likely to be skipped. Think about it, don't you do the same thing? I know I do.

This is crucial: Important points are usually lost in long paragraphs.

I'll bet you read my crucial point, didn't you? It's intended and prefaced with bold text, which implicitly tells you that it's important. Bury that line in a long passage of text and it doesn't have nearly the same impact. If you have a must-read key point to make, take steps to make sure readers don't skip over it.

If you have an important point to make, but you can't isolate it in one sentence, then headings may be the way to go. Headings draw visitors into your message. Think of headings as newspaper or advertisement headlines. They should be short and punchy, and sell the reader on reading the text that follows.

Another way to isolate a passage of text is by treating it as a pull quote. Isolate the whole paragraph by indenting it on each side. This can be done with a blockquote tag set or using CSS to add a margin to a paragraph or division element.

15.9 Clean Design

I DEFINE "CLEAN DESIGN" as well-focused, purposeful, uncluttered design. While white space is certainly a part of that, it's not the only factor that contributes to clean design. Some pages are so cluttered with information, images, links, and other items that users don't intuitively know where to focus their attention. It becomes a hunting expedition at that point, and the longer a hunting expedition is drawn out, more and more users will opt out of the hunting party to go elsewhere.

A clean design should visually lead users into the content you want them to concentrate on first on any given page. This can be accomplished through the use of color, a graphic, emphasized text, content placement, or other techniques.

To lead readers to the content you want them to read first, it helps to know where they tend to focus their concentration when they first arrive at a page. Eye tracking studies show that, as a general rule, readers view a page in an "F" pattern.

When following the F pattern, users scan from left to right across the top of the page first, creating the top piece of an imaginary giant letter F on the page. Their second focal point is about halfway down the page, where they'll read across the screen again, but not always all the way across the page as they do at the top. This tendency draws the lower horizontal piece of the letter F. Third, they read down the left side of the page, drawing the vertical piece of the letter F.

By this time, they've often picked the content to read or another page to access. If not, the patterns become less predictable regarding where their eyes go next. The point is, however, if you place your primary "catches" in one of these locations, there is a good chance users will read what you want them to read first—if the topic is of interest to them in the first place.

It's no coincidence that Google is the most popular search engine. Until Google came along, nearly all search engine landing pages were severely cluttered with information. Google's simple design is much easier to understand at a glance, so it's much easier to use. Therefore, Google quickly became the most popular search engine with a majority of users.

As Google's popularity rose, so did the number of search engines that started emulating its no-clutter style. Not many web sites can afford to have a home page as simplistic as a search engine's, whose primary purpose is more obvious than most other types of sites. But the simplicity does nicely illustrate how a clean design with plenty of white space is important. This type of design is simply more user friendly. Google's designers don't have to concern themselves with the F pattern because there is little else on the front page to consider.

A research study by Dr. Gitte Lindgaard at Carleton University shows that a user can have a "gut reaction" to a website in less than one second. This is a blink of the eye. The speed at which users form value judgments shows that these judgments are not based on cognitive thought, but on emotional reactions and intuition according to visual appeal. Furthermore, this initial judgment has a trickle-down effect that can influence subsequent value judgments, even those based on cognitive thought.

In a different study that Stanford University conducted with more than 2,600 participants, a "clean, professional look" was cited by 46.1 percent of participants when evaluating web sites for credibility. "Information design and structure" (presentation and navigation) was cited 28.5 percent of the time, and "information focus" was cited 25.1 percent of the time. In other words, clean design, good structure, and strong content meant credibility to 99.7 percent of the test subjects. That's pretty definitive by any standards.

By combining these three credibility fundamentals with the way users read web pages—scanning the page for catchwords and following the F pattern—you can optimize pages for the users' experience and your own purposes.

Other elements of clean design include maintaining focus and limiting page length. Maintaining focus was covered in Section 15.3: Writing YaYa earlier in this chapter. The ideal page length is subjective, but the idea is that you don't want pages that require a lot of scrolling or it can look like too much work to read. A wall of text can intimidate people into looking for shorter, more concise information elsewhere. By breaking up long pages into two or more pages, this problem is easily dodged.

A good rule of thumb is to keep pages to four or fewer screen lengths. That is, if a user has to scroll down more than the height of four screens, the page is probably too long. Of course, there are always exceptions, which I'll leave up to your judgment, but you are wise not to make too many exceptions without good reason.

The two final elements of clean design are using color effectively and providing adequate contrast for reading. We discussed color usage in Chapter 8: Color, Backgrounds, and Images, so we won't go into it again here. Except I will remind you that a business site shouldn't use a background image, with some wiggle room to that statement for a solid-colored, left-border style background that houses the navigation system or some other structured content. In all cases, any background image must be subtle—especially if there is text that must be read on top of it—and it must provide good contrast for reading.

To recap, a clean design includes these objectives:

- Focus on the mission
- Not too cluttered
- Adequate white space
- Built for scanning using the F pattern, catchwords, and emphasized text

- Good color coordination
- Good reading contrast
- No background image or very subtle background image
- Good navigation structure
- Reasonable screen length

15.10 Credibility

GOOD DESIGN HELPS YOUR SITE achieve credibility, and credibility is crucial to having any kind of success online. We briefly touched on credibility in the previous section, but now we'll go into more detail. Following is my list of 23 fundamentals of establishing credibility online.

1. **Show you're real.**

   One of the things consumers are most leery about is doing business with anonymous entities. It's relatively easy to set up an online scam, so users have good reason to be cautious. Placing your picture online, or pictures of key staff members, shows consumers there are real people behind the business.

2. **Include your bio and qualifications.**

   If you include a brief bio and any credentials or related experience with the personnel photos it demonstrates individuality and qualifications. Citing the expertise of your team is always a plus. Take care to only include staff members who are comfortable with having a blurb about them placed online. For example, a single woman living alone may not be comfortable with having any information about her posted. That's only natural and should be respected. Furthermore, individual home addresses and phone numbers should *never* be included online unless it's your own and you know what you're doing. Privacy is a valuable commodity and should not be taken for granted.

3. **Give your location.**

   Another part of showing you're real is to offer a physical address for your business. If people see you are willing to give a physical location, they have less reason to believe you may be a charlatan. After all, people who have reason to hide from the law or from people they have ripped off would never tell you or the authorities where to find them. If you're willing to disclose an address, there's less reason to doubt your sincerity. The exception is if your business location is your home address. For these I recommend using a P.O. Box. It's not as good as a street address, but it does give users a way to contact you in writing and a paper trail people know the authorities can trace if you turn out to be dishonest.

4. **Give your phone number.**

People are even more assured you'll be there for them if you give your phone number in case they have problems with a purchase from you. Of course, if you have a home business, you'll want to have a second number to use for the business—one you can turn off when you go to bed or stop working for the day. Remember, it's called the World Wide Web because it is *worldwide*. If you don't use a number you can turn off, you may well get phone calls any time of the night. Of course, if you can provide a toll-free number, that's all the better.

5. **Make verification easy.**

By citing references, information sources, and linking to authoritative material that supports your clams—I mean *claims*—you add to your credibility by indirect association. Your clams are on their own.

6. **Professional quality design.**

As I mentioned earlier, a user's first impression can take less than one second to form and can color the rest of his or her judgments about your site. A site that makes a good visual impression right out of the gate is crucial. This means a pleasing design and color scheme. If you use graphics, it means using professional quality custom graphics, not free clip art you can find online that can be seen on hundreds or even thousands of other web sites. The design should also be appropriate for the type of site you have. Using little smiley faces for bullet points on a plumbing site is not really appropriate, whereas using little pipe wrenches would be. Stick to the theme and play to your strengths.

7. Intelligent navigation.

A well thought-out navigation system that is consistent throughout the site is expected. Anything less is a red flag to a user. The more difficult it is to set up a usable and intuitive navigation system because of your site's content, the more crucial it is that you achieve that goal. The harder it is for users to find the content they are seeking, the more likely it is that it won't be found before they surf away to points unknown.

8. Unique and useful.

The two U's of credibility are *unique* content and *usefulness*. Content thieves may think there are so many web sites out there no one will know if they "borrow" content from others. That may be true when borrowing from low-traffic, amateur sites, but it's certainly not true for professional web sites with experienced webmasters. It's a relatively simple matter to find content thieves; it just takes a little bit of time. Users also recognize stolen content. When someone has an interest in a particular topic they frequent sites that address those topics and often recognize content they've seen elsewhere. On many different occasions, my loyal visitors have reported sites that had stolen my copyrighted content. If you can't write your own content, hire it done.

As for usefulness, this is pretty obvious. If your site isn't useful for something—if it has no purpose—it isn't destined for success.

9. Update your site.

Update your site regularly, at least twice a month, to show it isn't stagnant. This point is particularly relevant to sites that rely on repeat visitors. A one-page sales site built around one product doesn't need updating as often since the plan is to drive new visitors to the site to make sales rather than to have people coming back time and time again.

Having said that, even one-trick sales sites can benefit from updated content. By having a weekly tip or something similar that brings visitors back, those who don't buy immediately may buy later as they learn to trust you from repeated communication. That's why marketing experts say "the money is in the list" in reference to developing a mailing list. Repeat communication, even if it's one-way communication, helps build the trust that results in future sales.

10. **Use restraint.**

Use restraint when it comes to placing advertising on your site. Too many ads on one page, pop-up ads, and transition page advertisements become annoying quickly. A transition page ad displays when a user clicks a link expecting to find content and an advertising page displays first, leaving the user to find the link to continue.

Restraint also applies to written content. While writing about a topic you feel passionate about is normal, injecting too much emotion into your writing can reveal a lack of control and level-headed sensibility, rather than imparting your passion to the reader. Take care to prevent the emotional pendulum from swinging too far or cutting too deep.

Restraint in your writing style is important as well. Avoid excessive hype, unbelievable claims, and overt exaggerations. The fastest way to lose credibility is to make incredible claims without offering definitive proof to back them up.

Also, unless your site is political in nature, it's usually best to stay away from this hot-button topic unless you don't care if you alienate half your visitors. In the United States and many other countries, the population is split about evenly between those who identify with conservatives and those who identify with liberals. If you trot out your political views, you'll be trotting away from about half your potential customers. Save the politics for a more appropriate forum than your business site—unless your business caters to one particular ideology.

11. **Disclosures and disclaimers.**

As with traditional paper publishing, online publishers and writers should disclose any relationships, memberships, and associations that could call their objectivity into question. Full disclosure indicates honesty while nondisclosure can taint the message with suspicion.

Listing any relevant memberships, such as trade organizations, Better Business Bureau memberships, board memberships, and the like can add to your credibility. For example, at the time of this writing, I'm a Board Member of Mid-state Technical College's Marketing Board here in central Wisconsin. If I wrote an article about marketing, I'd be sure to list that membership to show I have at least a modicum of acknowledged expertise in the marketing field.

12. Date content.

Some types of content should be dated. News items, for example, should always be dated so readers know if it's relevant or not. Other types of content, such as free web graphics, don't need to be dated because it doesn't matter how old the images are or how old the pages they are on are; a person either likes and wants to use an image or not. Unless you plan to remove outdated content in a timely fashion, date content when the age of it is relevant to the reader.

13. Establish your expertise.

By either publishing your own newsletter or writing articles for other publishers, you help establish yourself as an expert in your field. Many newsletters depend on contributed content. Nearly all publishers will link from your article credits (also called a resource box, usually seen at the end of the article) to your web site. By getting your name and web site in front of lots of eyeballs that already have a relationship with the publisher, you "borrow" some of that publisher's credibility with his or her subscriber base.

14. Avoid jargon.

Write in everyday language—don't try to sound like an expert by using industry jargon. If people don't understand what you're saying, how can they trust what you're saying? If the use of jargon is a must, explain the jargon in the simplest terms possible to remove as much mystery as you can.

15. Post a privacy policy.

It's irresponsible to not have a privacy policy these days. A privacy policy details what you will and won't do with any information they provide to you. For example, responsible web site owners usually promise not to sell, trade, or give away your personal information to third parties. Potential customers want to know that any information they submit to you will not be misused. Study the privacy policies of several websites and develop one relevant for your purposes.

16. Respond promptly.

Try to answer all inquiries promptly. Knowing that you're there and will respond quickly eases the concerns a potential customer may have about doing business with you. Answering in a timely fashion can, however, become a real problem for one-person businesses that continue to grow in popularity. Take me for example: on a very busy day I receive as many as 500 emails. It's impossible for one person to conduct business as usual and answer that many emails, especially when many of them are technical in nature and require a lengthy or thoughtful answer. Sometimes you just have to do the best you can and take your lumps from the folks who aren't happy with you—but as they say in the sports world, it's a nice problem to have.

17. Use a secure server.

If you sell products or services online and take a customer's credit card information, you must use a secure server. A secure server encrypts the customer's credit card information to make it extremely difficult to impossible for unauthorized users to access. This not only establishes your credibility, but it protects your customer's private information, and that's *always* important!

18. Use testimonials and references.

Anytime you can use customer testimonials to laud your products or services helps establish your credibility with potential new customers. While you can solicit testimonials, I prefer to wait for customers to volunteer comments and then ask for their permission to use them. Testimonials labeled as "unsolicited" have more power. If you can get references from prior customers or experts in your field, so much the better—use them.

19. Make sure everything works.

Broken links, broken images, and other non-working items subtract from your web site's credibility. If you don't take the time to make sure your web site works properly, a user can rightly question whether your products and services will come as advertised or whether any information they provide will be secure.

20. Spellcheck and proofread.

Misspellings happen, but using spellchecking software will catch most of them for you. One or two misspellings every few pages isn't necessarily a deal breaker, but too many can call your professionalism and credibility into question, which can be a deal breaker. Using a spell-checker is important, but so is proofreading your pages. For example, the following sentence:

They're seams too bee mini airs hear.

...would pass a spellchecker, but not one word is correct. That's why proofreading your pages is important. You might catch mistakes the spellchecker can't.

21. Just be honest!

It sounds simple, and it is—just be honest. Nothing will destroy your credibility faster or more completely than running a dishonest business or lying to customers. A word to the wise should be sufficient...enough said.

22. Show your history.

Have an "about" page that tells a little of your company history. Even if your business is new, that's not a crime, and telling it the way it is may help. Include a mission statement that spells out your company philosophy and what your business is all about.

23. Show you care.

Donate some time, products, or services to good causes. Show people you care about more than just making the almighty dollar. There's a good reason so many business people have a current of altruism running through their character. The law of cause and effect brings good things back to those who sow good seeds.

According to The Pew Research Center, the credibility of the most news media outlets has fallen each year since 1998. In 2006, the last year data was available, less than 25 percent of those surveyed believed they could trust most or all of what the media reports. While that's really bad, the credibility of websites in general may not even be that good. It's even more important for webmasters to do all the things within their power to establish credibility.

15.11 Bad Design

ALONG WITH THE MANY THINGS you can do to enhance your web site design and credibility, there are many things you can do that negatively impact the design and credibility. Following is my list of 17 bad web design practices.

1. **Access time.**

   Excessive file sizes and/or slow server response times can make your site slow enough that many people will leave rather than wait for it to load. Studies show that you'll lose visitors after just eight seconds if your website still hasn't loaded to the point where it's usable. Placing all your content inside one giant table also slows your site down because many browsers won't display anything until the table content has completely downloaded. If you like using tables to design with, it's best to use several small tables rather than one big one.

2. **Buzzing and jumping.**

   Many sites get away from what made them popular in the first place. They try to incorporate the latest buzzwords and jump on the bandwagons of the latest trends, either diluting or moving away from their core appeal. Rather than building on the strengths that brought them success, they chip away at their very foundations by breaking the cardinal rule: if it ain't broke, don't fix it. That's not to say you can't branch out—you can, but not at the expense of neglecting what's already working.

3. Dead ends and under construction pages.

There's an old saying (old in Internet years, that is) that says, "no web site is ever finished, but each should be complete." Links that lead to dead ends—because you haven't added the content yet—should be avoided. Sometimes it's hard to avoid when redesigning a large site, but do try. Make a "coming soon" announcement if you must, but don't send users to nonexistent content if it's possible to avoid it.

Pages that have "under construction" signs were somewhat clever back in 1996 when they first appeared. Old cleverness is still old, but no longer clever.

4. Horizontal scrolling.

Few things annoy surfers more than having to scroll right, scroll left, scroll right, and so on to read content that is too wide for the average readers' screen. Horizontal scrolling is not only a nuisance, but it breaks up the flow of your message and other content. If you design using a fixed width and your design is greater than about 775 pixels wide, about half your visitors will have a horizontal scroll bar. At the time of this writing, about half your users will be surfing at a resolution of 800x600. The vertical scroll bar will take about 20 to 25 pixels of horizontal space, so 775 pixels is the maximum width to prevent scroll bars. Most everyone else who isn't using an 800x600 resolution is using a higher resolution so scrollbars won't be an issue. According to Browser News, fewer than 1 percent of web surfers use a resolution lower than 800x600, and that number will continue to fall as old computers are retired. Don't worry about the 1 percent.

5. Auto-play music.

Many people surf the Internet from work. If you force music on people, just about every office worker with speakers and coworkers present will immediately leave your site. Want more bad news? People like me, who usually have on their own choice of music or talk radio, leave the site as well. Your sound interferes with my listening choice, and there are a lot of people like me.

In addition, musical tastes are very diverse. No matter how popular the music you choose may be, it's a good bet that of those who initially stay on the site, at least half of them won't like your choice in music and may leave because they don't like what they hear. Is forcing your music on people so important that you don't care if you drive a major portion of your visitors away? If you think you must have music, let the user choose whether to play it and don't start it automatically.

6. **Browser-crashing code.**

Crashing isn't the issue it used to be because browser software is much more stable now. However, you still should check your site in several browsers to make sure any scripts, Java, or other "extra" technology doesn't cause a browser or operating system to crash. When testing on Windows, be sure to have several programs open at once as many people do, because each uses memory and a lack of memory resources is the cause of a great many crashes. As I'm writing this, I have six programs running (Word, Internet Explorer, Firefox, email, streaming audio, and TextPad). Just guessing, I'd say having five or six programs running at once isn't unusual. This is not an issue for Mac OS users.

7. **Splash screens.**

Splash screens are generally a waste of time. The webmaster is saying, "Look at my pretty picture," and the user is thinking, "Where's the content?" They add an unnecessary step between the users and the content they are seeking. Most experts agree that splash screens are all about the webmaster and show a lack of respect for the users' time. As one highly regarded web designer noted, "Splash screens are a sure sign of bad design."

8. **Poor content.**

This should probably be number one on the list. A web site with a lack of original, good quality information—or whatever the content is, depending on the purpose of the site—no matter how well designed, will be relegated to the scrapheap.

Quality content extends to your website's visuals, too. Cheap-looking graphics, awkward layouts, clashing colors, and too much visual clutter all contribute to the overall aesthetics of your website, and aesthetics are part of the content.

9. **Scrolling, blinking, and animation.**

Scrolling or blinking text, flashing colors—techniques designed to get attention—are often more annoying than attention getting. It doesn't do a lot of good to get people's attention if the result is that visitors develop a negative attitude about your presentation. Of course, there are always exceptions, but the general truth is reading text online is tiring enough for the eyes, it's best not to make it even more troublesome.

Animated graphics can be used successfully to get attention, but caution should be used here too. Animation that never ends becomes as irksome and distracting as scrolling and blinking text and flashing colors. Best to use sparingly, and don't let the animation run endlessly. Four or five loops are enough for animated graphics that are above the fold (in view on the first screen prior to scrolling). You can go longer for animations below the fold because a visitor won't see the first few loops.

10. **Page counters.**

From the beginning, professionals considered page counters to be amateurish. If you have a lot of traffic, using one looks either arrogant or phony. If you don't have a lot of traffic, do you really want people knowing that? You'll get more reliable traffic stats from the tracking software your web host provides or from your web site's log file.

11. **Poor grammar, spelling, and punctuation.**

You can get away with an error here and there, but there are people who will judge your professionalism by how well your site adheres to proper grammar, spelling, and punctuation. Too many obvious mistakes and your site will suffer a loss of credibility in some people's eyes.

Using slang such as the letter *u* in place of the word *you* or *l8ter* for *later* are practices kids use—and most adults don't like it. It has no place on a business web site.

Typing in all caps is a no-no, too. It's harder to read and is considered "shouting" online. Strive to make your points using language, not capitalization.

12. Linking to unexpected file types without warning.

When people click a link, they generally expect to see a new web page. When a webmaster links to an unexpected file type, such as a PDF file or Word document, you should explicitly advise visitors of the file type. A user may not have the software needed to open a non-HMTL file, so they will be waiting for a download for nothing.

Not only that, but some users won't like these other file formats, which weren't originally intended for reading content online. Forcing them on people by failing to offer a warning makes it that much harder to make a good impression.

Lastly, some of these alternate file types can contain viruses. Few people like being surprised by a file that could have a virus even if they have an antivirus program.

13. Visually deceptive advertising.

One current trend among advertisers is to use visually deceptive advertisements. A graphic image may be disguised as a helpful search box, a pop-up window may be designed to look like a genuine computer system alert, or a false virus warning may be displayed. All these and other deceptive practices put the web site selling these advertising placements in a bad light. By allowing deceptive advertising on your web site, you're basically telling your visitors that advertising money is more important to you than they are. Obviously, that's not a good practice.

14. Wrong conceptual approach.

A good many business web sites are built with a "me first" approach. That is, they design the site based on what they want, not what the consumer wants or needs. News flash—your visitors don't care about you, they care about what's in it for them. They may come to care about you in time, but when they first arrive at your site, you'd better show them what's in it for them or they'll find another site that will. Likewise, too much yakking about yourself or your company isn't going to be very interesting to most people. Put this kind of information on an "about" page for those who care, not on your home page for those who don't.

Don't write in officious, dry, corporate-style language unless your site specifically caters to business executives or technical people. Most people prefer a friendly, casual style of writing.

15. **Excess.**

The trend on some sites is to use a pop-up advertisement on every page. Even worse, some sites serve up two or three pop-ups from the same page. While I can empathize with the need to earn money, and advertising can be a legitimate income producer, we have to be careful that in our zeal to create income we aren't abusing our visitors.

A goal of most sites is to foster an atmosphere that encourages visitors to come back. Repeat visitors increase sales, web site popularity, and search engine rankings and bring other benefits to us. Put yourself in your visitors' shoes while designing or updating your site. If something about your site even moderately bothers you, it will bother your visitors even more.

Excess can apply to other things besides pop-up ads. Requiring too much information on a contact form, creating pages that never seem to end, playing music on every page, changing the site look from page to page, and many other things can all be forms of excess to avoid.

16. **Using too small a font size.**

Some web sites use fonts so small they must think everyone has perfect vision. If the font size is too small, some people will just sigh and go elsewhere. Tiny text is acceptable in disclaimers, copyright statements, and perhaps some sidebar uses, but the main body text should be big enough that most people can read it with relative ease.

Some argue that users can always set the text size larger in their browsers, but that won't work if the font size is set with CSS (as it should be). The font size control in the browser menu was designed for pre-CSS technology; it has no affect on text sized with CSS.

17. **Illegal use of copyrighted material.**

One of the biggest problems on the World Wide Web is people using copyrighted material without permission. The same person that wouldn't think of stealing a painting or shoplifting a music CD will take graphics or songs from web sites and use them as their own. Some may simply be ignorant of copyright law, but many others do know better—they just don't consider it stealing—but it is!

Here are five common myths about copyright law.

● **Myth 1:** If it doesn't have a copyright notice, it's free to use.

Fact: This was true at one time, but today most nations abide by the Berne copyright convention. Original works created after 1989 are copyrighted whether a notice is provided or not. This applies to web sites, too. Once a web site is published (placed online) it has copyright protection, provided it's using original content.

● **Myth 2:** If I make up my own story based on someone else's story, the new story copyrights belong to me.

Fact: These kinds of works are called derivative works. If you write a story using settings or characters from someone else's work, you need that author's permission. The lone exception is for parody.

● **Myth 3:** Copyright violation isn't a serious offense.

Fact: In the United States, a commercial copyright violation involving more than 10 copies or more than $2,500 is a felony. Fines and penalties can be over six figures.

● **Myth 4:** If I don't charge for it, it's not against the law to use it.

Fact: If you charge for it, penalties and awarded damages can be more severe. However, penalties and damages can be awarded whether you charge for content or not.

● **Myth 5:** Copyrights expire after three years.

Fact: A work that is created (fixed in tangible form for the first time) on or after January 1, 1978, is automatically protected from the moment of its creation and is ordinarily given a term enduring for the author's life plus an additional 70 years after the author's death, or until the author transfers the copyrights to another entity.

Lastly, facts and ideas can't be copyrighted, but the way those facts and ideas are presented and the system of implementation can be. You can write about anything that you research, as long as you use your own words and style of presentation.

It's impossible to please everyone, and it's been said that trying to do so is a recipe for failure. These rules of web design aren't designed to please everyone. They are offered only as a responsible guideline to please the majority of visitors.

15.12 Accessibility

IN RESPONSE TO A "Guess the Celebrity" contest on my web site, someone typed the following comment into the entry form (as a joke, I presume, because it was a visual-based contest):

"design your site for the blind — hahahaha"

What they probably didn't know is that blind people do access the Internet and do so without human help. How is this possible? They use software programs called screen readers. If you follow some basic design principles, you can create a site that is accessible to vision-impaired people, blind people, and people with other types of handicaps such as motor impairment.

1. Screen readers read from left to right. If you use tables, the information must be understandable that way. Table headers (<th>) should be used on data tables, but not layout tables.

2. Frames are a no-no. Most screen readers don't recognize when you change a frame and will not re-read that part of the screen. Of course, frames also kill your site with some search engines, so there's another reason to stay away from them.

3. Use *alt* text tags for all images that are part of the content (as opposed to images that are part of the design) so a screen reader can explain your graphics to the user.

4. Keep a high contrast between the text and background color.

5. Small link buttons are hard for motor-impaired people to click, so keep link buttons large enough to be clicked easily. Include alternative text links for any image links used.

6. Keep a consistent layout throughout your site.

7. Make sure the font size is large enough for most readers.

8. Finally, keep the page clean and uncluttered so it's easy to understand.

These are just the very basics. I'd have to add another chapter to give the topic a complete treatment, and there isn't room for that. If you're designing a site of particular interest to impaired users and would like to learn more about making it more accessible, I recommend reading the W3C standards at:

Web Content Accessibility Guidelines 1.0
http://www.w3.org/TR/WAI-WEBCONTENT

List of Checkpoints for Web Content Accessibility
http://www.w3.org/TR/WAI-WEBCONTENT/
checkpoint-list.html

15.13 Summary

THERE'S A LOT OF INFORMATION in this chapter, so here's a recap of the main points.

 Rule number one: content rules! Quality, original content should be an even higher priority than the website's appearance.

 Develop your own writing voice. Be yourself, but be your best self. Remember that surfers scan web pages looking for words and phrases that catch their attention. Design your pages for easy scanning. Keep your writing focused and terse.

 Plan your web site before attempting to design it. Remember to answer your visitor's most pressing concerns. What's in it for them? Can they trust you?

Consider employing preview-ability and usability testing to identify any potential problems before exposing your web site to the public.

 Create a site template that includes all the elements that will be common to every page. Validate the page with a validator so you're always starting a new page with validated correct syntax. Designate the template as a read-only file.

 Maintain consistency throughout your site. Keep the same look and primary navigation system from page to page. Secondary navigation can be implemented within distinct content sections as a supplement to the primary navigation system.

 Plan vertical and horizontal white space into your pages and follow the principles of clean design.

 You need to prove your credibility to visitors; they don't know that you're Roy Righteous or Edythe Ethical.

 Remember the checklists for good design and bad design. Adhere to as many of the good points as you can and avoid as many bad points as you can.

 While most people don't get too concerned with accessibility, I recommend you at least visit the two W3C accessibility pages listed and review the recommendations. You may learn something.

15.14 Chapter 15 Exercise

Now that you've read this chapter, you probably realize that some things about your project site couldn't be called good design. For example, the navigation isn't consistent throughout your site, and not all pages have the colorful header on the top with your organization's name.

- Your assignment for this chapter is to go back through all your pages and correct the inconsistencies.

- One thing you will need to do: On the framed page, change the frameset to nest the frames as shown in Section 12.11 so you can add the page header atop the framed content.

Have fun!

Publishing Your Web Site

16

16.1 Introduction

SOONER OR LATER YOU'LL PROBABLY want to publish your web site for the world to see. There are three main issues when it comes to publishing a web site:

- Obtaining a domain name
- Selecting a web hosting company
- Uploading your files to your web host

Be sure to secure a domain name before building your web site. Good domain names can be hard to find. It would be a disappointing surprise to build an entire web site around a name only to find some other entity is using that same name.

16.2 Obtaining a Domain Name

IF YOU'RE USING THIS BOOK in a classroom, your educational institution may offer space on their servers for your web site. That's fine for the purpose of learning to build your own web site.

There are also web sites whose business it is to offer free space for non-commercial purposes. This is OK if you only want a hobby site and are willing to tolerate the advertising they include on your site and the poor support that usually goes with free web site hosting.

Additionally, your ISP may offer you a small amount of web space for your web site. In these cases, your web site is usually listed under your ISP's domain name, and as such, the web address for your site is usually long and difficult to tell people. A typical web address on someone else's domain might look like this:

http://www.somedomain.com/users/~yourname/index.html

That's too unwieldy to be useful outside of the hyperlink context. In other words, it's difficult to pass on verbally, difficult to use in advertising or on business cards, and difficult to remember. In addition, it takes more work to type into a browser address bar, so users are more prone to making a typo that will cause the server to return a "file not found" error message, which means the user may think your site is no longer available.

All that may be acceptable if you're creating a site you expect to be used only by a few family members and friends to keep them up to date on your life. However, if you want to put forth a more professional image or start a commercial web site, you need your own domain name. Having your own domain name is better than having a site under someone else's domain name for several reasons:

- A shorter, easier to remember and use web address.
- Portability: If you ever move your site to another host, your domain name is still good. If you change hosts and your site uses another domain's name, your web address will change, so you'll lose all the links and bookmarks that point to your site.
- Most search engines no longer list sites that are sub-level sites of another domain; they only index the original domain, making promoting your site more difficult. Directories are also less likely to include your site if it doesn't have its own domain because free sites come and go quickly, causing link rot (broken links).
- A professional approach is mandatory for commercial sites, allowing you a small measure of credibility and trust without actually earning it yet. Without your own domain, commercial sites can be viewed with a measure of distrust —without earning that either.
- You'll have an email address at your own domain to use for most communications, allowing you to keep your ISP-provided email address private and mostly spam-free for family and friends.

- You can design your site as you please, with no space sacrificed for the advertising purposes of the host provider and fewer restrictions on how you may use it.

- Having your own domain means using a professional hosting service. A good web host will offer many more features and benefits than a free account provider will.

- For commercial sites, having your own domain may actually save you money. With the low cost of purchasing a domain and hosting, the benefits outweigh the costs without even considering sales. One example is that you can have multiple email accounts to efficiently sort your email. You might have: support@yourdomain.com, sales@yourdomain.com, and advertising@yourdomain.com. You may be a one-person business, but using different email addresses gives your business a "bigger than it is" perception.

- New businesses come online every single day of the year. The longer you wait, the harder it will be to find a quality domain name—and that's already difficult enough.

- Lastly, for most businesses, people expect you to have a web site with your own domain name.

Obtaining a domain name is easy—and difficult. That is, the actual purchase of a domain is simply a matter of filling out a few form fields and supplying your credit card information. However, finding a suitable domain name can be an exercise in frustration and perseverance.

Domain names are based on words. With millions of domains in existence, finding a word or combination of words that isn't already taken requires a lot of creativity and a little luck. If you want to find a single-word domain name that isn't already in use, you'll need a *lot* of luck.

I will give you some solid tips on finding a good domain name, but first you need to know what constitutes a good domain name. There are several components to a good domain name:

- It should be memorable and easy to spell. Being memorable is subjective. Many people think BoogieJack.com is a memorable and fun domain name. I suppose it is, but I bought it because I was already known as Boogie Jack. I wouldn't choose the name today because it doesn't tie in with my web site content, and having a tie-in with your content is a good idea whenever possible.

- It should be as short as makes sense, but not always as short as possible. For example, if your business is named *Jane's Persian Rug Bazaar*, the domain *janesrugs.com* is easier to remember than *jprb.com*.
- It has at least one keyword in it that is relevant to your site.
- It has an original top-level domain extension (.com, .org, or .net). There are many other domain extensions now, but people are not as familiar with them.
- Whenever possible, the domain name should be the same as the web site name, which ideally would be the same name as your business name.

It may not be possible to find a domain name with all of those components available. We just have to do the best we can. Still, a little creativity can go a long way toward coming up with a good domain name.

I recently purchased some new domain names, and more than a few people were surprised they were available because they are so simple. Those names are:

i-backgrounds.com

HTMLville.com

i-webmasters.org

Many web sites use an *i-* or *e-* before a good keyword (for *Internet* or *electronic*, the latter probably taken from the term e-commerce) to create a domain name with a single, high-quality keyword in it. As far as search engines are concerned, because of the hyphen (which search engines treat as a space), i-webmasters .org is on equal footing with webmasters.org (which wasn't available) as a keyworded domain name. Many domain seekers don't think of this simple trick.

There was a time when many experts thought hyphenated domains were a bad practice because people weren't used to seeing them. That's all changed now—a domain with a hyphen between two keywords is actually better, from a search engine standpoint, than two keywords run together.

For example, let's say you're trying to choose between the following two domain names:

blue-widgets.com

bluewidgets.com

Each domain has a benefit the other doesn't have. The hyphenated domain name is better for search engine rankings because nearly all search engines will treat the name as two keywords, making it extremely relevant for anyone searching for "blue widgets." Some search engines may break down bluewidgets.com into two keywords, but many will not. For the search engines that do not, the domain name is only relevant for people searching for "bluewidgets" as a single word, and not many do that. The benefit of the unhyphenated name is that it doesn't have a hyphen, because many people forget the hyphen when trying to remember a domain name. This isn't a factor for hyperlinks; it only comes into play when an address is verbally passed on or when someone is trying to remember a domain name they read about.

As you may have gathered, having a keyword in your domain name is an asset when it comes to search engine rankings. Because of space limitations I can't go into all the details of search engine rankings, but you can learn more about that topic on my www. BoogieJack.com site.

If the domain you really want is taken, consider adding an "s," a suffix, a prefix, or a descriptive noun to the name. I'm going to make up a word here to save me the time and trouble of hunting for a real example with the right qualifications. For this purpose, let's pretend that a "dirgle" is a mental practice for stimulating creative thinking and you want to build a web site teaching the practice. You checked dirgle.com and it was taken, and so were the .net and .org extensions.

You could try:

dirgle**s**.com, **mega**dirgle.com, dirgle**center**.com, **true**dirgle.com, etc.

You could try the .org and .net extensions, use hyphens, and try many other prefixes, suffixes, and add-on nouns, too. The point is, be creative. While single-word domains are extremely difficult to find, there are still plenty of good domain names for the creative thinker. One note about using hyphens in a domain name—don't use more than one. People are just getting accustomed to one-hyphen names; additional hyphens only add a new and unnecessary layer of unfamiliarity.

Finding a good domain name is often a case of trial and error. That is, you think up a bunch of domain names and then plug them into a domain search engine to see if they're taken. You can

> *Note*
>
> When I searched for a fictional word to use for an example of modifying a domain name, I tried seven different words I made up before finding a non-existent word that wasn't being used as a domain name. That's how hard it can be to find domain names.

double your brainpower by asking a friend or family member to help you think of domain names. The more people you ask to participate, the more you increase your brainpower.

For other help with creating a domain name, you'll find web addresses on my online resource page for this book. In case you're wondering why I don't include many web addresses in the book, I did that with the first edition only to regret it because one of the references went out of business. The domain name was then purchased by a porn company, which, of course, redirected users to an adult web site.

By keeping the references on my web site, I can control and update the information as needed and I don't have to worry about my readers encountering any nasty or unwelcome surprises. My resources page for this book is at:

www.BoogieJack.com/book/resources.html

Having said that, here are some online tools to help you find a domain name:

Expired Domains

You can search the expired domain names database at WhoIs. With this search, you enter a keyword to search for and receive a list of recently expired domains with your keyword in the name. Most of the domains aren't very good, but there are occasional gems and the list can inspire your own creativity. A deleted domain can have the added benefit of coming with some search engine listings and traffic, but I wouldn't expect too much from that. Some people sell small lists of expired domain names, but I've just told you how to search all the expired domains at no cost. You're welcome. ☺

Dislexicon

This online utility takes common words that you enter and adds suffixes and prefixes to them. It does a pretty decent job of finding short domain names that look like they could be real words. Plus, along with the new words, it tells you the meanings.

Word Mixer

This utility lets you enter up to five words to create new words from. The new words are less recognizable than the results from the Dislexicon utility, so they may not be as good as far as being memorable. Still, it can be a good tool for certain kinds of sites.

DomainsBot

This search engine is geared specifically to finding domain names—and it even tells you if the names it comes up with are available. This method works best if you're looking for a compound word rather than an invented or single word.

You'll also find a link on my resource page to ICANN-Accredited Domain Registrars, where you can enter any domain names you can think of and see if they're taken. You can purchase available domain names at these registrars as well.

The cost for registering a domain name varies from as low as $1.95 (on sale) to as much as $35 per year, depending on the registrar. On average, a top-level domain costs between $8 and $15 with most registrars. What's the difference between a domain purchased for $1.95 and one purchased for $35? Not much. The domain name works the same; the only differences are in some of the administrative features, the ease of use, and the quality of support.

Frankly, in my opinion, the best is not the most expensive. The most expensive registrar is a company I find very difficult to work with. You'll find my current recommendations on the resource page for this book, as well as the address for a web site that maintains an alphabetical list of all domain registrars.

Many hosting companies also offer domain registration. Most are OK to use, but you do have to be careful. Some hosts register themselves as the administrative contact. That means they own the domain, and some unscrupulous companies have been known to make it extremely difficult for you to transfer to a new host if you're not satisfied with their service. They may add unwarranted transfer fees as well, so if you use a hosting company to register your domain name, make certain they will list you as the administrative contact. Personally, I prefer to register domains through a domain registrar. I have several domains, purchased all through the same registrar, so I can manage them all at the same place.

In order for a company to exercise their trademark or servicemark rights,

> **WARNING!**
>
> The biggest danger in choosing a domain name concerns trademarks and servicemarks, sometimes collectively referred to as just marks. A trademark is a word, name, symbol, or "marking device" that is used with goods to indicate the source of the goods and to distinguish them from the goods of other entities. A servicemark is substantially the same as a trademark except that it identifies the source of a service rather than a product.

they have to take reasonable measures to protect them. Some companies are quite vigilant about it while others are not. Regardless, using another company's trademark or servicemark is an invitation for legal trouble to come a-calling. The average person wouldn't consider using a trademarked image, knowing that doing so would probably be illegal. What the average person may not realize, however, is that a word or phrase can be trademarked also.

A trademark is identified with the ™ symbol for trademark or the ® symbol for registered trademark. Many company names and product names are trademarked. For example, Painter™ is a trademarked product of Corel® Corporation, and the name Corel® itself is a registered trademark name of the company.

If you want to build a site offering Painter™ tutorials, you'd be wise to seek permission from Corel® Corporation to use the name Painter™ in conjunction with your tutorials. Some companies are quite accommodating as long as you aren't using their marks in a way they believe is damaging to the company or product while others are very restrictive. You never know until you ask.

As it pertains to domain names, if you wanted to bill yourself as a *painter tutor* and purchased "paintertutor.com" for a domain name, it would most likely be fine—if you were offering tutorials on house painting. But, you may run into problems with Corel® if you offered tutorials for Painter™ because "painter" as it pertains to their software is a trademarked word.

The U.S. Patent and Trademark Office is a good place to start checking for trademarks for any company with a U.S. presence. If in doubt, seek the advice of a professional or use an online Trademark Service to check. The U.S. Patent and Trademark web site is at:

www.uspto.gov

If you are considering buying an expired domain name, check the Internet Archive and look at old copies of the site to see if any trademarks are claimed. A search of the web using your favorite search engine should help, too. The Internet Archives may be accessed using the Wayback Machine, which is listed on my resources page.

If you violate a trademark, whether accidentally or intentionally, you may be required to surrender the domain name and possibly any monies earned while using it. It is obviously in your best interest to find a unique name without trademark or

Note

I don't know if Corel® is inclined to initiate cease and desist orders or legal action against those using their marks without permission or not; the point is, they would have the legal right to if they chose to, so prudence calls for obtaining permission in such cases.

servicemark restrictions, or obtain permission to use them if your site is planned around another company's products or services.

16.3 Selecting a Web Site Host

FOR A WEB SITE TO BE AVAILABLE on the Internet, it has to be located on a web server somewhere. That's where web hosting companies come into play. Thousands of web hosting companies exist, but the quality of services, features, technical support, and costs vary wildly. Choosing a good host can be a hit-or-miss proposition even for those well rehearsed in finding a new host.

There are several host-rating sites that supposedly rate the overall quality of web site hosts according to their own criteria. However, I would consider their ratings with a huge dose of skepticism. The three main reasons I have little trust toward these rating sites are:

- Many of them rate hosts in part or in total by visitor voting. A small number of disgruntled hosting clients, or the owner or employees of the hosting company, can skew the ratings one way or the other by repeated voting. Some of these sites claim they prevent voting repetition, but in most cases all you have to do is clear the cookies from your computer to vote again, and again, and again. Software robots may also be used to automate voting in some cases.

- Many hosts offer affiliate programs. An affiliate program pays you for sending customers to a business if the customer makes a purchase. Because of a negative experience I had with a highly rated hosting company that turned out to be a horrible web host, I suspect that at many rating sites the best-rated hosts are simply the ones that have the best-paying affiliate programs.

- I also have reason to believe many of the top-rated hosts merely buy their high rating and prominent placement from the host-rating sites, making their rating more of a disguised advertisement than a real rating based on services.

I think the best way to find a good host is to ask for recommendations from friends and from webmasters you trust. Even if the people you ask aren't the most experienced or knowledgeable about web hosting, they do know if they've had a good experience with their web host. Of course, the more experienced the web-masters you ask are, the more weight you should give their recommendations.

I do use one service to find web site hosts because the company is not affiliated with any host and does not accept advertising from hosts. Find My Hosting has a searchable database of hosts that have agreed to the Hosting Assured Code of Ethics. These guidelines are printed in the accompanying panel.

All Hosting Assured companies have agreed to abide by these guidelines. If a problem arises that you can't resolve with a Hosting Assured web host, Find My Hosting has a procedure to help mediate the problem. If the host simply is not living up to the guidelines, their Hosting Assured status will be removed.

While Find My Host can't guarantee a resolution to a problem, the Hosting Assured designation is another level of assurance that you're dealing with an ethical company and that you'll be treated fairly. You'll find a link to them on my book resource page.

Now that you know a little about how to find a host, you need to know what to look for from a host. First, let's look at the different types of hosting available.

Hosting Assured Code of Ethics

- All information and claims presented to the customer will be 100% accurate.
- All web-hosting services will be supplied as agreed.
- The customer will be treated with fairness and honesty.
- All planned service outages will be well communicated in advance.
- All communication with the customer will be timely and responsive.
- Every effort will be made to resolve all valid complaints in a professional and timely fashion.

1. Free Non-Virtual Hosting

If you need somewhere to host a personal web site, choosing a web host is a simple task. Many free hosts can give you space under their domain name.

Sample web address: http://www.thehost.com/ somedirectory/~yourname/index.html

There are a few drawbacks to this:

- Your web site address is usually long and hard to remember.
- You usually have to display advertising for the host.
- Web site extras such as CGI scripts, autoresponders, and other goodies are very limited or unavailable.
- The amount of web space dedicated to you is very limited.
- You're restricted in what you can do with the site. For example, most free hosts don't allow you to run a business or display advertising if you belong to an affiliate program.

- If you move your site, all the links and bookmarks pointing to it will be lost.
- Customer support is usually not very good or nonexistent.
- Reliability and performance can be quite spotty.

2. Free Virtual Hosting

If you are on a tight budget, but want to have a web presence, then free virtual web hosting may be the solution for you. You will be able to host your web site with your own domain name or as a sub-domain.

> Sample web addresses: http://www.yourname.com | http://yourname.yourhost.com

With this type of hosting, usually you have to display the host's advertising on your web site. If you move your site, all the links and bookmarks pointing to it will be lost if it's a sub-domain. If it's a true domain name that you own, however, your links and bookmarks will be preserved if you move your site. The drawbacks of free non-virtual hosting pretty much apply to free virtual hosting as well. The fact that it's free means your web site will not likely be a high priority to the host.

3. Virtual Hosting

Also called shared hosting, virtual hosting is the most common hosting solution. With virtual hosting, you're basically renting space on a server with other tenants (virtual hosting clients). You can choose from a variety of plans, features, and pricing. You use your own domain name and don't have to carry advertisements for the host in most cases. However, some very low-cost plans, typically under $2 to $3 per month, may require your site to display the host's advertising. With virtual hosting, you can change hosts with minimal hassle and you won't lose your incoming links or bookmarks. All my sites are hosted under this type of hosting.

4. Dedicated Server Hosting

A dedicated server means that you rent the use of a whole server. Since you are renting a machine instead of space on a shared machine, you have more control over what software is installed. Normally, dedicated servers are used by large sites that get an extraordinary amount of visitors or offer files that use a lot of bandwidth, such as audio or video files. This is not an inexpensive option as dedicated servers typically cost $100 per month or more. Renting a dedicated server isn't something you will want or need to do unless your site has developed an extremely strong presence and high traffic.

5. Reseller Web Hosting

Reseller plans let you act as a web hosting company and resell your web host's services under your own business name. If you're reading this book, this probably isn't something you're ready to do. You need a lot of experience to be a reseller because you need to provide technical support to your resold accounts and you need a good understanding of server control panels as well as a multitude of technical issues.

Most readers of this book will want to use virtual hosting. With a good host, this type of hosting provides the reliability, features, and low price most people want. Next, I'll discuss a few of the main features to base your hosting decision on.

Disk Space

Disk space is the amount of space you are allowed to use to store your web site files on your host's server. Most people buy more disk space than they actually need, but at today's prices that doesn't mean they're spending a lot of money doing it.

A typical web page usually runs about 40 to 50 kilobytes, not counting any graphics on it. At 50 kilobytes, it would take 250 HTML pages to equal 10 megabytes. Most hosts allow you to have way more than 10 megabytes of disk space. I'm using three different web-hosting companies at the time of this writing. All three allow more than 500 megabytes of disk space and all three cost $7.95 per month or less. The following chart shows you how all these "bytes" relate.

Disk Storage Terminology	
1 Byte	equals 1 text character
1 KB	1 kilobyte equals 1,000 bytes
1 MB	1 megabyte equals 1,000 kilobytes
1 GB	1 gigabyte equals 1,000 megabytes

Few people need more than 100 megabytes of disk space. On one of my sites I had more than 500 HTML pages and lots of graphics and still didn't use 100 megabytes of space. So don't overbuy on disk space unless the extra space comes with other features you need or want. You can always upgrade to a plan with more disk space at a later time.

Bandwidth and Data Transfer

The topics of bandwidth and data transfer are misleading to many people, even webmasters with a fair degree of experience. Many hosts offer unlimited bandwidth, and people take that to mean data transfer. But bandwidth and data transfer are two different things.

Bandwidth is the amount of data that can be piped out from the host at any given moment. It's their total data transfer capacity —but you share this capacity with everyone else renting server space from the host. When a host says you will have unlimited bandwidth, it's misleading. At best, it only means you have as much of the bandwidth that is available to them, but their bandwidth is not unlimited so yours can't be either. Plus, your site will share the bandwidth with other sites.

What hosts should say is that they won't place any artificial restrictions on your bandwidth. That, too, is misleading because if your site uses too much bandwidth, it can harm their other clients on the same server you share. To protect their other clients, they will likely request you to cut down on the bandwidth usage, place restrictions on the bandwidth you use, or require that you upgrade to a dedicated server at a much higher cost.

Data transfer is the amount of data that is piped out from the host on your behalf. Many hosts will claim unlimited data transfer as well, but there are limits. Hosts make that claim because it's reassuring and wins new customers—and because very few sites will approach the point at which data transfer usage is a problem.

Data transfer isn't something you will have to worry about unless your site becomes very popular, and at that point it's a nice problem to have. Most sites don't use more than 2 or 3 megabytes of data transfer per month. I didn't have to upgrade to a more expensive plan until my site started using about 15 gigabytes of data transfer a month. Today, all my accounts have a higher allowance than that at a lower cost than I was paying when 15 gigabytes was a problem. Times change.

You may be wondering just how much data transfer 15 giga-bytes is. For me, it was when my site was serving about 700,000 page views per month. Remember, many of my pages offer free graphics, and those pages use more data transfer than normal pages. As you can see, most sites will not have a data transfer problem.

Performance and Reliability

Performance can be hard to gauge due to a variety of factors, such as how many sites a host places on each server, how much empty disk space they keep on each server, the server configuration and software, the server processor speed and amount of memory, load balancing, etc. While you can request any information from a host you want, there is really only one thing that is of much use before trying them out—and that's the type of connections their servers have to the Internet.

Many hosts will tell you what kind of connections they have to the Internet. The following list shows some of the common connections you may see advertised and the amount of data each type of connection can move.

- T1: 1.544 megabits per second
- T3: 43.232 megabits per second (equal to 28 T1 lines)
- OC3: 155 megabits per second (equal to 84 T1 lines)
- OC12: 622 megabits per second (equal to 4 OC3 lines)
- OC48: 2.5 gigabits per seconds (equal to 4 OC12 lines)
- OC192: 9.6 gigabits per second (equal to 4 OC48 lines)

Obviously, the faster the connection, the faster the data transfer can be. But data transfer also depends on the type of connection the user has in accessing the Internet. A person connected to the Internet via a dial-up modem probably won't see much, if any, difference in how fast a site loads whether it's sent via a T1 line or an OC192 line because the data transfer is severely restricted on their end.

The real benefit of the higher data transfer rates is that an extremely busy server is less likely to get bogged down trying to pump out data through a pipeline that is too narrow for the amount of data requests it receives. The benefit is not necessarily in how fast your site downloads for a single user. In most cases, any of the OC lines will do an adequate job, but if a host offers OC48 or better, you're all but assured of high-speed reliability. A web host with OC3 or OC12 connections can be just as reliable if they don't overload their servers.

While we all like to spend as little as possible for web hosting, paying too little may mean poor performance as the super-low cost hosts tend to pack more sites onto a server than is practical for optimal server speed. Still, there are some very good hosts that have low pricing, and paying more doesn't necessarily mean higher speed. One thing you can do is check the speed of the sites they already host. Most hosts will give you addresses for some of the sites they host, but of course these may be sites they know to be fast rather than random sites. If you choose to do this, ask for the addresses of at least a dozen sites.

Reliability is something that varies. One person might have their server crash once and consider the host lousy while another might have excellent uptime with the same host. Again, that's why getting feedback and recommendations can be an important part of choosing a good web host. Most hosts advertise 98 to 99.9 percent uptime, but all hosts go down occasionally. It's when downtime is a regular occurrence or takes too long to remedy that you need to look elsewhere.

Support

It's hard to gauge a host's support when you don't have an account. You can send a few emails asking questions to see how fast they reply. You can also call and see how long it takes you to get through to a live person.

Some hosts only offer support by email. Others have support available by phone and email. With some, you must submit a support ticket. Some hosts offer support 24/7 while others have limited hours. Choosing the level of support your comfortable with is up to you. Not everyone needs support 24/7 as long as the help is reliable, effective, and available within a reasonable time frame.

Getting support isn't like walking into a department store and getting help from a sales person, so you'll probably be disappointed if you expect instant help. Support can take anywhere from 15 minutes (with a very good support team in place) to hours or even days (with a bad support team in place). If I can get help within an hour, I'm generally satisfied with that. That's not to say the problem will be resolved within an hour—just that someone will start working on it that soon. How long it takes to resolve the problem depends on the kind of problem you have. Some problems are more complex than others and require more time to troubleshoot and more experienced technicians.

Control Panel

A control panel lets you do things like add new email accounts to your domain, create password-protected directories, install a variety of CGI scripts (small software programs such as blogs, forums, etc.) with the click of a button, and perform many other tasks. Having a control panel with your site has become the norm, and it's very nice to have. I wouldn't use a host that doesn't offer a good control panel. My favorite control panel is the cPanel, although vDeck is pretty good too, as are many custom panels. Hosts that offer control panels usually have a demo panel so you can see what they do and how they work. Try them!

Server Operating System

When selecting a host, another consideration is whether to go with a Linux or a Windows server. Linux is usually cheaper for the hosting companies so the savings can be passed on to the customer. The many software modules that make up a server are also available for free so the administrator can install the required modules and leave out the others.

Windows systems, on the other hand, come as a complete package. They can be easier to work with for server administrators because much is preinstalled or automated. Each type of server has their own advantages and disadvantages. Both operating systems are good, but Linux is usually cheaper and less prone to problems. Personally, I prefer Linux servers. There are other server types too, but these are the most common.

FTP Enabled Server

There are two main ways to transfer files to your host's web server. One is using an online upload manager and the other is using file transfer protocol (FTP) software. While using an online file manager may seem simpler, FTP is usually much, much faster and isn't hard to use at all. I would never use a host that doesn't offer FTP uploading; it just takes too long the other way. After you read the section on uploading a web site, I'm sure you'll be comfortable with the idea of using FTP software.

Your Own CGI Bin

A CGI Bin, often listed as cgi-bin on the hosts features list, is a directory from which scripts are carried out. CGI scripts provide much of the functionality of most web sites. Every time you fill out a form, buy a product, use a forum or blog, or engage in a chat room conversation, you're running a script of one type or another. This feature is vital. Unless you plan to build a static site that will never offer any kind of user interactivity, do not sign up with a host that doesn't provide your own CGI Bin. Most hosts do.

To choose a hosting plan, first identify your needs. One thing is for sure—you'll pay for a poor choice over and over. Do your homework when choosing a web host and web-hosting plan!

Make a list of the features that are must haves and another list of things that would be nice to have. A host may make many options sound exciting, but will you use them? If not, there's no sense in paying extra for them.

Choose a host that allows you to upgrade your hosting package as your needs grow. For example, say you pick a host based solely on cost, but you know that in the future you will need a feature the host doesn't offer. It would be better to find a host now that offers a smaller plan for your current needs—plus offers the features you need later—than to take the cheapest price now only to have to find a new host later and move your site.

Price is one of the last things I consider when choosing a host. First, I select several hosts that offer the features I want and then I do my homework. When I've narrowed the list down to two or three hosts, then I consider the price. Of course, I do have a pricing framework to work within from the beginning. A host whose cheapest plan is several times more than the average for the same features will not be on my list.

One last thing about hosting—think twice about choosing a host that is also an ISP (provides Internet access). If the hosting servers use the same pipeline as the Internet access customers, your site can slow down as the number of users going online increases.

16.4 Uploading Files to Your Web Host

To have your web site online for the world to see, your web site files have to be uploaded to your web host's server. While some hosts offer an online upload manager, using one is a tedious process as each file must be selected one at a time using a "browse" process that requires you to drill down through your computer hierarchy for each file. Adding to the tedium is that many upload managers only allow you to upload one file at a time.

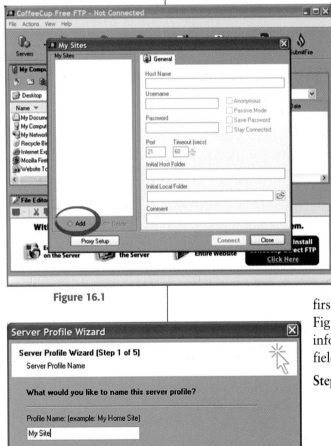

Figure 16.1

Using FTP (file transfer protocol) software, you can select a single file, multiple files, or even entire directories to upload all at once. Since you're only working with files on your computer until you click the upload button, selecting the files to upload is a much faster and more secure process.

This tutorial is based on Coffee Cup Free FTP, which is available from www.coffeecup.com. CoffeeCup Software makes a variety of quality software and they have a very good reputation. As the name implies, this FTP program is free.

When you run Free FTP for the first time, you'll see the set up shown in Figure 16.1. Since you haven't added the information for your web host yet, all the fields are blank.

Step 1:   The first thing you need to do is run the *Server Profile Wizard* to enter the information to connect to your web host. Start this process by clicking the *Add* button in the lower-left corner of the My Sites window, which is circled in red.

This will bring up the first dialog box of the Server Profile Wizard shown in Figure 16.2.

Figure 16.2

Step 2: Enter a name for your site on the server. In this example, I simply called it *My Site*, but if you plan to have more than one site you'll probably want to be more specific and enter your domain name here. This name has no function other than to identify the site you want to connect with.

Step 3: After entering your site name, click the Next button. This brings up the screen shown in Figure 16.3, where you enter your *Username* and *Password*. Your web host should have supplied these to you when you signed up to host your site with them.

  If you don't want to enter your password every time you use Free FTP to upload files to your web site, check the *Save Password* box.

Step 4: After entering your Username and Password, click the Next button. This brings up the screen shown in Figure 16.4 where you enter your *Hostname*. The host supplies your hostname, which is usually *ftp.yourdomain.com*, or .net or .org, depending on what kind of domain extension your site has. You can also enter the default folder (directory) name on the server that you want the program to open with.

Step 5: After entering your Hostname, click the Next button. This brings up the screen shown in Figure 16.5. If you use a proxy or socks server to access the Internet click the *Yes* button. If you don't, or if

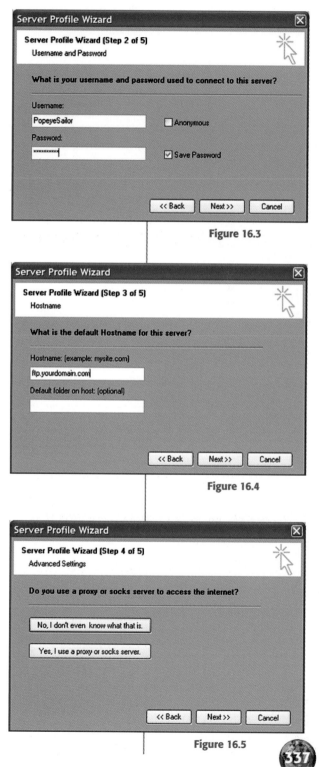

Figure 16.3

Figure 16.4

Figure 16.5

337

Figure 16.6

Figure 16.7

you don't know, click the *No* button. Most people do not.

The next screen will inform you that you've completed the setup; click the *Finish* button.

When you click the Finish button, the dialog box closes and you'll be back at the first screen you saw on startup, only now you'll have a site listed in the My Sites window, as shown in Figure 16.6.

Click the site you just added (if it isn't already highlighted). The information you just filled in will populate the information fields in the General tab. The *Connect* button will now be active. Click the *Connect* button to log in to your site via FTP.

Step 6: When you click the *Connect* button, Free FTP will log into your web site (if you entered all your data correctly). Figure 16.7 shows my computer logged into one of my web sites. To upload a file, first locate it on your computer, which is shown in the left pane. Navigate to the folder containing your web site.

The pane on the right side shows your web space on your web host.

Since this screen capture is one of my sites, there are all kinds of files in that window. Since you are just getting ready to upload your site, you'll probably have very little in that window. You'll probably have a folder that is named "www" or "public_html" or something similar. That would be the folder you upload your files to. Your web host should let you know when you sign up. Double-clicking a folder will open it.

Many hosts place a temporary index page as a placeholder in the folder where you should upload your files. When you upload your index page, it overwrites the temporary one—as long as they have the same file name and extension (otherwise you can delete the temporary index page when the time comes).

Step 7: Once you've opened the folder to your web site on your computer, and you've opened the folder on your host site, you're ready to upload a file. To do that, just click the file once to highlight it on your computer, and then click the *Upload* button at the top of the window. That's it; the file should upload to your web site space on your host's server. Easy!

You can also highlight a file on your host's server and download it to your computer by clicking the *Download* button; this is handy if you accidentally delete a file you want to keep.

In the free version of CoffeeCup Free FTP, some of the program features will be disabled, such as the *Edit* feature. Upgrading to the paid version will enable all features. You'll also see advertisements at the bottom of the program when you close it—but hey, that's a small price to pay for quality free software. If you don't like it, you can always buy the program or search for another FTP client.

At the top of the Free FTP window you'll see a button labeled *Auto*. When set on Auto, the program decides which mode is appropriate for uploading the file. Files are uploaded in either binary mode or ASCII mode. You're probably better off letting the program decide the correct mode most of the time. Just so you know, images are binary files so they should be uploaded in binary mode. HTML pages are text files so they should be uploaded in ASCII mode.

You can select multiple files and upload more than one at a time. To select a range of consecutive files, click the first file to highlight it, hold down the Shift key, then click the last file. The first and last file, plus all the files in between should be highlighted and will all upload at the click of the Upload button. To select multiple, nonconsecutive files, hold down the Control (Ctrl) key (Command key on Mac OS) and select each file individually. When you've selected all the files you want to select, release the Control/Command key. The individual files should remain highlighted and you can upload them by clicking the Upload button.

Mac OS users, my editor recommends the $25 Fetch FTP software. At the time of this writing they had a very nice online "tour" of the program showing you how to use it. You'll find Fetch at: www.fetchsoftworks.com.

16.5   Attracting Visitors to Your Site

BUILDING A WEB SITE is only half the task of establishing an Internet presence—promoting the site is the other half. Skipping the task of promoting your site means that few visitors will find it. There is no way to figure out how many web sites exist, but a conservative estimate is more than 40 million. As you can see, getting folks to visit your web site is no small undertaking. You should approach promoting your site as seriously as you approached building it.

Site promotion is 50 percent science, 50 percent art, and 50 percent luck. If you can add, you probably noticed that adds up to 150 percent—and that's how much effort you need to put into it! In this section, you'll learn what I've done to promote my site. I don't use all these techniques now that my site is well established and I have a vast network of online contacts, but these methods all helped me get started.

I intentionally focused on low-cost and free ideas to attract visitors to a web site. Most people reading this will be just starting out and probably working on a very limited budget. After all, I assume anyone with money to burn on promotion would not read a do-it-yourself book. If you do have money to burn, you might want to consider hiring professional marketing services.

I've rated each method of promotion on a scale of 1 through 5 stars, with 3 stars being the best. Um…just kidding. A 5-star rating is the most effective and a 1-star rating is the least effective —but that doesn't mean you should ignore that method. On the other hand, don't think any of these traffic-attracting methods will produce an instant influx of steady traffic. A continual stream of daily traffic is built a little at a time. Some methods, however, do provide surges of traffic that can last from a day to several days.

16.5.1 Search Engines

Search engines can be the steadiest and most prolific source of traffic for your web site, providing that your site ranks in the top 20 to 30 sites. After that, the benefit of a search engine listing begins to drop off dramatically because people have either found what they're looking for, have decided to refine their search, or have given up.

To rank highly in search engines, your pages need to be optimized for search engine ranking. Several things contribute to a high search engine ranking, some of which are within your control and some of which are not. Search engines change their ranking criteria on a regular basis, so the same sites aren't always on top—they need to show fresh content just like any other web site does. However, a well-optimized site can be found in the top listings on a regular basis when searching for some of the relevant keywords.

Most web design books don't even go into search engine optimization. A thorough treatment of the topic would take a full chapter, and I don't have that much space to devote to search engine optimization in this book. I can offer some general guidelines that will always have a measure of relevancy. For a more in-depth study of search engine optimization, you can visit www.BoogieJack.com and review my SEOS course to see if you're interested.

Following is a list of general principles for search engine optimization techniques. Each search engine doesn't necessarily align with each and every technique, just as each technique doesn't apply to every search engine. Most techniques apply to most search engines, but all are different and use a divergent set of criteria. Note that search engines are not the same as directories. Directories are human edited, and usually simply list the relevant sites in alphanumeric order so optimization techniques do not work.

 Content: The most important thing you can do for your search engine ranking is to have plenty of original, high-quality content.

 Theme: A web site with lots of quality content that follows a single theme will usually fair better than sites that cover multiple themes. The more focused your site is toward a unifying overall theme, the better it will rank for relevant searches.

 Keywords: Keywords and keyword phrases are the terms a searcher enters into a search engine to find a site with the type of content your site offers. Using plenty of keywords and keyword phrases throughout your text, and especially toward the top of pages, is food the search engines can feed on. Text that is emphasized on pages—for example, in heading tags or bold type—is given more weight by search engines. In other words, text that you display as important to visitors is considered important text to search engines.

Links: Incoming links, which are the links other web sites place to your site, are another important ranking criteria. Commonly called *link popularity*, the search engine wizards have rightly determined that the more links pointing to your site, the better your site must be. All incoming links are good, but links from sites that have the same theme as your site are even better.

Furthermore, the more popular the sites are that link to your site, the more important the search engine considers them. Therefore, the thing to do is try to convince as many sites as possible to link to your site—especially sites with the same theme and/or are popular sites. This usually means asking for reciprocal links, which simply means asking a webmaster to link to your site in exchange for you linking to their site. You scratch each others' backs, in a digital way.

When you're first getting started, you probably will have the best luck exchanging links with other sites that are fairly new and are trying to grow. Well-established sites are often reluctant to exchange links with new sites because it isn't a reciprocal trade. They have a lot more traffic, so they'd most likely be sending a lot more traffic to your site than your site could send to theirs. As your site grows, though, you can aim for bigger fish.

Meta tags: Meta tags are tags that tell the search engine about the page. They are placed within the <head> tag set of an HTML document. The two primary meta tags to be concerned with are the *description meta tag* and the *keywords meta tag*.

Some people say these meta tags aren't important any more. While it's true that they are not nearly as important as they used to be, there's still good reason to use them. Some search engines *require* the description meta tag. If you don't include it, they will not include your site in their database. As for the keywords meta tag, most search engines no longer count the keywords in this tag as keywords for your site, so they are not useful that way. Testing shows, however, that the keywords meta tag may help boost the theme of a web site with some search engines. At any rate, it doesn't hurt to use it with any search engine and it may help with some, so you might as well use it.

The description meta tag is written like this:

```
<meta name="description" content="Describe
the page this tag is on here. " />
```

This tag should describe the content of the web page. Some search engines use the text of this tag as the description of your web page in their listings—so take care to create a good description. A good description does two things: it gives an accurate description of the page content and it "sells" the page so searchers will click the link to it.

Some search engines lower your site's ranking if they repeatedly display your site but no one clicks to visit it. As a result, you should consider the description to be something of an advertisement that compels the searcher to click your link. The description should not read like an advertisement, though. It shouldn't be full of hype. Don't try to sell it with excess exclamation marks. Don't type words in all CAPITAL letters. Just write a thoughtful description that delivers enough interest to make people want to click the link.

The keywords meta tag is written like this:

```
<meta name="keywords" content="Enter,
your, keywords, here." />
```

Enter your keywords and keyword phrases one at a time, separated by a comma. Do not repeat any keyword more than three times. Search engines used to consider this as keyword stuffing (spamming) and penalized the practice. Since search engines no longer consider the content of this tag as keywords, they may no longer consider it negatively, but there's no reason to take a chance at having your site's ranking penalized.

Code Optimization: While I can't list every possible opportunity to optimize your code, I can show you the general principle. The idea is to use keywords in the source code in places where it is legal in HTML. For example, using the image alt tag to include keywords is one legal way to add keywords to code. For example:

```
<img src="dog.jpg" width="70 height="100"
alt="Dog grooming a poodle." />
```

Assume this image is on a site for a dog grooming service and the picture is of a poodle being groomed. We just legally added *dog grooming* and *poodle* as hidden keywords. Repeat this with all images, and in other hidden but legal attributes such as link titles, and you can see how easy it is to add dozens of quality keywords to a web page without actually displaying a lot of repetitive phrases to visitors.

 Site Map: A site map is sort of a super-index page. It lists all the pages on your site in one place. Including a site map and linking to it from your main page creates a convenience for visitors and food for search engines. It assures that your site will be fully indexed by many search engines. However, some search engines have a limit on the number of pages they will index from any one site, so if your site is more than 50 pages, list the most important 50 pages first.

Lastly:

- Submit your site to the major search engines by hand, one at a time.

- Make sure you follow all the rules for each search engine.

- Either buy software to submit your site to all the smaller directories and search engines, many of which you've never heard of, or hire a service to do that for you.

Some webmasters say it isn't necessary to submit your site to the small search engines because the traffic they offer is insignificant, but I disagree. While any one of them may be insignificant, because there are so many of them, they add up to a major traffic source when considered as a whole. For my site, it means about 10,000 to 20,000 unique extra visitors per month. That's a lot of traffic to ignore. If you're building a commercial site, that's a lot of sales you'll be missing if you ignore this traffic resource!

WARNING!

Beware of submission service hype!

Submission services may offer to submit your site on a schedule as a selling point to novice webmasters. They claim that you have to submit your site every so often for one reason or another. While I do offer a submission service, I don't offer recurring submissions because I don't believe in it.

If you resubmit your site too often or haven't made any significant updates since the last submission, the search engine could consider that spamming and lower your ranking or remove your listing. If you have a good position, resubmitting your site might cause it to fall in position. Resubmitting on a timetable is a sales pitch to make you think you're getting more for your money. I often leave my site untouched on search engines for two years or more and have noticed no loss of position other than the normal fluctuations.

You'll also hear, "We'll submit your site to five bazillion search engines!" The sheer numbers are also hype. Only a dozen or so search engines and directories are vital, several dozen more are fair, and the rest are worthless Free-For-All (FFA) link pages. There is nothing a search engine submission service can do for you that you can't do for yourself—except save you a good deal of time and work! If saving time and work is important, you may want to use this type of service. If saving money is more important, do it yourself.

16.5.2 Link Trading

I've already pointed out the importance of incoming links as far as search engine rankings go. Trading links also brings you traffic from the sites that include your link. Generally, the more traffic the site with your link gets, the more traffic you'll receive from them.

Some webmasters don't like to trade links. They fear that links tempt visitors to leave their site. That's flawed thinking…to my way of thinking. Every visitor will leave your site sooner or later—whether they enter a new web address in the address bar, select a bookmark, use the back button, or click a link that you provide—they are going to leave at some point and they are going to leave when they are ready to go.

If your content is good, visitors will leave your site later rather than sooner. If your content is bad, nothing you can do will keep them from leaving quickly. The best thing you can do is to provide quality links for users to surf when they are ready to leave. They may think more highly of your site for that alone and come back again to check out more. Whatever excellent content your site provides is an asset, even if that content consists of links leaving your site.

A request for a link to your site that gets positive results has several key elements. These may seem like common sense to you, but the overwhelming majority of requests I get contain very few of these key elements. Here are my tips for arranging link trades:

1. Follow instructions. Look around the site for any link request instructions. If you don't follow the instructions, you greatly reduce your chances of getting a link from that site.

2. Be to the point. In the subject line of your email request, get right to the point. Don't try to be cute or trick the person into reading your email.

   Subject: Link Trade Request

   ...will do the job. If they're interested, they'll act on it. If they're not, any tricks you use will ensure that your email is deleted without the desired response.

3. Make it relevant. Look the site over and find out what you have in common. Mention what you think your visitors would enjoy about the prospective trade partner's site, and then tie that in with what your site offers that would benefit their visitors. This shows that you've actually visited the site and have a clue about building quality traffic exchanges.

4. Use a direct and correct address. Look around to see if you can find the webmaster's name. Your email will be read with "friendlier eyes" if you start it off with "Hi Doug" instead of an impersonal salutation.

5. Be specific. In the body of the letter, include the name and URL of the site you're requesting to exchange links with:

   ...I've been enjoying your Boogie Jack web site at www.boogiejack.com, and...

   Believe it or not, the person you're writing to may not know what site you're talking about. I own several sites, for example, and I don't always know which site people are referring to when they write.

6. Be sincere and respectful. Don't write like you're old friends when you've never met, and don't go overboard on the flattery. Cite the reasons you should trade links and what you like about their site, but don't fake it. Insincerity can be spotted a mile away. That doesn't mean you can't compliment them—in fact, I recommend compliments if you can find something honest and positive to say. If you can, your genuineness will usually come through.

7. Make the first link. Link to the site before you request a link, and give the URL to the page where the link is. If they don't link back, consider leaving it on your link page anyway. It's still good content for your visitors.

8. Describe your site and give the URL. Give a brief and accurate description of your site along with the exact, full URL you'd like them to link to. You might also include the web page address of any link graphics in case they want to use a graphic. Not everyone will—in fact, most probably won't, so don't make the assumption that a webmaster will or should use a graphic link—even if you use a graphic for their site. Don't attach graphics to the email; just offer a link to the graphics in case they do want to use an image.

9. Give accurate contact information. For the extra-professional touch, include your phone number and mailing address along with your email address. No one has ever stopped by my house or bothered to call as a result of my including this information, but it looks professional in your request.

The bottom line is that you're showing respect and professionalism if you approach link requests this way. No one wants to trade links with a site that will be here today and gone tomorrow. That's extra maintenance we don't need. If you show some class, you create the impression that you're a real player and not just shooting arrows into the dark to see where they stick.

If you follow my guidelines, a webmaster will know from your email request that:

- You actually visited his or her site.
- You took the trouble to find out his or her name.
- You wrote a sincere letter, not just a form letter that you spammed dozens or perhaps hundreds of other webmasters with.
- That you've already linked to his or her site.
- That you're professional and sincere, and will probably not be the type of person that causes link rot or removes the link as soon as the site links back to yours.

This will put a webmaster in about as receptive a mood as possible, all without wasting his or her time. A few links at popular sites can be a nice traffic boost—and a nice search engine boost—so it's well worth the effort to go about it the right way.

There are also scripts to help manage link trading. If you install one, or have it installed for you, you only need to put an invitation to trade links with you on your site and let the people who visit your site submit their link. Most scripts require a site to add your link before they can submit their link to you. You get to approve whether or not their link is added so you needn't worry about inappropriate sites being added to your link page.

The only drawback to using scripts is that the links are often not what you'd call high-quality links. That's OK, though, as a dribble of traffic from a ton of sources equals a ton of traffic in due time. I recommend keeping two sets of links on separate pages or sections of your site—one for reciprocal links and one with featured links for the sites you write to exchange links with.

⭐ 16.5.3 Trade Sponsor Ads

This link-trading idea won't bring much traffic to your site because people tend to ignore advertising, which is why this technique is rated as least effective. More importantly, however, it can raise the prestige of your site.

Find sites with content that would appeal to the kinds of visitors your site is expected to attract. If the site has no paid advertising, offer to trade ads with them. You will really be trading links that look like paid advertising. They've probably never had an offer like that before, and may well love the idea of *looking* like a site that someone was interested in buying advertising on. You can trade text links or graphic links. Text links are often better than graphic ads, especially if the links can be placed in the context of an article.

Smaller sites can look as if they have a real paying sponsor, which can enhance their visitors' perceptions. As I said, this won't bring in a lot of traffic, but it should bring some traffic to both sites and every little bit helps.

This technique also helps you get started in networking and making contacts, which can lead to bigger things down the road. I was asked by a publisher to write my first book about web design because someone I met through networking recommended me to them. Now this book is in the third edition. Yahoo for me!

I've made many great contacts this way, and we've all helped each other grow as business entities and as people. While I will never meet most of these folks in person—because they are scattered all over the world—I'm still happy to call many of them good friends.

16.5.4 Awards

Years ago I would have rated this technique with 4 or 5 stars, but the glut of junk awards has caused awards to lose their meaning. Back in the day when they still meant something, my site won dozens of awards. It wasn't unusual to receive an extra 5,000 or more visitors in a single day due to winning a prestigious award.

Still, winning a good award can bring in a few hundred new visitors a day for a few days, and when your site is new, that's probably a lot more visitors than you're getting! A search at Google for "award sites" will turn up several possibilities.

The only awards worth applying for are from sites that list the winners. The other award sites are only in it to get links to their own sites. They are disparagingly referred to as "vanity" awards. All you have to do is ask for an award and you will get it from a vanity award site. In most cases, there is no judging criteria whatsoever for a vanity award and you'll receive no traffic from the awarding site.

Some sites that offer vanity awards even use autoresponders to answer your submission. An autoresponder is a software program that sends a predetermined message to anyone who sends a message to a specific email address. You apply for an award by email and almost immediately you get a reply stating you've won because your site is great. If you can send an email, you get a site award. Big whoop. There's no glory in that—and no traffic to gain by receiving it. It's ego fluff for the naïve and links for the award giver.

A legitimate award site, which lists the winners permanently or for a predetermined period of time, can bring a good deal of traffic. These awards are worth applying for when you're starting out as they can help bring a reasonable volume of traffic to your site for a short time. Read their judging criteria and apply for awards when you think your site passes muster.

Another way to create traffic to your site is to give out your own award. Before jumping into it, decide what type of sites you'd like to award and define your selection criteria. For best results, try to find an un-exploited or under-exploited niche topic related to your content. If your award is designed for a niche group, your chances of having sites apply for the award may be greater. Plus, the ones that do apply will be highly motivated.

Unless you already have a popular site, you'll probably need to start small, awarding home pages, new sites, and sites in early growth stages. I haven't seen many awards for beginners, so that's an idea. You can always aim higher, but don't be surprised if established sites say "thanks" but don't display your award. Well-established, quality sites have received so many awards that most don't bother displaying them any more. Although most sites still appreciate the gesture, posting awards becomes an unproductive task after a while. These sites spend their time on more productive activities such as developing new content.

A new webmaster, however, is often thrilled to receive an award and will display it proudly, usually with a link to your site. Not only do you get a link from a page you probably wouldn't have gotten one from, you get to make someone happy at the same time. It's really a win-win situation if you can devote the time and energy to it.

To increase the chances of having people apply for and display your award, you need to create a good-looking award graphic. If you can't design a nice award yourself, find someone who can. I used to offer that service when I first started out. All you have to do is ask the right person and he or she will design it for a reasonable price. Finding the right person can be as easy as emailing the webmaster of a site with nice graphics and inquiring about it. Depending on the complexity of the award graphic, expect to pay from $25 to $100. I wouldn't go any higher than that. Also, you don't have to wait for someone to apply for your award. You can seek out recipients and tell them how much you enjoyed their site. Stroke their ego a bit and offer them your award. It works if you don't aim too high (as I said, most popular sites have moved beyond the stage where awards are important to them).

If you offer an award, you need to list the winners on your site. If you don't, it will be perceived as a vanity award, meaning that fewer people will apply for it and fewer people will be willing to accept it if you seek them out.

Offering awards was one of the methods I used to build up my traffic—back when my site was averaging about 40 visitors a day. It helped me get started on the road to high traffic, and it can help you, too. Just don't forget to give visitors a way to apply for your award, either an email link or a form to fill out.

My site offers many link graphics for others to use to link to my site. A few of the more popular graphics are pseudo-award graphics. Many amateur webmasters love them, and it's something you might want to consider. Here are two examples of my pseudo-awards:

These and other pseudo-awards, as well as more standard style link graphics, are available for the taking on my Link to Boogie Jacks page.

16.5.5 Signature Files

A signature file is a message appended to the end of your emails. As long as you're initiating and replying to email, you might as well use a signature file to promote your site. Most email programs have a signature file feature. If yours doesn't, copy and paste your signature until you get an email program that does.

Signature files should be kept short. A good signature file will include your sign-off salutation, your web site address, and a line or two about your site or business service. You might also include your position or title, your email address, or other items that help identify you and may serve to impress.

Here's an example:

> All the best to you, Dennis
>
> Owner and CEO
>
> http://www.BoogieJack.com
>
> Boogie Jack's is a webmasters' resource site featuring free professional graphics, web design tutorials, one-of-a-kind software and other webmaster help.

Notice in the brief description at the end that I don't waste words. I get right to the "what's in it for them" part. I don't use statistics to show how popular it is and I don't list my awards, testimonials, or any other kind of "it's about me" information because they don't care about that. They want to know what's in it for them and that's what I give them.

An alternative signature is to use testimonials, another powerful advertising tool. If you have the right testimonial (that is short and to the point) you might try using it in your signature. The problem with including a testimonial in an email signature file is that you do have to keep it short. There is no room for explanations about the author of the testimonial and many recipients might think it's a company employee saying the niceties. I find it more effective to use the "what's in it for them" approach.

I've been online since 1996 and I still click links that look interesting in people's signature files. The only reason this method of site promotion isn't rated higher is because you have to send out a lot of email to receive a lot of traffic from it.

16.5.6 Start a Newsletter

If you write well and have knowledge about a topic others would want to learn about, a newsletter (also called an ezine) is a fantastic way to bring people back to your site again and again. Not only that, but a newsletter drives sales and helps establish your expertise in a field. You can also sell advertising space in it after it's grown some.

You don't have to be an expert in a field to start a newsletter about it. Believe me, you learn a lot as you go. You only have to know more than some folks, be willing to research, keep a fairly regular schedule, and produce quality content. You also need to have a passion for the topic—you'll soon grow tired of writing about something that doesn't truly interest you.

It takes a while to attract subscribers, but subscribers will help you earn more subscribers if you produce good content. They'll pass along your newsletter to others, and you can encourage them to help your newsletter grow by doing just that.

Don't worry about the numbers at first—just write the newsletter and give it a chance. I started my newsletter at the urging of my web site visitors, but I had only about a dozen subscribers for the first issue. I kept writing. After a few issues I hit 100 subscribers and that was so exciting! Now I have tens of thousands of subscribers, and it's still exciting!

Over the lifespan of my newsletter, *Almost a Newsletter,* I've received numerous requests to write an article on starting a newsletter. The approach that follows isn't the only approach. It's just my approach. Since *Almost a Newsletter* has received many honors, such as being named the Best Ezine of the Year and being mentioned as one of the top three ezines on the Internet in *Writers Digest Magazine*, obviously I've gotten a few things right along the way. Learn what you can from me, but remember that each of us is a unique personality. There is no sure-fire approach that will work for everyone.

There are many things to consider before you sign up a single subscriber. You need to decide what your newsletter is going to be about in general, and then break that down into specific columns. You need to lay out a template and decide if you'll send out the newsletter directly or keep it online and send out notices that the next issue is ready. (Hint: sending out notices is a lot easier to get past spam filters than a full newsletter is). Decide how often you plan to send it out, whether to write all the content yourself or have guest columnists, and whether to include advertising. You won't find paying advertisers at first, but you can advertise affiliate programs.

After this, write the first 10 issues. Why write 10 issues when you haven't even signed up one subscriber? Doing so will give you a great indication of whether or not you'll be able to sustain the interest and productivity it takes to publish on a schedule. You may decide it's a go, it's a no-go, or that you need to cut back from a planned daily ezine to a weekly or even monthly publication. It's also good practice.

If it's a go, you need to decide on list hosting. I don't recommend hosting the list on your own computer. This can lead to many problems, including complaints to your ISP that may cause you to lose your Internet access. When distributing a newsletter, you must understand that people will complain you spammed them with unwanted email, whether you did or not. People forget they signed up, or they find it easier to hit a button with their ISP's mail service to report a newsletter as spam rather than go through the unsubscribe process. It's not right or fair, but it happens to every online publisher.

When you're starting out, I recommend going with a free list hosting service such as Topica. Unless you're absolutely sure you're in it for the long haul and can generate and sustain subscribers and content consistently, it doesn't make much sense to spend money on list hosting when you can test the waters for free. Topica inserts their own advertising into your ezine to make it worth their while. Look for the free discusion lists on their site.

Many web hosts also let you have a small mailing list that is good enough to get you started.

Once your list grows enough that you want to move up to professional hosting, the transition is fairly easy—once you find the right host. The right host for me, however, may not be the right host for you. Prices range greatly depending on how often you send out to your list, how many subscribers you have, and what kind of features you need. You'll have to do your research to find the right host for your situation. You can spend as little as $10 or so per month to more than $500 per month on list hosting.

As with web sites, content is the first determining factor in whether or not your newsletter will be successful. There are many reasons a newsletter fails, but none succeed with lousy content. Many newsletters today are lost in a sea of sameness. Newsletters that don't focus on original content will drown in that sea. To keep a newsletter afloat requires original, high-quality content.

In my newsletter, I accept article submissions from other publishers and writers, but I only used three outside articles in the first seven years of publishing it. The articles that cross my desk are seldom innovative and new. Most are rehash after rehash of the same old stuff, offering no new information or original points of view. If I ran half the articles sent to me, I would guess my mailing list would be less than half its current size, and I surely wouldn't have won any awards for it. People just aren't going to stay subscribed to a publication that runs the same content found in dozens of other places.

Publishers who rely too heavily on guest articles are dooming their ezines to be the fodder of newbies. They will always be struggling to recruit new subscribers just to maintain their current subscriber level due to the high drop-out rate. Sales are greater with a base of loyal subscribers who have learned to trust you, so if your venture is commercial, losing subscribers means losing money. Eventually, these poor-performing newsletters are usually reinvented or closed down, and most are closed down because the publisher doesn't understand why it isn't working.

Who are you writing for? This is the first question you should ask yourself. If your answer is that you are writing for yourself, give it up. You must put your readers' interests first. You're writing for them. Not enough publishers view writing an ezine in the proper perspective. Writing an ezine is, or at least should be, a service to others. Smart publishers know that unless their ezine is a service to others, it's never going to be a very big deal. In the words of an old blues tune, "it ain't so much of a much."

To start getting subscribers, place your subscribe information on the front page of your web site and in other strategic locations. Mine is on almost every page of my web site. The more prominent you make it, the more subscribers you'll get.

Next, submit your ezine to sites that list ezines. You have to work on promoting your ezine just as you do your web site. This includes ezine listing sites, announcement lists, and search engines; you'll find a short list of these on the resource page for this book.

Building a special page on your site for your ezine, or building a site just for your ezine, will give it more prominence. Remember, if you're going to do it, it is worthy of a special location and special attention. Make it a big thing *before* it becomes a big thing to help it become a big thing! Archive sample issues or all your issues once you get going. If it's good, back issues help sell it.

Once you get going, you can trade ads with other newsletter publishers to help get new subscribers. When you're starting out, look for other startup or small circulation ezines to trade with. You won't find many ezines with 50,000 subscribers that want to trade ads with ezines with 50 subscribers. It's not fair for the other party.

To be readable in almost all email programs, format your ezine line length to 65 characters wide. TextPad allows you to set the line width. Then, if you distribute it as an email rather than as a link to a web page, make sure your email program's line width doesn't change your formatting. Send a test message to yourself first. Most email clients let you set the line length as well. I set mine slightly wider than the ezine.

Writing an ezine is hard work. You have to be able to consistently come up with topics and articles, and write in ways that are interesting. You can write about any topic. There is an audience for every subject, although the broader the appeal the more potential subscribers there are. You can do it! Anyone can write an ezine if they have the passion for it and the will to press on. If you've read this far, that might be you!

I don't want you to think publishing your own newsletter is all good, there is a downside to it as well.

- People subscribe and forget they subscribed. They'll get the first issue and then write nasty letters accusing you of spamming them and threatening to sue you, hurt you, or turn you in to "everyone" if you don't remove them yesterday.

- You'll get many requests to be removed from the subscriber list by people who refuse to follow unsubscribe instructions; it takes time and patience to deal with them.

- As your list grows, you'll get many "vacation responses" from people who send out automated replies to their email. Currently, I get about 200 to 250 automated replies every time I send an issue out. Add that to your regular email load plus spam, and it really becomes a time-consuming problem. Some publishers automatically remove subscribers who do this.

- Coming up with fresh, quality content regularly and on a schedule is a challenge.

- No matter what you write, someone will complain—and sometimes in language that would make a dictionary blush. It seems some people have a deep-seated need to try to show they are more intelligent than you and they subscribe to your publication just to look for things to complain about.

- Spammers will try to mail to your list. Unless you use professional list hosting, you need to learn all you can to prevent a spammer from tarnishing your good name.

- You may get more people wanting to advertise scams than legitimate products and services. It's your duty to try to weed out the scams and protect your subscribers. I turn down more would-be advertisers than I sell ad space to— but still, you can't catch them all. You won't be able to try every product and your subscribers will ultimately have to exercise their best judgment when responding to ads. Having said that, if they are upset with a product or service advertised in your ezine, some will blame you. Be kind when you educate them, but also remove any advertiser if the subscribers' complaints are legitimate.

 ## 16.5.7 Submit Articles to Newsletters

If you don't have the time or feel you can't produce quality ezine content on a regular schedule, then write articles whenever you can. Submit them to other ezine publications; this can be a big traffic booster.

The drawback to this is that you can't control who includes your articles or when they appear. In addition to not having to produce content so often, writing articles for different publications has other advantages. The articles could appear in ezines with large subscriber bases, producing a lot of targeted traffic for your site. Even if you do start your own ezine, you can—and probably should—still submit articles to other ezines to help increase your subscriber base. I do when I have time. Often, other publishers ask me for permission to use an article I wrote for my own newsletter or web site. That shows you there's a need for good content.

Writing articles for other publications can help establish you as an expert in your field, just as publishing your own newsletter can. If you write a good article that's included in a targeted ezine, it can bring a significant amount of traffic and new subscribers to your newsletter.

When you submit articles to other newsletters, your publicity comes in the way of a resource box (author's credits). A resource box is sort of an "about the author" blurb at the end of the article. Each ezine owner will set his or her own limit on the size the resource box can be, but it's usually in the range of five to eight lines. For example, a blurb about me in a resource box might look like this:

> Dennis Gaskill is an author, publisher, web site designer, and the creator and owner of the popular webmaster's resource site at BoogieJack.com. Visit his site to find the web design resources and the help you need, and sign up for his free newsletter for more articles like this one.

"BoogieJack.com" is usually linked to my web site so all the reader has to do is click the link to visit my site. A well-received article in a popular newsletter can bring in thousands of new visitors over several days. It's worth the effort.

 ## 16.5.8 Web Rings and Alliances

Web rings are groups of sites that join together in the common cause of cross-promotion. Rings are usually grouped together by a common theme such as graphics sites, poetry sites, women-only sites, or other common characteristics. All members display a graphic for the ring, which has links to the next site or the previous site in the ring. Each member site will also have a "List All Sites" link and a link to the ring home page so others can join.

Web rings can be a good way to generate traffic when you're just starting out, especially for non-commercial sites. They're not a good idea for business sites because they take away from the professionalism you want to project. A better idea for a business site is to create an alliance.

An alliance is an association of like-minded businesses that have similar target audiences and agree to promote each other through web site links or newsletter listings. Each site agrees to promote the others in a similar manner. Some freedom is usually given to allow for the various web site designs, but the reciprocity is roughly equal.

Alliances are rarely as obvious as web rings. Each site may simply place a row of buttons on their home page to the other sites involved, with no telltale label that it's a joint marketing effort.

Generally, you'll have to form your own alliances. But if you search for "web rings" at a good search engine, you should find several on most any topic. You'll find a short list of web rings on the resource page for this book on my site.

16.5.9 Newsgroups and Forums

Site promotion isn't limited to email and the web. An often overlooked but sometimes excellent way to bring in visitors is through newsgroup and forum postings. Newsgroups are public discussion groups sorted by topics, and are accessed through a part of the Internet called Usenet. Messages are presented in a list called threads, which show the original message and the responses to the message. You can follow an entire conversation or just read the messages you're interested in.

To access newsgroups, you'll need a newsreader. You can use Microsoft's Outlook Express email program, the email program built into Netscape, or the method I prefer, download a software program called a newsreader or news agent.

The messages in newsgroups are stored on news servers owned by ISPs, businesses, educational facilities, and other organizations. You can usually access newsgroups through your own ISP. Some ISPs have a small number, such as 5,000 or 10,000, while others carry more than 100,000 newsgroups.

Whatever your area of expertise or interest, your ISP will probably have several newsgroups on that topic. Use your expertise to promote your site or learn more about an area of interest so you can become an expert. Even if you don't think of yourself as an expert, you might be surprised to find that what you know is just what a less-experienced person is looking for—and to that person you will be an expert.

Depending on the group and the usefulness of your post, you can get anywhere from a handful to a few hundred new visitors over the course of a few days. Posts do expire, so you need to post once or twice a week to stay on top of a newsgroup. There is a right way and a wrong way to go about it, of course. The wrong way will get you a box full of flames (nasty, derogatory email).

You don't want to just post a notice to come and visit your site; that's how you get flamed. Blatant advertisements are considered spam to group regulars and they don't appreciate it. Start by lurking—that is, just monitor the group for a few days to get a feel for it. Read some of the posts and watch for a group etiquette or FAQ posting that explains the protocols of the group. If you don't see one, ask for it by posting a message yourself.

When you're comfortable with the group, look for messages asking questions you can answer. Give a thoughtful answer and include your URL and a brief description of your site in your signature file. If it's a good answer and a popular group, you may see an almost immediate surge in web site traffic.

If no one is posting questions you can answer, ask an intelligent question and leave your signature file with it. Newsgroups can be an excellent way to receive help as well as gain traffic by helping others. Do realize, though, that not everyone who answers will necessarily know what they're talking about.

Most newsreader programs require you to enter an email address to make posts. When posting to newsgroups, be prepared for an onslaught of spam if you don't take measures to stop it. Bulk emailers' use spiders on newsgroups to harvest email addresses. There are ways to avoid this spam trap. Suppose your email address is abc@123.com, you could change it to:

abcREMOVE_THESE_CAPS@123.com

Most users will know to remove the "REMOVE_THESE_CAPS" part of the address if they want to contact you, but the address is useless to bulk emailers. Or, many do as I do and just use a bogus address such as a@a.com unless they are seeking email replies.

359

Be careful in newsgroups. Binary files sometimes contain viruses. If you're just reading text messages you'll be safe, but downloading binary files is asking for trouble.

A forum is kind of like the online version of a good newsgroup, but with less spam and negligible virus problems. Newsgroups used to be far better than forums, but nowadays forums are at least on a par with newsgroups, and in many cases they are far better. As with newsgroups, forums exist on just about every topic you can imagine. To find a forum on a topic of interest, go to Google and enter "forum +*topic*" in the search field (replace the word *topic* with the actual topic you're interested in). Place the entire search term in quotation marks to narrow the results.

Forums work the same way as newsgroups as far as not blatantly advertising. Just leave your web site address in your signature line after a thoughtful reply or question. You are wise to lurk a while here, too, just to get the feel for the forum.

⭐ 16.5.10 Blogs

While I gave this method a three-star rating, the truth is, I could just as easily give it a one- or five-star rating. Blog is short for weB LOG. A blog is an online journal that is updated regularly and is intended for the general public. Blogs are used for social commentary and opinion articles, announcements, product reviews, business tools, and other less common purposes.

When blogs first started catching on, the media begin touting them as the next big thing on the Internet. Writers, marketers, news media, and many others hailed the power of the blog! It was a self-fulfilling prediction, because thanks to the hype, blogs caught on like wildfire.

The fact is, a blog can be a great asset, but it can also be an exercise in disappoinment. All the hype gave rise to overly optimistic expectations, which led to a lot of disillusioned bloggers (people who write blogs). I recently read that more blogs are abandoned each day than are started, so while blogging seems to be on the decline, that isn't necessarily bad news. A good quality blog only shines brighter when so many are of poor quality.

Many bloggers start their blogs with unrealistic expectations. Millions of blogs are little more than online diaries or excursions into vanity. That's OK if that's all you want from it—but many people expected the world to become excited about their every thought and the mundane routine of their lives. It just doesn't work like that. Now, we are seeing the shakedown of the blogging world, where those less dedicated to excellence are falling by the wayside.

Many elements go into having a successful blog, including: good writing, successful promotion, lots of incoming links, unique information, breaking news items, authenticity, frequent updates, and usefulness. To sum it all up, a successful blog is one that engages the reader.

Most blog readers are looking for information on specific topics. If you stick to a single general theme rather than writing about a plethora of topics, you'll be able to develop followers. The success of a blog depends greatly on returning readers because getting readers to your blog in the first place is the hard part.

Modern blog tools are quite sophisticated. They are content management systems that allow the blogger to focus on content rather than presentation. Blogs can even allow readers to add comments to the end of the blog post. By asking the reader questions and inviting them to leave comments, readers can become more engaged than they are when just reading a static web page. By turning the blog article into a two-way discussion with the author, readers feel like they're a part of the show and help build the popularity by linking to it and telling others about it.

If you have a blog, you should include your blog content in an RSS feed to increase readership and distribution. A lot of blog software does this automatically. RSS is discussed in Chapter 17: An Overview of Other Technologies.

Blogs can be an excellent asset to your online efforts, but they are not magic. They require hard work, quality content, unique content, frequent updates, patience, and perseverance to grow an audience.

16.5.11 Offline Promotion

While most people think of marketing their web site online, marketing your web site offline can be helpful as well, especially for brick-and-mortar businesses. For dirt-world businesses, wherever and whenever your company telephone number, address, and other information is printed, include your web site address. This includes but isn't limited to:

- Letterhead
- Business cards

- Yellow Pages ads
- Newspaper display ads
- Classified ads
- Invoices
- Sales receipts
- Product packaging materials
- Direct mailings
- Business checks
- Magnetic signs on your business transportation
- The entrance to your business or a display window
- T-shirts, hats, etc.
- Everywhere!

Any promotional material you produce should include your web site address. The wider the use of your Internet address, the more reach it will have.

Answering Machines

How many times have you heard an answering machine message that announces the company's web address? Not many— but including it can make sales for you. Perhaps your web site will answer the question the person was calling about. Or, by providing an email address or feedback/inquiry form on your site, you can give customers an alternate way to contact you. If potential customers contact you this way, you have their implied permission to market to them once in response to their inquiry. Since they represent a qualified lead at this point, it could be the difference between making and losing a sale.

Advertisements

I have already mentioned some forms of advertising, but other forms are equally relevant. Include your web address in any advertising you do. Other forms of advertising include, but are not limited to:

- Inserts and Flyers: Promotional brochures loosely inserted into magazines and newspapers or used as handouts and stuffed into bagged purchases.

- Joint Ventures: Enlist the cooperation of other local merchants with web sites to print a local Internet guide. You can share the cost of printing and all can distribute it. That's a very handy reference for a consumer to have next to their computer.

- Radio and Television Spots: Although this is a pricier option, it is likely to reach a larger audience and can drive significant traffic to your site. If your web site is professional looking, you might get local stations to trade advertising airtime or at least to discount it in return for promoting them on your site if your site is of local interest.

- Press Releases: If a newspaper picks up a story from a press release, the editors include only the information they care to. Therefore, be sure to include your web site address, emphasizing that the full story is on your web site. Newsworthy items for press releases include:

  - New launches (including a new web site)
  - New products or services
  - Business expansion
  - Employee promotions and new hires
  - Competitions
  - Industry news

Think Integration

Too many companies separate offline and online activities. They view their physical business as one entity and their web site as a separate entity. An integrated marketing approach is the most effective strategy.

Strategically placing signs for your web site in your physical store will not only generate more traffic to your web site, it shows the public you are a modern company interested in serving their needs in every way possible.

Print web cards for people to take, and place them by the cash register or in other high visibility locations. Web cards are simply business cards dedicated to your web site. If customers pick up your web card, they will likely visit your web site. The card should include your web site address and a brief, descriptive hook that makes them want to visit it. If you don't own a business, you may convince businesses related to your content to display your web cards (if you aren't in direct competition with them) in exchange for advertising them on your web site.

You can also use your web site to promote your physical store. Things such as printable coupons, special sales, Internet-only specials, or special events announced on your web site can increase walk-in traffic.

Barter

In case you haven't picked up on the idea, bartering can be a great way to promote your business or to cross-promote two or more businesses. The business world turns on deals, but much of the time small and local businesses fail to realize that trading services can be an excellent, low-cost way to help each other grow.

Be Creative

This section includes just a few ideas for increasing your web site traffic by integrating it with offline promotions. Be creative— you may make discoveries that will amaze you. If you make any traffic-building discoveries on your own, I hope you'll share them with me:

Boogie Jack
P.O. Box 603
1 Boogie Jack Road
Plover, WI 54467

Or send them to me via an email. You'll find my email address on the contact page on my web site. I won't print it here because I change it now and then when it starts getting too much spam.

Psst…there's a little trick in my mailing address for making your home business seem bigger than it is—name a road after it. As long as there's a P.O. Box in the address, that's where the mail will actually be delivered (according to our local postmaster).

16.6 Chapter 16 Exercise

YOUR PRACTICE SITE is about a professional organization, but some people learning web design are probably doing it to create a personal or family site. Since the project site you've been working on is complete, some of you may find the exercises for the final three chapters a little more appealing.

You get to create a personal home page or fun site about anything you like. You can use the fun stuff that isn't usually found on a professional site—such as colorful backgrounds, fun images, sounds, and whatever else you want to use—as long as the material is offered for public use. Still, you should follow the principles of good design and coding. Even if you are aiming to be a professional web designer, this final project is still good practice for you.

- For this chapter, do some surfing and find the background image, other images, sound files, and whatever else you want to use, and save them to your web space. You'll be making three pages, one for each of the remaining three chapters, including this chapter. The pages you'll make include the index page (home page), a content page, and a wrap-up page.

- Once you've found the items you want to use on your web site, lay out the basic page structure and save it as a read-only template. You can use the template to create the index page and other two pages from.

- Once you've created your template, open it and create your index page. It doesn't need to be a big project from a writing standpoint. Just write a paragraph or two about your topic (or more if you choose) and add links to the two pages that will be the assignments for the last two chapters. Since one is a content page and one is a wrap-up page, you might create links to content.html and wrap.html, or simply to page1.html and page2.html since this isn't going to be online for the general public and search engine optimization isn't necessary.

- Be sure to include the keywords and description meta tags, and practice using CSS with an external style sheet for most of your styles.

Now go have some fun!

An Overview of Other Technologies

17

17.1 Introduction

HTML, XHTML, AND CSS are the three main components of building a web page, but you can use many other technologies as well. This chapter gives you a brief overview of the most common technologies, but it does not teach the subject matter. Entire books have been written on each of these technologies, so there is no way to teach any of them, let alone all of them, in a single chapter.

You can find many good books on these topics as well as an abundance of online tutorials. While a classroom setting can make learning new skills easier, you can certainly teach yourself anything you want to learn if you locate the right teaching materials. One thing I should point out before you read this chapter is that some companies differentiate between designers and programmers. Designers create the structure and look while programmers create the back-end functionality. If you're building your own online empire, you might want to learn one or more of these additional technologies. If you're learning web design in hopes of being hired by a design firm or other business, look at the job market in your area before deciding which additional technologies to study. Do most firms expect a jack- or jill-of-all-trades or do most separate the duties? If they expect one person to know it all, keep learning. If they make distinctions between the two, you'd be wise to become a master of the side you'd rather work on—but supplement that with a general knowledge of the other side so you'll be better able to work with the team.

17.2 JavaScript

JAVASCRIPT IS A CROSS-PLATFORM, object-oriented scripting language that allows you to do things with web pages that can't be done with HTML alone. It is a simple programming language compared to many others, but it is more difficult to learn than HTML and CSS. Client-side JavaScript is embedded into HTML pages and executed on a user's computer, rather than on the server. There is server-side JavaScript, too, but its usage is rare and is almost always proprietary to specific servers and needs.

JavaScript allows executable functions to be distributed over the Internet, which means it offers a way to add interactivity and new functionality to web pages. JavaScript is an event driven programming language. In other words, it responds to events as they occur. The events can either be triggered by the user or automatically executed when a page loads or unloads (entering or exiting a page). JavaScript is also strongly tied to DHTML (Dynamic HTML), which is discussed later.

Many web sites offer copy-and-paste JavaScript code, so you don't really have to learn how to write JavaScript to use it on your web site. It does help to have a basic understanding of JavaScript so you can fix broken scripts or modify scripts to your own needs.

Many uses of JavaScript consist of little more than a few lines of code, or even a single line of code. For example, some users are very impatient. When they click an email form submit button to send an email message, if nothing happens right away, often they'll click the button again. This can result in you receiving two emails with the same message instead of just one. To prevent that from happening, you can add this single line of JavaScript to your sub-mit button:

```
onClick="alert('Success! Thank you for contacting us.')"
```

When the user clicks the submit button, the alert shown in Figure 17.1 immediately pops up (if they are using a JavaScript-capable browser, and most people are). This usually prevents users from clicking the submit button twice.

It's fairly easy to learn how to use such code snippets, even if you don't understand the concepts of the language. If you're learning web design for your own uses, you can prob-ably get by using code from copy-and-paste code sites. If you're

Figure 17.1

planning a career in web design, it's a good idea to learn to write your own JavaScript code.

Here are just a few things you can do with JavaScript:

- Process data on the user's computer without involving a server, which is very fast since no data has to travel between the user's computer and the server. It also helps prevent the server from slowing down by having to execute scripts.
- Add interactivity to tables, graphics, and other elements.
- Dynamically change content on the fly.
- Verify user input in forms.
- Activate alert messages or pop-up windows.
- Create simple, single-player games.
- Print the user's current date and time on a web page.
- Create a countdown or count-up event. For example, your web page could say "Only 7 more days until this sale ends." The next day it would say 6 days, then 5 days, etc. You don't have to change the web page text as the JavaScript does it for you.
- Create more dynamic menu systems.
- Create interactive calendars.
- Produce various effects on a web page.

That's just scratching the surface—you can do *a lot more* with JavaScript. I'm including three more code snippets to whet your appetite for learning more.

Change the Link Status Bar Message

When you place your cursor on a link, the link's URL usually displays in the browser's status bar. Using JavaScript, you can change what is displayed in the status bar. Many people use this to disguise affiliate links, but you can put any message there. For example:

```
<a href="http://www.somesite.com"

  onMouseover="window.status='Visit Some Site Now.';
return true">Some Site</a>
```

That's a normal link with a snippet of JavaScript (shown in red) added. With a link like that, when someone places the cursor on the link, the status bar displays "Visit Some Site Now." Note that the JavaScript code includes a set of double quotation marks with the text message enclosed in single quotation marks. This is how it should be—otherwise, enclosing the message in double quotation marks is interpreted as more code rather than as a message within the code. That would break the script.

One word of caution—if you need to use special characters such as an apostrophe in a message, the apostrophe needs to be prefaced with a backslash. For example:

```
onMouseover="window.status='Visit Boogie Jack\'s now.'; return true"
```

In JavaScript, the backslash tells the browser to print the character that follows rather than to interpret the character as code.

Mouseover Image Swap

The mouseover image swap JavaScript is commonly used for link buttons, but it can be used in other ways. The script allows one image to display until a user places his or her cursor on a link button, at which point a second, predetermined image displays. Many writers refer to image swapping as the "rollover effect."

```
1 <a href="page.html"
2 onMouseOver="document.MyImage.src='images/
  buttonOn.gif';"
3 onMouseOut="document.MyImage.src='images/
  buttonOff.gif';">
4 <img src="images/buttonOff.gif" name="MyImage" />
5 </a>
```

Note

The line numbers are not part of the code; they are there to assist in the explanation.

In Line 1, change "page.html" to the actual page you want the link button to open. In Line 2, change the "images/buttonOn.gif" to the actual path, name, and file type of the image. This button is the one that you want to display when a cursor rests on the button link. In Lines 3 and 4, change the "images/buttonOff.gif" to the actual path, name, and file type of the image that should display when the cursor is not on the button.

Preloading images

Since I showed you how to swap images using JavaScript, I should show you how to preload the images. Preloading the images allows the browser to store the images in the browser's cache memory. Without preloading the images, a short delay usually occurs in the image swap the first time each link button is rolled over because the browser only downloads images as they are needed for display. The secondary image is not needed until the OnMouseover event happens, thus causing a delay if images are not preloaded. Place the following code in the <head> section of the page.

```
1  <script type="text/javascript">
2  image1= new Image(120,34);
3  image1.src = "ImageName.gif";
4  image2 = new Image(120,34);
5  image2.src = "ImageName.gif";
6  </script>
```

The line numbers are not part of the code; they are there to assist in the explanation.

Line 1 opens the JavaScript. In Line 2, **image1** is a variable used for the process; it could be any name. If image 1 was a link to your contact page, you might label the variable as "contact" instead of image 1.

Still in Line 2, **new Image** tells the brower to be prepared to use a new image, and the *numbers in parentheses* are the image's *width* and *height*, in that order.

In Line 3, **image1.src** associates the new image 1 with its source, and **ImageName.gif** is the actual image name and extension. If the images are in another directory, include the path to the image before the image name and extension. If image 1 is for the contact button rollover, then ImageName.gif might be called "contact2.gif" assuming the first link button is named "contact.gif."

Lines 4 and 5 are for a second image. Repeat this procedure for as many images as you need. Just be sure to use unique variable names as shown here. Each image you want to preload must have a unique variable name.

Now, this works fine for a handful of images, but if you have a lot of images you might want to place the preload code in an external JavaScript file. To do that, open a new text file and enter the code from lines 2 through 5 only. Lines 1 and 6 are discarded because they are identified in a link to the external file. Once you've added all the image preload code to the blank text file, save it as: **preload.js**

The file name "preload" can be any name you choose, it just makes sense to name it something meaningful so you'll know what it is later. Be sure your text editor doesn't append a *.txt* to the end of the file name and extension.

To call the external file, place the following link in the <head> section of the web page:

```
<script src="preload.js" type="text/javascript">
</script>
```

This code will preload the images by calling the external file to the page, and it doesn't clutter up the <head> section of the page with line after line of JavaScript code.

17.3 Java

IN CASE YOU THINK JAVA and JavaScript are related because of their similar names, they are not. Although there are some similarities, Java is quite different from JavaScript. The programming language Java is a lot more powerful, far more complex, and unfortunately, a lot harder to master.

Java belongs in the same programming family as C, C++, and other more complex languages. To run a Java program, you need to commpile it; JavaScript requires no compiling. Since Java needs to be compiled, you need special software to write a Java applet (a small application).

The Java programming language and environment was designed to solve a number of problems in modern programming practice. It started as part of a larger project to develop advanced software for consumer electronics.

Java is a high-level programming language developed by Sun Microsystems. It is an object-oriented programming language similar to C++, but simplified to eliminate the features that caused common programming errors. Java source code files (files with a .java extension) are compiled into a format called bytecode (files with a .class extension), which can then be executed by a Java interpreter. Compiled Java code can run on most computers because Java interpreters and runtime environments, known as Java Virtual Machines, exist for most operating systems.

Java is a general purpose programming language with a number of features that make the language well suited for use on the World Wide Web. Small Java applications, called Java applets, can be downloaded from a Web server and run on your computer by any Java-enabled Web browser.

Java can be used to make all kinds of software applications: games, menu applets, animations, database applications, training applications, email programs, and probably just about any other kind of software application. Java applications are mostly designed to run on a web page, but they also can be desktop applications.

You have to be a little careful about using Java online because it does use the memory resources of the user's computer. Under-powered computers, computers with many programs open, and computers with memory leaks can crash when encountering a Java program that requires more memory than the computer has left to give. For this reason, I never use Java on web pages without first warning visitors that a particalur link has Java at the other end. This way, they can make an informed decision about whether or not they want to open that page.

In my opinion, Java is a nice programming language to know and has many uses—but it's not something you would use often in web design. Therefore, it's not the first skill I recommend to aspiring web designers. If you learn JavaScript, on the other hand, you might use that skill far more frequently.

17.4 DHTML

DYNAMIC HTML ISN'T A FORMAL programming language—it's a combination of HTML or XHTML with CSS, JavaScript (or another scripting language), and the Document Object Model. There are no formal W3C specifications for DHTML, which goes a long way toward explaining many of the problems associated with it.

The combination of code may sound like it's just a web page with JavaScript and CSS, but it's more than that. DHTML takes advantage of modern browser features that allow the browser to change a web page's look and style after it's been loaded, which is what makes the programming dynamic.

DHTML can do some marvelous things, like make incredible looking tool tips, display messages that "fly" into view and back off the screen, alter page content on demand after the page loads, make interactive menus that do incredibly cool tricks, create games and puzzles, create animated text, and many more snazzy things.

Sound interesting?

Before you get too hot and bothered about it, I'm going to have to throw a little cold water on the fire. Despite all the possibilities, DHTML isn't very useful—as of yet. It's still under development. What works in one browser will most likely not work in another browser for two reasons: (1) the browsers themselves are in different stages of development as to their level of support for DHTML, and (2) what they do support needs to be implemented using different methods (so even if two browsers support a particular effect, the code to make it work is different for each browser).

With DHTML itself under development, and with each browser offering differing implementations and levels of support, you can see it's probably going to be some time before DHTML is practical for general web design.

You can write multiple versions of DHTML and use a "browser detection" script so the browser implements the code it knows how to handle—but this means a lot of extra work for you and may cause unexpected behavior. Personally, it's my contention that any technology that requires tricks to be useful isn't ready for mainstream use, although I'm sure many good arguments could be made against that notion.

There are web sites that offer copy-and-paste DHTML code just as there are copy-and-paste JavaScript sites. The difference is, most JavaScript code works in all browsers, while most of the copy-and-paste DHTML code I've seen list which browsers the code works in (meaning it probably won't work in the browsers not listed).

If DHTML sounds interesting to you, I'd first master HTML and CSS, and then learn JavaScript. By then, DHTML may be practical to use on web sites. Don't be surprised, however, if it takes years to become universally compatible.

17.5 Flash

SINCE ITS INTRODUCTION IN 1996, Flash technology has grown in popularity as a method for adding animation and interactivity to web pages. In 2006, Adobe Systems bought Macromedia, the company that developed Flash. Adobe Flash (formerly Macro-media Flash), or simply Flash, now refers to both the Adobe Flash Player and to a multimedia authoring program used to create Flash content. Typical Flash content includes web applications such as navigation interfaces, graphically rich games, animated mini-movies, and advertisements.

Compared to other movie formats, Flash animated movies have the advantage of being small in file size so they load quickly. They are also more versatile because they can involve user inter-action, with different scenes playing out depending on which action a user takes.

Running Flash files

On the Web, Flash is played back by a web browser—so browsers require the Shockwave Flash plug-in to be usable. Many newer browsers come with the plug-in already included while most older browsers can be upgraded by installing the free plug-in. In addition to the required Shockwave Flash plug-in, the web server has to be configured with the correct MIME-type for dis-tributing Flash content. If you want to use Flash on a web site, you need to choose a host that offers the required MIME-type.

In addition to being displayed in a web browser, Flash movies can be converted to standalone executable files. This results in larger file sizes, but has the advantage of being able to run without a plug-in or separate native viewing application. Flash can also be converted to AVI, QuickTime, or animated GIF formats. In addi-tion, single frames can be exported as static images in a variety of formats.

Creating Movies in Flash

So how does Flash work?

Flash combines six basic elements that define its capabilities: vector graphics, text, streaming capability, a timeline, layers, and sound. Vector images and text can be created within Flash, while other graphics, along with sound files, can be imported.

Vector graphics (such as EPS files) are more efficient in Flash movies because they are based on mathematical computations rather than the pixel-by-pixel information used by bitmap graphics (such as GIF, JPG, and PNG files).

Vector graphics are scalable without affecting file size. For example, suppose the two squares in Figure 17.2 are separate

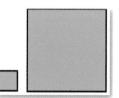

Figure 17.2

vector graphics. Both images have the same file size. The only difference between the two squares is the length of the sides. The length can be adjusted by mathematical calculations, which gives the graphics much smaller file sizes. In contrast, if these images are in one of the bitmap formats, the larger square has a much larger file size.

Flash movies are built on a "stage" that represents the area where the movie will display. Objects may float in and out of view, or make their appearance and disappearance in a variety of ways. A grid can be turned on and off to assist in positioning the elements of your movie.

A timeline is used to represent how the stage content changes over time. A timeline consists of a series of horizontal frames representing moments in time—similar to the frames of a movie reel or animation cels of a cartoon. You can create a movie frame by frame or create key frames and let Flash create the in-between frames for you. This technique is known as "tweening" and includes motion tweening or shape tweening. Motion tweening can modify the position, size, height-to-width ratio, rotation, color, and transparency of an object to simulate motion. Shape tweening modifies the shape of an object to transform it from one shape to another.

The timeline can also have vertically stacked layers. Having separate layers allows the movie to have multiple events occurring at once while providing the capability to edit one event without it directly affecting other events. Within the timeline, individual "scenes" can be used to divide the main timeline into shorter sequences, although using scenes may limit some of the features available.

Flash comes with a variety of drawing tools designed to create graphics with small file sizes, which in turn, keep the movie size down. There's a pencil tool, ink bottle tool, brush tool, paint bucket tool, eraser tool, and more.

There's also a text tool, which allows you to include various fonts, colors, and point sizes. Bold and italic type is included, and line spacing, kerning, and other formatting can be accomplished.

To conserve file space, Flash uses a "library" to store elements that are reused within a movie. The library has its own window, and the items in the library are called symbols. These symbols can be graphics, movie clips, and sound files.

When a Flash movie is exported, it can generate the HTML code needed to play the movie. Although this can be done manually, the Publish feature automates the many code options, including schemes for detecting the browser's ability to play Flash. For browsers not capable of playing Flash, it can create the code to deliver alternate content or take the visitor to a non-Flash page.

Drawbacks of Using Flash

Flash isn't without its drawbacks. Due to the increased use of Flash in online advertising, software has emerged that restricts Flash content. Sites that rely on Flash being available may find that many users are unable to access Flash-dependent web sites or site features.

The Flash Player has a long history of security flaws that, in theory, expose computers to remote attacks and problems with malevolent code. However, exploiting these flaws has only been at the proof-of-concept stage and has not translated into any known real-world problems yet.

For Internet users who are visually impaired and rely on screen readers, sites that use Flash may be difficult or impossible to use. While later versions of Flash support accessibility functions, many site designers may not create content with these considerations in mind.

Another consideration is that some Flash-authoring tools, particularly Adobe products, can be expensive.

17.6 RSS

RSS STANDS FOR A FEW DIFFERENT things depending on who's doing the telling, but the most widely accepted term is "Really Simple Syndication." Whatever the name attached to the abbreviation, RSS is yet another way to publish information online.

RSS gives webmasters a relatively easy way to syndicate their content and web site news, or to add syndicated content from others to their own web site. RSS content is written in XML (eXtensible Markup Language), and is called an RSS feed, RSS stream, RSS channel, or sometimes simply a web feed.

These feeds are viewed with software called feed readers or news aggregators. Some modern browsers also serve as RSS agents. In fact, by the time this book is actually in print or soon after, I think most of the major browsers will be able to serve as feed readers.

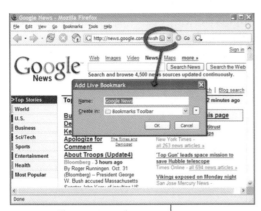

Figure 17.3

Some browsers, such as Firefox, not only serve as an RSS feed reader, but an icon displays in the address bar letting you know an RSS feed is available. In Figure 17.3, I circled the icon for an RSS Feed at Google News. Clicking the icon brings up the dialog box for subscribing to Google's news feed.

Firefox treats these news feeds as "live" bookmarks. The place where you saved the news feed bookmark in Firefox shows a folder with an expand arrow. When you expand the arrow, Firefox shows the latest entries for that particular web site, with the most recent news item on top.

All feed readers check news feeds the user subscribes to and then display a list of the updated articles found. Using RSS, webmasters can put content or news into a standardized format that can be fed to individual users who subscribe to the web site's news feed. Web sites looking for content can subscribe to the syndicated content to have it displayed on their own web site. The content you syndicate doesn't have to be traditional style news—opinion, tutorials, advice, and other content can be syndicated as well.

News feeds usually contain a title and brief summary of a news item or web site content along with a link to the news item or content itself. Entire articles can be supplied to the feed as well, depending on what the person creating the feed wants to do. For a news item, I might use RSS to announce a new product. Or, I could publish a web design tip every day or every week and offer this content for syndication for other sites. Other web sites looking for content could then subscribe to my syndicated news feed.

For publishers, RSS creates multiple entry points to their news items—entry points they probably wouldn't have without it, thereby increasing traffic to their web sites. For webmasters, they can add RSS feeds from other sites to their web sites as a way to have more content. It's really a win/win deal.

While using a browser as a feed reader is convenient, browsers are very basic and, to me, lacking in needed features. I prefer a full-featured feed reader for better usability and more options. There are many feed readers to choose from—some are free and some are commercial programs—and each offers different levels of complexity and features.

Essentially, there are two types of readers: application-based readers and web-based readers. Each type has its own benefits and drawbacks. With application-based readers comes more features and speed, but they lack mobility. With web-based readers, you sign up with a provider (some are free), which then allows you to check your news feeds from any computer. Access to web-based readers, however, comes at the cost of fewer features and less speed if you don't have a high-speed connection.

Figure 17.4

Figure 17.4 shows a screen capture of my news feeds at a free online reader provider called Bloglines. In the left pane is a list of all the news feeds I subscribe to. In the right pane is the latest news from the selected site; currently it's showing NASA breaking news. Clicking the headline for a news item in the right pane opens a new window with the story. RSS is pretty cool, and something I highly recommend both as a source of news and to syndicate your own content and news.

Currently, I use Bloglines for the portability, so I can't personally recommend an application-based reader. Instead, I'll name the popular ones: Google Reader, RSSOwl, GreatNews, Omea Reader, RSS Bandit, and SharpReader. Don't like any of those? Don't worry, just search for RSS Readers at Google or software sites and you'll find dozens of others to choose from.

By syndicating your content, it's much easier to get your information in the public spotlight. Instead of hoping someone who's been to your web site comes back after you update it, an RSS feed can tell them for you. In a sense, providing RSS feeds is like having newsletter subscribers, except you don't have to maintain a database of subscribers.

RSS builds web site traffic in one other way as well. A surfer who sees an RSS feed on one site might click on the content, which in turn sends the user to the web site that originates the news item. If you allow your content to be syndicated by other sites, RSS feeds can generate traffic to your site in two ways.

Sites that offer RSS feeds include many popular news sites such as Google and Yahoo, as well as other search engines, blogs, information portals, government agencies, magazines, book reviewers, libraries, music hit charts, technology-oriented web sites, and many other entities.

17.7 XML

XML, WHICH STANDS FOR Extensible Markup Language, offers a flexible method for sharing formatted information on the World Wide Web, intranets, print publications, wireless devices, and more. RSS uses XML to code news feeds, so you might think learning XML is a good idea if you're interested in syndicating your own content via RSS. But that's not necessarily the case. There are programs that generate the XML code needed for RSS feeds based on your input into form fields. There are also programs that will convert HTML pages into XML format for RSS feeds. If you only want to learn XML to create RSS content, in most cases I recommend using software to generate the RSS code.

Why? Because XML was specifically designed to be extensible, which means it was intended to allow the creation of user-defined, new markup, or elements. In other words, with XML the intent is to invent your own markup language. The guiding purpose of XML is not to mark up documents, but rather to define other document markup languages. So, as odd as this sounds, XML's main purpose is to create new markup languages based on XML.

When you use XML to create a new XML-based markup language, that language is technically called an "application" of XML. Learning XML is not really about XML itself, but instead it's about learning the rules for creating markup languages. That's just not something most of us will ever need or want to learn in order to design web sites.

While XML is more flexible than HTML, mainly because you can create your own elements and structural systems, most people find it more difficult to learn. Its best use may be for the organization of large quantities of specialized data, such as cataloging a library of books or a year-by-year history of NFL statistics, for example.

HTML is great for what it does, which serves most of our purposes, but the super-techie types found it too limited for their needs. They wanted something with the power and flexibility of SGML (Standard Generalized Markup Language) that was easy to use but better designed for online data exchange. They wanted a platform-independent language that was able to exchange data between different types of media, including the ability to process information not necessarily intended for human eyes.

And so, XML was devised. As a young markup language, as these kinds of things go, it is not without problems. One problem to overcome before it can become what it was intended to be is that many companies and individuals are creating extensions of XML that do not adhere to XML standards—yet this is one of the things XML was supposedly designed to avoid.

It is important to understand that XML is not a replacement for HTML. XML was designed to describe data while HTML was designed to display data.

Benefits of using XML include:

● With HTML, data is stored inside your HTML markup, but with XML data can be stored in separate XML files and read into the XML display page.

● Since XML data is really just plain text, it provides a software- and hardware-independent way to share data. This means data can be shared between different applications using different formats that once were incompatible.

● Learning XML makes it easier to learn to write wireless markup language (WML) for wireless devices such as mobile phones because WML is written in XML.

● It's a system independent, vendor independent standard.

● With good markup and a well-structured design, it can provide much better, more relevant search results.

● It's designed for high-volume data collections.

● It provides data reusability—one data source, multiple outputs.

On the human side, the need for XML programmers seems to be growing. A person with XML skills may command several thousand dollars more per year than a non-XML programmer, at least until the market is saturated.

17.8 Perl, PHP, ASP, and JSP

PERL, PHP, ASP, AND JSP ARE ALL scripting languages used to write small server-side software programs that reside on the host server and provide functionality to a web site. Typical script applications include: shopping carts, web page counters, email processors, database management, random content generators, guest books, polls, forums, site search engines, advertisement rotators, quizzes, and more.

As you might guess from the preceding list, these scripting languages can be used to create almost any web application you need. A script typically takes input from the user and then processes that information. It may generate a temporary web page based on the input, such as the pages of a purchase process when using a shopping cart. Or, it may produce content embedded in a static web page, such as a random quote or advertising rotation. Or, a script may simply save data to a database, such as a name and email address when someone subscribes to a newsletter.

This type of programming presents some unique security concerns that pose possible security breaches. If the wrong person discovers security holes in the scripts you use, the results could be very severe. For example, a spammer could exploit a mail script to send unauthorized, unsolicited emails by the thousands or millions. Your web site host will probably discover it before you do—and would waste no time shutting down your site temporarily until you fixed the security problem.

Other breaches might result in a non-paying customer gaining free access to your commercial software. Someone else might be after your customer information or may simply want to deface your web site to show that he or she can.

While you can learn the basics of these scripting languages online, because of these security concerns I highly recommend taking courses from a local college or tech school where they'll teach proper script security. I haven't seen too many online courses that teach security with the seriousness it warrants. However, taking a free online course as an introduction would probably help you breeze through the courses in the classroom—and then everyone will think you're so *very* smart!

You'll also find many free scripts online. Some of them are very good, and some are very bad. Be careful about the free scripts you choose to use. Don't just grab the first script you find. Instead, find several that look promising and then research them online for any known security problems.

17.9 Databases

A DATABASE IS A COLLECTION OF DATA organized for convenient storage and retrieval. Data comes in many forms, including but not limited to numbers, text, graphics, and even multimedia.

Databases help organize data in ways that help simplify our workload—and our lives. You already use databases on a regular basis. Each time you look up a number in the phone book, look up the meaning of a word in a dictionary, or query a search engine, you are using a database.

From the users' perspective, traditional phone books and dictionaries are paper-based databases, but on the publisher's computer system they are computerized. Of course, there are many computerized databases that you probably use as well. The address book in your email program is an example of a small database. If you keep track of your finances in a program such as QuickBooks, that's another database you use.

On your computer, databases are fairly easy to use—because the software is already written and all you have to do is make entries. Databases play a vital part in the online world. Sites such as Amazon, Barnes & Noble, CD Universe, eBay, Tiger Direct, NFL, MLB, NBA, and virtually every search engine and directory as well as every online retailer makes use of databases to some extent. They are vital components of many web sites, and without them many web sites would be out of business instantly.

As noted, many scripting languages can make use of small databases. For heavy-duty database compilations, however, or for more versatility and utility, a more robust environment is needed. Originally, databases were simple flat files. This means that the information was stored in one long text file, called a tab-delimited file. Each entry in a tab-delimited file is separated by a special character, such as a vertical bar (|). Here's an example:

FirstName, LastName, ClockNo, JobTitle, YearsEmp|Dan, White, 534, welder,9|Doug, Jackson, 332, labor.3|Annette, Burns, 873, bookkeeper.15|Fred, Jennings, 329, press operator,18|Kirsten, Malloy, 499, line leader.12|Barry, Langford, 517, shift manager,12|

As you can see, you'd have to search sequentially through the entire file to gather related information, such as job titles or employee numbers. Just imagine having to comb through a list of several hundred or several thousand names in a file like that.

Along came relational databases, which allow you to easily find specific information and let you sort data by field. They can also generate reports that contain only certain fields from each record. For example, in the following relational database, you could sort employee records by missed days of work to reward those with perfect attendance.

First Name	Last Name	Hire Date	Age	Days Absent	Authorized
Bill	Cummings	2/21/1989	42	0	0
John	Fisher	5/9/1997	28	3	3
Cheryl	Roland	12/2/1991	37	2	1
Andrew	Herman	7/15/2005	21	5	5
Marcus	Rindleman	5/23/1983	58	0	0

As you can see, relational databases are stored in table-like structures. The columns are called fields and the rows are called records. The data is stored in these fields and records. With this database, you could easily print a list of only the employees with perfect attendance.

Relational databases comprise most of the databases you will be involved with in web programming. The most common language used by relational databases is SQL, or Structured Query Language. If you want to build databases for your site, or want to get into the server programming side of the web, I strongly encourage you to learn SQL and/or MySQL database management.

17.10   Conclusion

THE INFORMATION IN THIS CHAPTER represents only a small sample of the most well-known technologies an aspiring web designer may want to learn. This chapter is a very short representation of a very long list. There are dozens, perhaps hundreds, of other skills a person could learn. From Ajax to Zope, there are far too many things you could learn to even mention them all. And the fact is, for most people, there's little need to know most of them because few employers would require such extensive knowledge.

Rather than picking technologies to learn for the sake of learning, find out what would be useful to you. You can do that without researching them all. A good way to learn which technologies are most in need is to peruse online employment sites to see what the requirements are for the fields you are interested in.

By reviewing various job position requirements, you'll have real-world examples of what skills are in need.

While knowing technologies is one consideration, many jobs also require experience or training in specific software, too. Be sure to consider that when thinking about skills to acquire. For example, I just searched one job posting site for "web designer" postings. I compiled nine different postings and came up with this list of software they require proficiency with:

- Photoshop
- Illustrator
- ImageReady
- Flash
- Dreamweaver
- Word
- Excel
- Outlook
- WinZip
- PowerPoint
- Fireworks

On the programming side, the only languages mentioned were HTML, CSS, PHP, and JavaScript. None of them even listed XHTML, so knowing that would be a feather in your cap at the firms looking for web designers that I observed.

As you can see, while there's a lot you could learn, proficiency with relatively few technologies are required for employment—at least according to the job postings I reviewed.

17.11 Chapter 17 Exercise

IN THE LAST CHAPTER, you started a personal or fun site of your choosing. For this chapter, you will make your only content page for that site:

- Talk about whatever you want on this page. If it's a personal site, you might talk about your family and friends or your interests. If it's a fun site, go with the flow—the content isn't really important here so don't spend too much time on the creative writing part. The important thing is that you are practicing your newly acquired skills in layout and design.

- Be sure to link back to the home page and to the wrap-up page from this page, and include the keyword and description meta tags.

Bonus Chapter

18

18.1 Introduction

THIS CHAPTER INCLUDES A VARIETY of tips and tricks that I've found useful in some way. Basically, these are just good things to know that seem to fit better here than in the flow of content in other places in the book.

18.2 Netiquette

THE WORD *NETIQUETTE* IS A MARRIAGE of the two words "Internet" and "etiquette." As you might have guessed, it describes proper etiquette on the Internet. The people who use and contribute to the Internet represent a melting pot of ideas, opinions, and cultures. As such, it has been likened to the days of no rules and no authorities in the Wild West.

While that may be true for some, the vast majority of users quickly adapt to an unwritten code of conduct. Most users voluntarily follow these rules, both as a courtesy to others and to be respected by others. If you want to be accepted by the majority of the online community, and especially among the movers and shakers of the industry, you need to follow these accepted standards.

Most of these rules are simple common sense, but they are often overlooked. There is no official set of rules, no central place to learn the rules, and no one authority to go by. What follows is my interpretation of the rules of netiquette based on my experience. While these rules are expressed in my words, they are common knowledge to many.

- Don't send mass, unsolicited commercial email (UCE). This is known as spam, and is hated far and wide. Plenty of spammers exist, but they are so afraid of being known and hated as spammers that they use elaborate ruses to hide their true identities. Laws have changed, too, and massive fines and jail time can be levied against those caught. In one case reported by IDG News Service, a San Francisco company was fined $900,000 for spamming; in the same article, four men indicted in New York face up to 30 years in prison for using spam to scam people out of money.

- Don't type in all CAPITAL LETTERS. It's considered the equivalent of shouting at someone face to face. It's also harder to read text in all caps because after a lifetime of word shape recognition, we're just not used to reading all capital letters. When we encounter it, we have to slow down to read the message.

- When sending messages to people you don't know, keep it short and to the point. Many people are very busy and don't have time to read rambling, unfocused messages.

- Do not use deceptive subject titles in your emails as an attempt to trick people into reading them. Also, don't mark messages as urgent when they are not.

- When quoting others or replying to ezine publishers and other lengthy emails, edit out all but the relevant portion of the message you're replying to. This saves the recipient time and trouble and may determine whether your message is answered or not.

- Never send messages to multiple recipients in such a way that each recipient can see everyone the message was sent to—unless you're certain all the parties know each other and won't mind. New users who forward false virus warnings are almost always guilty of this. It's a breach of privacy to share contact information that has been entrusted to you with people who don't know each other.

- Never, EVER forward a virus warning unless you verify it first. About 99.9 percent of the virus warnings you receive by email are hoaxes. When you forward these bogus warnings, you only perpetuate lies. Never forward chain letters either. You can lose your credibility and your Internet access if enough people complain to your ISP.

● Never assume the message you're sending will only be read by the person you intend it for. Never write anything you'd be ashamed or embarrassed to see on the evening news—or in your mother's hands!

● Never send HTML email without permission. HTML email isn't compatible with all email clients so it looks like HTML source code to some recipients. They often delete it without reading it rather than trying to decipher the message from the gibberish. Among the other reasons not to send HTML email:

   ● It is slower to download. People like me who regularly receive hundreds of emails per day don't need the delays.

   ● It takes up more space on the recipient's computer.

   ● It costs people who pay for Internet access by the hour more money to download it. While that's not a big problem in the United States, it is in some foreign countries.

   ● It ties up bandwidth and slows down the Internet.

Note

This list could go on and on. Just trust me, never send HTML email to strangers and check with your friends first to see if it's welcome.

● Never add anyone to a mailing list without his or her permission.

● Never EVER send file attachments with email without asking if it's OK first. The only exception to this is the vcard (virtual business card).

● Never harshly criticize someone in public forums. If you have issues with a person, take it up with him or her in private.

● Never blatantly advertise in newsgroups or forums.

● Cite all quotes and references; respect copyrights.

● Many consider attaching return receipts to email messages an invasion of privacy. A return receipt means that when someone opens your message, his or her email program sends you a notification that the message was opened.

● Be careful what you write! A user can't see your facial expressions or hear your vocal inflections. Your token joke might easily be taken as an insult. Remember, once your words are written and sent, the recipients can save them. Your words may come back to haunt you!

● The Golden Rule applies on the Net just like in real life. Do unto others as you would have them do unto you. Think before acting.

- You are the center of your universe, but not everyone else's universe. When you write to someone hoping for a little of his or her time, don't expect an instant reply. People have other concerns. Be patient and respectful. One person wrote to me complaining that she asked me a question yesterday and hadn't received a reply yet. The messages were actually about 11 hours apart. The user went on to tell me how I should shut down my site if I wasn't going to reply promptly, and went on and on about *her* problems. The user was looking to me for help, and then became rude when she didn't get a response fast enough to suit her. Do you think I helped her? If you said no, you win a pebble from my aquarium. Send $5 to me for shipping and handling to claim your prize.

- Don't be confrontational. There is intelligent life out there. If you're a troublemaker, you will sooner or later be on the ugly end of a verbal whooping, with your only recourse to slink away and lick your wounds.

- Share. Everyone starts out on the Internet as a newbie. Others probably helped you along the way. When the opportunity arises, give back.

- Be forgiving. Everyone makes mistakes. Don't play it up to be bigger than it is.

- Keep your ego and power in check. No one likes a bully and no one likes to be lorded over. Remember, there are real people with real hearts and feelings behind all the email addresses and web sites. Be somebody—but be somebody you'd like if you were the other person!

As you can see, netiquette primarily consists of treating your fellow men and women as you would like to be treated—with respect and dignity. When all you see in front of you is your computer, it's easy to forget there is flesh and blood on the other end of your communications.

Your words can make a person's day—or ruin it. I encourage everyone to be a builder and not a destroyer in life. Anyone can insult and degrade others; it doesn't even take brains. But it does take an ounce of courage and a pound of heart to help build up others. That's something missing in many people's lives: someone to encourage them and give them a shred of respect to hang on to. When it comes down to basics, everyone wants to be liked. You can feed that need and be an everyday, unsung hero.

18.3 Spotting an Email Hoax

MISGUIDED INDIVIDUALS USUALLY INTEND email hoaxes as pranks. In reality, they are nuisances that make you look silly for forwarding them to others. They can range from warnings about nonexistent viruses to bogus rewards for forwarding the email to cruel letters that play upon the readers' sympathy for dying or missing children.

A few commonalities will help you spot possible hoaxes. For example, many hoaxes use technical sounding language, claim associations with people of authority, or mention personal acquaintances.

A hoax may say something like, "…this destructive virus uses mathematical analytics to reallocate binary data fields that will burn out your hard drive through infinite loop interrupt requests."

Yeah, whatever.

Or, a hoax may claim, "This happened to my girlfriend's brother so I know it's true," or they may reference corporate officers, doctors, lawyers, and other official types. The hoax writer may even sign the letter as one of these people to make it seem official and important sounding. The writers try to make their hoaxes seem real by association.

Any email that says, "Pass this letter on to everyone you know," should raise a huge red flag. That's how hoaxes are spread —by well-intentioned but misguided email users. Another red flag is a message that purports to be an FCC warning or other governmental agency warning. The FCC does not issue warnings, nor do most governmental agencies.

In short, don't forward any warnings that you haven't investigated for authenticity. The resource page for this book lists a few sites where you can investigate the authenticity of this kind of email. Again, the resource page for the book is at:

http://www.BoogieJack.com/book/resources.html

18.4 Converting RGB Color to Hex Code

MOST GRAPHICS PROGRAMS will give you the RGB value of a color, but some won't give you the hex value, which most webmasters use for coding color on web pages. Windows 95 and later provides a way for you to find the hex value of any RGB color.

1. Click the Start button on the task bar. Choose Program Files, then choose Accessories, then choose Calculator.

2. Make sure *Scientific* mode is checked in the *View* menu.

3. Across the top are seven radio buttons, a group of four and then a group of three. In the first set, click the radio button for *Dec* (decimal). In the second set, click the radio button for *Degrees*.

4. Next, follow these instructions to convert an RGB number to a hex code:

   a. Enter a value for the Red field (for example, 159).

   b. Click the Hex radio button. The number will change to 9F—the red hex value.

   c. Go back and change the radio button to Dec.

   d. Enter a value for the Green field (for example, 122).

   e. Click the Hex radio button. The number will change to 7A—the green hex value.

   f. Go back and change the radio button to Dec.

   g. Enter a value for the Blue field (for example, 223).

   h. Click the Hex radio button. The number will change to DF—the blue hex value.

So from the RGB color values of:

    Red: 159, Green: 122, Blue: 223

We have calculated the exact hex color value of:

    #9F7ADF

If you're not sure what color you want, try using one of the color utilities on my site to help you choose one or more colors. There is also a conversion chart and color charts in Appendix C.

Note

On Mac OS, open the Utilities folder inside the Applications folder. There you will find the Digital-Color Meter application. With it open, choose RGB as Hex Value, 16-bit from the menu. Then, simply point at anything on your computer to get the pixel's hex value. Any open image, the desktop, a web page—anything is fair game.

18.5 Creating Smart Passwords

IN YOUR LIFE ONLINE, you'll need to use passwords with regularity. Most people want a password that is easy to remember, such as their birth date, their maiden name, a child's name, their dog's name, and things like that. The trouble with that is, if it's easy to remember, it can also be easy to guess.

Many people also tend to use the same password for everything so they don't have to remember several different ones. I made that mistake in the early days, but there's a problem with that too. If someone learns or guesses your one password, they will have access to everything you use the password for (at least everything they know you use it for).

It's better to use a unique user name and password for each and every place you need them, and to make them hard to guess. Keep a list on paper of all your user names and passwords as you collect them. Each time you create a new user name and password, add it to the list immediately. In case you missed it, I am recommending actual hard copy here—if you keep the list on your computer, it can be accidentally deleted, become corrupt, be overwritten, or lost if your hard drive fails. Obviously, you'll need to keep the paper in a safe place—not stuck to, say, a bulletin board over your desk so it can be stolen right along with your laptop.

A good password consists of a mix of uppercase and lowercase letters, plus numbers. Some web sites and software programs also allow extra characters (@ $ %, etc.), which makes passwords even harder to crack. Be sure to use more than the minimum number of characters required. The more characters you use, the harder it is to guess or to hack with a password attack tool.

Some people use a system to create unique passwords. A comedienne friend of mine uses a name that is easy for her to remember, but then moves each character over and up a row on the keyboard. Doing this, the name "Anthony" becomes "Qh5y9h6," which is much harder to guess than Anthony.

You can create your own system, just remember to make your passwords hard to guess and keep track of them off your computer in case of any computer problems.

18.6 Windows Explorer Thumbnails

IF YOU WANT AN EASY WAY to view thumbnails of images, but I don't want to buy or install any new software, then I have a tip for you. In some versions of Windows you have an option that's pretty nifty.

Open Windows Explorer and right-click the folder in the left pane with the graphics you want to view as thumbnails, and then choose Properties. Check the box at the bottom that says Enable Thumbnail View. Click Apply.

Next, left-click the folder in the left pane to have it open in the right pane. Now, click the View menu and notice that the Thumbnails command is added to it. Simply choose Thumbnails from the View menu to display thumbnails of all compatible file types, including HTML pages.

If you don't see the Thumbnails command, close Windows Explorer and then reopen it and it should be there. You may also need to close and reopen Windows Explorer to actually see the thumbnails once you've set a folder to display them.

You will need to perform these steps for each individual folder that you want to enable the thumbnail view for.

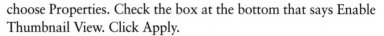

18.7 Better Graphics for AOL Users

AOL USERS OFTEN WRITE TO ME about poor image quality or complain that when they try to save a GIF or JPG image it turns into an .art file. This is because, by default, AOL browsers are set to display compressed images, which don't look as nice. The browser saves the images in its own proprietary format, thus the .art images resulting from GIF and JPG files. All is not lost though—you can correct this browser behavior.

Here is how to turn off AOL image compression:

1. Click My AOL at the top of the screen.
2. Click Preferences.
3. Click WWW.
4. Click Web Graphics.
5. Uncheck Use Compressed Graphics.
6. Click Apply.

If you return to a previously visited page, AOL will load the old compressed graphics from the cache. A browser's cache is where web pages you've visited are temporarily stored on your computer. If you revisit any of these pages before the stored pages expire, you may be viewing pages that are on your computer rather than on the site, so you can still see the old, compressed graphics. To change that, you need to clear out your temp files while you are still in MY AOL/Preferences. To do that:

1. Click General.

Note

On Mac OS, any image that has a preview displays as a thumbnail by default.

2. Click Delete Files.

3. Click Apply.

Enjoy the web in glorious full color.

18.8 Installing CGI Scripts

THIS SECTION IS INTENDED FOR THOSE with little or no experience installing CGI scripts. It only covers installing ready-made scripts you can find at free script resources; it does not cover customizing scripts for your own purpose.

Most CGI scripts are written in a programming language called Perl. Although other languages can be used to create CGI scripts, Perl is by far the most common, so this section focuses on Perl scripts.

A Perl script is actually a text file written in the Perl language and saved with a .cgi extension (or .pl extension for some scripts). CGI scripts are server-side scripts, which means the scripts are executed on the server with only the output of the script shown in the browser. This is the opposite of most JavaScripts, which are usually contained within an HTML page and executed by the viewer's computer (client-side).

These instructions are subject to change because of browser changes after this book was written. If so, you may have to explore the menus to find where or how to make the changes. You could also use a search engine to find current instructions.

Requirements

1. Before looking for scripts, first check to see if your web host supports them and that you have permission to use them. Some services don't allow them—especially free hosts. If you see a folder called cgi-bin or cgibin when you upload your HTML files, then you are most likely allowed to use them. With some hosts, you may have to request that they create a CGI directory for you as it's not always included by default (even with hosts that allow and support cgi scripts). A few hosts may even want to test and approve any scripts before allowing you to use them.

2. You also need a text editor to edit the script (Notepad on a PC, or TextEdit on Mac OS). You won't have to edit much, if anything, but you will need a text editor and not a word processor. A word processor may add formatting to the saved file, which will break the script.

3. You'll also need an FTP program such as CoffeeCup's Free FTP covered in Chapter 16: Publishing Your Web Site. CGI scripts should be uploaded in *ASCII* mode.

4. A little bit of common sense and perseverance helps since CGI can be frustrating, especially if you're new to it.

Configuration

The first thing you need to know is the path on your server to the Perl interpreter. If you have a cgi-bin already in place, there may already be a script in it. View the script to see the correct path to Perl. It will be the first line. You may also find the path in the FAQ pages, setup message, or support documents provided by your web host.

The most common error made by webmasters new to installing CGI scripts is having the path to Perl incorrect. When you open the script you want to try out, the first line should look something like this:

#!/usr/bin/perl ...or... #!/usr/local/bin/perl

This may or may not have to be changed. The path has to be the correct one for your server or it won't work. About half the time, the script you download will have the right path. If you don't check, however, somehow Murphy's Law always seems to apply.

Check for More

While you've got the script open to check the path to Perl, look at the top of the script for comments regarding any other variables that need to be configured. Often there are none, but occasionally you'll find one or more. Comments in Perl are the lines that start with the hash mark/pound sign (#).

This is a comment in a Perl script.

Comments often read across multiple lines.

Each line that starts with # is a comment…

except the first line, which is the path to Perl.

Occasionally, the path to your site must be specified somewhere in the script, and you'll find directions on this in the comments. The path is not the same thing as the web address

(URL). My URL is http://www.boogiejack.com, but the path to my site ON THE SERVER is like this:

/mmt/web/users/boogiejack/www

This example probably won't work on your server, even if you change the domain name from mine to yours. The paths are different at almost every web host. With some FTP clients you'll be able to see the complete path in the window above the server-side files when you connect. Otherwise, check your web host's support, FAQ, or setup pages.

Installation

Once you've configured the script for your server, it's time to upload it. When uploading CGI scripts, you must upload them in ASCII mode. Here's a memory trick: ASCII and CGI both end in the letter "i" so that's the mode to upload a CGI script. The other option is binary mode, which is used for images and other types of binary files.

Many hosts only allow CGI scripts to be executed from the cgi-bin, so you should upload the script to that directory. After uploading the script, you must set the correct file permissions for the script and any other directories and files the script uses.

Understanding File Permissions

UNIX servers allow you to set different levels of access to a file for different groups of people. In terms of file access, there are three groups and three different permission types each group can receive. You don't really have to understand this part to set permissions—if you know what permissions the script should have—but I'll show you anyway. Feel free to skip down to "Setting Permissions" if you're in a hurry.

The groups are:

User: The "user" group consists only of the owner of the file (your hosting account).

Group: The "group" group (Tricky English, huh? Pay attention!) consists of the other users on the server—you can usually remove their permissions entirely if you think it is necessary.

Other: The "other" group consists of everyone else—most importantly, the web server falls into the "other" category.

The permissions are:

Read: The "read" permission allows a user or program the ability to read the data in a file.

Write: The "write" permission allows a user or program the ability to write new data into a file, and to remove data from it.

Execute: The "execute" permission allows a user or program the ability to execute a file, if it is a program or a script.

Setting Permissions

Permissions are set with a UNIX command called CHMOD. Don't worry; you don't have to know UNIX server commands as this can be accomplished quite easily with your FTP client. You'll have to check with the place you got the script from or with any help files or comments within the script to see what permissions are needed. Most scripts require a permission of 755. If the script you're using doesn't indicate it, try 755.

To set file permissions using WS_FTP:

1. Left-click the script to highlight it.

2. Right-click on the highlighted file and a drop-down list will open.

3. Choose *chmod* from the list.

Figure 18.1

Figure 18.1 shows a screen capture of the dialog box for setting file permissions.

Some FTP programs, including some versions of WS_FTP, show the numeric value of the file permissions you've checked off. I'm using one that doesn't show the numeric value—so I can show you how to figure it out on your own.

Each group and permission has an assigned number. A script author will usually tell you what permission to the set the script for, but that doesn't tell you which groups to check to arrive at the number. You can determine the correct permission number using basic math.

Permission Assignments:

```
400   read by owner
040   read by group
```

```
004   read by anybody (other)
200   write by owner
020   write by group
002   write by anybody
100   execute by owner
010   execute by group
001   execute by anybody
```

Look again at the screen capture in Figure 18.1 and compare the checked boxes to the list of permission assignments. Add up the numbers of the boxes with checkmarks. The total will tell you what permission setting the example script would have.

What number did you get? You should have gotten 755, which is a common setting.

Here's an exercise for you. You have a script that calls for the following permissions:

```
Owner:  read, write, execute
Group:  read, write
Other:  read, execute
```

Before looking at the following chart for the answer, see if you can add up the correct numbers according to the permission assignments and come up with the correct CHMOD setting number.

Here is the answer worked out in living grayscale for you:

	Read	Write	Execute	Totals
Owner	400	200	100	700
Group	040	020	000	060
Other	004	000	001	005
File Permission (chmod) #:		765		

You peeked at the answer without trying to work it out for yourself, didn't you?

Tsk, tsk. How are you going to learn that way?

As you can see, if you add up the subtotals in the right-hand column in this table, you get a file permission of 765. The numbers in each column were taken from the permission assignments shown previously.

Here's a handy chart of the most commonly used CHMOD settings.

| **Legend:** r = read   w = write   x = execute | | | |
Permission #	Owner	Group	Other	What it Means...
777	r w x	r w x	r w x	Writable Directory
755	r w x	r x	r x	Standard (non-writable) directory/executable file
666	r w	r w	r w	Writable File
644	r w x	r	r	Readable File

Troubleshooting

If you're reading this section, you're probably inexperienced at installing CGI—and the bad news is that many things can go wrong. To compound the problem, whatever is wrong won't likely be obvious to you. Following are the three most common errors and likely causes.

- **403 Permission Denied:** Error 403 is as much of a sure thing as you'll find. You get this error when you forget to change the file permissions of the script or you changed them to the wrong setting.
- **404 File Not Found:** The actual file (the script) was not found. This is the same error you get for broken links. You probably entered the link incorrectly somewhere.
- **500 Internal Server Error:** You don't want this one! Don't do it! It will blow up the server!

The last one is the most common error, and also the worst one to correct. It may be an error in the script itself, but not always. Read the documentation for the script very carefully and make sure you followed each step correctly. Go back through all the configuration and installation steps and try to find out what is incorrectly configured. Of course, this assumes you have a good script to begin with. It could also be a programming error by the script author; although that isn't common, it does happen. Most authors will test their scripts thoroughly before releasing them to the public.

If you have access to the log files on your server, find one called *error_log* and check the end of that file. You need to check it right after you discover your script doesn't work. When a script fails to execute, errors are logged in that file and they may give you a clue about what went wrong.

The problem might be something peculiar to your web host as well, so read the documentation your host provides. If you can't find anything there, you might check with your host's support services. As a last resort, you could contact the script author. Be sure you've gone through all the other means of troubleshooting first before contacting the script author, especially if it's a free script. The author may help you, but may ask for a fee for the service.

Finally, make sure any scripts you use work before linking to them for public access/use. If you serve up a broken script, it causes the clock on the user's computer to skip ahead four years. People really don't like aging that fast.

Whew! That was a humdinger, wasn't it? Yea, you loved it though. You'll find a complete listing of server errors in Appendix E: Troubleshooting Chart.

18.9 Stop Directory Snooping

SUPPOSE YOU HAVE A DIRECTORY named "Software" where you keep programs for paying customers to download. Hang on if you don't have a commercial site—this tip does apply to you, too.

If you don't have an index page in that directory, the entire contents of that directory may be open to the public. If someone bought one program and noticed it was downloaded from the Software directory, and then wanted to see what else you have, he or she could type this URL into the browser:

http://www.yoursite.com/Software/

Without an index page in that directory, some servers will return a list of everything in the directory, including subdirectories. The person would have access to any directory on your server and could download anything he or she wanted.

Even if you don't have a commercial site, you can still have vulnerable directories that you don't want the general public to have access to. Perhaps you have a secret family page, a private journal, or other things you don't want to be publicly available.

The solution is to put an index.html page in *all* of your directories. The index page could have a *"You've been busted!"*

notice. You might use a script that identifies their IP addresses and tells them they've been logged so you can scare them a little. You could also put up a "*Restricted Access*" notice. Or, you could do what I do: Place a redirect page there so that if users try to gain access to your directories, they'll get shuttled to your home page instead. In some directories, I shuttle them off to one of my other sites. Let them try to figure that one out.

18.10 Disable Smart Tags

THIS IS ONE OF THOSE "just in case" kind of tips. A few years ago Microsoft developed a technology they call Smart Tags. Smart Tags add links to Microsoft sites and partner sites in places on your site where you never intended for links to be. There was a considerable uproar over many aspects of Smart Tags.

One of the objections was that by altering web site content, Microsoft was violating copyright protection laws. Another was that Microsoft was effectively advertising on web sites without compensating the web site owner. Another was that it made it seem as if the web site or owner was endorsing whatever product, service, or company Microsoft linked to, including Microsoft itself.

The uproar caused Microsoft to back off from the idea, but that doesn't mean they've abandoned it all together. This extremely bad idea—at least for everyone except Microsoft and their favored partners—may come back somewhere down the road. Besides that, just because Microsoft is no longer distributing Smart Tag–enabled browsers doesn't mean there aren't Smart Tag–enabled browsers still in use.

You can prevent Smart Tags from appearing on your pages in browsers that have the capability. Just add the following meta tag to the <head> section of your pages and Smart Tags will not appear.

```
<meta name="MSSmartTagsPreventParsing" content=
"true" />
```

18.11 Disable the Image Toolbar

INTERNET EXPLORER 6 and later has an Image Toolbar built into it. If you hover your cursor over an image, a floating Image Toolbar pops up and allows users to save the image, email the image to a friend, or print the image. The fourth option on the

Figure 18.2

Toolbar is for opening the *My Pictures* folder on your computer. Figure 18.2 shows the Image Toolbar.

Not all images will activate the toolbar. The image must be at least 130x130 pixels, and the image cannot be a background image or an image map.

If you use a "no-right click" script to stop people from stealing your graphics, it won't stop anyone from grabbing your image via the floating Image Toolbar. As a result, a lot of webmasters were concerned that IE made image theft all too easy.

To their credit, Microsoft did include a way for webmasters to prevent the Image Toolbar from activating on their sites. To their discredit, they put the burden on the webmasters to turn it off—because it's on by default. To my knowledge, other than Microsoft, I was the first publisher to offer instructions on how to turn this feature off.

Used with a no right-click script, your images can be as safe as they were before the Image Toolbar. That's not to say there aren't still ways to steal your images—because there are—but it does return things to the previous level of difficulty and required know-how.

To turn off the Image Toolbar for individual pictures, use either:

```
<img src="pic.jpg" galleryimg="no" />
<img src="pic.jpg" galleryimg="false" />
```

To turn off the Image Toolbar for all the images on a Web page, add either of the following meta tags to the HEAD section of the page:

```
<meta http-equiv="imagetoolbar" content="no">
<meta http-equiv="imagetoolbar" content="false">
```

Note

You should still use the width, height, and alt attributes. I left them out of the examples for the sake of simplicity.

If you turn off the Image Toolbar functions for all the images on a Web page, you can enable them for individual images by setting the "galleryimg" attribute to *yes* or *true*:

```
<img src="pic.gif" galleryimg="yes">
<img src="pic.gif" galleryimg="true">
```

That's faster than including individual tags for each image if there are one or two that you want to let people grab, but you don't want them to grab the majority of your images.

Note

You can only turn off elements that use the <img> tag; it doesn't affect other graphics encoded using the <embed> or <object> elements.

If you turn the Image Toolbar off, you may occasionally encounter users that complain you're taking control of their browser behavior. They may feel that's an invasion of their rights, but remember, it's their browser, but *your* web site. As the owner of the web site, you are completely within your rights to decide whether to allow the Image Toolbar.

Many people don't like the Image Toolbar and wish it wouldn't display. Fortunately, you can disable its display in your browser preferences. To turn the Image Toolbar on or off in your own browser:

1. On the *Tools* menu of Internet Explorer, click *Internet Options*.
2. Click the *Advanced* tab, and then scroll down to the *Multimedia* area.
3. Uncheck the *Enable Image Toolbar* checkbox.
4. Click OK, and then restart Internet Explorer.

You can also disable the Image Toolbar on a per session basis. To do that:

1. Point to a picture to activate the Image Toolbar.
2. Right-click the Image Toolbar and then choose *Disable Image Toolbar*.
3. To turn off the Image toolbar for the current session, choose *This Session*. To turn off the Image Toolbar for all sessions, choose *Always*.

18.12 Server Side Includes

SERVER SIDE INCLUDES, OR SSI for short, offers a marvelous method for adding site navigation or other elements to all the pages of a site via one file. For example, on most of my sites the navigation is added to each web page via SSI. To add a new site section, I only need to change my one *navigation.ssi* file; that change is automatically reflected on all the pages of my site that are linked to that SSI file.

To use SSI, your web host needs to have your server enabled for SSI. Many hosts enable it automatically, so you can test it for yourself without their help. If it doesn't work, then request that the host enable SSI. You can also enable it yourself in some control panels; you may want to check that if you have a control panel with your hosting plan.

For SSI to work, most hosts require that you name HTML pages with a .shtml extension instead of .html or .htm. They can, however, enable your server so that all pages, regardless of the page extension, can run SSI. This is what I prefer, primarily because many of my sites were built before I learned about SSI, and I don't want to break incoming links by renaming the pages with a different file extension.

To include SSI on a page, place the following at the location on the page where you want the SSI file to appear.

```
<!--#include file="ssi_files/navigation.ssi"-->
```

This example references a file named "navigation.ssi," which is located in the folder (directory) called "ssi_files." Of course, you need to use the correct path and file name for the file you want to add via SSI or it won't work.

That's all there is to adding a navigation system to a page using SSI—as long as your web site is SSI enabled (and if necessary for your server, the page is named with a .shtml extension).

The only thing left to do is create the actual navigation.ssi file you are referencing. This file simply contains whatever code you would actually place on the page if you weren't using SSI. For example, for links to show up like this:

Home Page | Contact Me

Create the navigation.ssi file with only this in it:

```
<div style="text-align: center;">
<a href="index.html">Home Page</a> |
<a href="contact.html">Contact Me</a>
</div>
```

If those are the only links you want in your navigation system, that's all you need to include. Save the file with a **.ssi** extension, such as "*navigation.ssi*" and it's finished.

In an SSI file, you can use any standard HTML code that you use on a web page. Just don't start it off with the <html> declaration and don't go through the *head*, *title*, and *body* routine. Those are presumably on the page you're inserting the SSI into, so you don't need to repeat them. Add only the code that you want to place in the spot on the page you're inserting the file into.

Note

Some text editors will automatically add a .txt extension to a file when you try to save it as "something.ssi," leaving you with "something.ssi.txt" instead. To prevent the .txt extension from being added, place the file name and extension in quotation marks when you save it. For example, **"linkbox.ssi"**.

18.13 Your Worst Enemy

WHEN IT COMES TO CONTENT WRITING, believe it or not, your harshest critic, your worst enemy, is probably you. I've already mentioned (how many times now?) that content is an extremely critical factor in online success. What I haven't mentioned is that many people write something, then judge it or themselves too harshly, and go feed the cat.

Feeding the cat, mowing the yard, doing the dishes, and other chores are things that need done, but make sure you're not using these things as an excuse to quit. Whether as an individual or business entity, you can make a unique contribution to the web. Simply share what you know about the things that interest you.

It doesn't really matter whether it's scrapbooking, fishing, small engine repair, hair styling, portrait painting, interior design, pottery, horticulture, candy making, women's issues, men's issues, finances, geology, geography, travel, boating, health, sports, or anything else that interests you. The point is that if you think it's interesting, it's a sure thing that others will find it interesting, too.

Building good content means putting some of yourself out there—out where others may criticize you or your work. Remember, while you're not anonymous online, chances are you will never meet 99.99 percent of the people who you make contact with via your web site. Some people live to criticize others; it's just the way they are. It shouldn't matter. It's not what anyone says about you or to you; it's how you internalize it that makes a difference.

So when you've written something you're unsure about, be careful not to judge it harshly out of fear of criticism. Put it online and give it a trial—you can always remove it later. Don't be afraid to be yourself, because you are remarkable whether you realize it or not. You're a wonderful person, so let your light shine. I'd bet money that self-criticism and self-judgment has killed more creative ideas than criticism from outside sources. Don't be your own worst enemy by sabotaging your own creativity and interests.

18.14 How to Ask For Help— Intelligently

MANY PEOPLE ARE WILLING TO HELP others out, but how you go about asking for that help can make the difference in whether you actually get help or remain frustrated. To help yourself get help, do these things *before* contacting an individual or company with a help question:

1. Try to find an answer by surfing their web site, including any FAQ pages, tutorial pages, forums, and help files; check any emails, manuals, or download instructions you may have received associated with the site or product.

2. Try to find an answer by searching the web using a good search engine.

3. Try to find an answer by trial-and-error experimentation.

4. Try to find an answer by asking a skilled friend.

5. Try to find an answer by reading the source code.

Once you've done those things, tell the person or site what you've done to try to find the answer on your own before submitting your question. This shows them you're not just a lazy sponge soaking up people's valuable time to save your own.

I can get up to 500 emails in one day. It's not usually that high, but it happens from time to time. I regularly get a lot more email than I possibly have the time to answer. I have no choice but to not answer some emails. Guess whose emails are the first to be deleted without answer? It's those who write with questions that are already answered on my web site. If you're not going to try, why should I when I'm buried in email as it is? I like to help people, but there's only so much time each day that I can donate to that end.

Once you're ready to ask a question, think about how to word it. Set the stage for the recipient. I get email every week from people who write something like, "I tried the code in your tutorial on [topic] and it didn't work. What did I do wrong?"

How the heck would I know? I didn't watch you make the page. I don't even know where the page is located. For all I know the person may have tattooed the code on their forehead. A question like that is like saying, "I lost my wallet. Where is it?" There's no way to answer it.

Write clearly, using correct spelling, punctuation, and grammar (as best you can). I know one web site owner who won't reply to anyone who writes in what he calls "Lazy Mary" style. He believes people who are careless and sloppy writers are usually careless and sloppy at thinking, coding, and following instructions. He says answering questions for a Lazy Mary is often unproductive and unrewarding; he'd rather spend his time on people who are more thoughtful.

While that may seem a little harsh, I know from experience there's some truth to it. I've had people buy downloadable products, and then reply to my email that includes the download instructions, asking where to download the product! All they had to do was *read* the email instead of *skimming* it. So then I enlarge the link and make it bold so they can't miss it, and politely tell them to follow the bold link.

When sending questions to strangers by email, always send it in plain text format. Busy people don't want to wait for your fancy graphics to download, and they may not get your email if you try to make it look like a web page. Web pages are web pages, and emails are emails. Just because you can make an email look like a web page doesn't mean you should. It's the mark of an amateur. Many webmasters, including myself, use email filters to weed out junk mail and viruses. One of the filters I use is for file size limitation. If your email's file size is too big, indicative of viruses and spam, it's deleted at the server and I'll never see it. HTML email can fall victim to that same filter.

That may sound cold, but you have to understand that my email address is probably in thousands of address books. On Windows, many viruses are set to send themselves to everyone in the address book of an infected computer. When one of these email viruses was running rampant, I would get hundreds of viruses each day for several days until it cooled off. Between my antivirus software and my filters, I rarely get viruses by email anymore. You do what you have to do.

To ask for help intelligently, remember:

 Describe your problem or bug in detail. Don't assume the recipient will know what you're talking about because of his or her experience or expertise. Many problems can have multiple causes.

 At the same time, don't be overly wordy. If you want to know why the picture of your Aunt Emma looks distorted, Joe Expert doesn't need to know that she is really nice, makes a great cherry pie, and spent her last vacation on the moon. Well, maybe the moon thing is worth mentioning.

 If computer related, describe any recent changes to your computer or software configuration, such as a new software installation or uninstallation. Include what operating system you're using and what specific software the problem is in. Many people who need help with software don't realize the company may sell multiple programs.

 If it's a web design question, don't include the code in an email unless the recipient asks you to. It might cause a problem or get deleted by spam filters. Put the code on a web page and send the URL. Use comment tags in the source code to mark the code in question. By making it easier for someone to help you, you'll be more likely to get help.

 If your problem is with software, don't blast the company for faulty software or assume it's buggy unless you're very sure. There are probably tens of thousands of people using the software who have no problems. With so many combinations of software, operating systems, system configurations, and user skills out there, it's impossible to write software that won't run into problems on at least one computer. Be kind, be patient, and let the vendor help you.

 Describe your problem in chronological order, starting with what you did, what the symptoms are, and any error messages that displayed. Also, make sure the problem wasn't just an anomaly. Sometimes something flukey happens but never happens again.

 If you are trying to find out how to do something technical, begin by describing the goal. People often get stuck on what they think is the right path—or the only path—to their goal, when there may well be a better option.

 Don't flag your email as urgent, even if it is to you. Your priorities and problems are not necessarily the recipient's priorities and problems. Claiming urgency can be counterproductive because it may be viewed as a selfish attempt to elicit special attention. It's like cutting in line at the movie theater—and a lot of people don't like that kind of behavior.

 Politeness never hurts, and it often helps. Saying "please" and "thank you" is still important to many people, including me. Remember, if you are asking for help, you are asking for someone's time. Time is limited. We only get so much time in our lives, so you're really asking for a piece of someone's life when you ask for their time. If you're smart, you'll show respect for such a costly request.

18.15 Maintain a Save File

THOUSANDS AND THOUSANDS of people buy downloadable software but fail to protect their investment. Once they install the software and it is working, they're happy and go on with life. Then somewhere down the road they get a new computer, the hard drive dies in the old one, or a file becomes corrupted—something happens that requires them to reinstall their software—but where did they put that user name and registration code?

Unable to find it, they write to the vendor for a new registration code. Sometimes they get one, sometimes not. If the vendor has the user on file, there may be a service fee for reissuing registration information.

Of course, not all vendors keep a record of registered users. Or, some vendors keep a list of registered users for some products, but not every product. Vendors can also lose their lists of registered users due to a hard-drive failure or corrupt file of their own. That happened to me once, and my backup file was corrupt as well.

When the person seeking a new registration code discovers the vendor doesn't keep a list of registered users, they blame the vendor for the problem, but that's just wrong. Once the vendor delivers the product and registration code, and it's working on your computer, the vendor's obligation is complete. It's up to you to protect your investment.

You wouldn't expect a record store to replace a CD because you lost the one you bought, so don't expect an Internet vendor to replace something you bought either—especially if you have no proof of purchase. People try to scam vendors all the time, claiming they've paid for something they haven't. It's your purchase and your responsibility to take care of it.

Print out any emails the vendor sends that include download instructions and registration codes. Print out any receipts as proof of purchase. Save these printouts in a folder in a file cabinet or wherever you save important papers. If you're living in a dorm room or apartment where your privacy is not guaranteed, consider buying a lock box to store important papers.

Don't stop there, though. Create a file with all the user names and passwords you use for everything. Keep a current copy printed out and stored in a safe place. I do that, and when I had a hard-drive failure I was mighty glad I had taken the time to do it. Because of that one printed file, I had all the information I needed in one convenient location to set up my email program with all my email accounts and my FTP accounts and to reinstall all my software with the correct user names and registration codes.

I also had all the passwords and user names I needed for the forums I visit and every other web site where a user name and password is needed. I had everything I needed right there because I was smart enough to think ahead—and I was back in business in no time.

That saved a great deal of time and trouble because I didn't have to hunt for my critical information. I didn't have to write to vendors and hope I could get new registration codes. I didn't even have to go online to download the software again because I had it backed up on CD. Be smart and be responsible—don't be angry with someone for not taking care of you if you haven't bothered to take care of yourself.

Now that you've read this, you're smart enough to think ahead too. You just have to do it. Printing out a list of all the user names, passwords, registration codes, login names, product names and web addresses for the products, and any other related information is one of the smartest things you can do to protect your investments of time and money.

For pros, I recommend a daily backup of your entire system instead of having to reinstall everything. Now that you know that, what are you waiting for?

18.16 Colored Scrollbars

THE ABILITY TO USE CSS to change the appearance of a browser's scrollbar is not officially sanctioned CSS. In fact, the W3C specifically states that these are illegal CSS properties.

However, colored scrollbars are supported by the latest versions of Internet Explorer, Opera, and perhaps other browsers. Because it is such a popular option, I feel compelled to include the instructions here.

> **WARNING!**
> Perhaps the W3C will include the scrollbar properties in a future version, but until that time I must warn you that changing the scrollbars may cause your page to fail validation. Whether that matters to you is your choice. As for me, I enjoy using them.

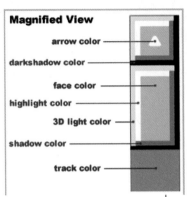

Magnified View

arrow color

darkshadow color

face color

highlight color

3D light color

shadow color

track color

Figure 18.3

In Figure 18.3 you can see the various parts of the scroll-bar. Changing the color is simply a matter of using CSS to program a new color for each of the scrollbar properties. Browsers that do not support the scrollbar properties simply ignore the code.

The scrollbar properties for the main browser window are set using the *body* selector, although the scrollbar appearance for iframes and form textarea boxes can be altered as well.

You can change all the scrollbar properties, or just one or more properties as you see fit. You can only use a background color for scrollbars as background images are not supported. Here's how to set all the scrollbar properties using an external style sheet.

```
body {scrollbar-face-color: #423626;
      scrollbar-highlight-color: #000000;
      scrollbar-3dlight-color: #000000;
      scrollbar-darkshadow-color: #000000;
      scrollbar-shadow-color: #000000;
      scrollbar-arrow-color: #A7C2B1;
      scrollbar-track-color: #000000;}
```

If you set two or more of the scrollbar properties, list them in the order shown.

18.17 Chapter 18 Exercise

Ah...THE LAST EXERCISE OF THE BOOK, the mysterious "wrap-up" page you are to make. In my personal worldview, the happiest people are those who appreciate what they have, be it a little or a lot. The unhappiest are those who have little gratitude for their blessings.

Your instructor for this class works hard, and does so more out of a desire to help advance others than for monetary gain or personal recognition. Those dedicated to teaching others often receive very little gratitude from those whom they help, so please use your wrap-up page to offer a few words of thanks to your instructor for his or her services, time, and energy.

That's it, nothing complicated, no restrictions or requirements; just make a page thanking your instructor for what he or she does so well. Without those dedicated to teaching others, we'd be decades, if not centuries, behind where we are now.

HTML and XHTML

A

In this appendix, you will find:

- HTML and XHTML Elements, Attributes, and Values
- Deprecated and Obsolete Elements and Attributes
- Proprietary Elements and Attributes
- Element Compatibility and DTD Chart
- Valueless Attribute Chart
- DOCTYPE Declarations

Note

It's not practical to show every possible value for the style attribute that can be used with each HTML element. That would easily double the size of this book and unnecessarily increase the price. Appendix B: Cascading Style Sheets should fill in most of the blanks.

These charts include some elements and attributes that are not covered in the tutorial sections of the book. This is due to space constraints or the rarity of use/need for some items, and because some items are proprietary. To learn more about any elements and attributes, visit the W3C site at: www.w3.org.

Core Attributes

THIS CHART SHOWS THE HTML *core attributes*, which can be used with *any* HTML element except:

<base> | <basefont> | <head> | <html> | <meta> | <param> | <script> | <style> | <title>

Core Attribute	Description
class="…"	Identifies the CSS class to be used for the element. **Value:** Any class defined in an embedded or external style sheet.
id="…"	Assigns a unique identifier to an element. **Value:** No set value. Use any unique id you prefer, but it must begin with a letter (*A–Z* or *a–z*) and may be followed by any number of letters, whole numbers, hyphens, underscores, colons, and periods.
lang"…"	Designates a human language using an ISO 639 two-character name; dialect sub-code is optional in some languages.
style="…"	Begins an inline style definition. Refer to Appendix B: Cascading Style Sheets for selector properties and values or *Chapters 4, 6*, and *7* for detailed CSS instructions.
title="…"	Sets the tool tip text (pop-up balloon) text for an element. **Value:** A text message used to describe the content of the element; title content is shown in a pop-up balloon in some browsers and read aloud by screen readers.

Important Note: Rather than listing the core attributes with every eligible element in the HTML/XHTML chart on this page, I chose not to repeat them to avoid redundancy. This will make it easier to find the other elements and attributes. Just remember, the core attributes can be used with any element except the ones listed on page 413 (unless "none" is listed in the attribute column, in which case no attributes may be used with the element).

HTML and XHTML Elements, Attributes, and Values

THE FOLLOWING CHART LISTS in alphabetical order the HTML and XHTML elements along with each element's attributes and possible values. Three dots ("...") indicate where you insert one of the possible values you want to assign to the attribute.

Note

In these charts, multiple value options are separated by the pipe (|) character. Tag pairs are shown in the Elements column. Empty tags are tags that have no separate closing tag. These are shown with the XHTML method of closing them. *Example:*
 If for some reason you do not want your document to be XHTML compliant, remove the space/backslash from the end of the empty tag. *Example:*

Element	Attributes	Description / Possible Values
<!-- Comment -->	none	A comment tag lets you insert comments into your source code that are not displayed on the visible page.
<!DOCTYPE>	none	Specifies the document type definition (DTD). This is the only tag that should be capitalized. See the full DOCTYPE code at the end of this appendix.
<a> </a>		Anchor tag set, used to create links.
	accesskey="..."	Accessibility keyboard character. **Value:** Any single character from the document's character set.
	charset="..."	Character encoding of the linked document. **Value:** Any Universal Character Set.
	coords="..."	Used to set the coordinates of a hot spot on an image map. The values are numerical values that depend on the shape and location of the hot spot. See *Section 9.14: How to Make an Image Map* in *Chapter 9: Links and Multimedia* for instructions to determine coordinates.
	href="..."	Encodes the URL of the linked resource. **Value:** URL to any online file.
	hreflang="..."	Specifies the language of the linked document. **Value:** The language code specified in the destination document. Seldom used.

Element	Attributes	Description / Possible Values
	name="..."	Assigns a unique name to an element. **Value:** No set value. Use any unique name you prefer, but it must begin with a letter (*A–Z* or *a–z*) and may be followed by any number of letters, whole numbers, hyphens, underscores, colons, and periods.
	rel="..."	Specifies the forward link type. **Values:** alternate | stylesheet | start | next | previous | contents | index | glossary | copyright | chapter | section | subsection | appendix | help | bookmark *Note:* If more than one value is used, they should be separated by a single space.
	rev="..."	Specifies reverse link type. **Values:** alternate | stylesheet | start | next | previous | contents | index | glossary | copyright | chapter | section | subsection | appendix | help | bookmark *Note:* If more than one value is used, they should be separated by a single space.
	shape="..."	Specifies the shape of an image map hot spot. **Values:** rect | circle | poly
	target="..."	Sets the target window or frame for the link. **Values:** _blank | _parent | _self | _top | the name assigned to a frame | any name to open a new window with that name
	type="..."	Content advisory. **Value:** Any registered MIME type.
\<abbr> \</abbr>		Designates an abbreviation.
\<acronym> \</acronym>		Designates an acronym.
\<address> \</address>		Designates an address.
\<area />		Defines an image map hot spot.
	alt="..."	Provides alternative text for non-graphical browsers. **Value:** Description of linked content.
	coords="..."	Sets a comma-separated list of coordinates for the hot spot.
	href="..."	Encodes the URL of the linked resource. **Value:** URL to any online file.
	nohref="nohref"	Specifies the region has no link. **Value:** No other values.

Element	Attributes	Description / Possible Values
	shape="..."	Specifies the shape of an image map hot spot. **Values:** rect | circle | poly
	target="..."	Sets the target window or frame for the link. **Values:** _blank | _parent | _self | _top | the name assigned to a frame | any name to open a new window with that name
\<b> \</b>		Designates bold text.
\<base />		Specifies an absolute URL that acts as the base URL for resolving relative links.
	href="..."	Specifies the base URL. **Value:** Any web address on your site.
	target="..."	Designates the frame or window the link should open in. **Values:** _blank | _parent | _self | _top | the name assigned to a frame | any name to open a new window with that name
\<bdo> \</bdo>		Bidirectional override to change the direction of text flow.
	dir="..."	Sets the direction the text should be rendered in. **Values:** ltr | rtl *Note:* ltr = left to right | rtl = right to left
\<big> \</big>		Increases text size.
\<blockquote> \</blockquote>		Designates long quotations.
	cite="..."	Indicates the source of the quotation. **Value:** URL to source of quotation.
\<body> \</body>		Encloses the page content to be displayed.
\ 		Creates a single line break.
\<button> \</button>		Creates a clickable form button.
	accesskey="..."	Accessibility keyboard character. **Value:** Any single character from the document's character set.
	disabled="disabled"	Disables the button to prevent click action. **Value:** No other values.
	name="..."	Assigns a unique name to an element. **Value:** No set value. Use any unique name you prefer, but it must begin with a letter (*A–Z* or *a–z*) and may be followed by any number of letters, whole numbers, hyphens, underscores, colons, and periods.

Element	Attributes	Description / Possible Values
	tabindex="..."	Designates the element's tabbing order. **Value:** Any positive number not already used or 0 (zero) to remove the element from the tabbing order.
	type="..."	Specifies which button type is used. **Values:** button | reset | submit
	value="..."	Assigns the initial value to the button. **Value:** Text to include upon form submission.
`<caption> </caption>`		Provides a table caption.
`<cite> <cite>`		Designates a citation.
`<code> </code>`		Used to display code samples.
`<col> </col>`		Defines a column or group of columns within a colgroup.
	span="..."	Designates the number of columns in the group. **Value:** The number of columns included.
	width="..."	Designates the width of the columns. **Value:** Numerical value in pixels or as a percentage.
`<colgroup> </colgroup>`		Defines a group of columns within a table.
	span="..."	Designates the number of columns in the group. **Value:** The number of columns included.
	width="..."	Designates the width of the columns. **Value:** Numerical value in pixels or as a percentage.
`<dd> </dd>`		Encloses a definition description in a definition list.
`<del> </del>`		Marks text for deletion with a strike-through.
	cite="..."	Provides URL to additional information containing an explanation about why the document was changed. **Value:** URL to explanatory document.
	datetime="..."	Indicates the date and time of the document change.
`<dfn> </dfn>`		Denotes the defining (first) instance of a term.
`<div> </div>`		Generic container element for dividing and aligning sections of a page.
`<dl> </dl>`		Containers for a definition list. Definition lists are not bulleted or numbered.
`<dt> </dt>`		Encloses the definition term in a definition list.

Element	Attributes	Description / Possible Values
<em> </em>		Marks text for emphasis.
<fieldset> </fieldset>		Used to control a group of form elements.
< form> </form>		Encloses the elements of an interactive form.
	accept="..."	Used to specify the content types accepted by the server in processing the form. **Values:** text/html | image/png | image/gif | image/jpg | video/mpeg | text/css | audio/basic *Note:* These are only examples; for a complete list, download the list of registered MIMETYPES from the W3C web site.
	accept-charset="..."	Designates the character encoding accepted by the server when the form is processed. **Value:** Any Universal Character Set.
	action="..."	Designates the URL to the form processing script. **Value:** The location of the form processing script on the server.
	enctype="..."	Designates how the form element values are to be encoded for processing. **Values:** text/html | text/plain *Note:* These are only examples; for a complete list, download the list of registered MIMETYPES from the W3C web site.
	method="..."	Determines the method of form processing. **Values:** get | post
	name="..."	Sets the name of the form. **Values:** No set value. Use any unique name you prefer, but it must begin with a letter (*A–Z* or *a–z*) and may be followed by any number of letters, whole numbers, hyphens, underscores, colons, and periods.
	target="..."	Sets the destination frame or window where the form output should be sent. **Values:** _blank | _parent | _self | _top | the name assigned to a frame | any name to open a new window with that name
<frame> </frame>		Defines a single frame within a frameset.
	border="..."	Sets the border thickness. Set this to zero to remove the frame border. *Note:* This is not W3C legal, but it works better than the legal attribute for removing a border in most browsers. **Value:** Any number, measured in pixels.

Element	Attributes	Description / Possible Values
	frameborder="…"	Supposed to turn the frame border on or off. Browser support is spotty. **Values:** 1 | 2 *Note:* 1 = visible | 2 = invisible
	longdesc="…"	Provides URL of optional document with a long description of the frames content. **Value:** URL to descriptive document.
	marginheight="…"	Sets the distance between the top and bottom of the frame and the frames content. **Value:** Numeric value as measured in pixels.
	marginwidth="…"	Sets the distance between the left and right sides of the frame and the frames content. **Value:** Numeric value as measured in pixels.
	name="…"	Assigns a unique name to an element. **Value:** No set value. Use any unique name you prefer, but it must begin with a letter (*A–Z* or *a–z*) and may be followed by any number of letters, whole numbers, hyphens, underscores, colons, and periods.
	noresize="…"	Sets whether the user may resize the frame. **Values:** yes | no
	scrolling="…"	Sets whether a frame's scrollbars will be shown. **Values:** auto | yes | no
	src="…"	Defines the URL of the document to be displayed in the frame when the frameset is first loaded. **Value:** URL of the document.
<frameset> </frameset>		Container element for one or more frames.
	cols="…"	Sets the frame columns and widths within a frameset. **Value:** Width is set in pixel units or percentage; or use an asterisk to let the browser decide.
	rows="…"	Sets the frame rows and heights within a frameset. **Value:** Width is set in pixel units or percentage; or use an asterisk to let the browser decide.
<h1> </h1> (largest) - *thru* - <h6> </h6> (smallest)		Establishes heading text. Headings come in six sizes: h1, h2, h3, h4, h5, and h6.
<head> </head>		Encloses the document head section. Content in the head section typically contains information about the document, CSS code, or JavaScript.

419

Element	Attributes	Description / Possible Values
	profile="..."	Provides a link to additional metadata about the document. **Value:** URL to secondary document.
\<hr />		Creates a horizontal rule (line) across the page.
\<html> \</html>		Encloses a hypertext markup language document.
	dir="..."	Sets the direction of text flow for the page. **Values:** ltr | rtl *Note:* ltr = left-to-right | rtl = right-to-left
	lang="..."	Specifies the language used. **Value:** Any two-letter ISO language name.
\<i> \</i>		Displays enclosed text in italic type.
\<iframe> \</iframe>		Creates an inline sub-window.
	frameborder="..."	Sets whether a frame border will be drawn. **Value:** 1 | 0 *Note:* 1 = border | 0 = no border
	height="..."	Sets the height of the iframe window. **Value:** Numeric value, as measured in pixels.
	longdesc="..."	Indicates the location of a document providing a long description of the iframe contents. **Value:** URL to the document.
	marginheight="..."	Sets the space between the top and bottom edges of the frame and the frame content. **Value:** Numeric value, as measured in pixels.
	marginwidth="..."	Sets the space between the side edges of the frame and the frame content. **Value:** Numeric value, as measured in pixels.
	name="..."	Assigns a unique name to an element. **Values:** No set value. Use any unique name you prefer, but it must begin with a letter (*A–Z* or *a–z*) and may be followed by any number of letters, whole numbers, hyphens, underscores, colons, and periods.
	scrolling="..."	Sets whether frame scrollbars will be shown. **Values:** auto | yes | no
	src="..."	Defines the URL of the document to display in the frame when the page is first loaded. **Value:** URL of the document.
	width="..."	Sets the width of the iframe window. **Value:** Numeric value, as measured in pixels.

Element	Attributes	Description / Possible Values
<img />		Inserts an inline image into the document flow. **Value:** URL to the image.
	alt="..."	Provides a short description of the image. **Value:** Short text description of the image for users without graphical browsers and users who surf the web using screen readers.
	height="..."	Sets the height of the image. **Value:** Numeric value, as measured in pixels.
	ismap="ismap"	Designates the image as a client-side image map. **Value:** No other values.
	longdesc="..."	Indicates the location of a document providing a long description about the image. **Value:** URL to the document.
	name="..."	Assigns a unique name to an element. **Value:** No set value. Use any unique name you prefer, but it must begin with a letter (*A–Z* or *a–z*) and may be followed by any number of letters, whole numbers, hyphens, underscores, colons, and periods.
	src="..."	Defines the URL to the image. **Value:** URL of the image.
	usemap="..."	Associates map coordinates and links with the image used as an image map. **Value:** The value of the name attribute given to the associated image.
	width="..."	Sets the width of the image. **Value:** Numeric value, as measured in pixels.
<input />		Designates an input field in a form element.
	accept="..."	Used to specify the content types accepted by the server in processing the form. **Value:** text/html	image/png	image/gif	image/jpg	video/mpeg	text/css	audio/basic *Note:* These are only examples; for a complete list, download the list of registered MIMETYPES from the W3C web site.
	accesskey="..."	Accessibility keyboard character. **Value:** Any single character from the document's character set.
	alt="..."	Provides a short description of the form element if the "type" is set to "image." **Value:** Description of the image for non-graphical browsers and screen readers.

Element	Attributes	Description / Possible Values
	checked="checked"	When the input value is a *radio* button or *checkbox* the form element is preselected. **Value:** No other values.
	disabled="disabled"	Disables the form element. **Value:** No other values.
	maxlength="…"	Sets the maximum number of characters for an element when the value of the type attribute is *text* or *password*. **Value:** Any positive numeral.
	name="…"	Designates the name of the parameter sent with the submitted data. **Value:** No set value. Use any unique name you prefer, but it must begin with a letter (*A–Z* or *a–z*) and may be followed by any number of letters, whole numbers, hyphens, underscores, colons, and periods. Typical values are descriptive, such as "email", "state", or "name".
	readonly="readonly"	Prevents users from modifying an input field. **Value:** No other values.
	size="…"	Sets the initial width of the control. The width is given in pixels except when the *type* attribute has the value "text" or "password". In that case, its value refers to the number of characters the user is allowed to enter into the field. **Values:** Any positive number as measured in pixels for text or password fields or any positive number for the desired maximum character count.
	src="…"	Points to the source of the image for fields in which image use is allowed. **Value:** The URL to the image.
	tabindex="…"	Designates the element's tabbing order. **Value:** Any positive number not already used; use 0 (zero) to remove the element from the tabbing order.
	type="…"	Sets the type of input field for the element. **Values:** button | checkbox | file | hidden | image | password | radio | reset | submit | text
	usemap="…"	Associates map coordinates and links with the image used as an image map. *Note:* Support is spotty with input element. **Value:** The value of the name attribute given to the image.

Element	Attributes	Description / Possible Values
	value="..."	Sets the default value of the input field. **Value:** Text string of your choice.
<ins> </ins>		Denotes text inserted into a document.
	cite="..."	Points to the document explaining the text insertion. **Value:** URL to the document.
	datetime="..."	Specifies the date and time of the inserted text. **Value:** Date and time of change.
<kbd> </kbd>		Denotes text to be input by the user.
<label> </label>		Used to label a form element.
	accesskey="..."	Accessibility keyboard character. **Value:** Any single character from the document's character set.
	for="..."	Associates a label with another control. **Value:** Must match the value of the id attribute of the associated control element.
<legend> </legend>		Encloses text as a caption for a field set.
	accesskey="..."	Accessibility keyboard character. **Value:** Any single character from the document's character set.
<li> </li>		Designates a list item for ordered and unordered lists.
<link> </link>		Creates a relationship between the current document and the linked-to document. May *only* be used in the HEAD section of the page.
	charset="..."	Character encoding of the linked document. **Value:** Any Universal Character Set.
	href="..."	Points to the external file. **Value:** The URL to the file.
	hreflang="..."	Specifies the language of the linked document. **Value:** The language code specified in the destination document. Seldom used.
	media="..."	Denotes the intended destination medium for style information. It may be a single media descriptor or a comma-separated list. **Value:** all | aural | braille | handheld | print | projection | screen | tty | tv

423

Element	Attributes	Description / Possible Values
	rel="..."	Specifies the forward link type. Commonly used to link to external style sheets. **Values:** alternate | stylesheet | start | next | previous | contents | index | glossary | copyright | chapter | section | subsection | appendix | help | bookmark *Note:* If more than one value is used, they should be separated by a single space.
	rev="..."	Specifies reverse link type. **Values:** alternate | stylesheet | start | next | previous | contents | index | glossary | copyright | chapter | section | subsection | appendix | help | bookmark *Note:* If more than one value is used, they should be separated by a single space.
	target="..."	Sets the target frame or window for the link. **Values:** _blank | _parent | _self | _top | the name assigned to a frame | any name to open a new window with that name
	type="..."	Denotes the MIME type of the external document. **Value:** Any registered MIME type.
<map> </map>		Defines a map containing hot spots in a client side image map.
	name="..."	Specifies the name of the image map. **Value:** The name used for the image that will be the image map.
<meta />		Denotes additional information about the document. Must be placed in the HEAD section.
	content="..."	Used in conjunction with the *name* attribute to enter content relevant to the name. **Value:** Text dependent on the name (type) of content of the meta element. *Examples:* If the name value is "keywords," the content is a comma-separated list of keywords relevant to the document; if the name value is "description," a description of the web page content is entered.
	http-equiv="..."	Sometimes used in place of name attribute. HTTP servers use this to gather information for HTTP response message headers. **Value:** HTTP response header name.

Element	Attributes	Description / Possible Values
	name="..."	Provides a descriptive word for the type of *content* listed in the associated content attribute. **Values:** No set value, typical names include: keywords, description, or author.
	scheme="..."	Denotes the profile scheme used to interpret the content attribute. **Value:** See [ISO8879] on the W3C web site for possible values.
\<noframes> \</noframes>		Provides alternate content for browsers that do not support frames.
\<noscript> \</noscript>		Provides alternate content for browsers that do not support client-side scripts.
\<object> \</object>		Embeds an object into the page. Objects include: applets, images, sound files, video, etc.
	archive="..."	Denotes the URL of an archive containing resources used with or by the object. **Value:** URL to archive.
	classid="..."	Supplies the URL to the object to be embedded. **Value:** URL to object.
	codebase="..."	Specifies the base path used to resolve relative links within the object. **Value:** URL of object's base path.
	codetype="..."	Denotes the MIME type of the object's code. **Value:** Any registered MIME type.
	data="..."	Denotes the location of the object's data. **Value:** URL to object's data file.
	declare="declare"	Declares an object without instantiating (finding an instance of) it. The object must be instantiated by a subsequent OBJECT definition referring to this declaration. **Value:** No other values.
	height="..."	Sets the height of the object. **Value:** Any positive number, measured in pixels.
	name="..."	Designates the name of the parameter that is sent with the submitted data. **Value:** No set value. Use any unique name you prefer, but it must begin with a letter (*A–Z* or *a–z*) and may be followed by any number of letters, whole numbers, hyphens, underscores, colons, and periods.

Element	Attributes	Description / Possible Values
	standby="..."	Message to show while the object is loading. **Value:** Your text message.
	type="..."	Specifies the content type for the data specified by the *data* attribute. This attribute is optional but recommended if data is specified since it allows the user agent to avoid loading information for unsupported content types. **Value:** Any registered MIME type.
	usemap="..."	Associates map coordinates and links with the image used as an image map. **Value:** The value of the name attribute given to the image.
	width="..."	Sets the width of the object. **Value:** Any positive number, measured in pixels.
<ol> </ol>		Encloses an ordered list.
<optgroup> </optgroup>		Provides the mechanism to group <option> elements logically within a <select> group.
	disabled="disabled"	Disables the element. **Value:** No other values.
	label="..."	Specifies a label for the option group. **Value:** Text string of your choice.
<option> </option>		Encloses an option within a form select field. **Value:** No set value. Options depend on the purpose of the select list.
	disabled="disabled"	Disables the option. **Value:** No other values.
	label="..."	Specifies a label for the option. **Value:** Text string of your choice.
	selected="selected"	Preselects an option (which can be changed by the user). **Value:** No other values.
	value="..."	Sends the content of the value to the form processor instead of the option text. **Value:** Text string of your choice.
<p> </p>		Encloses a paragraph, creating a double-spaced line between the content above and the content below.

Element	Attributes	Description / Possible Values
<param />		Sends a parameter value to an applet.
	name="..."	Denotes a unique name identifier. **Value:** No set value. Use any unique name you prefer, but it must begin with a letter (*A–Z* or *a–z*) and may be followed by any number of letters, whole numbers, hyphens, underscores, colons, and periods.
	type="..."	Denotes the MIME type of the external document. **Value:** Any registered MIME type.
	value="..."	Denotes the value of the parameter. **Value:** Text string.
	valuetype="..."	Designates the value type of the value attribute. **Value:** data | object | ref *Note:* For ref, the value is the URL pointing to the data; for object, the value is the name of the object in the document.
<pre> </pre>		Defines enclosed text as preformatted.
<q> </q>		Defines enclosed text as a short, inline quotation.
<samp> </samp>		Denotes enclosed text as literal characters, that is, as sample program code, scripts, etc.
<script> </script>		Encloses a client-side script. May appear in the HEAD or BODY of document, or as a link to an external file. Usually used for JavaScript. **Value:** The actual script or URL to the script.
	charset="..."	Character encoding of the linked document. **Value:** Any Universal Character Set.
	defer="defer"	Defers the execution of the script. **Value:** No other values.
	src="..."	Points to an external script. **Value:** URL to the script.
	type="..."	Denotes the MIME type of the external document. **Value:** Any registered MIME type.
<select> </select>		Creates a drop-down selection list.
	disabled="disabled"	Disables the form element. **Value:** No other values.
	multiple="multiple"	Allows multiple selections from the list. **Value:** No other values.

Element	Attributes	Description / Possible Values
	name="..."	Denotes a unique name identifier. **Value:** No set value. Use any unique name you prefer, but it must begin with a letter (*A–Z* or *a–z*) and may be followed by any number of letters, whole numbers, hyphens, underscores, colons, and periods.
	size="..."	Changes the drop-down list into a scrollable window. **Value:** Any number greater than zero. The number set is how many list options appear in the window before the user has to scroll.
	tabindex="..."	Designates the element's tabbing order. **Value:** Any positive number not already used, or 0 (zero) to remove the element from the tabbing order.
\<small\> \</small\>		Decreases text size.
\<span\> \</span\>		Creates a generic container to apply styles to.
\<strong\> \</strong\>		Emphasizes the enclosed text, usually in bold.
\<style\> \</style\>		Defines global style sheets for the document.
	media="..."	Denotes the intended destination medium for style information. It may be a single media descriptor or a comma-separated list. **Value:** all | aural | braille | handheld | print | projection | screen | tty | tv
	type="..."	Defines the MIME type. **Value:** text/css *Note:* the value is not a misprint; the value is both *text/css*, not either | or.
\<sub\> \</sub\>		Displays enclosed text as subscript.
\<sup\> \</sup\>		Displays enclosed text as superscript.
\<table\> \</table\>		Creates a table. The table is further defined by rows and columns.
	border="..."	Sets the border width for the table. **Value:** Any positive number within reason.
	cellpadding="..."	Sets the distance in pixels between the table data cell edges and the content of the cell. **Value:** Any positive number within reason.
	cellspacing="..."	Sets the distance in pixels between the individual table data cells. **Value:** Any positive number within reason.

Element	Attributes	Description / Possible Values
	frame="..."	Specifies which sides of the frame surrounding a table will be visible. **Values:** above | below | border | box | hsides | lhs | rhs | void | vsides **Descriptions:** above = top side only | below = bottom side only | border = all four sides | box = all four sides | hsides = top and bottom sides | lhs = left hand side | rhs = right hand side | void = no frame | vsides = right and left sides
	rules="..."	Denotes whether the inner grid lines are drawn. **Values:** all | cols | groups | none | rows
	summary="..."	Provides a description of the table's content. **Value:** Text string.
	width="..."	Sets the width of the table. **Value:** Any positive number, measured in pixels.
<tbody> </tbody>		Organizes table rows into logical groups for formatting. Follows thead and tfoot in code.
	align="..."	Sets the horizontal alignment of the content within the table data cells. **Values:** left | center | right | justify | char
	char="..."	Sets the character to be used if the align attribute is set to *char*. **Value:** Any character. A decimal is the most commonly used character, which is used to align numbers (dollars and cents, for example) on a vertical axis centered on the decimal point.
	charoff="..."	Specifies the offset distance (in pixels) from the alignment character set in the char attribute. **Value:** Numeric value.
	valign="..."	Sets the vertical alignment of the content within the table data cells. **Values:** baseline | bottom | middle | top
<td> </td>		Encloses the content of a table data cell.
	abbr="..."	Used to designate an abbreviated version of the cell's content. **Value:** Text string.
	align="..."	Sets the horizontal alignment of the content within the table data cells. **Values:** left | center | right

429

Element	Attributes	Description / Possible Values
	char="..."	Sets the character to be used if the align attribute is set to *char*. **Value:** Any character. A decimal is the most commonly used character, which is used to align numbers (dollars and cents, for example) on a vertical axis centered on the decimal point.
	charoff="..."	Specifies the offset distance (in pixels) from the alignment character set in the char attribute. **Value:** Numeric value.
	colspan="..."	Sets the number of columns the table data cell will span. **Value:** Any numeric value up to the number of columns in the table.
	headers="..."	List of table headers associated with the table data cell. **Value:** A space-separated list of cell names; those cells must be named by setting their *id* attribute.
	rowspan="..."	Sets the number of rows the table data cell will span. **Value:** Any numeric value up to the number of rows in the table.
	scope="..."	Specifies the set of data cells for which the current header cell provides header information. This attribute may be used in place of the headers attribute, particularly for simple tables. **Value:** col | colgroup | row | rowgroup
	valign="..."	Sets the vertical alignment of the content within the table data cells. **Value:** bottom | middle | top
<textarea> </textarea>		Creates a multi-line text input box in a web form. Any text included within the tag set will be displayed inside the text box on the web page.
	accesskey="..."	Accessibility keyboard character. **Value:** Any single character from the document's character set.
	cols="..."	Sets the width of the text area in characters. **Value:** Any positive number. The width of the text area box is approximately the number of characters that can be typed without wrapping to the next line.
	disabled="disabled"	Disallows the user to modify the text area. **Value:** No other values.

Element	Attributes	Description / Possible Values
	name="..."	Denotes a unique name identifier. **Value:** No set value. Use any unique name you prefer, but it must begin with a letter (*A–Z* or *a–z*) and may be followed by any number of letters, whole numbers, hyphens, underscores, colons, and periods.
	readonly="readonly"	Specifies the text area as read only; the user is not allowed to modify or add content. **Value:** No other values.
	rows="..."	Sets the height of the text area. **Value:** Any positive number. Height is increased by one line for each row added.
	tabindex="..."	Designates the element's tabbing order. **Value:** Any positive number not already used, or 0 (zero) to remove the element from the tabbing order.
<tfoot> </tfoot>		Encloses the content of a table footer.
	align="..."	Sets the horizontal alignment of the content within the table data cells. **Values:** left | center | right | justify | char
	char="..."	Sets the character to be used if the align attribute is set to *char*. **Value:** Any character. A decimal is the most commonly used character, which is used to align numbers (dollars and cents, for example) on a vertical axis centered on the decimal point.
	charoff="..."	Specifies the offset distance (in pixels) from the alignment character set in the char attribute. **Value:** Numeric value.
	valign="..."	Sets the vertical alignment of the content within the table data cells. **Values:** baseline | bottom | middle | top
<th> </th>		Encloses the content of a table header cell. Works like a table data cell except the header text is rendered in bold type by most browsers. Headers are usually used across the top row and/or down the left (first) column.
	abbr="..."	Used to designate an abbreviated version of the cell's content. **Value:** Text string.

Element	Attributes	Description / Possible Values
	align="..."	Sets the horizontal alignment of the content within the table data cells. **Values:** left | center | right
	axis="..."	Used to place a cell into conceptual categories. Primarily used for speech-based user agents. **Value:** Comma separated list of category names.
	char="..."	Sets the character to be used if the align attribute is set to *char*. **Value:** Any character. A decimal is the most commonly used character, which is used to align numbers (dollars and cents, for example) on a vertical axis centered on the decimal point.
	charoff="..."	Specifies the offset distance (in pixels) from the alignment character set in the char attribute. **Value:** Numeric value.
	colspan="..."	Sets the number of columns the table data cell will span. **Value:** Any numeric value up to the number of columns in the table.
	headers="..."	List of table headers associated with the table data cell. **Value:** A space-separated list of cell names; the cells must be named by setting their *id* attribute.
	rowspan="..."	Sets the number of rows the table data cell will span. **Value:** Any numeric value up to the number of rows in the table.
	scope="..."	Specifies the set of data cells for which the current header cell provides header information. This attribute may be used in place of the headers attribute, particularly for simple tables. **Value:** col | colgroup | row | rowgroup
	valign="..."	Sets the vertical alignment of the content within the table data cells. **Values:** bottom | middle | top
\<thead> \</thead>		Encloses the content of a table header.
	align="..."	Sets the horizontal alignment of the content within the table data cells. **Values:** left | center | right | justify | char

Element	Attributes	Description / Possible Values
	char="..."	Sets the character to be used if the align attribute is set to *char*. **Value:** Any character. A decimal is the most commonly used character, which is used to align numbers (dollars and cents, for example) on a vertical axis centered on the decimal point.
	charoff="..."	Specifies the offset distance (in pixels) from the alignment character set in the char attribute. **Value:** Numeric value.
	valign="..."	Sets the vertical alignment of the content within the table data cells. **Values:** baseline | bottom | middle | top
<title> </title>		Denotes the title of the document. The text in the title tag set is displayed in the title bar of the web browser and is used as the link text at some search engines. The title is placed in the HEAD of the document. The title element is not the same as the title attribute.
<tr> </tr>		Establishes a row within a table. A row may have any number of table data cells, but must have at least one.
	align="..."	Sets the horizontal alignment of the content within the table data cells. **Values:** left | center | right
	char="..."	Sets the character to be used if the align attribute is set to *char*. **Value:** Any character. A decimal is the most commonly used character, which is used to align numbers (dollars and cents, for example) on a vertical axis centered on the decimal point.
	charoff="..."	Specifies the offset distance (in pixels) from the alignment character set in the char attribute. **Value:** Numeric value.
	valign="..."	Sets the vertical alignment of the content within the table data cells. **Values:** baseline | bottom | middle | top
<tt> </tt>		Renders text in teletype (monospaced font face).
<ul> </ul>		Encloses an unordered list.

Note: If you check the W3C site for information about attributes, be sure to crosscheck with the element chart. As I was researching for the most up-to-date information, some attributes would be listed as deprecated in one chart but not the other. Everyone makes mistakes.

Deprecated and Obsolete Elements and Attributes

THE FOLLOWING CHART SHOWS an alphabetical list of elements or attributes that have either been declared deprecated or obsolete. Deprecated elements and attributes may still be used but are not recommended. Obsolete elements should not be used as browsers and other user agents are not required to support them. In all cases, other elements or style sheets can achieve the same purpose as the deprecated or obsolete items.

Legend: D = Deprecated | O = Obsolete

Deprecated or Obsolete Element	Description/Recommendation	D or O
applet	Java applet; use <object> instead.	D
basefont	Sets base font size; use CSS instead.	D
center	Centers content; use CSS instead.	D
dir	Directory list; use an unordered list instead.	D
font	Sets font; use CSS instead.	D
listing	Denotes listings; use <pre> instead.	O
isindex	Creates a single-line text input widget; use the <input> element with type="text" attribute and value instead.	D
menu	Creates a menu list; use an unordered list instead.	D
plaintext	Denotes text as plain text; use <pre> instead.	O
s	Strike-through text; use CSS instead.	D
strike	Strike-through text; use CSS instead.	D
u	Underlined text; use CSS instead.	D
xmp	Example text; use <pre> instead.	O

NOTE: The attributes in the following chart are not obsolete with all elements, just the ones listed.

Deprecated or Obsolete Attribute	Deprecated for use with these elements:
align	applet, caption, div, h1, h2, h3, h4, h5, h6, hr, iframe, img, input, legend, object, p, table
alink	body
alt	applet
archive	applet
background	body
bgcolor	body, table, td, th, tr,
border	image, object

Deprecated or Obsolete Attribute	Deprecated for use with these elements:
clear	br
code	applet
codebase	applet
color	basefont, font
compact	dir, dl, menu, ol, ul
face	basefont, font
height	applet, td, th
hspace	applet, img, object
language	script
link	body
name	applet
noshade	hr
nowrap	td, th
object	applet
prompt	isindex
size	basefont, font, hr
start	ol
text	body
type	li, ol, ul
value	li
version	html
vlink	body
vspace	applet, img, object
width	applet, td, th, pre

Proprietary Elements and Attributes

T HE FOLLOWING CHART SHOWS proprietary elements and attributes. Proprietary items have been developed by a browser vendor and are not officially recognized by the W3C. If you were familiar with web design prior to obtaining this book, you will probably recognize some of these items.

Some proprietary items work only in the browser of the vendor that developed it, while some have been picked up and supported by other browsers. Only a handful of browsers are well-known, but there are actually dozens of different browsers. Most of the proprietary codes were developed by either Internet Explorer or Netscape Navigator, so I identify which browser supports the code. In cases where both browsers support the proprietary code, chances are good most browsers will support it. Where Netscape is identified, it refers to older versions of Netscape. You can switch the latest version between the Internet Explorer and Firefox rendering engines.

> **Important Note:** In the chart below, only the *attributes* are proprietary *unless otherwise noted.* Unless noted, all elements are official W3C recognized elements.

Legend: IE = Internet Explorer | N = Navigator

Element	Attributes	Description	IE/N
<area />			
	notab="notab"	Excludes this form element from being included in the tabbing order. **Value:** No other values.	IE
	taborder="..."	Sets an area's (image map hot spot) tabbing order. **Value:** Any positive number not already used.	IE
	target="..."	Sets the target frame or window for an image map link. **Values:** _blank | _parent | _self | _top | the name assigned to a frame | any name to open a new window with that name.	IE / N
<bgsound />	- proprietary element -	Plays a background sound. Because it's a proprietary element, all attributes are proprietary. Some support in some other browsers, but not good.	IE
	balance="..."	Designates how the sound will be balanced between speakers on a stereo setup. **Value:** Numeric value from *-10000* to *10000* with zero (0) as equal balance.	IE
	delay="..."	Designates the number of seconds to delay before playing the sound. **Value:** Any positive whole number.	IE
	loop="..."	Determines how many times the sound will repeat. **Value:** Numeric value | infinite	IE

Element	Attributes	Description	IE/N
	src="..."	Specifies the location of the sound file. **Value:** URL to the file.	IE
	volume="..."	Sets the initial volume. **Value:** Numeric value from -10000 to 0 with zero being the default value.	IE
\<blink\> \</blink\>	- proprietary element -	Causes text to blink. Very annoying!	N
\<body\> \</body\>			
	bgproperties="fixed"	Keeps the background from scrolling. **Value:** No other values.	IE
	bottommargin="..."	Sets the bottom page margin size as measured in pixels. **Value:** Any positive whole number.	IE
	leftmargin="..."	Sets the left page margin size as measured in pixels. **Value:** Any positive whole number.	IE
	marginheight="..."	Sets the top and bottom page margin size as measured in pixels. **Value:** Any positive whole number.	N
	marginwidth="..."	Sets the left and right page margin size as measured in pixels. **Value:** Any positive whole number.	N
	rightmargin="..."	Sets the right page margin size as measured in pixels. **Value:** Any positive whole number.	IE
	topmargin="..."	Sets the left page margin size as measured in pixels. **Value:** Any positive whole number.	IE
\<caption\> \</caption\>			
	valign="..."	Sets the vertical position of the caption. **Values:** top | bottom	IE
\<comment\> \</comment\>	- proprietary element -	Same as \<!-- comment --\>, which should be used instead.	IE
\<div\> \</div\>			
	nowrap="nowrap"	Prevents wrapping within the division. **Value:** No other values.	IE
\<embed\> \</embed\>	- proprietary element -	Used to embed an object such as a sound or video file. The W3C recommends using \<object\> for this, but \<embed\> is actually supported better by the major browsers at the time of this writing.	IE / N

Element	Attributes	Description	IE/N
	align="..."	Denotes the alignment of text flow around the embedded object. Values of LEFT and RIGHT specify a "floating" horizontal alignment. The other values specify vertical alignment. **Values:** Left | Right *or* Absbottom | Absmiddle | Baseline | Bottom | Middle | Texttop | Top	IE / N
	border="..."	Sets a border around the applet, measured in pixels. **Value:** Any whole number.	N
	disabled="..."	Determines whether the controls are disabled for the user. **Values:** True | False	IE / N
	height="..."	**REQUIRED:** Sets the height. **Value:** Any positive whole number.	IE / N
	hidden="..."	Determines if the object will be visible or hidden. A value of true overrides the height and width and hides the object. **Values:** true | false	IE / N
	hspace="..."	Sets the empty space to the left and right of the object. **Value:** Any whole number.	N
	name="..."	Assigns a name to the object. **Value:** No set value. Use any unique name you prefer, but it must begin with a letter (*A–Z* or *a–z*) and may be followed by any number of letters, whole numbers, hyphens, underscores, colons, and periods.	IE / N
	palette="..."	For Windows platform only. Denotes foreground and background colors. **Values for IE:** Any two colors separated by the pipe (|) character. **Values for N:** foreground | background	IE / N
	pluginspage="..."	Provides the location for a document with information about installing a required plug-in associated with the object. **Value:** URL to document.	N
	pluginurl="..."	This attribute overrules the PluginsPage attribute and indicates the URL of a Java Archive. **Value:** URL to archive file.	N

Element	Attributes	Description	IE/N
	src="..."	**REQUIRED:** The source of the embedded object. **Value:** URL to the object.	IE / N
	type="..."	Specifies the MIME type. **Value:** Any registered MIME type.	N
	units="..."	Sets the unit of measurement for the height, width, hspace, and vspace attributes. **Values:** pixels | en	IE / N
	vspace="..."	Sets the empty space to the left and right of the object. **Value:** Any whole number.	N
	width="..."	**REQUIRED:** Sets the height. **Value:** Any positive whole number.	IE / N
<frame> </frame>			
	bordercolor="..."	Sets the color of the frames borders. **Value:** Any hexadecimal or named color value.	IE / N
<frameset> </frameset>			
	border="..."	Sets the thickness of the border. **Value:** Any positive number, measured in pixels.	IE / N
	bordercolor="..."	Sets the color of the borders for the current frameset. **Value:** Any hexadecimal or named color value.	IE / N
	frameborder="..."	Enables or disables borders. **Values:** 1 (enabled) | 2 (disabled)	IE / N
	framespacing="..."	Sets the thickness of the frame for the current frameset. **Value:** Any positive number, measured in pixels.	IE
<hr />			
	color="..."	Sets the color of the rule. **Value:** Any hexadecimal or named color value.	IE
<ilayer> </ilayer>	- proprietary element -	Defines an inline layer. **Value:** Your own content.	N
	above="..."	Places the layer above another named layer. **Value:** Any named layer.	N

Element	Attributes	Description	IE/N
	background="..."	Designates a background image. **Value:** URL to background image.	N
	below="..."	Places the layer above another named layer. **Value:** Any named layer.	N
	bgcolor="..."	Sets a background color for the layer. **Value:** Any hexadecimal or named color value.	N
	clip="..."	Sets the viewable area of the layer. If the CLIP attribute is omitted, the clipping rectangle is the same size as the HTML content of the layer. A layer will expand to contain all of its content by default. **Values:** A comma-separated list of numeric values representing the pixel coordinates of the viewing rectangle. Origin values are at the top, left corner. *Format 1*: CLIP="left,top,right,bottom" *Format 2*: CLIP="right,bottom" (left and top values default to zero.)	N
	height="..."	Specifies the height of the layer's content and serves as a reference for child layers. **Values:** A numeric value representing a pixel width or a percentage relative to the containing layer/window.	N
	left="..."	Sets the coordinate position of the left side of the layer in relation to a parent layer if present; if no parent layer exists, the value is relative to the main document window. **Value:** Any positive numeric value.	N
	name="..."	Assigns a name to the object. **Value:** No set value. Use any unique name you prefer, but it must begin with a letter (*A–Z* or *a–z*) and may be followed by any number of letters.	N
	overflow="..."	Specifies what should happen if the ilayer's content exceeds its area. **Value:** clip	none	N
	pagex="..."	Specifies the horizontal (X) coordinate of the left boundary position of the current layer. **Value:** Numeric value specifying screen position.	N

Element	Attributes	Description	IE/N
	pagey="..."	Specifies the vertical (Y) coordinate of the left boundary position of the current layer. **Value:** Numeric value specifying screen position.	N
	src="..."	Allows you to specify another source for the content. **Value:** URL to the other source.	N
	top="..."	Sets the coordinate position of the top edge of the layer in relation to a parent layer if present; if no parent layer exists, the value is relative to the main document window. **Value:** Any positive numeric value.	N
	visibility="..."	Sets whether to show, hide, or inherit the visibility from the containing element. **Values:** hide | show inherit	N
	width="..."	Sets the width of the layer in pixels. **Value:** Any positive numeric value.	N
	z-index="..."	Sets the layers position in the stacking order. **Value:** Any unused numeric value.	N
<img />			
	lowsrc="..."	Specifies a low-resolution image to be loaded first. **Value:** URL to the low source image.	N
<input />			
	notab="notab"	Removes the input widget from the tabbing order. **Value:** No other values.	IE
	taborder="..."	Sets the tabbing order. **Value:** Any positive number not already used.	IE
<keygen />	- proprietary element -	Used to generate a security key.	N
	challenge="..."	Specify a challenge string for verification. **Value:** Alphanumeric characters.	N
	keytype="..."	Specifies the type of encryption to use to verify the KEYGEN element. **Value:** RSA | DSA	N
	name="..."	Denotes a unique name for the keygen apparatus. **Value:** Alphanumeric name.	N

Element	Attributes	Description	IE/N
\<layer> \</layer>	- proprietary element -	Defines a layer.	N
	above="..."	Places the layer above another named layer. **Value:** Any named layer.	N
	background="..."	Designates a background image. **Value:** URL to the background image.	N
	below="..."	Places the layer above another named layer. **Value:** Any named layer.	N
	bgcolor="..."	Sets a background color for the layer. **Value:** Any hexadecimal or named color value.	N
	clip="..."	Sets the viewable area of the layer. If the CLIP attribute is omitted, the clipping rectangle is the same size as the HTML content of the layer. A layer will expand to contain all of its content by default. **Values:** A comma-separated list of numeric values representing the pixel coordinates of the viewing rectangle. Origin values are at the top, left corner. *Format 1*: CLIP="left,top,right,bottom" *Format 2*: CLIP="right,bottom" (left and top values default to zero.)	N
	height="..."	Specifies the height of the layer's content and serves as a reference for child layers. **Values:** A numeric value representing a pixel width or a percentage relative to the containing layer/window.	N
	left="..."	Sets the coordinate position of the left side of the layer in relation to a parent layer if present; if no parent layer exists, the value is relative to the main document window. **Value:** Any positive numeric value.	N
	name="..."	Assigns a name to the object. **Value:** No set value. Use any unique name you prefer, but it must begin with a letter (*A–Z* or *a–z*) and may be followed by any number of letters.	N
	overflow="..."	Specifies what should happen if the layer's content exceeds its area. **Value:** clip | none	N

Element	Attributes	Description	IE/N
	pagex="..."	Specifies the horizontal (X) coordinate of the left boundary position of the current layer. **Value:** Numeric value specifying screen position.	N
	pagey="..."	Specifies the vertical (Y) coordinate of the left boundary position of the current layer. **Value:** Numeric value specifying screen position.	N
	src="..."	Allows you to specify another source for the content. **Value:** URL to the other source.	N
	top="..."	Sets the coordinate position of the top edge of the layer in relation to a parent layer if present; if no parent layer exists, the value is relative to the main document window. **Value:** Any positive numeric value.	N
	visibility="..."	Sets whether to show, hide, or inherit the visibility from the containing element. **Values:** hide | show | inherit	N
	width="..."	Sets the width of the layer in pixels. **Value:** Any positive numeric value.	N
	z-index="..."	Sets the layers position in the stacking order. **Value:** Any unused numeric value.	N
\<marquee\> \</marquee\>	- proprietary element -	Creates a scrolling text message (also works with images).	IE
	align="..."	Aligns the marquee to the surrounding content. **Value:** bottom | middle | top	IE
	bgcolor="..."	Sets a background color for the layer. **Value:** Any hexadecimal or named color value.	IE
	behavior="..."	Sets the marquee behavior style. **Value:** alternate | scroll | slide	IE
	direction="..."	Sets the direction. **Values:** left | right | down | up	IE
	height="..."	Sets the height in pixels. **Value:** Any positive numeric value.	IE

Element	Attributes	Description	IE/N
	hspace="..."	Sets the cushion of space to the left and right of the marquee area. **Value:** Any positive numeric value.	IE
	loop="..."	Sets the number of times the marquee repeats. **Values:** numeric value | infinite	IE
	scrollamount="..."	Sets the distance in pixels for the scroll action to move. **Value:** Numeric value.	IE
	scrolldelay="..."	Sets the delay (in milliseconds) between each movement. **Value:** Numeric value	IE
	truespeed="truespeed"	Sets the exact SCROLLDELAY values to be honored. If not present, all delay values less than 59 are rounded to 60 milliseconds. **Value:** No other values.	IE
	vspace="..."	Sets the cushion of space to the left and right of the marquee area. **Value:** Any positive numeric value.	IE
	width="..."	Sets the width in pixels. **Value:** Any positive numeric value.	IE
<meta />			
	charset="..."	Denotes the character set to use. **Value:** Any Universal Character Set.	IE
<multicol></multicol>	- proprietary element -	Specifies that all content will be displayed in multi-column format, with columns having equal width and content distributed evenly to achieve roughly equal column heights.	N
	cols="..."	**REQUIRED:** Sets number of columns. **Value:** Any positive numeric value.	N
	gutter="..."	Sets the distance in pixels between columns. **Value:** Any positive numeric value.	N
	width="..."	Documentation indicates this sets the width of each individual column, but in practice it seems to set the total width of all columns. **Values:** width in pixels | percentage	N
<nobr></nobr>	- proprietary element -	No line breaks are permitted in enclosed text.	IE / N

Element	Attributes	Description	IE/N
<noembed> </noembed>	- proprietary element -	Provides alternate content for browsers that don't support the <embed> tag.	IE / N
<object> </object>			
	notab="notab"	Removes the object from the tabbing order. **Value:** No other values.	IE
<server> </server>	- proprietary element -	Defines a server-side JavaScript file. **Value:** The actual script.	N
<spacer />	- proprietary element -	Creates an empty space.	N
	align="..."	Aligns a spacer in one of two ways. **Method 1:** *If the value is set to:* absbottom | absmiddle | baseline | bottom | middle | texttop | top ...the surrounding text lines up with that value. **Method 2:** *If the value is set to:* left | right ...against the page margin, the text will flow around the image.	N
	height="..."	Sets the height of a block spacer. **Value:** Any positive numeric value.	N
	size="..."	Sets the length, in pixels, of a horizontal or vertical spacer. **Value:** Any positive numeric value.	N
	type="..."	Sets the type of spacer it is. **Value:** block | horizontal | vertical	N
	width="..."	Sets the width, in pixels, of a block spacer. **Value:** Any positive numeric value.	N
<table> </table>			
	background="..."	Sets a background image for the entire table. **Value:** URL to the image.	IE / N
	bgcolor="..."	Sets the background color for the entire table. **Value:** Any hexadecimal or named color value.	IE / N
	bordercolor="..."	Sets the border color for the entire table. **Value:** Any hexadecimal or named color value.	IE / N

Element	Attributes	Description	IE/N
	bordercolordark="..."	Sets the dark border color for the table to simulate a 3-D appearance. **Value:** Any hexadecimal or named color value.	IE
	bordercolorlight="..."	Sets the light border color for the table to simulate a 3-D appearance. **Value:** Any hexadecimal or named color value.	IE
	cols="..."	Denotes the number of columns in the table. May allow complex tables to download faster. **Value:** Actual number of columns.	IE / N
	height="..."	Sets the height of the table. **Value:** Any positive numeric value.	IE / N
	hspace="..."	Sets the amount of empty space on the left and right side of the table. **Value:** Any positive numeric value.	N
	nowrap="nowrap"	Prevents wrapping within the table data cells. **Value:** No other values.	IE
	valign="..."	Sets the vertical alignment for the table. **Value:** bottom | baseline | center | top	IE
	vspace="..."	Sets the amount of empty space on the top and bottom sides of the table. **Value:** Any positive numeric value.	N
\<td> \</td>			
	background="..."	Sets a background image for the table data cell. Overrides background image and color set in the \<table> tag. **Value:** URL to the image.	IE / N
	bgcolor="..."	Sets the background color for the table data cell. **Value:** Any hexadecimal or named color value.	IE / N
	bordercolor="..."	Sets the border color for the table data cell. **Value:** Any hexadecimal or named color value.	IE / N

Element	Attributes	Description	IE/N
	bordercolordark="..."	Sets the dark border color for the table data cell. **Value:** Any hexadecimal or named color value.	IE
	bordercolorlight="..."	Sets the light border color for the table data cell. **Value:** Any hexadecimal or named color value.	IE
<textarea> </textarea>			
	wrap="..."	Sets the word wrapping within the text area. **Values:** off | physical | virtual *Physical:* Displays/sends wrapped text. *Virtual:* Displays but does not send text in the wrapped state.	N
<th> </th>			
	background="..."	Sets a background image for the table header cell. Overrides background image and color set in the <table> tag. **Value:** URL to the image.	IE / N
	bgcolor="..."	Sets the background color for the table header cell. **Value:** Any hexadecimal or named color value.	IE / N
	bordercolor="..."	Sets the border color for the table header cell. **Value:** Any hexadecimal or named color value.	IE / N
	bordercolordark="..."	Sets the dark border color for the table header cell. **Value:** Any hexadecimal or named color value.	IE
	bordercolorlight="..."	Sets the light border color for the table header cell. **Value:** Any hexadecimal or named color value.	IE
<tr> </tr>			
	background="..."	Sets a background image for the table row. Overrides the background image and color set in the <table> tag. **Value:** URL to the image.	IE / N

Element	Attributes	Description	IE/N
	bgcolor="..."	Sets the background color for the entire row. **Value:** Any hexadecimal or named color value.	IE / N
	bordercolor="..."	Sets the border color for the table row. **Value:** Any hexadecimal or named color value.	IE / N
	bordercolordark="..."	Sets the dark border color for the table row. **Value:** Any hexadecimal or named color value.	IE
	bordercolorlight="..."	Sets the light border color for the table row. **Value:** Any hexadecimal or named color value.	IE
	nowrap="nowrap"	Disables word wrapping for all the cells in the row. **Value:** No other values.	IE / N
<wbr />	- proprietary element -	Denotes a breaking point, if needed, within a <nobr> tag set.	IE / N

Element Compatibility and DTD Chart

IN THE COLUMNS FOR IE AND NETSCAPE, the number listed indicates which browser version first started supporting the element. Later versions will also support the element. The DTD column shows which DOCTYPE declaration(s) supports the given element.

Legend: IE = Internet Explorer | NN = Netscape Navigator | S = Strict DTD | T = Transitional DTD | F = Frameset DTD

Element	Description	IE	NN	DTD
<!-- ... -->	Defines the body element	3.0	3.0	STF
<!DOCTYPE>	Defines the document type			STF
<a>	Defines an anchor	3.0	3.0	STF
<abbr>	Defines an abbreviation		6.2	STF
<acronym>	Defines an acronym	4.0	6.2	STF
<address>	Defines an address element	4.0	4.0	STF

Element	Description	IE	NN	DTD
<area>	Defines an area inside an image map	3.0	3.0	STF
<b>	Defines bold text	3.0	3.0	STF
<base>	Defines a base URL for all the links on a page	3.0	3.0	STF
<bdo>	Defines the direction of text display	5.0	6.2	STF
<big>	Defines big text	3.0	3.0	STF
<blockquote>	Defines a long quotation	3.0	3.0	STF
<body>	Defines the body element	3.0	3.0	STF

	Inserts a single line break	3.0	3.0	STF
<button>	Defines a push button	4.0	6.2	STF
<caption>	Defines a table caption	3.0	3.0	STF
<cite>	Defines a citation	3.0	3.0	STF
<code>	Defines computer code text	3.0	3.0	STF
<col>	Defines attributes for table columns	3.0		STF
<colgroup>	Defines groups of table columns	3.0		STF
<dd>	Defines a definition description	3.0	3.0	STF
<del>	Defines deleted text	4.0	6.2	STF
<div>	Defines a section in a document	3.0	3.0	STF
<dfn>	Instance definition, the defining instance of the enclosed term	3.0		STF
<dl>	Defines a definition list	3.0	3.0	STF
<dt>	Defines a definition term	3.0	3.0	STF
<em>	Defines emphasized text	3.0	3.0	STF
<fieldset>	Defines a fieldset	4.0	6.2	STF
<form>	Defines a form	3.0	3.0	STF
<frame>	Defines a sub-window (a frame)	3.0	3.0	F
<frameset>	Defines a set of frames	3.0	3.0	F
<h1> to <h6>	Defines header 1 to header 6	3.0	3.0	STF
<head>	Defines information about the document	3.0	3.0	STF
<hr>	Defines a horizontal rule	3.0	3.0	STF
<html>	Defines an html document	3.0	3.0	STF
<i>	Defines italic text	3.0	3.0	STF
<iframe>	Defines an inline sub-window (frame)	4.0	6.0	TF

Element	Description	IE	NN	DTD
<img>	Defines an image	3.0	3.0	STF
<input>	Defines an input field	3.0	3.0	STF
<ins>	Defines inserted text	4.0	6.2	STF
<kbd>	Defines keyboard text	3.0	3.0	STF
<label>	Defines a label for a form control	4.0	6.2	STF
<legend>	Defines a title in a fieldset	4.0	6.2	STF
<li>	Defines a list item	3.0	3.0	STF
<link>	Defines a resource reference	3.0	4.0	STF
<map>	Defines an image map	3.0	3.0	STF
<meta>	Defines meta information	3.0	3.0	STF
<noframes>	Defines a noframe section	3.0	3.0	TF
<noscript>	Defines a noscript section	3.0	3.0	STF
<object>	Defines an embedded object	3.0		STF
<ol>	Defines an ordered list	3.0	3.0	STF
<optgroup>	Defines an option group	6.0	6.0	STF
<option>	Defines an option in a drop-down list	3.0	3.0	STF
<p>	Defines a paragraph	3.0	3.0	STF
<param>	Defines a parameter for an object	3.0	3.0	STF
<pre>	Defines preformatted text	3.0	3.0	STF
<q>	Defines a short quotation		6.2	STF
<samp>	Defines sample computer code	3.0	3.0	STF
<script>	Defines a script	3.0	3.0	STF
<select>	Defines a selectable list	3.0	3.0	STF
<small>	Defines small text	3.0	3.0	STF
<span>	Defines a section in a document	3.0	4.0	STF
<strong>	Defines strong text	3.0	3.0	STF
<style>	Defines a style definition	3.0	4.0	STF
<sub>	Defines subscripted text	3.0	3.0	STF
<sup>	Defines superscripted text	3.0	3.0	STF
<table>	Defines a table	3.0	3.0	STF
<tbody>	Defines a table body	4.0		STF
<td>	Defines a table cell	3.0	3.0	STF
<textarea>	Defines a text area	3.0	3.0	STF

Element	Description	IE	NN	DTD
<tfoot>	Defines a table footer	4.0		STF
<th>	Defines a table header	3.0	3.0	STF
<thead>	Defines a table header	4.0		STF
<title>	Defines the document title	3.0	3.0	STF
<tr>	Defines a table row	3.0	3.0	STF
<tt>	Defines teletype text	3.0	3.0	STF
<ul>	Defines an unordered list	3.0	3.0	STF
<var>	Defines a variable	3.0	3.0	STF

Valueless Attributes

A VALUELESS ATTRIBUTE, sometimes called a minimized attribute, is an attribute that has no value added to it in HTML. An example is the *checked* attribute for a form input checkbox, which is used to preselect the checkbox element. For example:

<input type="checkbox" value="Red" name="Color" **selected** />

In that example, *selected* is a valueless attribute as it has no = *"value"* associated with it. Valueless attributes are not valid in XHTML, so to make them compliant the attribute is repeated as the value of itself. This chart shows the valueless attributes and how they should be written for XHTML compliance.

Valueless Attribute	How to Make It XHTML Compliant
checked	checked="checked"
compact	compact="compact"
declare	declare="declare"
defer	defer="defer"
disabled	disabled="disabled"
ismap	ismap="ismap"
multiple	multiple="multiple"
nohref	nohref="nohref"
noresize	noresize="noresize"
noshade	noshade="noshade"
nowrap	nowrap="nowrap"
readonly	readonly="readonly"
selected	selected="selected"

DOCTYPE Declarations

IF YOU WANT TO ADD A DOCTYPE declaration at the beginning of your page (before the opening HTML tag), add one of the following choices, depending on which HTML version you want your page graded against.

HTML 3.2

Version 3.2 is an old version of HTML, and as such should not be used for new web pages since they may contain code that isn't authorized. Any *one* of the following is acceptable for HTML 3.2:

```
<!DOCTYPE HTML PUBLIC "-//W3C//DTD HTML 3.2 Draft 19960821//EN">
<!DOCTYPE HTML PUBLIC "-//W3C//DTD HTML 3.2 Draft//EN">
<!DOCTYPE HTML PUBLIC "-//W3C//DTD HTML 3.2 Final//EN">
<!DOCTYPE HTML PUBLIC "-//W3C//DTD HTML 3.2//EN">
```

HTML 4.0

This is the previous version of HTML. I still wouldn't recommend it for new pages. If you choose to use this version of HTML, use the first DOCTYPE if the site does not use frames; use the second one if it does use frames.

```
<!DOCTYPE HTML PUBLIC "-//W3C//DTD HTML 4.0 Transitional//EN"
   "http://www.w3.org/TR/REC-html40/loose.dtd">

<! DOCTYPE HTML PUBLIC "-//W3C//DTD HTML 4.0 Frameset//EN"
   "http://www.w3.org/TR/REC-html40/frameset.dtd">
```

HTML 4.01

This is supposedly the *final* version of HTML. The HTML 4.01 Strict DTD includes all elements and attributes that have not been deprecated or do not appear in frameset documents. For new documents that adhere to HTML version 4.01 and do not include deprecated elements or attributes, use this document type declaration:

```
<!DOCTYPE HTML PUBLIC "-//W3C//DTD HTML 4.01//EN"
   "http://www.w3.org/TR/html4/strict.dtd">
```

The HTML 4.01 Transitional DTD includes everything in the strict DTD *plus* deprecated elements and attributes (most of which concern visual presentation). For most folks, I recommend using this document type declaration:

```
<!DOCTYPE HTML PUBLIC "-//W3C//DTD HTML 4.01 Transitional//EN"
   "http://www.w3.org/TR/html4/loose.dtd">
```

The HTML 4.01 Frameset DTD includes everything in the transitional DTD plus frames. For framed sites, use this document type declaration:

```
<!DOCTYPE HTML PUBLIC "-//W3C//DTD HTML 4.01 Frameset//EN"
   "http://www.w3.org/TR/html4/frameset.dtd">
```

Cascading Style Sheets

Main CSS Property and Value Charts

THIS SECTION IS DIVIDED into two main groups, with the two groups further divided into several property-based groups. The main group consists of the CSS properties with the most widespread support; they are likely to be the charts you reference the most frequently.

After the main group of charts is a secondary group of charts consisting of properties that are used less frequently by most web-masters, are proprietary, or don't yet have widespread browser support. I made an exception for the chart showing the scrollbar properties. While changing the appearance of the browsers scroll-bar is unofficial code, I feel compelled to include it in the main group because of its popularity among webmasters.

Key

In the *values* listings in the following charts, there are three types of values:

1. **Keyword:** A keyword value means you use one of the keywords for the property value. These are indicated by normal text. For example, in setting a background-attachment property, I might use the keyword "fixed" as the value.

2. **Reference:** A reference word, such as *length*, means you substitute the proper value for the reference word. For example, where it says *length*, you use a CSS unit of length in place of the word *length*. In writing the code for a font size, I could write *14px* in place of *length*; or in writing a border color I might write *blue* in place of a value listed as *named color*. Reference words are indicated by *italic* type.

3. **Inherit:** Inherit is actually a keyword value, but it means the property inherits its value from its parent element.

Note

The code examples are formatted like this: {background-color: #7de55b;}. This shows you how to format the property and value, but it does not include the selector. In an external style sheet, you might use that same code example as the background color for a paragraph, a division, for the entire web page, or with many other elements. To use this code example as the background for a heading, you'd write: h1 {background-color: #7de55b;} in a style sheet. It's not practical to list all the selectors available for each style property. I trust after reading this book you have a good handle on that, but when in doubt, experiment! Experimentation and discovery are fun and rewarding. You could also consult the W3C web site.

Background Color and Image Properties

Property	Description	Values
background-attachment	Sets whether a background image will scroll with the page or remain fixed in place as the page is scrolled.	fixed | scroll | inherit
	Example: {background-attachment: fixed;}	
background-color	Sets the background color. *Color value* can be a hexadecimal color value or RGB color value.	*color value* | *named color* | transparent | inherit
	Example: {background-color: #7de55b;}	
background-image	Sets a background image.	URL to image
	Example: {background-image: url(images/marble.jpg);}	
background-position	Specifies the position of a background image. With a value pair of '0% 0%', the upper-left corner of the image is aligned with the upper-left corner of the viewing port. A value pair of '100% 100%' places the lower-right corner of the image in the lower-right corner. With a value pair of '5px 3px', the upper-left corner of the image is placed 5px to the right and 3px below the upper-left corner of the viewing port.	*percentage* | *length* | inherit -or - **Horizontal keywords:** left | center | right **Vertical keywords:** top | center | bottom
	Example: {background-position: right top;} **Example:** {background-position: 100% 100%;}	
background-repeat	Sets whether a background image is repeated, and if so, how it's repeated. *Repeat-x* tiles the background horizontally only. *Repeat-y* tiles the background vertically only.	repeat | repeat-x | repeat-y | no-repeat | inherit
	Example: {background-repeat: repeat-y;}	
background	Shorthand property for setting any or all of the above five background properties in one declaration.	**Order:** color | image | repeat | attachment | position
	Example: {background: #d557e3 url(bg.gif) fixed;} *Note:* You don't need to set all properties, just the ones you want.	

Box Model Properties (applies to all block-level elements)		
Property	**Description**	**Values**
border	Shorthand property for setting the border *width*, *style*, and *color* for all four borders in one declaration. *Width length* refers to a unit of measurement such as pixels. *Style* refers to one of 10 styles set by keyword reference. Width, style, and color values are separated by a space.	**Value order:** width | style | color **Width Values:** thin | medium | thick | *length* **Style values:** dashed | dotted | solid | double | groove | ridge | inset | outset | none | hidden **Color values:** *hexadecimal color |RBG color | named color*
	Example: {border: 2px solid rgb(123,220,85);} **Example:** {border: thin dotted #d33ca5;}	
border-top **border-right** **border-bottom** **border-left**	Properties for setting the width, style, and color of each border individually. May set any one, any two, any three, or all four borders. If setting more than one border, they should be listed in the order shown. *Width length* refers to a unit of measurement such as pixels. *Style* refers to one of 10 styles set by keyword reference. Width, style, and color values are separated by a space.	**Value order:** width | style | color **Width Values:** thin | medium | thick | length **Style values:** dashed | dotted | solid | double | groove | ridge | inset | outset | none | hidden **Color values:** *hexadecimal color |RBG color | named color*
	Example: {border-top: 3px dashed red;}	
border-color	Sets the color of all four borders in one declaration.	*hexadecimal color |RBG color | named color*
	Example: {border-color: #442a75;}	
border-top-color **border-right-color** **border-bottom-color** **border-left-color**	Properties for setting the color value of each border one at a time. May set any one, any two, any three, or all four border color properties. If setting the color for more than one border, list them in the order shown.	*hexadecimal color |RBG color | named color*
	Example: {border-color-top: red; border-color-bottom: blue;}	

Property	Description	Values
border-style	Sets the style of all four borders in one declaration.	dashed | dotted | solid | double | groove | ridge | inset | outset | none | hidden
	Example: {border-style: inset;}	
border-top-style **border-right-style** **border-bottom-style** **border-left-style**	Properties for setting the style of each border one at a time. May set any one, any two, any three, or all four border style properties. If setting the style for more than one border, they should be listed in the order shown.	dashed | dotted | solid | double | groove | ridge | inset | outset | none | hidden
	Example: {border-left-style: solid;}	
border-width	Sets the width of all four borders in one declaration.	thin | medium | thick | *length*
	Example: {border-width: 3px;}	
border-top-width **border-right-width** **border-bottom-width** **border-left-width**	Properties for setting the width of each border one at a time. May set any one, any two, any three, or all four border width properties. If setting the width for more than one border, they should be listed in the order shown.	thin | medium | thick | *length*
	Example: {border-right-width: medium;}	
margin	Shorthand property for setting all four margins around an element. If only one value is listed, it applies to all sides. If two values are given, the top and bottom margins are set to the first value and the right and left margins are set to the second. If three values are given, the top is set to the first value, the left and right are set to the second, and the bottom is set to the third. If four values are given, they apply to the top, right, bottom, and left, in that order.	*length* | *percentage* | inherit | auto Length is any CSS unit of length; percentage is in respect to the width of the containing block.
	Example: {margin: 15px;}	
margin-top **margin-right** **margin-bottom** **margin-left**	Properties for setting the margin for each side one at a time. May set any one, any two, any three, or all four margin properties. If setting more than one, list them in the order shown.	*length* | *percentage* | inherit | auto Length is any CSS unit of length; percentage is in respect to the width of the containing block.
	Example: {margin-left: 3%;}	
padding	Shorthand property for setting the padding on all four sides between the containing element and the content.	*length* | *percentage* | inherit
	Example: {padding: 7px;}	

Property	Description	Values
padding-top **padding-right** **padding-bottom** **padding-left**	Properties for setting the padding for each side one at a time. May set any one, any two, any three, or all four padding properties. If setting more than one, list them in the order shown.	*length* | *percentage* | inherit
	Example: {padding-top: 3px; padding-left: 5px;}	

Font and Text Properties		
Property	**Description**	**Values**
color	Sets the element's foreground color, which almost always applies to the font color.	*hexadecimal color* | RGB *color* | *named color*
	Example: {color: black;}	
font	Shorthand property for setting most font properties in one declaration. The included properties are: font-style | font-variant | font-weight | font-size *or* font-size/line-height | font-family You may set any number of the font properties, but they should be declared in that order. *Size and family are required.* When setting the font size, you may specify the font-size or the font-size/line-height, but not both. See example 2 for visual reference. Values should be separated by a space. Multiple values for font-family should be separated by commas. *Relative size* is as it relates to the parent font size or default font size. Values are: larger | smaller. *Length* refers to any CSS unit of length, such as pixels or ems (ems are defined in the CSS Units of Measurement table later in this appendix). *Percentage* refers to a percentage of the parent font size or default size. *Line height* specifies the minimal height of line boxes within the element. *Font family* refers to a specific typeface or a style of type, such as serif.	**Font-style values:** normal | italic | oblique | inherit **Font-variant values:** normal | small-caps | inherit **Font-weight values:** normal | bold | bolder | lighter | 100 | 200 | 300 | 400 | 500 | 600 | 700 | 800 | 900 | inherit **Font-size values:** xx-small | x-small | small | medium | large | x-large | xx-large | *relative-size* | *length* | *percentage* | inherit **Font-family values:** *family name* | *generic name* ***Family names*** are specific fonts, such as Arial, Verdana, etc. ***Generic names*** are: serif | sans-serif | cursive fantasy | monospace
	Example: {font: normal 16px Verdana, Arial, sans-serif;} **Example:** {font: 14pt/20pt Arial;} *(14pt/20pt=size/line height)*	

Property	Description	Values
font-family	Sets the font face (typeface) used. Using a family name requires the font be installed on the user's computer. If it's not available and only one family is listed, the default font will be used. Multiple fonts may be listed, separated by commas. The user agent will display text using the first font listed that it finds installed on the user's computer.	**Font-family values:** *family name* | *generic name* **Family names** are specific fonts, such as Arial, Verdana, etc. **Generic names** are: serif | sans-serif | cursive | fantasy | monospace
	Example: {font-family: Broadway, Castellar, fantasy;}	
font-size	Sets the font size. *Relative size values:* larger | smaller	**Font-size values:** xx-small | x-small | small | medium | large | x-large | xx-large | *relative-size* | *length* | *percentage* | inherit
	Example: {font-size: 14px;}	
font-style	Defines the style of the font face.	normal | italic | oblique | inherit
	Example: {font-style: italic;}	
font-variant	Allows the use of small capital letters.	normal | small-caps | inherit
	Example: {font-variant: small-caps;}	
font-weight	Sets the weight (heaviness) of the font. Note that some of you probably won't see any difference between some weights due to software or system limitations or the font size used.	normal | bold | bolder | lighter | 100 | 200 | 300 | 400 | 500 | 600 | 700 | 800 | 900 | inherit
	Example: {font-weight: bold;}	
letter-spacing	Allows you to change the spacing between characters of text. *Length* refers to any CSS unit of length, such as pixels or ems.	normal | *length* | inherit
	Example: {letter-spacing: 2px;}	
line-height	Allows you to change the spacing between lines of text. A number can either be a whole number or a decimal. It may be preceded by a "-" or "+" to denote a positive or negative value.	normal | *number* | *length* | *percentage* | inherit
	Example: {line-height: 110%;}	

Property	Description	Values
text-align	Sets the horizontal alignment of text.	left | right | center | justify | inherit
	Example: {text-align: justify;}	
text-decoration	Sets the text decoration property. A value of none is often used to remove the underline from links. *Note:* Blink isn't well supported.	underline | overline | line-through | blink | none
	Example: {text-decoration: line-through;}	
text-indent	Sets the amount of indentation for the first line of text. Usually used to indent the first line of paragraphs.	*length* | *percentage* | inherit
	Example: {text-indent: 7px;}	
text-transform	Transforms the case of the text. The value of capitalize makes the first letter of each word a capital letter.	capitalize | uppercase | lowercase | none | inherit
	Example: {text-transform: lowercase;}	
vertical-align	Sets the vertical position of text with respect to the surrounding content. *Percentage* raises (positive value) or lowers (negative value) the box by a percentage of the 'line-height' value. *Length* raises (positive value) or lowers (negative value) the box by the distance given.	baseline | sub | super | top | text-top | middle | bottom | text-bottom | *percentage* | *length* | inherit
	Example: {vertical-align: middle;}	
white-space	Sets how white space (blank spaces, new lines, tabs) is handled. *Normal* collapses whitespace and breaks lines as needed. *Pre* prevents collapsing of whitespace. Lines are only broken at newlines in the source code. *Nowrap* collapses whitespace but suppresses line breaks. *Pre-wrap* prevents collapsing of whitespace. Lines are broken at newlines in the source code. *Pre-line* collapses whitespace. Lines are broken at newlines in the source code and where necessary.	normal | pre | nowrap | pre-wrap | pre-line | inherit
	Example: {white-space: pre;}	
word-spacing	Sets the spacing behavior between words. *Length* refers to additional spacing between words in addition to the default spacing unless a negative value is used.	normal | *length* | inherit
	Example: {word-spacing: 1px;}	

List Properties

Property	Description	Values
list-style	Shorthand property for defining all list styles in one declaration. **Style options:** list-style-type list-style-position list-style-image By specifying a list *type* and a list *image*, the type will be used only if the image is unavailable or for browsers without graphics capabilities. Separate each value with a space.	***Type* values:** disc | circle | square | decimal | decimal-leading-zero | lower-roman | upper-roman | lower-alpha | upper-alpha | none | inherit ***Position* values:** inside | outside | inherit ***Image* values:** *URL* | none | inherit
	Example: {list-style: disc url(image.jpg) outside;}	
list-style-image	Sets an image as a bullet for graphical browsers.	*URL* | none | inherit
	Example: {list-style-image: url(images/bluestar.gif);}	
list-style-type	Sets the list item marker (bullet type). The decimal-leading-zero value is poorly supported at the time of this writing. *Note:* Greek, Georgian, and Armenian alphabets are also available. See the W3C web site for details.	disc | circle | square | decimal | decimal-leading-zero | lower-roman | upper-roman | lower-alpha | upper-alpha | none | inherit
	Example: {list-style-type: decimal;}	
list-style-position	Sets the list item marker's position.	inside | outside | inherit
	Example: {list-style-position: inside;}	

Scrollbar and Cursor Properties

Property	Description	Values
cursor	Sets the cursor image to be used. *Note:* To have the same cursor throughout the page, set it for the *BODY* element; otherwise, set different cursors for different elements to have more than one type. *Note:* Some browsers may support other cursor types. Also, the *progress* cursor will show as the *wait* cursor on many systems.	*URL* | auto | crosshair | default | pointer | move | e-resize | ne-resize | nw-resize | n-resize | se-resize | sw-resize | s-resize | w-resize | text | wait | help | progress | inherit
	Example: {cursor: crosshair;} **Example:** {cursor: url(images/mycursor.cur);}	
scrollbar-3dlight-color	Sets the color of the left edge and top edge of the slider bar.	*hexadecimal color* | *RBG color* | *named color*
	Example: {scrollbar-3dlight-color: #3398de;}	

Property	Description	Values
scrollbar-arrow-color	Sets the directional arrow color at the top and bottom of vertical scrollbars, and at the right and left ends of horizontal scrollbars.	*hexadecimal color | RBG color | named color*
	Example: {scrollbar-arrow-color: green;}	
scrollbar-base-color	Sets the color of the slider bar tray and arrow button face.	*hexadecimal color|RBG color | named color*
	Example: {scrollbar-base-color: rgb(147,0,33);}	
scrollbar-darkshadow-color	Sets the color of the outer bottom and right edges of the slider bar.	*hexadecimal color|RBG color | named color*
	Example: {scrollbar-darkshadow-color: #bbc558;}	
scrollbar-face-color	Sets the color of the slider bar.	*hexadecimal color|RBG color | named color*
	Example: {scrollbar-face-color: maroon;}	
scrollbar-highlight-color	Sets the color of the inner top and left edges of the slider bar.	*hexadecimal color|RBG color | named color*
	Example: {scrollbar-highlight-color: #a393cd;}	
scrollbar-shadow-color	Sets the color of the inner bottom and right edges of the slider bar.	*hexadecimal color|RBG color | named color*
	Example: {scrollbar-shadow-color: rgb(122,49,109);}	

NOTE: Scrollbar properties are set for the BODY element. See Section 18.16: Colored Scrollbars in Chapter 18: Bonus Chapter for details.

Table Properties

Property	Description	Values
border-collapse	Sets whether the table cells will each have separate borders or if the borders between cells will collapse into a single border.	collapse | separate | inherit
	Example: {border-collapse: collapse;}	
border-spacing	If border-collapse is set to separate or not used, this determines the distance between the individual table cells. If one value is given, that value is used on both the vertical and horizontal borders. If two values are given, the first value sets the horizontal spacing and the second value sets the vertical spacing. *Note*: This property isn't well supported yet.	*length* | inherit
	Example: {border-spacing: 2px 4px;}	

Property	Description	Values
caption-side	Sets the alignment for the caption. Some references include *right* and *left* as values too, but the W3C indicates *text-align* should be used to set the caption to the right or left. *Note*: This property isn't well supported yet.	top | bottom | inherit
	Example: {caption-side: top; text-align: left;}	
empty-cells	If border-collapse is set to separate or not used, this sets whether to display empty cells or not. *Note*: This property isn't well supported yet.	show | hide | inherit
	Example: {empty-cells: hide;}	
table-layout	Defines the algorithm used to draw the table. Auto draws the table after all the table cells have been read; fixed draws the table after the first row of table cells has been read.	auto | fixed | inherit
	Example: {table-layout: fixed;}	

Secondary Charts

Aural Properties (audio styles for aural browsers)		
Property	**Description**	**Values**
azimuth	Defines the location of the sound in a spatial landscape (not the location of the sound file) as to how elements (such as headings and other text) will be read aloud in aural browsers.	*angle* | left-side | far-left | left | center-left | center | center-right | right | far-right | right-side | behind | leftwards | rightwards | inherit
	Example: {azimuth: 45deg;}	
cue	Adds sound to an element. Cue is shorthand for setting 'cue-before' and 'cue-after'. If two URLs are given, the first is 'cue-before' and the second is 'cue-after'. If only one URL is given, it applies to both properties.	*URL* | none | inherit
	Example: {cue: url(sound1.wav) url(sound2.wav);}	
cue-after	Adds a sound to be played after an element.	*URL* | none | inherit
	Example: {cue-after: url(sound.aiff);}	
cue-before	Adds a sound to be played before an element.	*URL* | none | inherit
	Example: {cue-before: url(sound.au);}	
elevation	Sets the vertical elevation of the sound, such as above or below the listener.	*angle* | below | level | above | higher | lower | inherit
	Example: {elevation: above;}	

Property	Description	Values
pause	Adds a pause before or after an element is read. Pause is shorthand for setting 'pause-before' and 'pause-after'. If two values are given, the first value is 'pause-before' and the second is 'pause-after'. If only one value is given, it applies to both properties. Time may be given in seconds (s) or milliseconds (ms).	*time* | *percentage* | inherit
	Example: {pause: 250ms 200ms;}	
pause-after	Adds a pause after an element is read.	*time* | *percentage* | inherit
	Example: {pause-after: 20%;}	
pause-before	Adds a pause before an element is read.	*time* | *percentage* | inherit
	Example: {pause-before: 5s;}	
pitch	Sets the average pitch (frequency) of the speaking voice.	*frequency* | x-low | low | medium | high | x-high | inherit
	Example: {pitch: 110hz;}	
pitch-range	Sets the pitch range (variation in pitch) on a scale of 0–100. The lower the value, the more monotone the voice. The higher the value, the more animated the voice.	*number* | inherit
	Example: {pitch-range: 60;}	
play-during	Specifies a background sound to be played behind an element's spoken content.	*URL* | mix | repeat | auto | none | inherit
	Example: {play-during: url(backgroundmusic.wav);}	
richness	Specifies the richness or brightness of the speaking voice using a value from 0–100. The higher the value, the richer the voice. The lower the value, the softer the voice.	*number* | inherit
	Example: {richness: 34;}	
speak	Specifies how (or if) the text will be spoken.	normal | spell-out | none | inherit
	Example: {speak: spell-out;}	
speak-numeral	Controls how numerals are spoken. Digits speak each numeral individually, so "23" would be read as "two three." Continuous speaks the full number, so "23" would be read as "twenty-three."	digits | continuous | inherit
	Example: {speak-numeral: continuous;}	

Property	Description	Values
speak-punctuation	Sets whether punctuation is spoken aloud. Code means punctuation is spoken; none means punctuation is not spoken.	code | none | inherit
	Example: {speak-punctuation: none;}	
speech-rate	Specifies the speech rate (tempo). *Number* refers to how many words per minute are spoken on average.	*number* | x-slow | slow | medium | fast | x-fast | faster | slower | inherit
	Example: {speech-rate: 140;}	
stress	Controls the height of speech inflection on a scale from 0–100, with 50 being average.	*number* | inherit
	Example: {stress: 60;}	
voice-family	Sets the kind of speaking voice that is used. The W3C web site is rather vague on specific voices. It cites examples such as *announcer, male; Juliet, female;* or names such as *comedian, trinoids, carlos, lani.* It doesn't, however, list any parameters for determining specific voices.	**Generic voices:** male | female | child **Specific voices?**
	Example: {voice-family: female;}	
volume	Sets the volume of the voice. The *number* value ranges from 0–100, with 100 being full volume.	*number* | *percentage* | silent | x-soft | soft | medium | loud | x-loud | inherit
	Example: {volume: medium;}	

Display Properties		
Property	Description	Values
clip	Sets which portion of an element is displayed. Element must be absolutely positioned.	*shape* | auto | inherit
	Example: {clip: rect(15px, 140px, 145px, 15px);}	
display	Controls how an element is displayed.	inline | block | list-item | run-in | inline-block | table | inline-table | table-row-group | table-header-group | table-footer-group | table-row | table-column-group | table-column | table-cell | table-caption | none | inherit
	Example: {display: inline;}	

Property	Description	Values
height	Sets the height of an element.	*length* | *percentage* | auto | inherit
	Example: {height: 400px;}	
min-height	Sets a minimum height for an element.	*length* | *percentage* | inherit
	Example: {min-height: 3in;}	
min-width	Sets a minimum width for an element.	*length* | *percentage* | inherit
	Example: {min-width: 50cm;}	
max-height	Sets a maximum height for an element.	*length* | *percentage* | inherit | none
	Example: {max-height: 500mm;}	
max-width	Sets a maximum width for an element.	*length* | *percentage* | inherit | none
	Example: {max-width: 88px;}	
overflow	Tells the browser how to handle content that overflows the containing element's size.	visible | hidden | scroll | auto | inherit
	Example: {overflow: scroll;}	
visibility	Sets whether the box generated by an element is rendered. Values have the following meanings: **Visible:** The generated box is visible. **Hidden:** The generated box is invisible but still affects layout. **Collapse:** If used on elements other than table rows, row groups, columns, or column groups, *collapse* has the same meaning as *hidden*.	visible | hidden | collapse | inherit
	Example: {visibility: hidden;}	
width	Sets the width of an element.	*length* | *percentage* | auto | inherit
	Example: {width: 99px;}	

Layout Properties		
Property	**Description**	**Values**
bottom	Sets how far an absolutely positioned element's bottom edge is offset above the bottom of the containing block.	length | *percentage* | auto | inherit
	Example: {bottom: 12px;}	

Property	Description	Values
clear	Places an element after a floating element.	none | left | right | both | inherit
	Example: {clear: right;}	
float	Positions an element and allows other content to flow beside the element. The typical use is to float an image so text flows beside it.	left | right | none | inherit
	Example: {float: left;}	
left	Sets how far an absolutely positioned element's left edge is offset to the right of the left edge of the containing block.	*length* | *percentage* | auto | inherit
	Example: {left: 2%;}	
position	Sets the model for how an element is placed on the page. For the *relative* and *absolute* values, it's usually used with one or more of these properties: *top* | *right* | *bottom* | *left* as shown in the example on the next line.	static | relative | absolute | fixed | inherit
	Example: {position: absolute; top: 20px; left: 40px;}	
right	Sets how far an absolutely positioned element's right edge is offset to the left of the right edge of the containing block.	*length* | *percentage* | auto | inherit
	Example: {right: 5cm;}	
top	Sets how far an absolutely positioned element's top edge is offset below the top edge of the containing block.	*length* | *percentage* | auto | inherit
	Example: {top: inherit;}	
z-index	Sets the order in which overlapping elements are stacked.	auto | *integer* | inherit
	Example: {z-index: 1;}	

Outline Properties		
Property	**Description**	**Values**
outline	Shorthand property for setting an outline's width, style, and color.	**Color values:** *hexadecimal color* | *RBG color* | *named color* | invert | inherit **Style values:** dashed | dotted | solid | double | groove | ridge | inset | outset | none | inherit

Property	Description	Values
		Width values: thin | medium | thick | *length* | inherit
	Example: {outline: 3px dashed black;}	
outline-color	Sets the outline color of an element.	*hexadecimal color* | *RBG color* | *named* *color* | invert | inherit
	Example: {outline-color: invert;}	
outline-style	Sets the outline style for an element. This is used to create outlines around visual objects such as buttons, form fields, images, etc.	dashed | dotted | solid | double | groove | ridge | inset | outset | none | inherit
	Example: {outline-style: groove;}	
outline-width	Sets the width of the outline. Note that some outline styles will not display properly if the width you set is too narrow.	thin | medium | thick | *length* | inherit
	Example: {outline-width: thick;}	

Printing Properties

Property	Description	Values
page	Specifies a specific page type to use when displaying an element box using the @page rule.	auto | *identifier*
	Example: @page {size: 8.5in 11in;}	
page-break-after	Specifies how page breaks should be controlled after an element.	auto | always | avoid | left | right | inherit
	Example: {page-break-after: always;}	
page-break-before	Specifies how page breaks should be controlled before an element.	auto | always | avoid | left | right | inherit
	Example: {page-break-before: auto;}	
page-break-inside	Denotes the page-breaking behavior inside an element's rendering box. Page breaks are not allowed in absolutely positioned elements.	avoid | auto | inherit
	Example: {page-break-inside: avoid;}	
marks	Specifies the printing marks to be rendered outside the page box.	crop | cross | none | inherit
	Example: {marks: none;}	
size	Sets the orientation or dimensions of the page box. For length, if only one unit is listed it creates a square print box. See the example on the next line for a standard print size.	*length* | auto | portrait | landscape | inherit
	Example: {size: 8.5in 11in;}	

Property	Description	Values
orphans	Sets the minimum number of lines for an orphaned paragraph fragment.	*integer* | inherit
	Example: {orphans: 4;}	
widows	Sets the minimum number of lines for a widowed paragraph fragment.	*integer* | inherit
	Example: {widows: 5;}	

Pseudo-Classes

Pseudo-class	Description
a:link	Allows you to apply styles to unvisited links.
a:visited	Allows you to apply styles to visited links.
*element***:active**	Allows you to apply styles to an element being activated by the user. This is usually applied to links, but some browsers support the pseudo-class with other elements.
*element***:hover**	Allows you to apply styles to an element when the user has the cursor resting (hovering) on the element. This is usually applied to links, but some browsers support the pseudo-class with other elements.
*element***:first-child**	Allows you to apply styles to the first child/descendent of an element.
*element***:focus**	Allows you to apply styles to an element when it has received focus from the cursor or keyboard. This is usually applied to form elements.
*element***:lang**	Allows you to set a specific language with an element.

Pseudo-Elements

Pseudo-element	Description
*element***:after**	Inserts content before an element. For example, this code: *h4:after {content: "Sale ends June 20th.";}* would insert "Sale ends June 20th." after each h4 heading. This allows you to change the date, remove the text, or whatever after each h4 element by only making one change in your external style sheet.
*element***:before**	Inserts content after an element. It works the same as the *:after* pseudo-element.
*element***:first-letter**	Allows you to set a style for the first letter in an element. For example, if your default text size was 14 pixels, you could have the first letter of each paragraph be 18 pixels tall by using: *p:first-letter {font-size: 18px;}*
*element***:first-line**	Allows you to set a style for the first line in an element.

At-rules

What are at-rules?

At-rules extend the CSS rules syntax beyond simple selector/declaration rule sets. At-rules start with an '@' character followed by an identifier (for example, '@import'). What follows depends on the specific type of at-rule. See the W3C web site for details.

Item	Description
@**charset** "*character_set*"	Sets the character set for an external style sheet. This rule, if used, must be on the first line of an external style sheet, cannot be preceded by any characters, and cannot be included in an embedded style sheet.
	Example: @charset "ISO 8859-1";
@**font-face**	Denotes a font to embed in the HTML document. This at-rule allows you to use fonts that might not be available on the user's system. The *URL* must point to an embedded OpenType font file (.eot or .ote format). Don't count on this working in most browsers.
	Example: @font-face {font-family: Pristina; src: url(http://domain.com/font_file.eot);}
@**import**	Imports a style sheet document into the current style sheet.
	Example: @import url("SomeName.css");
@**media**	Specifies style rules to be rendered only with specified media.

	Example: @media print
	{
	    body {font-size:8pt;}
	}

@**namespace**	Declares namespace prefixes for use in CSS selectors.
	Example: @namespace Name url("http://www.domain.com");
@**page**	Sets any or all of the following: *dimensions*, *page orientation*, and *margins* of a page box.
	Example: @page {margin: 2cm portrait}

Miscellaneous Items	
Item	**Description**
#**id**	Creates an id class.
*	A single asterisk used in place of a selector is a universal selector. Any rule set on the universal selector applies to all eligible elements. For example: * {*color: red;*} renders all text elements in the color red unless overruled by another style rule.
.**name**	Creates a class that can be used with any element, where *name* can be any name you choose for the class.

Item	Description
/* your comments */	Allows you to insert comments into your style sheet code.
content	This property is used with the *:before* and *:after* pseudo-elements to generate content before or after an element. Content values include: normal | none | *string* | *URL* | *counter* | attr(*identifier*) | open-quote | close-quote | no-open-quote | no-close-quote | inherit
element.**name**	Creates a class for the element, where *name* can be any name you choose to call the class.
element1 > element2	Creates a parent/child relationship. Element 2 is a child of element 1, the parent element.
element1 element2 *etc.*	Creates a nested set of elements. Nested elements are separated by a space.
element1, element2, *etc.*	Creates a group of selectors. Group selectors are separated by a comma.
quotes	Sets the type of quotation marks to be used with the *q* (quote) element. Quotation marks options include:

Character	ISO 10646 code (hex)	Description
"	0022	Quotation mark [ASCII double quotation mark]
'	0027	Apostrophe [ASCII single quotation mark]
‹	2039	Single left-pointing angle quotation mark
›	203A	Single right-pointing angle quotation mark
«	00AB	Left-pointing double angle quotation mark
»	00BB	Right-pointing double angle quotation mark
'	2018	Left single quotation mark [single high-6]
'	2019	Right single quotation mark [single high-9]
"	201C	Left double quotation mark [double high-6]
"	201D	Right double quotation mark [double high-9]
„	201E	Double low-9 quotation mark [double low-9] (Note the difference in vertical alignment)

Item	Description
style **! important**	Sets the style rule as important, overriding the usual cascading order. Overrides user style sheets.

CSS Units of Measurement

MANY CSS PROPERTY VALUES use various units of measurement. The following reference chart will help you to understand the various units, including some not discussed in the tutorial sections of the book due to space constraints or rarity of use.

Units of Measurement: Color	
Color Unit	**Description**
name	A named color. All browsers recognize the following 16 officially sanctioned named colors: aqua | black | blue | fuchsia | gray | green | lime | maroon | navy | olive | purple | red | silver | teal | white | yellow In addition, all modern browsers recognize the X11 color names. See Appendix C: Color Charts for the full list of X11 color names. Note that in using named colors there may be slight variations in color from browser to browser. **Example:** {color: blue;}
#rrggbb	The six-digit alphanumeric hexadecimal color model, where rr is the red value, gg is the green value, and bb is the blue value. **Example:** {color: #49c7ab;}
#rgb	The compressed RGB hexadecimal color model. In essence, each color value of the compressed model equate to listing the same color value twice in the six-digit model. For example, the #rgb color of #d57 is the same as writing #dd5577 in the six-digit hexadecimal model. **Example:** {color: #93a} (same color as: #9933aa)
rgb(*red, green, blue*)	The decimal color model, where (*red, green, blue*) is replaced with a color number value from 0–255 for each color. **Example:** {color: rgb(133, 57, 241);}
rgb(*r%, g%, b%*)	The RBG percentage model in which each color value is expressed as a percentage of the maximum color value. **Example:** {color: rgb(7%, 88%, 19%);}

Units of Measurement: Length	
Length Unit	**Description**
%	Percentage. Percentages refer to x-percent of the size of the parent element.
auto	A keyword unit that instructs the browser to determine the size.
cm	A centimeter. Centimeters may be expressed in whole numbers or decimals.

Length Unit	Description
em	Borrowed from print media, an em unit is a value equal to the height and width of the capital letter "M" of the browser's default font.
ex	Similar to an em unit, an ex unit is a value equal to the height of the lowercase letter "x" of the browser's default font.
in	An inch. Inches may be expressed in whole numbers or decimals.
mm	A millimeter. Millimeters may be expressed in whole numbers or decimals.
pc	A pica. A pica may be expressed in whole numbers or decimals. *Note:* There are 6 picas in an inch.
pt	A point. A point may be expressed in whole numbers or decimals. *Note:* There are 72 points in an inch.
px	A pixel. It represents the smallest unit of length the output device is capable of displaying. Often considered as a single dot on a computer screen by laypersons, although this isn't quite an accurate description.
xx-small	A keyword for an extra-extra-small font size.
x-small	A keyword for an extra-small font size.
small	A keyword for a small font size.
medium	A keyword for a medium font size.
large	A keyword for a large font size.
x-large	A keyword for an extra-large font size.
xx-large	A keyword for an extra-extra-large font size.

Units of Measurement: Angles

Angle Unit	Description
deg	The angle expressed in degrees.
grad	The angle expressed in gradients.
rad	The angle expressed in radians.

Units of Measurement: Time

Time Unit	Description
ms	Time in milliseconds. A millisecond is one-thousandth of a second.
s	Time in seconds.

Units of Measurement: Frequency

Frequency Unit	Description
hz	Frequency in hertz.
khz	Frequency in kilohertz. A kilohertz is 1,000 hertz.

CSS Terms and Definitions

T HE FOLLOWING CHART INCLUDES some common CSS terms and their definitions you may see in this book or in other references. This is not an all-inclusive list, but it covers what I believe are the most common terms you'll run across and may not understand.

CSS Term	Definition
ancestor	An ancestor is an element that is higher up in the document tree that is related (connected) to the current element.
block	Same as declaration.
cascade	The cascade, or cascading order, is the set of rules used to determine which rule to apply when an element has conflicting rules.
child	A child is an element that is directly below and related (connected) to the current element.
declaration	A *declaration, declaration block*, or simply just *block* is the rule you set for an element. It starts with the left curly brace and ends with the right curly brace, and includes everything in between. **Example:** *{margin: 3px; font-size: 12px;}*
descendent	A descendant is an element that is lower in the document tree that is related (connected) to current element.
document tree	Each web page document structure is defined as a document tree. Each element in this tree has exactly one parent, with the exception of the root element, which has none. The <html> element is considered the root element, or trunk, of this tree. This "tree" is an analogy to a human family tree, with ancestors, descendants, parents, children, and siblings. Within a human family tree, a person can be described in many ways. The same person can be a descendant of their ancestors, a child of their parents, and may also be a parent, a sibling, and so on. In the same way, elements on a web page often have multiple descriptions within the document tree.
escape (mechanism)	The character set for CSS is Unicode, which includes thousands of characters that keyboards aren't capable of directly typing. When an author wants to use a character that cannot be directly entered from the keyboard, a special escape mechanism allows for this. Use of the backslash character ("\") indicates that what follows is an escape sequence for a Unicode character. The backslash can also be used to avoid parsing of CSS syntax characters such as the semicolon (;).
inherit	Inheritance allows style properties to be taken (inherited) from other elements. This practice helps keep style sheets smaller and more manageable because an author doesn't have to code separate rules for every element used.
parent	A parent is an element that is directly above and related (connected) to the current element.

CSS Term	Definition
property	The aspect of the selector that the rule will affect, such as color or size.
rule set	A rule set is the selector or selectors, plus the declaration block. **Example:** *div {font-family: Arial; font-size: 12px;}* **Example:** *h1,h2,h3 {color: red; text-decoration: underline;}*
selector	The HTML element that a rule will be applied to.
shorthand property	Allows an author to set several separate CSS properties in one declaration.
sibling	A sibling is an element that shares the same parent with another element.
stacking level	In CSS 2.1, an element has its position in three dimensions, vertical, horizontal, and depth. When positioned elements overlap, the stacking level is the order of depth of the elements. In other words, it's the order in which the elements stack up from top to bottom. The stacking level is determined using the z-index property.
user agent	Not specific to just CSS, a user agent is any program that interprets a document written in the document language and displays the document, reads it aloud, causes it to be printed, converts it to another format, etc.
viewport	Not specific to CSS, the viewport is the window or viewing area in which content is viewed.

Color Charts

BECAUSE COLORS DISPLAYED on a monitor use the RGB (red, green, blue) color model and colors that are printed on paper use the CMYK (cyan, magenta, yellow, and black—the four process ink colors) color model, the colors shown here may not appear the same as they display on your monitor. Some RGB colors cannot be recreated in the CMYK color model, so the closest color that *can* be created is substituted. This holds true for all the color charts in this appendix.

In this appendix, you will find:

- 216 Browser-Safe Colors Chart
- Named Colors Chart
- Grayscale Colors Chart
- RGB to Hexadecimal Conversion Chart

216 Browser-Safe Colors Chart

IN THE 216 BROWSER-SAFE COLORS chart, the six-digit alphanumeric line at the top of each color square is the hexadecimal value for that color. Under that are the individual red, green, and blue values.

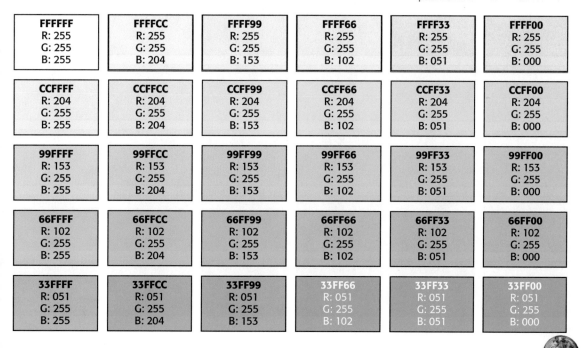

FFFFFF	FFFFCC	FFFF99	FFFF66	FFFF33	FFFF00
R: 255	R: 255	R: 255	R: 255	R: 255	R: 255
G: 255	G: 255	G: 255	G: 255	G: 255	G: 255
B: 255	B: 204	B: 153	B: 102	B: 051	B: 000
CCFFFF	CCFFCC	CCFF99	CCFF66	CCFF33	CCFF00
R: 204	R: 204	R: 204	R: 204	R: 204	R: 204
G: 255	G: 255	G: 255	G: 255	G: 255	G: 255
B: 255	B: 204	B: 153	B: 102	B: 051	B: 000
99FFFF	99FFCC	99FF99	99FF66	99FF33	99FF00
R: 153	R: 153	R: 153	R: 153	R: 153	R: 153
G: 255	G: 255	G: 255	G: 255	G: 255	G: 255
B: 255	B: 204	B: 153	B: 102	B: 051	B: 000
66FFFF	66FFCC	66FF99	66FF66	66FF33	66FF00
R: 102	R: 102	R: 102	R: 102	R: 102	R: 102
G: 255	G: 255	G: 255	G: 255	G: 255	G: 255
B: 255	B: 204	B: 153	B: 102	B: 051	B: 000
33FFFF	33FFCC	33FF99	33FF66	33FF33	33FF00
R: 051	R: 051	R: 051	R: 051	R: 051	R: 051
G: 255	G: 255	G: 255	G: 255	G: 255	G: 255
B: 255	B: 204	B: 153	B: 102	B: 051	B: 000

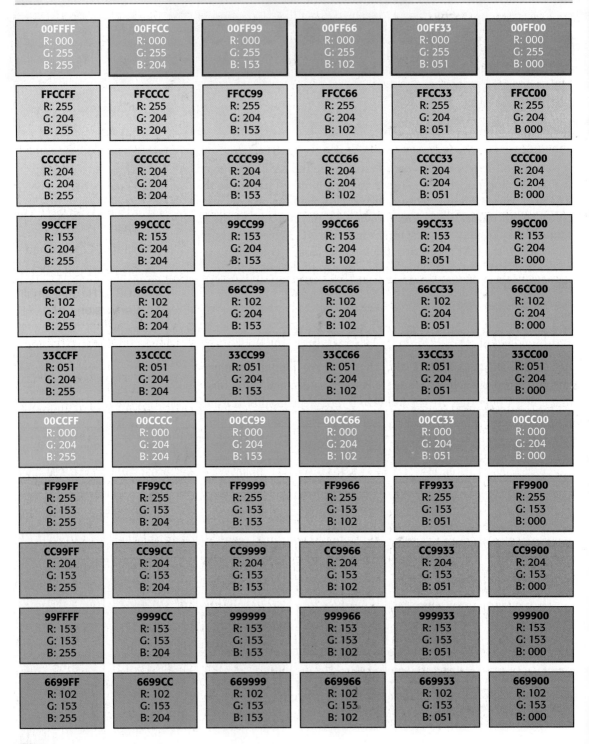

00FFFF	00FFCC	00FF99	00FF66	00FF33	00FF00
R: 000	R: 000	R: 000	R: 000	R: 000	R: 000
G: 255	G: 255	G: 255	G: 255	G: 255	G: 255
B: 255	B: 204	B: 153	B: 102	B: 051	B: 000
FFCCFF	**FFCCCC**	**FFCC99**	**FFCC66**	**FFCC33**	**FFCC00**
R: 255	R: 255	R: 255	R: 255	R: 255	R: 255
G: 204	G: 204	G: 204	G: 204	G: 204	G: 204
B: 255	B: 204	B: 153	B: 102	B: 051	B 000
CCCCFF	**CCCCCC**	**CCCC99**	**CCCC66**	**CCCC33**	**CCCC00**
R: 204	R: 204	R: 204	R: 204	R: 204	R: 204
G: 204	G: 204	G: 204	G: 204	G: 204	G: 204
B: 255	B: 204	B: 153	B: 102	B: 051	B: 000
99CCFF	**99CCCC**	**99CC99**	**99CC66**	**99CC33**	**99CC00**
R: 153	R: 153	R: 153	R: 153	R: 153	R: 153
G: 204	G: 204	G: 204	G: 204	G: 204	G: 204
B: 255	B: 204	B: 153	B: 102	B: 051	B: 000
66CCFF	**66CCCC**	**66CC99**	**66CC66**	**66CC33**	**66CC00**
R: 102	R: 102	R: 102	R: 102	R: 102	R: 102
G: 204	G: 204	G: 204	G: 204	G: 204	G: 204
B: 255	B: 204	B: 153	B: 102	B: 051	B: 000
33CCFF	**33CCCC**	**33CC99**	**33CC66**	**33CC33**	**33CC00**
R: 051	R: 051	R: 051	R: 051	R: 051	R: 051
G: 204	G: 204	G: 204	G: 204	G: 204	G: 204
B: 255	B: 204	B: 153	B: 102	B: 051	B: 000
00CCFF	**00CCCC**	**00CC99**	**00CC66**	**00CC33**	**00CC00**
R: 000	R: 000	R: 000	R: 000	R: 000	R: 000
G: 204	G: 204	G: 204	G: 204	G: 204	G: 204
B: 255	B: 204	B: 153	B: 102	B: 051	B: 000
FF99FF	**FF99CC**	**FF9999**	**FF9966**	**FF9933**	**FF9900**
R: 255	R: 255	R: 255	R: 255	R: 255	R: 255
G: 153	G: 153	G: 153	G: 153	G: 153	G: 153
B: 255	B: 204	B: 153	B: 102	B: 051	B: 000
CC99FF	**CC99CC**	**CC9999**	**CC9966**	**CC9933**	**CC9900**
R: 204	R: 204	R: 204	R: 204	R: 204	R: 204
G: 153	G: 153	G: 153	G: 153	G: 153	G: 153
B: 255	B: 204	B: 153	B: 102	B: 051	B: 000
99FFFF	**9999CC**	**999999**	**999966**	**999933**	**999900**
R: 153	R: 153	R: 153	R: 153	R: 153	R: 153
G: 153	G: 153	G: 153	G: 153	G: 153	G: 153
B: 255	B: 204	B: 153	B: 102	B: 051	B: 000
6699FF	**6699CC**	**669999**	**669966**	**669933**	**669900**
R: 102	R: 102	R: 102	R: 102	R: 102	R: 102
G: 153	G: 153	G: 153	G: 153	G: 153	G: 153
B: 255	B: 204	B: 153	B: 102	B: 051	B: 000

3399FF R: 051 G: 153 B: 255	**3399CC** R: 051 G: 153 B: 204	**339999** R: 051 G: 153 B: 153	**339966** R: 051 G: 153 B: 102	**339933** R: 051 G: 153 B: 051	**339900** R: 051 G: 153 B: 000
0099FF R: 000 G: 153 B: 255	**0099CC** R: 000 G: 153 B: 204	**009999** R: 000 G: 153 B: 153	**009966** R: 000 G: 153 B: 102	**009933** R: 000 G: 153 B: 051	**009900** R: 000 G: 153 B: 000
FF66FF R: 255 G: 102 B: 255	**FF66CC** R: 255 G: 102 B: 204	**FF6699** R: 255 G: 102 B: 153	**FF6666** R: 255 G: 102 B: 102	**FF6633** R: 255 G: 102 B: 051	**FF6600** R: 255 G: 102 B: 000
CC66FF R: 204 G: 102 B: 255	**CC66CC** R: 204 G: 102 B: 204	**CC6699** R: 204 G: 102 B: 153	**CC6666** R: 204 G: 102 B: 102	**CC6633** R: 204 G: 102 B: 051	**CC6600** R: 204 G: 102 B: 000
9966FF R: 153 G: 102 B: 255	**9966CC** R: 153 G: 102 B: 204	**996699** R: 153 G: 102 B: 153	**996666** R: 153 G: 102 B: 102	**996633** R: 153 G: 102 B: 051	**996600** R: 153 G: 102 B: 000
6666FF R: 102 G: 102 B: 255	**6666CC** R: 102 G: 102 B: 204	**666699** R: 102 G: 102 B: 153	**666666** R: 102 G: 102 B: 102	**666633** R: 102 G: 102 B: 051	**666600** R: 102 G: 102 B: 000
3366FF R: 051 G: 102 B: 255	**3366CC** R: 051 G: 102 B: 204	**336699** R: 051 G: 102 B: 153	**336666** R: 051 G: 102 B: 102	**336633** R: 051 G: 102 B: 051	**336600** R: 051 G: 102 B: 000
0066FF R: 000 G: 102 B: 255	**0066CC** R: 000 G: 102 B: 204	**006699** R: 000 G: 102 B: 153	**006666** R: 000 G: 102 B: 102	**006633** R: 000 G: 102 B: 051	**006600** R: 000 G: 102 B: 000
FF33FF R: 255 G: 051 B: 255	**FF33CC** R: 255 G: 051 B: 204	**FF3399** R: 255 G: 051 B: 153	**FF3366** R: 255 G: 051 B: 102	**FF3333** R: 255 G: 051 B: 051	**FF3300** R: 255 G: 051 B: 000
CC33FF R: 204 G: 051 B: 255	**CC33CC** R: 204 G: 051 B: 204	**CC3399** R: 204 G: 051 B: 153	**CC3366** R: 204 G: 051 B: 102	**CC3333** R: 204 G: 051 B: 051	**CC3300** R: 204 G: 051 B: 000
9933FF R: 153 G: 051 B: 255	**9933CC** R: 153 G: 051 B: 204	**993399** R: 153 G: 051 B: 153	**993366** R: 153 G: 051 B: 102	**993333** R: 153 G: 051 B: 051	**993300** R: 153 G: 051 B: 000

6633FF R: 102 G: 051 B: 255	**6633CC** R: 102 G: 051 B: 204	**663399** R: 102 G: 051 B: 153	**663366** R: 102 G: 051 B: 102	**663333** R: 102 G: 051 B: 051	**663300** R: 102 G: 051 B: 000
3333FF R: 051 G: 051 B: 255	**3333CC** R: 051 G: 051 B: 204	**333399** R: 051 G: 051 B: 153	**333366** R: 051 G: 051 B: 102	**333333** R: 051 G: 051 B: 051	**333300** R: 051 G: 051 B: 000
0033FF R: 000 G: 051 B: 255	**0033CC** R: 000 G: 051 B: 204	**003399** R: 000 G: 051 B: 153	**003366** R: 000 G: 051 B: 102	**003333** R: 000 G: 051 B: 051	**003300** R: 000 G: 051 B: 000
FF00FF R: 255 G: 000 B: 255	**FF00CC** R: 255 G: 000 B: 204	**FF0099** R: 255 G: 000 B: 153	**FF0066** R: 255 G: 000 B: 102	**FF0033** R: 255 G: 000 B: 051	**FF0000** R: 255 G: 000 B: 000
CC00FF R: 204 G: 000 B: 255	**CC00CC** R: 204 G: 000 B: 204	**CC0099** R: 204 G: 000 B: 153	**CC0066** R: 204 G: 000 B: 102	**CC0033** R: 204 G: 000 B: 051	**CC0000** R: 204 G: 000 B: 000
9900FF R: 153 G: 000 B: 255	**9900CC** R: 153 G: 000 B: 204	**990099** R: 153 G: 000 B: 153	**990066** R: 153 G: 000 B: 102	**990033** R: 153 G: 000 B: 051	**990000** R: 153 G: 000 B: 000
6600FF R: 102 G: 000 B: 255	**6600CC** R: 102 G: 000 B: 204	**660099** R: 102 G: 000 B: 153	**660066** R: 102 G: 000 B: 102	**660033** R: 102 G: 000 B: 051	**660000** R: 102 G: 000 B: 000
3300FF R: 051 G: 000 B: 255	**3300CC** R: 051 G: 000 B: 204	**330099** R: 051 G: 000 B: 153	**330066** R: 051 G: 000 B: 102	**330033** R: 051 G: 000 B: 051	**330000** R: 051 G: 000 B: 000
0000FF R: 000 G: 000 B: 255	**0000CC** R: 000 G: 000 B: 204	**000099** R: 000 G: 000 B: 153	**000066** R: 000 G: 000 B: 102	**000033** R: 000 G: 000 B: 051	**000000** R: 000 G: 000 B: 000

Named Colors Chart

aliceblue	antiquewhite	aqua	aquamarine
azure	beige	bisque	black
blue	blueviolet	brown	burlywood
cadetblue	chartreuse	chocolate	coral
cornflowerblue	cornsilk	crimson	cyan
darkblue	darkcyan	darkgoldenrod	darkgray
darkgreen	darkkhaki	darkmagenta	darkolivegreen
darkorange	darkorchid	darkred	darksalmon
darkseagreen	darkslateblue	darkslategray	darkturquoise
darkviolet	deeppink	mediumturquoise	deepskyblue
dimgray	dodgerblue	firebrick	floralwhite
forestgreen	fuchsia	gainsboro	ghostwhite
gold	goldenrod	gray	green
greenyellow	honeydew	hotpink	indianred
indigo	ivory	khaki	lavender
lavenderblush	lawngreen	lemonchiffon	lightblue
lightcoral	lightcyan	lightgreen	lightgrey
lightpink	lightsalmon	lightseagreen	lightskyblue
lightslategray	lightsteelblue	lightyellow	lime

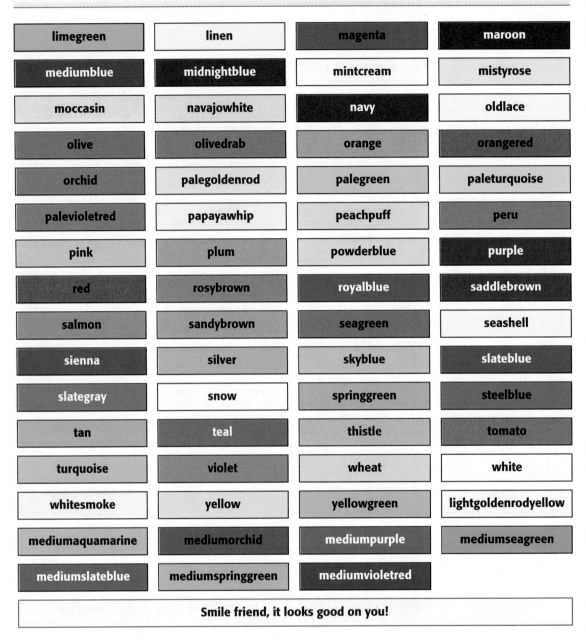

limegreen	linen	magenta	maroon
mediumblue	midnightblue	mintcream	mistyrose
moccasin	navajowhite	navy	oldlace
olive	olivedrab	orange	orangered
orchid	palegoldenrod	palegreen	paleturquoise
palevioletred	papayawhip	peachpuff	peru
pink	plum	powderblue	purple
red	rosybrown	royalblue	saddlebrown
salmon	sandybrown	seagreen	seashell
sienna	silver	skyblue	slateblue
slategray	snow	springgreen	steelblue
tan	teal	thistle	tomato
turquoise	violet	wheat	white
whitesmoke	yellow	yellowgreen	lightgoldenrodyellow
mediumaquamarine	mediumorchid	mediumpurple	mediumseagreen
mediumslateblue	mediumspringgreen	mediumvioletred	

Smile friend, it looks good on you!

Seeing these colors reminds me of mankind. We're all different colors, too—if only we could coexist as peacefully. ☺

Grayscale Colors Chart

I T'S KIND OF AN OXYMORON, isn't it—grayscale colors? I could have written it as Grayscale Chart, but that doesn't sound as colorful.

#000000	#111111	#222222	#333333
#444444	#555555	#666666	#777777
#888888	#999999	#AAAAAA	#BBBBBB
#CCCCCC	#DDDDDD	#EEEEEE	#FFFFFF

Notice a pattern in those hex codes? Here are a few more patterns for you to really get your little ol' heart pounding with excitement.

#272727	#353535	#616161	#959595
#2E2E2E	#4F4F4F	#7B7B7B	#9D9D9D
#A5A5A5	#B9B9B9	#C3C3C3	#D8D8D8
#ACACAC	#BFBFBF	#DADADA	#FCFCFC

You can produce shades of gray by repeating the two letter/number combination found in the 1–2 position of the hex code in the 3–4 and 5–6 positions. Any two letter/number combinations repeated in each position makes a grayscale color, or solid white (FFFFFF) or solid black (000000).

RGB to Hexadecimal Conversion Chart

THE FOLLOWING CHART HELPS YOU easily convert RGB color values into hexadecimal values. Just look up the individual red, green, and blue RGB numbers in the left column and the number next to it in the right column will be the hexadecimal equivalent. Once you convert all three RGB numbers, you'll have the six-digit hexadecimal number. Nifty, swifty!

RGB	Hex	RGB	Hex	RGB	Hex	RGB	Hex	RGB	Hex	RGB	Hex	RGB	Hex	RGB	Hex
0	00	32	20	64	40	96	60	128	80	160	A0	192	C0	224	E0
1	01	33	21	65	41	97	61	129	81	161	A1	193	C1	225	E1
2	02	34	22	66	42	98	62	130	82	162	A2	194	C2	226	E2
3	03	35	23	67	43	99	63	131	83	163	A3	195	C3	227	E3
4	04	36	24	68	44	100	64	132	84	164	A4	196	C4	228	E4
5	05	37	25	69	45	101	65	133	85	165	A5	197	C5	229	E5
6	06	38	26	70	46	102	66	134	86	166	A6	198	C6	230	E6
7	07	39	27	71	47	103	67	135	87	167	A7	199	C7	231	E7
8	08	40	28	72	48	104	68	136	88	168	A8	200	C8	232	E8
9	09	41	29	73	49	105	69	137	89	169	A9	201	C9	233	E9
10	0A	42	2A	74	4A	106	6A	138	8A	170	AA	202	CA	234	EA
11	0B	43	2B	75	4B	107	6B	139	8B	171	AB	203	CB	235	EB
12	0C	44	2C	76	4C	108	6C	140	8C	172	AC	204	CC	236	EC
13	0D	45	2D	77	4D	109	6D	141	8D	173	AD	205	CD	237	ED
14	0E	46	2E	78	4E	110	6E	142	8E	174	AE	206	CE	238	EE
15	0F	47	2F	79	4F	111	6F	143	8F	175	AF	207	CF	239	EF
16	10	48	30	80	50	112	70	144	90	176	B0	208	D0	240	F0
17	11	49	31	81	51	113	71	145	91	177	B1	209	D1	241	F1
18	12	50	32	82	52	114	72	146	92	178	B2	210	D2	242	F2
19	13	51	33	83	53	115	73	147	93	179	B3	211	D3	243	F3
20	14	52	34	84	54	116	74	148	94	180	B4	212	D4	244	F4
21	15	53	35	85	55	117	75	149	95	181	B5	213	D5	245	F5
22	16	54	36	86	56	118	76	150	96	182	B6	214	D6	246	F6
23	17	55	37	87	57	119	77	151	97	183	B7	215	D7	247	F7
24	18	56	38	88	58	120	78	152	98	184	B8	216	D8	248	F8
25	19	57	39	89	59	121	79	153	99	185	B9	217	D9	249	F9
26	1A	58	3A	90	5A	122	7A	154	9A	86	BA	218	DA	250	FA
27	1B	59	3B	91	5B	123	7B	155	9B	187	BB	219	DB	251	FB
28	1C	60	3C	92	5C	124	7C	156	9C	188	BC	220	DC	252	FC
29	1D	61	3D	93	5D	125	7D	157	9D	189	BD	221	DD	253	FD
30	1E	62	3E	94	5E	126	7E	158	9E	190	BE	222	DE	254	FE
31	1F	63	3F	95	5F	127	7F	159	9F	191	BF	223	DF	255	FF

Reminder: There are millions of colors you can use. Visit www.BoogieJack.com and surf to the web design area for some color utilities to help you select the exact color you want.

ASCII Character Chart

A SCII IS AN ACRONYM for American Standard Code for Information Interchange. Your computer can only understand numbers, so ASCII code is the numerical representation of a character. The ASCII characters are also known as HTML Extended Characters.

Not all characters have a corresponding keyboard key, so they must be accessed in another manner. You'll find instructions for accessing these extended characters after the character chart. Note that not all font sets contain all character entities. Many font sets contain no more than the uppercase and lowercase English characters, numerals, and basic punctuation marks.

In this appendix, you will find:

- ASCII Character Chart
- How to Access Extended Characters on Windows
- How to Access Extended Characters on Mac OS X
- Entering Extended Characters into HTML Documents

ASCII Character Chart

Entity	Entity Name	HTML Code	Description
		&#01; - &#08;	Unused
				Horizontal tab

		
	Line feed

		&#11; - &#31;	Unused
		 	Space
!		!	Exclamation point
"	"	"	Double quote
#		#	Number sign
$		$	Dollar sign
%		%	Percent sign
&	&	&	Ampersand
'		'	Single quote
(		(	Left parenthesis
)		)	Right parenthesis
*		*	Asterisk
+		+	Plus

483

Entity	Entity Name	HTML Code	Description
,		,	Comma
-		-	Hyphen
.		.	Period
/		/	Forward slash
0		0	Zero
1		1	One
2		2	Two
3		3	Three
4		4	Four
5		5	Five
6		6	Six
7		7	Seven
8		8	Eight
9		9	Nine
:		:	Colon
;		;	Semicolon
<	<	<	Less-than sign
=		=	Equal sign
>	>	>	Greater-than sign
?		?	Question mark
@		@	At sign
A		A	Capital a
B		B	Capital b
C		C	Capital c
D		D	Capital d
E		E	Capital e
F		F	Capital f
G		G	Capital g
H		H	Capital h
I		I	Capital i
J		J	Capital j
K		K	Capital k

Entity	Entity Name	HTML Code	Description
L		L	Capital l
M		M	Capital m
N		N	Capital n
O		O	Capital o
P		P	Capital p
Q		Q	Capital q
R		R	Capital r
S		S	Capital s
T		T	Capital t
U		U	Capital u
V		V	Capital v
W		W	Capital w
X		X	Capital x
Y		Y	Capital y
Z		Z	Capital z
[		[	Left square bracket
\		\	Back slash
]		]	Right square bracket
^		^	Caret
_		_	Underscore
`		`	Grave accent
a		a	Lowercase a
b		b	Lowercase b
c		c	Lowercase c
d		d	Lowercase d
e		e	Lowercase e
f		f	Lowercase f
g		g	Lowercase g
h		h	Lowercase h
i		i	Lowercase i
j		j	Lowercase j
k		k	Lowercase k

Entity	Entity Name	HTML Code	Description
l		l	Lowercase l
m		m	Lowercase m
n		n	Lowercase n
o		o	Lowercase o
p		p	Lowercase p
q		q	Lowercase q
r		r	Lowercase r
s		s	Lowercase s
t		t	Lowercase t
u		u	Lowercase u
v		v	Lowercase v
w		w	Lowercase w
x		x	Lowercase x
y		y	Lowercase y
z		z	Lowercase z
{		{	Left curly brace
|		|	Vertical bar
}		}	Right curly brace
~	˜	~	Tilde
▪		&#127;	Not defined
€		€	Euro
▯			Unknown
‚	‚	‚	Single low quote
ƒ		ƒ	Function symbol
„	&dbquo;	„	Double low quote
…		…	Ellipses
†	†	†	Dagger
‡	‡	‡	Double dagger
ˆ		ˆ	Circumflex accent
‰	‰	‰	Per mille symbol
Š		Š	Capital esh
‹	‹	‹	Left single angle quote

Entity	Entity Name	HTML Code	Description
Œ		Œ	OE ligature
			Unused
Ž		Ž	Capital ž
			Unused
			Unused
'	‘	‘	Left single quote
'	’	’	Right single quote
"	“	“	Left double quote
"	”	”	Right double quote
•		•	Small bullet (heavy middle dot)
–	–	–	En dash / Minus sign
—	—	—	Em dash
~	&tilde	˜	Tilde
™	™	™	Trademark symbol
š		š	Lowercase š
›	›	›	Right single angle quote
œ		œ	Ligature for oe
			Unused
ž		ž	Lowercase ž
Ÿ	Ÿ	Ÿ	Uppercase y umlaut
			Nonbreaking space
¡	¡	¡	Inverted exclamation point
¢	¢	¢	Cent
£	£	£	Pound sterling currency sign
¤	¤	¤	Currency sign
¥	¥	¥	Yen currency sign
¦	¦	¦	Broken vertical bar
§	§	§	Section symbol
¨	¨	¨	Umlaut
©	©	©	Copyright symbol
ª	ª	ª	Feminine ordinal indicator
«	«	«	Left angle quotation mark

Entity	Entity Name	HTML Code	Description
¬	¬	¬	Not sign
-	­	­	Soft hyphen
®	®	®	Registered symbol
¯	¯	¯	Macron
°	°	°	Degree sign
±	±	±	Plus/minus sign
²	²	²	Superscript 2
³	³	³	Superscript 3
´	´	´	Acute accent
µ	µ	µ	Micro sign
¶	¶	¶	Paragraph sign
·	·	·	Middle dot
¸	¸	¸	Cedilla
¹	¹	¹	Superscript 1
º	º	º	Masculine ordinal indicator
»	»	»	Right angle quotation mark
¼	¼	¼	One-quarter fraction
½	½	½	One-half fraction
¾	¾	¾	Three-quarters fraction
¿	¿	¿	Inverted question mark
À	À	À	A grave accent
Á	Á	Á	A accute accent
Â	Â	Â	A circumflex
Ã	Ã	Ã	A tilde
Ä	Ä	Ä	A umlaut
Å	Å	Å	A ring
Æ	Æ	Æ	AE ligature
Ç	Ç	Ç	C cedilla
È	È	È	E grave
É	É	É	E acute
Ê	Ê	Ê	E circumflex
Ë	Ë	Ë	E umlaut

Entity	Entity Name	HTML Code	Description
Ì	Ì	Ì	I grave
Í	Í	Í	I acute
Î	Î	Î	I circumflex
Ï	Ï	Ï	I umlaut
Đ	Ð	Ð	Eth
Ñ	Ñ	Ñ	N tilde
Ò	Ò	Ò	O grave
Ó	Ó	Ó	O acute
Ô	Ô	Ô	O circumflex
Õ	Õ	Õ	O tilde
Ö	Ö	Ö	O umlaut
×	×	×	Multiplication sign
Ø	Ø	Ø	O slash
Ù	Ù	Ù	U grave
Ú	Ú	Ú	U acute
Û	Û	Û	U circumflex
Ü	Ü	Ü	U umlaut
Ý	Ý	Ý	Y acute
Þ	Þ	Þ	Thorn
ß	ß	ß	SZ ligature
à	à	à	a grave
á	á	á	a acute
â	â	â	a circumflex
ã	ã	ã	a tilde
ä	ä	ä	a umlaut
å	å	å	a ring
æ	æ	æ	ae ligature
ç	ç	ç	c cedilla
è	è	è	e grave
é	é	é	e acute
ê	ê	ê	e circumflex
ë	ë	ë	e umlaut

Entity	Entity Name	HTML Code	Description
ì	ì	ì	i grave
í	í	í	i acute
î	î	î	i circumflex
ï	ï	ï	i umlaut
ð	ð	ð	Eth
ñ	ñ	ñ	n tilde
ò	ò	ò	o grave
ó	ó	ó	o acute
ô	ô	ô	o circumflex
õ	õ	õ	o tilde
ö	ö	ö	o umlaut
÷	÷	÷	Division symbol
ø	ø	ø	o slash
ù	ù	ù	u grave
ú	ú	ú	u acute
û	û	û	u circumflex
ü	ü	ü	u umlaut
ý	ý	ý	y acute
þ	þ	þ	Thorn
ÿ	ÿ	ÿ	y umlaut

How to Access Extended Characters in Windows

THERE ARE SEVERAL WAYS TO ACCESS extended characters. Windows computers have a *Character Map* utility located in the *Systems Tools* folder, which is in the *Accessories* folder in the *Programs* menu (*Programs > Accessories > System Tools > Character Map*). By opening the Character Map utility, you can view all the characters in any installed font and copy any character to the Windows clipboard.

You can also type an extended character directly into a document. In the previous chart, the third column shows the HTML code for a character. For example, *©* is the HTML code for the copyright symbol. In that code, the number "169" is also the ASCII character number. To type a copyright symbol directly into a document, hold down the *Alt* key and type 169 on the numbers pad, then release the Alt key. The "numbers pad" is the numbers keypad on the right side of the keyboard, not the numbers above the alphabet keys. On some systems you may need to add a zero in front of the number, so if typing "169" doesn't work try holding down the Alt key and typing "0169" on the numbers pad. If the font set you're using in the document has that character entity, it will be entered into the document when you release the Alt key. If the font set doesn't have that character entity, it will usually display a hollow square (⬚) in its place. This occurs less often as operating systems and programs add Font Fallback support, a feature that automatically finds the character in another font (if possible).

How to Access Extended Characters in Mac OS X

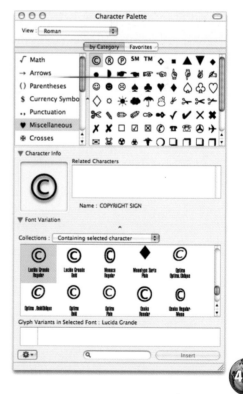

MAC OS X HAS A CHARACTER PALETTE that displays and inserts extended characters. To use it:

1. Go into the *International* settings inside *System Preferences*.

2. Click *Input Menu* and check *Character Palette*.

3. The Input Menu should now be displayed as a flag icon near the clock in the upper-right corner of the menu bar.

4. Open a program and select the font, then click the flag icon and choose Show Character Palette.

5. Locate the character you want in the palette, and then double-click it to insert it into text.

Entering Extended Characters into HTML Documents

TYPING A CHARACTER ENTITY (also known as a glyph) directly into the source code for an HTML page isn't the recommended way of placing the symbol on the page. For HTML, it is recommended that you either enter the entity name if it has one; or the HTML code for it. In the case of the copyright symbol, you could use either *©* or *©* to place it on a web page.

Troubleshooting Chart

Web Server Error Chart

In this appendix, you will find:
- Web Server Error Chart
- HTML Troubleshooting Chart

WHEN YOU CLICK A LINK ON A WEB PAGE, you are sending a data packet to a server somewhere. These data packets can be routed through several different servers and data stream pipelines before they reach the host server. Once they reach the host server, the process is reversed and the requested data is sent back, possibly through a different set of servers and pipelines.

This process is actually fairly efficient, but sometimes the data packets can be lost or caught in an information bottleneck where it times out. This usually results in the famous "404 – Page Not Found" error message. Often, simply reloading the page with the error message, which resends the data packet, will solve the problem and load the page.

Of course, there are also legitimate server errors. The following chart lists the server errors and offers a brief explanation of what they mean.

Error Code	Error	Explanation
Error 400	Bad Request	The request could not be understood by the server, often due to incorrect syntax.
Error 401	Unauthorized	The server has determined that you are not authorized to view the page requested. This can be because of coding errors or intentional restrictions.
Error 402	Payment Required	This message means a charging specification has not been met. A suitable ChargeTo header must be implemented before access is granted.
Error 403	Forbidden	The request is for something forbidden, which is not the same as needing authorization. This error code is often used as a catchall error message used when no other response is applicable. It can also indicate that you're trying to access a part of the server that the host has disallowed access to. If this happens on your web site, try CHMOD-ing the file permissions to "read" for all users.

Error Code	Error	Explanation
Error 404	Not Found	The server can't find a match for your request. If this happens on your site, make sure the web address (URL) has proper text case, spelling, punctuation, and file extension, and make sure that file paths are correctly coded. Be sure you are using the forward slash (/) and not the backward slash (\). If the error occurs on someone else's site, try simply reloading the page. Your data packet (link request) may have been lost or it may have timed out due to heavy Internet traffic or a slow server response.
Error 405	Method Not Allowed	The method specified is not allowed for the resource identified by the request.
Error 406	Not Acceptable	The resource identified by the request is incapable of generating a response according to the accept headers sent in the request.
Error 407	Proxy Authentication Required	Similar to the 401 error (Unauthorized), this indicates that the user must first authenticate with the proxy server.
Error 408	Request Timeout	The user did not produce a request within the time limit the server is programmed to wait.
Error 409	Conflict	The request could not be completed due to a conflict. This error is used in situations when it is anticipated the user may be able to resolve the conflict and resubmit the request.
Error 410	Gone	This is a web maintenance message. It notifies the web-master of the site containing the link that the resource is intentionally unavailable. The site owner of the resource wants remote links to that resource removed.
Error 411	Length Required	The server refuses to accept the request without a defined content length.
Error 412	Precondition Failed	The precondition mandated was not met. This allows servers to prevent the requested method from being applied to a resource other than the one intended.
Error 413	Request Entity Too Large	This is a server refusal to process a request because the request entity is larger than the server will process. The server may close the connection to prevent the client from continuing the request. This also helps prevent unauthorized resource usage.
Error 414	Request-URI Too Long	The server refuses the request because the Request-URI is longer than the server can interpret.
Error 415	Unsupported Media Type	The request is in a format not supported by the server.

Error Code	Error	Explanation
Error 500	Internal Server Error	The request could not be processed due to an internal server error. The server encountered an unexpected condition that prevented it from completing the request.
Error 501	Not Implemented	The server doesn't support the function requested. This is the standard response when the server doesn't recognize or understand the request or it isn't capable of supporting the request.
Error 502	Bad Gateway	The server encountered an invalid response from the up-stream server it accessed in attempting to fulfill the request. In this case, the server is acting only as a gateway or proxy server.
Error 503	Service Unavailable	The server is currently unable to handle the request due to temporary overload or maintenance of the server. This implies it's a temporary condition and service will be restored to normal after a period of time.
Error 504	Gateway Timeout	The server did not receive a timely response from the up-stream server it attempted to access to complete the request. In this case, the server is acting only as a gateway or proxy server.
Error 505	HTTP Version Not Supported	The server does not support the HTTP protocol version used in the request. The response may contain a description of why it is not supported and which protocols that server supports.

HTML Troubleshooting Chart

THE FOLLOWING HTML TROUBLESHOOTING chart offers possible solutions to the most common problems new web authors encounter.

Problem	Possible Solutions
Broken images.	• Check that the capitalization (uppercase/lowercase pattern) is correct. Image names, file extensions, and the image path to your server are case sensitive. • Check the file path; many times people have the image coded to a location on their own computer rather than on the server. • Be sure you uploaded the image in binary mode. • Check your typing as misspellings do break your code. Be sure you didn't accidentally type something like "igm src" instead of "img src." • Check that you have referenced the right image extension. Many times people will type .gif or .jpg as the extension when the image is actually saved as the other type. • Check that you're using a universally supported image type, either JPG or GIF.
I can view the images on my site, but other people can't view all of them.	You probably have the image path set to your own hard drive. You'd be able to see the image because it's on your hard drive in the location your code indicates, but others can't see them because they don't have access to your hard drive.
Unexpected layout.	Check your code. Unexpected results are often caused by a simple code error such as leaving out one end of the quotation marks (") in an HTML tag.
Page doesn't display or only displays to a certain point and is then blank.	Check for any unclosed tables. Internet Explorer forgives you for forgetting to close table tags, but Netscape does not. Any open table in a page viewed with Netscape will cause the content not to display from the beginning of the open table on. If your page is a framed page, make sure you closed the framesets.
My page shows up on my computer but not online.	• Make sure you didn't include any illegal characters in your file name or directory name. Spaces and some characters are illegal in file and directory names. • Did you remember to upload the file? If so, did you upload it in ASCII mode? • Did you use the correct case and file extension? File names, file extensions, and folder names are case sensitive.

Problem	Possible Solutions
Code is showing up on the page.	• If it's a left arrow bracket (<) or right arrow bracket (>), chances are you typed in two brackets at the beginning or end of a tag. For example, <<font...> would cause one < to show up on the page. • If the whole page is showing up as code, make sure you saved the page as .html and that your text-editing program didn't add a .txt extension on the end. • Check that you started the page with the <html> declaration and ended it with the </html> tag.
There's an extra table cell off to the side of my table.	Somewhere in your code you have an extra and unnecessary table cell or you have spanned too many columns with one or more cells.
My brakes squeak.	This is a warning device built into your vehicle. When you hear that, your brake linings probably need replaced.
There's a blue "tick" after one of my links.	You either have a space at the end of the linked text or image (before the </a> tag) or you have a hard return in the link.
I made changes on my web site but they're not showing up.	• Your browser or ISP may be caching the page. Click the reload or refresh button on your browser. It's sometimes necessary to reload a page three or four times to get the new page. • If that fails, try emptying your browser history folder and retrying. • If that fails, check with your ISP to see if they are serving cached pages instead of fresh pages.
My pages are loading in the wrong frame.	Check your target tags and frame names. They must correspond exactly, and each link should include a target.
A table is sandwiched between paragraphs of text instead of the text wrapping around the table.	• If you used the deprecated *align="left"* or *align="right"* attribute and value in the <table> tag, try moving into the future and use the CSS float property to align tables. • If you did use the float property, check to be sure you don't have a *clear all* property and value on another floating element that is forcing the text down the page.
The links to my favorite sites aren't working.	• Check that you have used the full web address of the site rather than a relative path, which would point to your own web site. • Check that the site is up and running—sites often go down for a few minutes or an information packet can become lost or time out. Try reloading the page. • Check your syntax; confirm that you've included the quotation marks around the addresses. Also, remember that "a href" is two words, not one.

Problem	Possible Solutions
My link points to the wrong site!	You've probably forgotten to close a previous link on the page. Check to be sure the </a> tag is included after each link.
All my text looks like a link.	You've forgotten to close a link. Look at the point in the code where the link begins to find the place to cancel the link tag.
All my text after a list remains indented.	You've left a list tag open. Be sure to proofread your code and then send me a dollar for all this troubleshooting.
I used a lot of CSS on my page and it looks great in [pick your browser], but crummy in [pick another browser].	Older versions of most browsers had very spotty support for CSS. You're preferred browser may be more modern than the browser that isn't working for your site. Be sure you are using modern browsers, not only for the one you use, but also the ones you proof your web sites with. Newer versions of browsers also offer better security.
People are complaining that my site is too slow.	• Well they've certainly got a lot of nerve! Check that your images are optimized and are not too large, that your page isn't too long, and that you've included image size tags and proper code. If your page is 40K or under including the graphics, then it's definitely not your page. • It could be that your server is bogged down with heavy traffic. Or, it might be that or another site that your site shares the server with is slowing the server down. Or, your site may be hosted with substandard equipment that's causing poor performance. • Is it slow for you, too? The visitor's ISP could be suffering from too many users, or the user has a bad connection.
Sometimes this stuff just seems too hard to learn.	Write <increase target="brainpower" /> on your pillow and you'll magically get smarter as you sleep.
My CGI script isn't working.	• Check to ensure the path to Perl at the beginning of the script is correct. • Make sure you uploaded it in ASCII mode. • Make sure the correct file permissions are set. • If it's a new script, especially if it was a free script, the problem may be with the script itself.
My site is down. What should I do?	• First, make sure your site is actually down and that it's not something at your end. Check other sites to see if you can access them. If not, the trouble is with your computer or your ISP. If you can't access other sites, contact your ISP. • If you can access other sites, wait 10 or 15 minutes and try your site again. Often, little problems occur that seem to self-correct in a short time. If you still can't access your site, contact your web hosting company.

Problem	Possible Solutions
I linked to graphics on another site and they're not working.	Good! You should never link to graphics on another site. That's stealing bandwidth and it's illegal. Why should someone else have to pay for your web site's bandwidth? You were lucky if all they did was disallow the link. They could have taken you to court, reported you to your web host provider (possibly causing you to lose your site), reported you to your ISP (possibly causing you to lose your Internet access), or uploaded another image—a nasty image—in place of the one you linked to, making you look like a pervert or an idiot. Never link to any files on someone else's site unless they give you permission to do so.
The first link on my index page is to my Brain Café. I thought it would be my most popular section, but hardly anyone clicks the link to check it out.	It could be that they don't understand what's at the other end of the link. Brain Café? What does it mean? Cutesy names should include a descriptive caption so your visitors understand what they are, rather than leaving them to guess at what the content is. There are so many choices of where to go and what to do on the Internet that not many people are willing to play guessing games. Most want to know what to expect before they get there.
Whenever I get into the shower the phone rings.	This is called the law of attraction. You're attracted to the shower just before the phone rings because you're a little ringy-dingy.

The most common cause of page malfunctions is simple typing mistakes. Check and recheck your code, or use an HTML validator to help you find errors on your pages. If you use a validator, it may require a DOCTYPE declaration at the beginning of the document. The DOCTYPE tells the browser which version of HTML to validate your page against. See the end of Appendix A: HTML and XHTML for DOCTYPE options to add to pages.

You'll find many HTML validators online and some that you can install on your own computer. If you want to try the toughest of them all, go to: http://validator.w3.org.

Don't be too discouraged if the W3C's validator lists a ton of warnings and errors—it probably will. I've not seen many pages that pass without several warnings. In the past, I even ran a few of the W3C's own web pages through their own validator and found a page or two that didn't pass.

Browsers are much more tolerant, so a few warnings need not be viewed as a horrible thing—but receiving warnings is a good way to learn. Some warnings may not be avoidable, but you should fix any errors you can. Some errors, such as those caused by affiliate codes, may not be something you can fix. If that happens, you'll have to choose between having a page that validates or removing the affiliate until they can provide code that validates.

Glossary

This glossary defines common terms you'll encounter while designing web sites or surfing the Internet. It does not include HTML and CSS terms, which have their own reference charts.

A

Absolute Address The full address of a file. The address is the physical location of the file on a computer. See also, *relative address*.

Access Provider An Internet service provider (ISP) that provides local access to the Internet.

Adware Software that is free to the user, but supported by advertisers.

Anchor A named point (anchor) on a web page that specifies where a link will go. All links use the anchor tag.

Animated GIF A series of images shown one after another to simulate animation.

Announcement List A mailing list that restricts who may send messages to the list of subscribers.

Apache Apache is an open-source web server software application. Open-source means many different individuals and companies can and have contributed to its development. It is designed as various sets of modules, which allows administrators to choose which features they wish to use.

Applet A small Java program embedded into a web page.

ASCII American Standard Code for Information Interchange. The lowest common denominator method for transferring information with almost universal support.

ASP (1) Active Server Pages: A form of programming available only on servers that run the Windows NT operating system. (2) Application Service Provider: A company that creates business software applications and makes them available on a subscription basis to other businesses.

Atom An evolving protocol for content syndication and distribution. Like RSS feeds, Atom is an XML-based platform, but is more advanced.

Attachment A file attached to an email message that can be sent to any other email account. Attachments can be any type of file—including text, graphics, fonts, programs, compressed files, etc.

Attribute An aspect of an HTML tag that is modified with a value.

Autoresponder (or Infobot) A type of email account that automatically responds to requests for information with a prewritten message. See also, *smart autoresponder*.

B

Backbone High-speed lines that are the basis of data transfer capabilities within a network.

Bandwidth The amount of data you can send through a connection. Usually measured in kilobits per second (Kbps).

Baud A measurement of how fast data flows through a modem or router.

Binary File A file that is not in ASCII text format, such as an image or a program.

Bit A single binary piece of information, consisting of a 1 or 0 (zero).

Blog Short for weB LOG, a blog is an online journal. Blogs are typically updated daily, with "bloggers" ranging from amateur writers to professional journalists and book authors. Blog content can be specific to a topic or simply daily musings, rants, and ramblings about anything the writer feels compelled to comment on. Blog postings are usually arranged in chronological order with the most recent entries featured most prominently.

Bookmark (or Favorite) A feature included in browsers such as Microsoft Internet Explorer and Safari that allows you to save addresses of your favorite web sites and quickly access pages of interest.

Broadband Ultra-high speed Internet connections. There is no minimum defined speed of what makes a broadband connection, but in general any DSL or cable connection is considered broadband.

Browser See *Web Browser.*

Bulletin Board An electronic message center that usually serves a specific interest group. You access a bulletin board through the Internet, and then read or post messages to relate to others who frequent the specific board. Bulletin boards are often topical in nature.

Byte A unit of data that is eight binary digits (8 bits) long.

C

Cache A location on a computer that stores recently visited web pages so they can be accessed faster. When returning to a recently visited web site, you may be viewing a page from the computer's cache rather than fresh content, depending on how the browser is configured.

Cascading Style Sheets See *CSS.*

CGI Acronym for *Common Gateway Interface.* A scripting language that allows HTML pages to interact with programming applications.

Chat Room An area on the Internet where people can communicate in real time. As users type their messages, they appear on-screen along with messages from other visitors to the chat room.

Client-side Image Map An image that is divided into clickable regions; each region can be linked to a different file.

Compression A technology used to make files smaller so they transmit faster over the Internet and take up less hard drive space. To use a compressed file, you must expand it. Compressed files are often called zipped or stuffed files.

Cookie A cookie is a bit of information sent by a web server to a user's computer that is later fed back to the server in order to enhance a web site's functionality or a user's experience. A cookie may be used to remember log-in information, user preferences, shopping cart wish lists, etc. Cookies can be stored temporarily in computer memory or semipermanently on the user's hard drive until an expiration date has passed. Contrary to newbie fears, cookies do not send copies of your email to the FBI, your bank account information to the Nigerian Mafia, or pictures of your most embarrassing moment to *The National Enquirer.*

CPM Cost per thousand impressions. A pricing method usually used for pricing advertising impressions. For example, a $5 CPM means that $5 is paid for every 1,000 displays of an advertisement on a web site. CPM is also used for mailing lists—one impression usually equals one email address the mailing is sent to.

CSS Cascading Style Sheets. A web page formatting language that gives greater control and more flexibility in page design than is possible with only HTML, including the ability to use a single file as a central control mechanism over the layout of an entire web site.

Cyberspace A sweeping term used to refer to anything on the Internet.

D

Dedicated Server A computer that runs only one type of server software and is usually configured according to the user's specifications. Dedicated servers are typically used for high-traffic web sites that need dedicated processing power.

Demoware Programs you can download and use for evaluation. Often, some features are disabled until you actually pay for the program. Demoware is sometimes disparagingly called *crippleware.*

DHTML Dynamic HyperText Markup Language. DHTML is a combination of HTML, JavaScript, and CSS used together to create unusual page effects and dynamic functionality.

Digerati A word combined from digital literati, digerati refers to people thought to be the movers and shakers in the Internet world.

Digital Electronic information that uses on/off sequences to convey information.

Discussion List A moderated or unmoderated mailing list that allows any member to send messages to the other members (subscribers).

DNS Domain Name Server. A method of indexing the Internet based on site names. DNS is sometimes referred to as *domain name system.*

DNS Aliasing The Internet relies on Domain Name Servers (DNS's) to translate domain names into IP addresses. Every web hosting company must have a domain name server.

Domain Name The name that defines your web site's address online. A domain name is much like a trademark or a license. It allows people to find a web site by name instead of by number (IP address). Domain names must be unique—only one of each name can exist in the world. Domain names can be 67 characters long, including the domain extension at the end, but not including the "http://www" at the beginning.

Downloading The process of copying files from the Internet onto a computer or removable media (Flash drive, iPod, etc.) via a variety of methods such as with a web browser, FTP software, or Telnet.

DSL A technology that utilizes unused frequencies on copper telephone lines to transmit data at high speeds.

E

E-commerce Short for electronic commerce, it means to conduct business online.

Email Short for electronic mail, email is a method for sending messages along with attachments such as letters, sales notices, brochures, pictures, and countless other things over the Internet.

Email Alias Sometimes called a forwarding account, this type of account forwards emails sent to the alias account to another account.

Email POP Account See *POP.*

Encryption A process of scrambling information so it is unusable to all but the intended users.

Ethernet A common method of networking computers in a Local Area Network (LAN).

Extranet An intranet that is accessible to computers that are not part of a company's own network. While public access isn't allowed, virtual partners could, for example, have limited to full access to a partner network site.

F

FAQ Frequently Asked Questions. A list of common questions and answers about a web site, individual, company, or specific topic.

Firewall Software or hardware that creates a protective barrier between an individual user's computer or a company's internal network and the rest of the Internet.

Flame A fiery (read angry) complaint sent via email. Often generated when sending unsolicited email or posting commercial ads to noncommercial areas of the Internet.

Form A web page that has input fields for a user to submit information.

Frames A feature that divides a web page into separate windows, each of which can be scrolled independently. Many search engines cannot index framed sites well.

FreeBSD An operating system that is a version of UNIX. FreeBSD runs on Intel microprocessors and powers the servers of the web's largest sites.

Freeware Software that is free.

FrontPage A Microsoft Office program for web site creation and management that lets users manipulate and publish web pages with little to no knowledge of HTML. In December 2006, Microsoft replaced FrontPage with Expression Web.

FTP File Transfer Protocol. A means of uploading files to the Internet or downloading files to a computer.

G

Gateway A hardware or software mechanism or configuration that allows communication between two dissimilar protocols.

GIF Graphics Interchange Format. A common image format that allows up to 256 colors. GIF images work best for text, sharp lines, and large areas of continuous color. GIF images support transparency and can be displayed in rapid succession to simulate animation.

Gigabyte Depending on the source referenced, it's either 1000 or 1024 megabytes.

H

Helper Application An application that is launched to view files that browsers can't parse (such as videos).

Hit A request from a browser to a server. A web page with 14 images will count 15 hits, one for the main page and 14 for the images (one per image). Hits are often confused with other measurements, such as page views or users.

Home Page Originally, a home page was the browser's start page. That evolved to meaning personal web sites for a short time, but nowadays the most common meaning is the main web page (index page) for any web site.

Host A company that provides server disk space to other companies and individuals so their web sites are available on the Internet.

HTML (HyperText Markup Language) The simple programming language that allows formatted pages to display on the World Wide Web via a web browser.

Hyperlinks See *HyperText Links.*

HyperText Links A method of embedding a URL into an object, such as a segment of text or an image. When this object is clicked, the browser activates the embedded URL to retrieve the linked file.

I

ICANN The Internet Corporation for Assigned Names and Numbers. An organization recognized by the U.S. government in November 1999 to administer the Internet's core technical functions and foster competition among domain name registrars.

IDE Integrated Drive Electronics. A standard connector for connecting computer peripherals.

Internet The catchall word used to describe the massive worldwide network of computers. The word "Internet" literally means, "network of networks." In itself, the Internet is comprised of thousands of smaller regional networks scattered throughout the globe.

InterNIC Internet Network Information Center. InterNIC began as a cooperative effort between the U.S. government and Network Solutions, Inc. They were initially responsible for registering and maintaining the com, net, and org top-level domain names on the World Wide Web.

Internet Service Provider See *ISP*.

Intranet A private network of computers in which access from the outside is restricted.

IP Address Internet Protocol Address. The numerical addresses that relate to a specific domain name, which may identify one or more IP addresses. The format of an IP address is a 32-bit numeric address written as four sets of numbers separated by periods. Each number can be from zero to 255. For example, 204.17.42.69 could be an IP address.

IRC Internet Relay Chat. A massive network of text-based chat channels (rooms) and their users all across the world.

ISDN Integrated Digital Services Network. A type of phone line that can handle both analog and digital data that is used for higher-speed Internet access. If you have ISDN, you can use the same line for talking on the phone and accessing the Internet simultaneously.

ISP Internet Service Provider. A company that provides local access to the Internet and may provide hosting services as well. Also known as a local dial-up provider or access provider.

IT Information Technology. IT is a very broad term referring to everything from computer hardware to software programming to network management.

J

Java A general programming language developed by Sun Microsystems in response to problems encountered with the C++ language. Suited for use on the web, Java is intended to produce simple, cross-platform, high-performance, multi-threaded, dynamic programs.

JavaScript A movie script about the coffee industry... just kidding. A popular client-side, interpreted scripting language used to bring additional functionality and interactivity to web pages.

JPEG Joint Photographic Experts Group. A common image compression format capable of including more than 16 million unique colors. JPEG images, recognizable by the file name extension .jpg, are best suited for textures, photographs, and gradients.

JSP Java Server Pages. A scripting language similar to ASP and PHP, JSP allows the use of Java on the server side to produce dynamic web pages.

K

Kbps Kilobits per second. The transfer rate of information from one point to the next. A kilo equals 1000—unless you're referring to computers, when it sometimes refers to 1024 bytes of binary data.

L

LAN Local Area Network. A LAN is a computer network limited to a confined space, such as within a building, one floor of a building, or just to certain offices scattered about a building.

Linux A widely used, open-source operating system with many similarities to UNIX. Very adaptable, there are versions of Linux for most types of computer hardware from desktops to IBM mainframe systems. "Open-source" means the source code is available to anyone and many different individuals and companies can and may have contributed to its development.

Listserv A registered trademark of L-Soft International, Inc., Listserv is the most common type of mailing list software in use.

Login The account name used in combination with a password to gain access to a secured computer area. Also refers to the act of logging in.

M

Mac An Apple Macintosh computer such as an iMac, G5, MacBook, or MacBook Pro.

Mbps Megabits per second. Equal to 1000 Kbps.

Megabyte Usually refers to one million bytes, technically it's 1024 kilobytes.

MIME Multipurpose Internet Mail Extensions. MIME is a set of standards for defining the types of files attached to email messages. For example, HTML files have a MIME type of text/html.

Modem Modulator/demodulator. A device to convert digital signals to analog for transfer over phone lines.

MRA Multiple-recipient alias. An email alias account that forwards mail to multiple email addresses.

MSQL Mini Structured Query Language. A lightweight database engine designed to provide fast access to stored data with low-memory requirements.

Multimedia Content in the form of images, sound, video, or animation.

N

Navigation A system of links used to access web pages and other files on the Internet.

Network Two or more computers connected so they can communicate with each other.

Netiquette The art of employing common courtesy while using email, newsgroups, forums, and other Internet resources.

Newbie A somewhat affectionate term used to describe someone new to the Internet.

Newsgroup An individual newsgroup within Usenet.

NIC Network Information Center. In general, an NIC is any office that manages information for a network. The most well-known NIC is the InterNIC, which was where new domain names were registered in the early days of the Internet. That process has since been decentralized to several private companies.

NT A Windows operating system designed to act as a server in network settings.

O

Open Content Copyrighted information that is licensed to individuals and companies under specific terms of use, allowing the re-use of the information under the conditions set forth in the license.

Open Source Software Open source software is software in which the source code is available to the public so that they may examine it and try to add new features, enhance existing functionality, or build new versions of the software.

Operating System An operating system (OS) is what runs your computer. Most computer users have most likely heard of Windows, DOS, or Mac OS. These are operating systems that are normally used on private individual computers. A computer that is used as a web server must also have an operating system.

Opt-in List Email addresses of people who have agreed to receive email messages, usually ezines or announcement lists.

P

Pageview The display of a web page by a user agent. Counting the total pageviews offers a good measure of web site popularity.

Password A secret code that allows a user to access a restricted area.

PC Personal Computer. A general term for IBM-compatible computers running the Windows operating system. The term is historical; IBM no longer manufactures personal computers.

PDF Portable Document Format. An Adobe Acrobat proprietary file type; these files are cross-platform (Windows and Mac OS) and are useful in electronic publishing, prepress, and information sharing.

PERL Popular Extraction and Report Language. Designed for processing text, this popular programming language is also used for creating interactive web sites.

Permalink Formed by combining the words *permanent* and *link*, a permalink is a link that points to a specific blog post rather than to the page where the original post occurred (since that page may no longer contain the posting).

PHP PHP is a programming language for creating web server software that interacts with HTML. PHP code is read and processed by the web server software instead of by the web browser software on the user's computer, as with HTML.

Pixel A pixel is the basic unit of programmable color on a computer display or in a computer image.

Plug-in A program that is not part of the original software. For example, Macromedia Flash, Real Audio, and a number of other companies have browser plug-ins to make web sites more interactive. Also refers to components added to software programs such as Corel Photopaint and Adobe Photoshop that extend a program's capabilities.

Podcasting Formed by combining *iPod* and *broadcasting*, a podcast is a form of audio broadcasting via the Internet.

POP Post Office Protocol. An email account for sending and receiving email. When email is sent to a POP account, the mail is stored on the server until the user logs in with their email software and downloads it. (Same as Email POP and POP account.)

POP Account See *POP.*

Protocol Specific rules governing how data is exchanged between two electronic devices.

Public Domain Works in the public domain are available to the public at no charge because their copyrights, trademarks, or patents have expired or somehow been nullified. This may include information on government sites. This does not include information that is publicly visible on private or commercial web sites. Just because it's there, does not mean you may copy it for your own site or publications without permission from the copyright holder.

R

RAM Random Access Memory. The most common type of memory used by computers and other devices. The "random" part means that any byte of memory can be accessed without touching the preceding bytes. RAM is commonly known as the amount of memory that is available to programs.

RealAudio/RealVideo RealMedia technology that allows you to stream audio and video from your site.

Registrar A company or organization that registers domain names. Previously, Network Solutions was the only domain name registrar, but competition for registrars opened up in November 1999. Now, dozens of registrars exist globally. ICANN is the new governing body for registrars.

Relative Address An Internet address defining the path to a file within a domain (rather than using the full Internet address). For example, a link to a page within your own site can use a relative address rather than an absolute address.

Remove List A file containing the email addresses of those who have asked to be removed from a mailing list.

Resolution The number of pixels per inch that an image is saved with or that a monitor can display.

Router On the Internet, a router is a mechanical device or software that determines the network path a data packet should be sent to in order to reach its destination.

RSS Real Simple Syndication. RSS is a protocol for the syndication and sharing of content.

S

Search Engine A web site providing searchable index of content on the web. Search engines are consistently ranked among the most popular sites on the Internet because they help people find what they are looking for.

Secure Server A web site that uses encryption technology to protect information being transferred over the Internet.

SEO Search Engine Optimization. SEO refers to the practice of optimizing web pages so they rank as high as possible in search engine returns.

Servlet Server Side Java that replaces CGI and allows access to Java functionality from both client-side and server-side web applications.

Servlet Container A program that plugs into your web server and allows it to serve Servlet and JSP (Java Server Page) technologies. These are small programs that provide similar functionality to Microsoft's Active Server Page.

Shareware Software that you may download and use at no initial charge. If you like the software and want to keep using it, some form of payment is usually required. Shareware is sometimes referred to as nagware, as it often prompts you to register if you keep using it.

Sig File Signature File. Contact information and marketing materials in a brief format at the end of an email message. Sig files are the only accepted way to advertise within newsgroup posts.

Sit File A compressed file usually produced with Allume Systems' StuffIt, which is available for both Mac OS and Windows. Most versions of StuffIt Expander, included with StuffIt, can unstuff both .zip and .sit files.

Smart Autoresponder Smart autoresponders are similar to standard autoresponders, but they can send multiple emails at varying intervals of time, from one hour apart to many days apart.

SMTP The server address of the account through which you send email.

Spam The practice of sending massive amounts of email promotions or advertisements (and scams) to people who have not asked for it. Also refers to the messages received as such. Spam email lists are often created by harvesting email addresses from discussion boards, newsgroups, chat rooms, IRC, and web pages. Spam is universally hated by almost everyone except the spammer.

Spyware Software that is installed on a user's computer without the owner's knowledge and consent. It usually comes hidden in freeware software programs, and then monitors and reports back how the victim uses his or her computer.

SQL Structured Query Language. SQL is a specialized computer language for sending queries to databases.

SSL Secure Sockets Layer. SSL protects transmissions over the World Wide Web from spectators by encrypting the data while it is transmitted. SSL works through a certificate that authenticates the domain. With this certificate, secure transmissions on the server are "certified" and valid. Many web sites use this protocol to obtain confidential user information, such as credit card numbers. Web pages that require an SSL connection start with (https:) instead of (http:).

Storefront To sell your products on the web, you must build an electronic storefront where users can browse your products, put desired products into an electronic shopping cart, and then check out to pay for the items in the cart.

Streaming This technology promises quick access to media content without waiting for files to download. Downloading requires files to be sent to the user's computer in their entirety before they can be played. Streaming sends files to the user's computer in such a way that they can begin viewing or listening to the file after an initial buffer is set. Downloaded files remain on the user's computer until deleted by the user; when a streaming file ends, no data is left behind on the user's machine.

Sub-domain Anything that appears before your master domain in the URL, such as: http://www.yourchoice.masterdomain.com.

Surfer Slang for a person browsing the web.

Surfing The act of browsing the web.

T

Table A formatting method for arranging web page content into orderly rows and columns.

Tag A term that generally refers to an HTML element. *Tag set* refers to the start and end tags.

TCP/IP Transmission Control Protocol/Internet Protocol. The set of protocols that allows the web, Telnet, FTP, email, and other services to function between computers using varied networks and operating systems.

Terabyte 1000 gigabytes, give or take a giggle or two.

Telnet A program commonly used to remotely control web servers. The Telnet program runs on your computer and connects your computer to a server on the Internet. You can enter commands through Telnet to be executed as if you were entering them directly on the server console. Telnet requires a valid user name and password.

Templates A web page format designed to accept information from someone by simply typing or pasting content into it. It enables a less-skilled (or non-skilled) web site owner or newsletter operator to post regular updates without having to do any programming and without the danger of messing up the site's code. A template can also be the shell of a page, containing all the elements common to each page on a site, saved as a read-only file. You can start new pages from the template to save time and ensure consistency.

Tracking Code The means by which you keep track of the response generated by marketing messages. Often expressed as a department number, operator code, extension, or specific email box.

Trojan Horse A computer program hidden inside another program or a program disguised to trick people into running it—for example, a program may appear to be a song, game, or some other file, but in reality it performs another, usually malicious, function.

U

UCE Unsolicited Commercial Email. Informally and disparagingly referred to as spam.

Undeliverables Email returned to the sender when the person at the other end has closed their account, has a full email box, or provided you with a faulty address.

Unique User One user identity. When talking about the number of unique users to a web site over a specific time frame, this counts each user as one visitor, no matter how many times he or she may return. A web site that has the same 1000 users returning every day will have 30,000 user sessions in a month, but only 1000 unique users for that month. This statistic is a good measure of site popularity.

UNIX A popular multi-user, multi-tasking operating system developed at Bell Labs in the early 1970s. Due to its portability, flexibility, and power, UNIX has become the leading operating system for Internet server workstations.

Uploading Taking files from your computer or disk and sending them to the Internet. Generally, this is done through FTP or a template provided by your host. You need to upload files to put your site's pages on the Internet. Many sites also offer online templates or forms to let you simply paste in the information and put it in their pages.

Upstream Provider A larger, faster Internet provider that gives connectivity to local or smaller ISPs.

URI Uniform Resource Identifier. Same as *URL*.

URL Uniform Resource Locator (sometimes referred to as Universal Resource Locator). This is the address at which you can find a specific web site or file.

Usenet A collection of newsgroups, and the system to index and access them.

User Agent Any device capable of accessing the World Wide Web, such as a browser, cellphone, screen reader, or other device or software.

User Session A person visiting a web site over a short period of time. Usually, a user session is considered ended if there is no activity from that user for 30 minutes or so.

USP Unique Selling Proposition. The reasons a consumer should use your products rather than a competitor's products.

UUENCODE Short for UNIX to UNIX Encode(ing), this is a method for converting files from binary format to ASCII format so they can be sent via email.

V

Virtual Server A web server that shares computer resources among many clients (hosted sites) on a single machine. Virtual web servers provide low-cost web hosting services since dozens or even hundreds of small web sites can reside on one computer.

Virus Malicious computer code that infects a computer, often by replicating itself via email, that might display messages, install other software or files, corrupt or delete software or files, send confidential and private information to third parties, give the virus creator remote access to your computer, and more. Viruses cause millions of dollars of damage and losses each year.

Visitors The people who come to a web site.

VPN Virtual Private Network. VPN usually refers to a network that is, in part, connected via the Internet, but the data sent across the Internet is encrypted so the network is "virtually" private.

W

Web Browser A software program that allows your computer, once connected to the Internet, to retrieve documents from web servers around the world, translate the HTML code in the documents, and display the information on-screen.

Web Designer A person who creates web sites. Web designers may use web-authoring software, an HTML editor, or a simple text editor to create the actual pages, or they may design the overall look and let a webmaster do the actual coding. Web designers are usually proficient with web graphics and images.

Web Developer The person who develops the interface between the front and back end of a web site. Although web developers may be web designers as well, they typically have more database, CGI, and computer engineering experience.

Webmaster A very broad term generally meaning anyone who builds web sites. The scope of webmaster duties varies greatly. For a small company, the webmaster may design and build the site, market it, and handle all Internet-related activity. For a large company, it could have as little meaning as the person who answers email inquiries.

Webmaster Service Provider A company in the business of providing webmaster services to clients on a contract basis.

Web Page Any one particular page that is accessed via the World Wide Web. Web pages comprise a web site, and are distinct from other pages by their URLs (web addresses).

Web Server A computer on the World Wide Web (connected to the Internet backbone) that stores HTML documents that can be retrieved via a web browser or other user agent. An Internet backbone is a larger transmission line that carries data gathered from smaller lines, such as a local phone line or cable that interconnects with it.

Web Site A location on the World Wide Web. Each web site contains a home page, which is the first document or page users see when they enter the site. The site may contain any number of additional documents.

Wi-Fi Wireless Fidelity. Wi-Fi refers to a form of wireless communication, essentially meaning "Wireless Ethernet."

Worm A worm is similar to a virus, but it doesn't infect other programs. Like a virus, it makes copies of itself to infect other computers, and may alter, install, or destroy files and software programs.

www (World Wide Web) Also known as simply the web, this is the graphical, fastest-growing part of the Internet. It is sometimes disparagingly referred to as the World Wide Wait because of slow Internet connections, slow servers, or slow web sites.

X

XML eXtensible Markup Language. XML, a widely used system for defining data formats, provides an efficient way to define complex documents and data structures such as catalogs, news feeds, glossaries, inventories, real estate, etc.

XUL eXtensible User-interface Language. XUL is a markup language based on XML, and is used to define what the user interface will look like for software.

Z

Zip File A compressed file format. A zip file may contain one or more files, which are compressed to save space or allow for faster transmission to others.

Index